A Celebration of Young Poets

New Jersey – Spring 2006

Creative Communication, Inc.

A Celebration of Young Poets
New Jersey – Spring 2006

An anthology compiled by Creative Communication, Inc.

Published by:

CREATIVE COMMUNICATION, INC.
1488 NORTH 200 WEST
LOGAN, UT 84341

Printed in the United States of America

ISBN 10: 1-60050-027-7
ISBN 13: 978-1-60050-027-5

Foreword

Welcome! Thank you for letting us share these poems with you.

This last school year we surveyed thousands of teachers asking what we could do better. We constantly strive to be the best at what we do and to listen to our teachers and poets. We strongly believe that this is your contest. Several changes were made to this anthology as we adapt to what was requested.

In this and future editions of the anthology, the Top Ten winners will be featured on their own page in the book. Each poet that is included in this book is to be congratulated, however, the Top Ten Poets should receive special recognition for having been chosen as writing one of the best poems. The Top Ten Poems were selected through an online voting system that includes thousands of teachers and students. In a day and age where television programs use viewer voting to determine which contestant is the winner, it is appropriate that our poetry winners are chosen by their peers.

Over the years we have had many parents contact us concerning the privacy of their children. The comments focus on the fact that publishing a poet's name, grade, school name, city and state with each poem is too much information. We want to address these concerns. In the Fall 2005 edition of the anthology, we made the decision to only list the poet's name and grade after each poem. Whereas we received many calls and letters concerning the issue that we were publishing too much information, we received thousands of calls and letters requesting that we again publish more information to include a student's school name and state with each poem. Therefore, for this and future editions we will publish each student's name, grade, school name and state unless specifically instructed not to include this information. Just as this information is included in a school yearbook, we provide this information in this literary yearbook of poetry. This decision hopefully makes it easier to find classmates in the book and brings appropriate recognition to the schools.

We are proud to provide this anthology. In speaking to the poets in our anthologies we have found that our anthologies are not stuffy old books that are forgotten on a shelf. The poems in our books are read, loved and cherished. We hope you enjoy reading the thoughts and feelings of our youth.

Sincerely,
Gaylen Worthen, President
Creative Communication

WRITING CONTESTS!

Enter our next POETRY contest!
Enter our next ESSAY contest!

Why should I enter?

Win prizes and get published! Each year thousands of dollars in prizes are awarded in each region and tens of thousands of dollars in prizes are awarded throughout North America. The top writers in each division receive a monetary award and a free book that includes their published poem or essay. Entries of merit are also selected to be published in our anthology.

Who may enter?

There are five divisions in the poetry contest. The poetry divisions are grades K-3, 4-6, 7-9, 10-12, and adult. There are three divisions in the essay contest. The essay division are grades 4-6, 7-9, and 10-12.

What is needed to enter the contest?

To enter the poetry contest send in one original poem, 21 lines or less. To enter the essay contest send in one non-fiction, original essay, 250 words or less, on any topic. Each entry must include the writer's name, address, city, state and zip code. Student entries need to include the student's grade, school name and school address. Students who include their teacher's name may help the teacher qualify for a free copy of the anthology.

How do I enter?

Enter a poem online at:
www.poeticpower.com
or
Mail your poem to:
    Poetry Contest
    1488 North 200 West
    Logan, UT 84341

Enter an essay online at:
www.studentessaycontest.com
or
Mail your essay to:
    Essay Contest
    1488 North 200 West
    Logan, UT 84341

If you are mailing your poetry entry, please write "Student Contest" at the top of your poem if you are in grades K-12. Please write "Adult Contest" at the top of your poem if you are entering the adult division.

When is the deadline?

Poetry contest deadlines are December 5th, April 5th, and August 15th. Essay contest deadlines are October 17th, February 15th, and July 17th. You can enter each contest, however, send only one poem or essay for each contest deadline.

Are there benefits for my school?

Yes. We award $15,000 each year in grants to help with Language Arts programs. Schools qualify to apply for a grant by having a large number of entries of which over fifty percent are accepted for publication. This typically tends to be about 15 accepted entries.

Are there benefits for my teacher?

Yes. Teachers with five or more students accepted to be published receive a free anthology that includes their students' writing.

For more information please go to our website at **www.poeticpower.com**, email us at editor@poeticpower.com or call 435-713-4411.

Table of Contents

Spring 2006 Poetic Achievement Honor Schools

* Teachers who had fifteen or more poets accepted to be published

The following schools are recognized as receiving a "Poetic Achievement Award." This award is given to schools who have a large number of entries of which over fifty percent are accepted for publication. With hundreds of schools entering our contest, only a small percent of these schools are honored with this award. The purpose of this award is to recognize schools with excellent Language Arts programs. This award qualifies these schools to receive a complimentary copy of this anthology. In addition, these schools are eligible to apply for a Creative Communication Language Arts Grant. Grants of two hundred and fifty dollars each are awarded to further develop writing in our schools.

Allen W Roberts Elementary School
New Providence
Mrs. Signorelli*

Assumption School
Atco
Karen Gulla*
Bill Saul

Bartle Elementary School
Highland Park
Dara Botvinich
Elizabeth Kauffman
Rachel R. Pasichow

Belhaven Avenue Middle School
Linwood
Amy Winterbottom
Mrs. Yakopcic*

Byram Township Intermediate School
Stanhope
Paula Firmender
Ginette Garrity
Elisa Nesnay

Chatham Middle School
Chatham
Miss Anderson*
J. Stasiuk

Cherry Hill Elementary School
River Edge
Sandy Lautz
Julia Mahoney*

Christ the Teacher School
Fort Lee
Vicki Cooke*
Linda Gambino
Marie Raas*
Kim Winter

Christa McAuliffe Middle School
Jackson
Mr. Convery
Nancy Dell'Osso*

Community School of Bergen County
   Teaneck
      Deborah Buonomo
      Bonnie Kreielsheimer
      Martine McGowen
      Rita Salemo

Durban Avenue Elementary School
   Hopatcong
      Carol Procter*

Elizabeth F Moore Elementary School
   Seabrook
      Mrs. Nicosia-Jones*

Evergreen Elementary School
   Plainficld
      Gina Iacocca
      Ms. Prince
      Zena D. Young

Fieldstone Middle School
   Montvale
      S. K. Boyle*
      Katherine Grasso*

Franklin Elementary School
   Bloomfield
      Marion Armenti
      Lcah Gialanella*

Franklin Park Elementary School
   Franklin Park
      Eleanor Hoeflinger*

Franklin Township Elementary School
   Washington
      Jennifer Fischer
      Linda Milson

Gilmore J Fisher Middle School
   Ewing
      Regina Wachter*

Holy Saviour School
   Westmont
      Sr. Bianca Camilleri*
      Helen Guittar

Hopatcong Middle School
   Hopatcong
      Joanne Canizaro*
      Krista Reynolds
      Mrs. Spear

Immaculate Conception Regional School
   Bridgeton
      Frances Davis
      Jeanne Huber

Immaculate Conception Regional School
   Franklin
      Linda Pohlmann
      Deborah Sowden*

Indian Hill Elementary School
   Holmdel
      Denise Aquinas
      Mrs. Archinaco
      Miss Boyle
      Kathy Bradley
      Beth Catania
      Mrs. Dike
      Kevin Dillon
      Mrs. Giusti
      Mrs. Loschenko
      Mrs. MacConnell
      Mrs. Sadowski
      Carol Stehn
      Ms. Sullivan
      Dee Talarico
      Mrs. Walton

John F Kennedy Elementary School
   South Plainfield
      Cynthia Severino*

John Hill School
   Boonton
      Bevin Hughen*

Katharine D Malone Elementary School
   Rockaway
      Mrs. Beck*
      Mrs. Jaremack

Little Egg Harbor Intermediate School
Little Egg Harbor Township
Elizabeth Bacskai*
Clare Gallagher*
Jean Kuderski*
Regina Nielsen*
Mike Vaughn*

Lower Alloways Creek Elementary School
Salem
Mrs. Harris*

Mansfield Township Elementary School
Columbus
Mrs. English
Mrs. Kidd
Mr. Mersinger
Karen Omiatek
Mrs. Rudinsky
Mrs. Tellefsen
Jessica Winters

Most Holy Redeemer School
Westville
Jane Earnest*

Mother Seton Inter Parochial School
Union City
Adrian Cortes*
Lorraine DePinto
Yesenia Espinosa
Darling Magner
Marisol Rodriguez

North Dover Elementary School
Toms River
Rosa A. Fisher*

Old York Elementary School
Branchburg
Rhonda Sherbin*

Our Lady of Mount Virgin School
Middlesex
Patricia Langton*
Noreen McHale*
Linda Myers*
Mrs. Rospopa*

Perth Amboy Catholic Intermediate School
Perth Amboy
Mrs. Fiedler
M. Gibney
K. Kenney
Rita Novak
K. Stewart

Pioneer Academy of Science
Clifton
Marie Duda*

Pond Road Middle School
Robbinsville
Linda Biondi*

Ridgeway Elementary School
Manchester
Diane DeMarco
Marge Jennings*

Robert B Jaggard Elementary School
Marlton
Mrs. Holden*

Robert L Craig Elementary School
Moonachie
Judy Sullivan*

Roosevelt Elementary School
Kearny
Jeanine Doffont*

Roosevelt Elementary School
Rahway
Deborah Prakapas*

Sacred Heart Elementary School
South Amboy
Sister M. Immaculata Biskner*

Sacred Heart School
Rockaway
Joyce Baio*

Saints Mary and Elizabeth Academy
Linden
Nellie Cummins*

Salt Brook Elementary School
  New Providence
    Madeline Brooks*
    Mr. Fama
    Carolyn Zirpoli*

Sandman Consolidated Elementary School
  Cape May
    Judy Mohler
    Kimberly Whittington

Sicomac Elementary School
  Wyckoff
    Gail Cordello
    Stacey Juliano
    Mrs. Laurent
    Heather Ocampo
    Susan Pettoni
    J. Rickettson

Solomon Schechter Day School
  New Milford
    Cynthia Bibergal*
    Gayle Helfgott*

Springfield Township School
  Jobstown
    Mrs. Batchler
    Mrs. Byrne
    Wendy Kolev*
    Miss Lueckel*
    Nancy O'Leary
    Patty Sepessy*
    Patricia Wendler

St Augustine of Canterbury School
  Kendall Park
    Gayle M. Geiger*
    Kathleen Lakarosky

St Augustine Regional School
  Ocean City
    Ms. Morris*

St Helena School
  Edison
    Christine Latch*

St John's Academy
  Hillsdale
    Joan Mitchell*

St Joseph Grade School
  Toms River
    Jamie Blanz
    Patricia Bodden
    Lynn Palguta
    Mrs. Saluccio

St Joseph School
  Bogota
    Anita Coppock
    Angela Yannotti

St Joseph's School
  West Orange
    Eda M. Sully*

St Mary's School
  New Monmouth
    Maryann Johnson*
    Donna LaSasso*
    Ms. Walsh

St Rose of Lima School
  Freehold
    Mary Ann Caputo*
    Josephine Emmich*
    Mrs. McLearen*

St Rose of Lima School
  Haddon Heights
    Felicia Ferri
    Joan Maguire*

St Veronica Elementary School
  Howell
    Mrs. J. Nelson*
    Mrs. Pace*
    Mrs. Pawlicky
    Linda Rhodes*

Stonybrook Elementary School
Kinnelon
Mrs. Catalano
Mr. B. Kane
S. Kukan
Linda Taylor

Sundance School
North Plainfield
Ms. Betsy
Carina Beyer
Gina Schiano*

Tamaques Elementary School
Westfield
Michael Chodroff
Mrs. Truselo

The Red Bank Charter School
Red Bank
Lorna Breiter*

Thomas Jefferson Middle School
Lodi
Joyce Napolitano
Amanda Sheldon*

Toll Gate Grammar School
Pennington
Carol Chalela*

Township of Ocean Intermediate School
Ocean
Joanne DeVito*
Christine Fogler
Pamela S. Murphy

West End Memorial Elementary School
Woodbury
Claudia Cremeens
Claire Frapaul
Krista Javadi
Mrs. Jess
Mr. Jess

William Davies Middle School
Mays Landing
Annmarie Benson*
Daniel Weber*

Woodcliff Middle School
Woodcliff Lake
Susan Dym*

Woodlynne School
Woodlynne
K. Murphy*

Language Arts
Grant Recipients
2005-2006

After receiving a "Poetic Achievement Award" schools are encouraged to apply for a Creative Communication Language Arts Grant. The following is a list of schools who received a two hundred and fifty dollar grant for the 2005-2006 school year.

Acushnet Elementary School – Acushnet, MA
Admiral Thomas H. Moorer Middle School – Eufaula, AL
Alta High School – Sandy, UT
Alton R-IV Elementary School – Alton, MO
Archbishop McNicholas High School – Cincinnati, OH
Barbara Bush Elementary School – Mesa, AZ
Bellmar Middle School – Belle Vernon, PA
Bonham High School – Bonham, TX
Cool Spring Elementary School – Cleveland, NC
Douglas Elementary School – Liberty, KY
Dumbarton Middle School – Baltimore, MD
Edward Bleeker Jr High School – Flushing, NY
Emmanuel/St. Michael Lutheran School – Fort Wayne, IN
Floyds Knobs Elementary School – Floyds Knobs, IN
Fox Creek High School – North Augusta, SC
Friendship Jr High School – Des Plaines, IL
Gibson City-Melvin-Sibley High School – Gibson City, IL
Hamilton Jr High School – Hamilton, TX
John F. Kennedy Middle School – Cupertino, CA
John Ross Elementary School – Edmond, OK
MacLeod Public School – Sudbury, ON
McKinley Elementary School – Livonia, MI
Monte Cassino School – Tulsa, OK
New Germany Elementary School – New Germany, NS
North Beach Elementary School – Miami Beach, FL
Paradise Valley High School – Phoenix, AZ
Parkview Christian School – Lincoln, NE
Picayune Jr High School – Picayune, MS
Red Bank Charter School – Red Bank, NJ
Sebastian River Middle School – Sebastian, FL
Siegrist Elementary School – Platte City, MO

Language Arts Grant Winners cont.

Southwest Academy – Baltimore, MD
St. Anthony School – Winsted, CT
St. John Vianney Catholic School – Flint, MI
St. Paul the Apostle School – Davenport, IA
St. Rose School – Roseville, CA
St. Sebastian School – Pittsburgh, PA
Sundance Elementary School – Sundance, WY
Thorp Middle School – Thorp, WI
Townsend Harris High School – Flushing, NY
Warren Elementary School – Warren, OR
Washington High School – Washington Court House, OH
Wasilla Lake Christian School – Wasilla, AK
Woodland Elementary School – Radcliff, KY
Worthington High School – Worthington, MN

Young Poets
Grades 4-5-6

Note: The Top Ten poems were finalized through an online voting system. Creative Communication's judges first picked out the top poems. These poems were then posted online. The final step involved thousands of students and teachers who registered as online judges and voted for the Top Ten poems. We hope you enjoy these selections.

Top Poem Grades 4-5-6

The Crazy Pet Store

It all started when I was sweeping the floor.
All of a sudden, two people walked into the store.

Before I could stop them they opened a cage.
Out ran a puppy, young in age.

He spun around, chasing his tail.
The parakeets' wings began to flap and flail.

Their cages opened, and out they flew.
I caught a bird, but the cats ran free, too!

The little kittens went for the fish tanks,
And dog food jars slipped off their planks.

Mushy dog food splattered all over my head!
The rodents ran out of their cages, with a chinchilla who led.

I snatched up a monkey who tried to run free.
But suddenly, a bird left an unpleasant surprise on me!

An hour later, the store was clean.
I'm glad it's over, that's all I mean!!

Chelsea Brennan, Grade 5
St John's Academy

Top Poem Grades 4-5-6

I Wish

I wish I could change the World Trade Center from going down,
But I can't.
I wish I could change it so no one would die in that accident,
But I can't.
I wish I could change the pain in people's hearts,
But I can't.
I wish I could change the horrible things that happened,
But I can't.
I wish I could change the world into a better place,
Maybe I can't, but I can try.

Maura Keefe, Grade 5
Liberty Corner Elementary School

Top Poem Grades 4-5-6

If Once You Slept in the Forest

If once you slept in the forest,
You'll never be quite the same;
You may look as you looked before,
And go by the same old name.

You may watch TV, turning from channel to channel,
You may listen to the radio.
But you'll see the dawn break and,
Hear the rustling leaves.

You may go and play at your friend's house,
Or draw on a piece of paper.
But you'll play with sticks and stones,
And draw in the dirt.

Oh, you want to know why
There is such a change in you,
But once you have slept in the forest,
You'll never be quite the same.

David Liao, Grade 4
Edward H Bryan Elementary School

Top Poem Grades 4-5-6

Puzzle Piece

One little puzzle piece
Lying in the mud
One little puzzle piece
Picked up by a soul
Not knowing what lay uncompleted
Could it be a river
Filled with water
Could it be a raindrop
Dropping from Heaven
Two little puzzle pieces joined their brother
What could it be
That light blue tint
A raindrop from Heaven
An angel's tear
So painful, so sad
Unable to bear

Chanthia Ma, Grade 6
Chatham Middle School

Top Poem Grades 4-5-6

Chocolate Cake for Breakfast!

When I wake up each morning, my mom is wide awake.
She makes me things for breakfast, packs lunch for me to take.

One day it was my dad's turn to make me something good.
He got up nice and early, just like he knew he should.

He read the note from mommy, which told him what to do,
"Make something nice and healthy, like eggs and pancakes, too."

But Dad was much too tired, he wanted something quick.
He looked around the kitchen for something else to pick.

And then he saw the chocolate cake that mom had made last night.
He thought about what's in it, and his brain turned on a light.

What did we get for breakfast? Why don't you try and guess.
A giant slice of chocolate cake, my dad he is the best!

Mom asked Dad what he fed us, he told her eggs and stuff.
He never mentioned chocolate cake, he thought that was enough.

Joseph Mattero, Grade 4
Wedgwood Elementary School

Top Poem Grades 4-5-6

If I Were the Ocean

If I were the ocean,
My bleached blue hair would wave in the wind.
I'd wash up on the tiny white crystals of sand
And gently carry them back to their beds.
I'd watch over the sea life like a magnifying glass.
My sleek, shiny coat of salty water would shimmer in the blazing hot sun.
At night, when I am alone, I quietly whisper to the moon.
If I were the ocean.

Katherine Miras, Grade 4
Sicomac Elementary School

Top Poem Grades 4-5-6

Middle Child

Being a middle child is like being the frosting inside an Oreo cookie
You're always in the middle
You're the different one…you're always the white filling while your siblings
are the chocolate cookies
Everyone always likes the chocolate cookies better than the frosting
Then you meet the occasional one or two people that like the filling
That is how life is like for the middle child

There are only two parents and three kids
I think you are one parent short…
that's how life is for the middle child

The middle child is always the good one
The one who gets the good grades
The one who doesn't get in trouble
but the middle child doesn't get much attention either
That's how life is for a middle child

Jayna Patel, Grade 6
Sampson G Smith Intermediate School

Top Poem Grades 4-5-6

Books

Books can take you to the unknown
Make another world your very own
Take you to places where your mind can fly
Around the world and into the sky

Travel through space as an astronaut
Experience places that time forgot
Dive the seas or mountains you climb
Meet people from another place or time

Reading opens door after door
So many places and ideas to explore
It won't be an airline ticket you'll need
Just pick up a good book and read

Dean Rexines, Grade 5
Old York Elementary School

Top Poem Grades 4-5-6

What Is a Poem?

What is a poem if it does not rhyme?
A poem is a thought, a place, a time
A poem can express our true emotion
A feeling deep down like love and devotion

A poem paints a picture in one's mind
A magical place you'll never find
A poem can fulfill your every desire
And your soul it will attempt to inspire

With poetry you can chuckle or cry
Dab the tear from the corner of your eye
Poetry can be simple or make you tongue-tied
When you read a great poem you are satisfied

Jenna Schwartz, Grade 4
Old York Elementary School

Top Poem Grades 4-5-6

A Kite Takes Flight

The wind gets us ready, prepared for flight,
Into the clouds brilliant and white.
Free as a bird, light as a feather,
March is perfect kite-flying weather!
Up with the wind, turn with a twist.
The tail is controlled by string and a fist.
Dodging and swooping like a wave in the sky.
What could be better than flying that high?
Up with a gust, down with a dive,
This kind of weather makes me feel alive.
The air is still crisp; the sky is bright blue.
Flying a kite is more fun with you!

Annie Shaffer, Grade 5
Sacred Heart School

Penguins

Cute, fluffy, cuddly
Swim, waddle, slide, funny birds
Black, yellow, white coats
They're the coolest birds for me
Patrick Williams, Grade 4
Middle Township Elementary School #2

Baseball

B aseball in the spring is fun.
A ll-star baseball is hard.
S ilver bats are the best.
E verybody loves baseball.
B alls go flying everywhere.
A ll of the people have a good time.
L aughing at baseball games.
L ucky hits and runs.
Tucker Merkler, Grade 4
John F Kennedy Elementary School

Wind

W ind blows from the east coast.
I n the fall, leaves get blown away.
N ow it is winter now.
D own there are snowflakes.
Michael Healy, Grade 4
Community School of Bergen County

February

F lower
E very thing about love
B lack history month
R osaura's birthday
U and me on Valentine's Day
A lways together
R oses
Y ou and me and love
Melissa Torbor, Grade 6
Gilmore J Fisher Middle School

The Sounds of the City

Cabs beep, beep through the streets
People yell, "Taxi, taxi please."
Wind says, "Hello, hello good people."
Subway roars, roars underground
City…yells…yells…just…yells!
Dylan Palmer, Grade 6
Little Egg Harbor Intermediate School

Sis

There once was a sis named Jamie,
Who would always try to blame me.
We went to dance class,
She ran and broke glass.
So dance class ended for Brandi.
Brandi Esters, Grade 4
West End Memorial Elementary School

Joy

Joy is magenta.
It smells like freshly cut flowers.
It looks like a birthday party.
It tastes like chocolate fudge brownies from your favorite bakery.
It sounds like your dog's happy barks when you walk through the door.
Joy feels like you're walking through the colors of a rainbow with the wind
blowing your hair.

Noelle Brennan, Grade 6
St Rose of Lima School

When the Ball Meets the Bat

When the ball meets the bat,
Crack! It makes a sound like that;
The "Crack!" keeps on flyin',
just like the roar of a lion

When it goes over the fence, the people stand up and cheer,
like they had won the World Series, like it was the end of the year;
The people are like animals, wild and loud
and the team is happy, excited, and proud…
Now the score was one to nothing,
and the game had really become something

That day, the boy who hit the homerun earned a nickname,
because he had put his team ahead in that nail-biting game;
They called him Boom-Boy from then on,
which he liked better than his real name, Don

And because of that life-changing game,
he was given eternal youth fame;
And whether it was April, June, or December,
Boom-Boy would always remember…
When the ball meets the bat,
Crack! It makes a sound like that
Michael Colfer, Grade 6
St Veronica Elementary School

The Lazy Cat

The kitten next door would just sit on the floor
Licking her paws all day
But when I would say "Come on let's play"
She would "meow" and then look away
She would just sit there she would never move
When I tried to give her a treat she would just disapprove
She kept getting fatter every day
I don't think she likes me anymore I think she wants me to go away
But one day she wasn't there I wondered where she went
I searched everywhere for her even in the vent!
She was nowhere to be found had she gone to the vet?
If she didn't come back, I'd be very upset.
The day she came back, it wasn't just her…
She wasn't fat anymore, and she had a whole litter!
I couldn't believe it…I got to keep one!
Taking care of this one will be so much fun
Mikal Frater, Grade 6
Sampson G Smith Intermediate School

Summer

Flip-flops. Cute tops.
Sunshine. Pool time!
Ice-cream. Sunscreen.
No school. Summer's cool!
Short shorts. Summer sports.
Sand, heat burns your feet.
Cartoons. Sand dunes.
Bronzed tans. Portable fans.
Sunglasses. Beach bashes.
The radio's playing all the songs we know…
READY…SET…GO!

Anne Stevens, Grade 5
St Rose of Lima School

Best Friends Forever

I always write her a letter
And she replies back to me.
Whatever happens,
We are always still friends.
Friends are kind and thoughtful.
They care about you too.
She is also very funny,
She makes me laugh too.
I always trust her,
And she trusts me too.
She would always say to me,
That she's my best friend.
I will always agree with her.
I will never forget my friend.
Friends are like gifts.
Friends believe in honesty,
They are loyal.
When she told me that I was her best friend,
Yes, I agree
And it will never end.
Best friends forever.

Louise Ivy Merin, Grade 5
North Dover Elementary School

Red Beauty (Red Robin)

I am known as Red Beauty,
I glide across the sky,
I smell the nature so sweet.
The chirping of my mouth still rings in my head,
Relaxing on the trees, I am being admired.
People snap pictures and smile,
I sing a sweet song,
And hop away in a matter of minutes,
To keep them awaiting my return.
I fly a great deal,
The wind under my wings is all I feel,
Red Beauty, Red Robin,
So gentle and charming,
With only my song so astounding.

Deanna Bochicchio, Grade 6
The Red Bank Charter School

Fall

All is quiet.
The only noises are my pencil scratching against paper,
birds chirping,
trees rustling in the wind,
and the music you will always have
if you are quiet and listen.
I feel like dancing.
Everything is so quiet and perfect here.
No mistakes have been made.
Here it is,
a fresh start,
a new world!
Here it is,
the freedom you have always longed for.
Here it is,
the perfect place
I have always wanted.

Arlien Ricciardi, Grade 5
Lyncrest Elementary School

Color

Blue is the sparkling ocean water,
Red is a preschooler's teeter-totter.

Gold is a girl's shiny hair,
Brown is a new teddy bear.

Green is a four-leaf-clover,
Yellow is a lab when he rolls over.

Orange is the cheeks of a clown,
Purple is a color that never makes you frown.

Pink is a cute baby girl,
Black is a Chinese curl.

White is a piece of paper
Vanilla is a yummy wafer.

All these colors you will find,
If you follow your mind.

What are colors to you?

Blair Sliazis, Grade 5
St Dominic Elementary School

Outside

Outside the leaves are blowing.
The wind is blowing in your face.
Playing outside with the leaves,
It's starting to get dark and kids are going home.
Each day the night is coming earlier and earlier.
Also it is getting colder and colder.
Winter is coming again.

Andrew Delgado, Grade 6
Thomas Jefferson Middle School

Jerry, the Greyhound
Jerry the greyhound
Is big and strong
And likes to run all day long
He is fast and swift
And a wonderful gift
He has four paws and sharp claws
And racing is his cause
He is the one
Whose day is always done
He's sleepy and tired
My racing dog's retired
Bridget Zaleski, Grade 6
Springfield Township School

Summer
I like summer everyone should
I like summer whoopi-do
I like summer it's very hot
I like summer there's not much rain
I like summer we get to play
I like summer there is no school!
Fernando Salgado, Grade 6
Gilmore J Fisher Middle School

Animal
Fox
Big tail, small head
Running, jumping, catching
It's a weird animal
Mammal
Michael Pascale, Grade 4
Katharine D Malone Elementary School

Autumn Activity
Leaves falling softly
Like a gentle spring rain
A blur of orange, yellow, and brown
Tumbling through the air

Leaves tickling my face
Then floating to my feet
A chorus of crunching
Echoes in my ears

Leaves dancing across the street
Like a fall parade
Cara Ehlenfeldt, Grade 6
Olson Middle School

What Makes a Hero
H ere fighting for our freedom
E verything counts
R ough, tough, and always alert
O verall we all care about our troops!
Alexa Rae Reisen, Grade 5
Byram Township Intermediate School

This Moment
Your life is happy today,
This very moment, this day.
You can't help but smile,
This is something you've put into a file.
Feeling you could fly, so high,
Never let this moment pass by.
Forbid this moment from going away,
Forever it will stay.
Maybe in your mind,
Or some days your heart will find,
That your days may give way,
But this memory will always stay.
Sarah Gordon, Grade 6
Fieldstone Middle School

School
School is so cool,
Like playing in a pool.
We use books,
That gives us looks.
We use pencils,
And at lunch we use the utensils.
School is so fun,
When we play in the sun.
This is what I like about school
Where all my friends are cool
Joshua White, Grade 5
Most Holy Redeemer School

Braces
Braces, braces, braces.
They're on people's faces.
They straighten your teeth,
and make them neat.
But you can never eat!!
Meredith Brooks, Grade 5
Roosevelt Elementary School

Bright Shimmering Moon
I wonder what I will catch in my net?
Will it be happiness or greatness?
I jump up like a kangaroo
And swing my net
I look inside
And see
A bright, shimmering full moon
Shimmering like a vase
Filled with millions of diamonds
Sparkling in the night
I leap up with joy
I tip over my net
And let my moon free
Just like it should be.
Avery Manville, Grade 5
Salt Brook Elementary School

In My Net
I took out my net
And went holding it high,
Walked right into the forest
And looked up in the sky.

I closed my eyes so tight
And swung my net,
I clapped the lid of my jar
On tight and walked home
Carrying my treasure with delight.

I took off the lid
And waited with bated breath
As my catch zoomed
Around the room
And finally it came to me
And revealed itself to me.

I peered at it, it grinned at me,
For it was my hopes, my dreams,
And my love, all zooming 'round
The room with me.
Madeline Ketley, Grade 5
Salt Brook Elementary School

Good Old Sunny Days!!
On this
Bright, beautiful day
The sun shines
Like a glowing star.

The park is…
Full of surprises.
Teeny babies hop!
Children play
Tired as anything

As I
Swing softly
I feel suspended
In thin air.
Birds cheerfully chirp.
Parents laugh loudly!

Oh what a
Thrilling day!!
Olivia Mohnacs, Grade 5
Robert B Jaggard Elementary School

Life
Life is like a hot bath.
It feels good while you're in it.
But the longer you stay,
the more wrinkled you get.
Simon Wang, Grade 6
Bartle Elementary School

Love Is a Seesaw

Love is a seesaw.
Relationships never balance.
It takes a thousand different humans,
to balance love out.
This is just fun and games,
until you find that one special one.

Cara Vitale, Grade 6
Township of Ocean Intermediate School

Waves

As blue as the ocean,
Which has waves and curves,
Surfers love to ride,
In the blue ocean,
With strength,
While on a wave,
Speeding down the crystal water,
And having wind push against your face,
You hope that you will make it through the
Waves and curves.

Jeffrey Coluccio, Grade 5
Laura Donovan Elementary School

Leaves

Crunch, crunch, crunch, crunch, crunch,
go the beautiful fall leaves
as we play in them.
Beautiful, orange, red, green.
Crunch, crunch, crunch, crunch, crunch.

Deepshikha Das, Grade 4
Mansfield Township Elementary School

My Lord

O Lord, O Lord,
Don't you know?
O Lord, O Lord,
I love you so.

You were born in a stable in a faraway land,
But you are as near to me as my own hand.

Mary and Joseph raised you right.
You are the one I pray to at night.

Teaching God's word was your special mission.
You healed the sick better than a physician.

To save souls You died and rose,
That is why my heart glows!

O Lord, O Lord,
You are so bright.
O Lord, O Lord,
I wish to hold you tight.

Matthew Pluta, Grade 4
Assumption School

A Day in the Life as a Soccer Ball

The whistle is blown
the game begins
I decide to see my dear friend cleat
But why did he
Kick me again?
Soaring in the air
I spot my other friend Net
Tired and dizzy of rolling
I decide to stop by
for a quick snack of dirt
But what's this?
I can't stop!
I keep going and going
until I ran Net right in the face
The whistle is blown
the game ends
I'm put away for another day
Tomorrow,
the kicking and bruising and rolling and flying
starts all over again.

Billy Gilroy, Grade 5
Salt Brook Elementary School

Rivers…

Days like today people are still polluting the beautiful rivers.
To me the river is quiet, calming, and fun.
The fish in the river are also harmed too.
The bass are beautiful and the trout are jumping
And still no one cares about the river.

Tommie Clark, Grade 6
Christa McAuliffe Middle School

Growing Up

Growing up is very hard,
So much to do like writing cards,
Maybe just a little challenge,
To get life to our advantage.
Eating ice cream in the summer,
And younglings saying playing is funner.
Schooling and so much homework,
Though kids prefer to have no work!
Big bad bullies stealing money,
Though in movies it is funny.
To get our pay we have to say,
"Okay Mom I'll work on Sundays."
Sunday, Monday, Tuesday, Wednesday,
Tons of workin' 'till my birthday.
Doing good deeds to get our attention,
But then your dad is going to a convention.
Falling down and breaking bones,
Then for comfort you get a gnome.
So here we are living our upbringing,
Keeping our pants on from all the stinging,
Living our life with no blundering.

Peter Viereck, Grade 5
Liberty Corner Elementary School

Kindness

Kindness is like a rose
When we're kind it blooms its blossoms
We give and care for each other

Kindness is like a wall
It can never be broken
It's like a barrier in our hearts

Kindness is like love
But sometimes stronger
We all have kindness

Kindness is everywhere
Don't forget it, but most of all
Kindness is US!
Anthony Arroyo, Grade 6
The Red Bank Charter School

Right and Wrong

Right
Correct, honest
Honoring, becoming, defending
Laws, liberty, incorrect, untrue
Abusing, blaming, injuring
Misinformed, sin
Wrong
Peter Falgiano, Grade 4
Our Lady of Mount Virgin School

Chocolate, Oh Yeah

Chocolate, chocolate
I love it so
I eat it when I stay
I eat it on the go.

Candy bars, M&M's
It doesn't matter to me
I eat them in my room
I eat in them in a tree.

Pour it on ice cream
With sprinkles on top
I eat it with my mom
I eat it with my pop.

I like it on strawberries
Man, it tastes so good
I eat it hungrily
I eat like I should.

Chocolate brownies
Chocolate cake
Give me more
For goodness sake!
Bria Waller, Grade 5
Roosevelt Elementary School

Chocolate ice cream
Chocolate ice cream,
Sitting in its cone.

Chocolate Ice Cream

Melted by the hot yellow sun,
And it's all my own!

Chocolate drops
D
R
I
P
P
I
N
G
Down,
And then SPLAT on the
GROUND
Now it's time to take a lick,
So I'll hurry up and do it quick
Finally my ice cream is ready to go down south,
So I'll open up my big wide mouth!!

Alyssa Raiola, Grade 6
Chatham Middle School

What I Love About the Beach

I love the beach, the sand at my feet, the salty smelling air.
I love going swimming in the cold water, and the water going through my hair.
I love the hot sun; it burns on my face, it feels so good, oh how I love this place.
I love looking for shells on the hot sand. I love holding them in the palm of my hand.
I hate when I have to go, and the fun day ends, I hope one day I can come here again.
Christine Unanue, Grade 5
St John's Academy

Armageddon

I am Armageddon.
I wonder when it will happen.
I hear constant war cry.
I see a pre Armageddon.
I want no more warfare.
I am Armageddon.

I pretend Armageddon never will happen.
I feel the cold steel of the war blade.
I touch the cold blood of soldiers who died in valor.
I worry the chaos of war will never end.
I cry for the death of innocent people.
I am Armageddon.

I understand the reckless death of the soldiers who died in valor.
I say "Death to all who oppose me!"
I dream for the future of Armageddon.
I try to prevent Armageddon.
I hope Armageddon never happens.
I am Armageddon.

Shane F. Donovan, Grade 6
John Hill School

Tsunami Terror

I am an undulating motion.
When you hear about me you are in caution.
I make a roaring noise,
and I will wash away all your toys.
If I wash you away,
I will have to pay.
I start at the beach,
and when I am over, your clothes may need bleach.
I'm very salty,
and quite naughty.
My dad is a tornado, my mom is a storm,
and they make my sister a hurricane for sure.
I am a terror, no doubt about,
when people see me, they run and shout.
Now I have to go back to sea.
This will be the end of me.

Rachel Lauren Schwartzman, Grade 5
Solomon Schechter Day School

My Dream

I often dream of being rich
and wishing for new things for my room.
I think of helping my family
and I dream of going on a family vacation.
I feel happy!
I often dream of being rich.

Michael Guallpa, Grade 4
Evergreen Elementary School

What Is Red?

Red is the color of blazing fire.
Red is the color of my mom's hair.
Red is the color of bright lipstick.
Red is the color of yummy peppers and tomatoes.
Red is the color of beautiful roses.
Red is the color of M&M's.

Kristen Zaccardi, Grade 5
Sicomac Elementary School

Stress

Stress is blue
It smells like sour milk in your refrigerator
It looks like a list of chores that can't be done
It tastes like metal being stuffed in your mouth
It sounds like a cat's nails screeching on a chalkboard
Stress feels like the weight of the world is on your shoulders

Matthew Allen, Grade 6
St Rose of Lima School

Love

Love is patient,
Love is not proud.
It is peaceful,
Peaceful as the night sky.

Samantha Hulmes, Grade 6
Lower Alloways Creek Elementary School

On the Field

Standing, running, jogging on the soccer field
with all of my faith to win.
Who should I pass it to?
As I feel the bitter cold, I look around,
and see parents screaming to their children,
encouraging them to have fun.
When I shoot, I hear my cleat pound the ball,
echoing in the distance.
Watching the ball speed past the goalie,
and into the goal, the only thought I have is,
GOAL! GOAL! GOAL!
I can now see the happiness in my teammates eyes,
thinking now that we will win.
As the final whistle blows,
my heart gets filled with joy.
It will be a game to remember.

Conor Pellas, Grade 5
Salt Brook Elementary School

All Things Green

Green is crayons and paint
and a stomachache.
Green is the taste of green M&Ms.
Candles and mints smell green.
Roller coasters make me feel green.
Green is the sound of country music and Greenday.
Green is a field, forest, and Greenland.
St. Patrick's Day is also green.
Green is grass.

Jessica Molnar, Grade 6
Thorne Middle School

Friends

Friends are like a river,
    Changing every day.
They don't make you quiver
    All through life from day to day.
A friend shares their dreams of the future,
    As they trickle down the bank,
Moving or staying
    Ever changing.
Memories that are unforgettable,
    You will always share with them.
You don't know what the future holds
    You can only dream.
'Cause friends can't stay forever
    But you can hold the memories.
Friends are like a river
    Changing every day!
A good friend won't forget you
    No matter what you say.
The worry stays all of your days.
    Yes, a friend is like a river
Ever changing. Yes, changing every day!

Jennifer Mattson, Grade 6
Walter T. Bergen Middle School

Mom!

Mom, she cares for me every day,
She lets me go outside and play,
She is my favorite hero,
She never is a zero!
Allyson Hicks, Grade 4
Katharine D Malone Elementary School

Little Brothers Are Pests

Little brothers look innocent
but looks deceive
'cause little brothers throw things
and kick and scream.

Little brothers seem nice
but that's not true
they're mean and nasty
and they spit, too.

Little brothers are kind
but that's part of their attack
'cause they are out to get you
when you turn your back.

Little brothers should listen,
be helpful, and nice
they should love you forever
and take your advice.

Are you listening, Colby?
Kyle Golden, Grade 5
Roosevelt Elementary School

Princess, My Dog

Princess is my favorite dog
In the whole wide world
Sometimes she's as boring as a log
But it makes me love her more
She loves to run around and play
But most of the time she sleeps all day
Every now and then I lay with her
I love her cute, soft, fluffy fur
After she and I play a lot
My dog P gets massive knots
As much fun as my dog and I can have
But when she bites me it makes me mad
Even though I know
That my dog can't talk
I know she's always there for me
To inspire me to be the best I can be
Princess is so special
To me and my family
I love my dog so dearly
My favorite dog named P
Sarah Culp, Grade 5
North Dover Elementary School

Hair

Last night
I got a haircut
It was a really, really
short haircut
People started laughing
When they saw my hair
So, now
My name is
The Hooded One
Since I started
hiding my hair
So, if you see me
call me
The Hooded One
Until my really, really short hair
Grows back.
Teddy Koutros, Grade 4
Ridge Ranch Elementary School

Special Person

Mom
Happy, honest
Painting, drawing, writing
She always makes me so happy
Special
Raul Flores, Grade 5
Ridgeway Elementary School

Coala

Adorable, chunky
Sleeps, runs, mooches
Sleeps fifteen hours a day
My dog
Timothy Vogel, Grade 4
Mansfield Township Elementary School

Princess

Fluffy, cuddle,
runs, jumps, walks
keeps you company
dog
Chrysoula Manetas, Grade 4
Mansfield Township Elementary School

Summer

Summer is the best
I love going in the pool
Sometimes I dig in the sand
Summer is cool.

Summer is time to play
I hate going back to school
So all I have to say is…
I hate homework and closing the pool.
Laurel Bates, Grade 4
St Mary's School

Staring

As we sit all 'round at a table
Quiet as mice
All staring, staring
Nerves a wreck
Then a whisper…
It's probably about me,
Me, abnormal, different,
Strange in a way.
They talk as if it's behind my back.
But it now pains my face, a blow
Words of hate, discomfort
All because of our human instinct to…
Gossip.
When it starts, it never
Stops.
Anat Mano, Grade 6
Bartle Elementary School

Soccer

This game is like a vicious war
where you fight, fight,
and fight for the ball. You kick,
kick, and kick at the small ball.

Cards happen as often
as a school day.
And when you score a goal,
your team goes wild every time.
Zachary Buchanan, Grade 4
Middle Township Elementary School #2

In the Park

The sun is rising,
Birds are chirping in the park,
Squirrels play nearby.
Madeline Hourican, Grade 4
St Mary's School

Seasons

Fresh flowers blooming everywhere
Shining bright sun warms us with care
Green valleys are a feast for the eye
Birds and bees soar through azure skies

Bright crimson leaves float to the ground
Falling swiftly without a sound
Chilling cool breezes wrap us in
Warm blankets cover us with a grin

Swirling white snowflakes, one of a kind
Two of the same, you never can find
Wonderful sleigh rides, such a delight
Joy lasting throughout the frosty night
Gabriella Mongelli, Grade 6
Woodcliff Middle School

Where What When

I can eat 2 big bags of French fries.
In an hour
I do it at my mom's
I can do it at my grandmom's and at my grandpop's
I can do it at my aunt's and uncle's
I can do it at my cousin's house
I love French fries
Sometimes I get mad if I can eat that many fries
But they're so good sometimes.
I even fry extra fries with it.

Ikeda Collins, Grade 5
Elizabeth F Moore Elementary School

A Knee-Shattering, Bone-Crushing Activity

My favorite hobby to do is ski
My debut was when my mom taught me
Instead of skiing for free
You have to pay a fee
You also have to really be careful
Not to bust a knee
The most important rule in skiing is to keep your ski parallel

The sights you see are like
Riding on a bumble bee
The mountains that you ski on are exceedingly enormous
One day I might want to teach kids to ski

When I go down the hill I used to yell, "wee"
After skiing I like to have some hot tea
I also have an unbelievable bowl of meaty chili
I also like to keep my freezing hands near the burning fire
My favorite hobby to do is to ski

Ryan Listro, Grade 6
Fieldstone Middle School

Summer at the Beach

Have you ever touched the beach?
I have.
I remember the splish-splashy cold water,
The touch of the hot steamy sand
On my face, hands, arms, bathing suit, legs, and feet.
Flying a homemade kite with my family
In the warm cozy air.
Walking on the mossy green jetties and jumping into the water.
Have you ever touched the beach?
I have.

Elise Palermo, Grade 4
Edward H Bryan Elementary School

Science

Science is my favorite class
I like it even more than reading and math.
And if you don't like your science class,
that's too bad for you 'cause mine is a blast.

Jared Alexander, Grade 6
Gilmore J Fisher Middle School

My Dream

I often dream of being a policeman,
and wishing for a fast police car.
I think of making the world a better place,
and, when I dream of things I should be.
I feel delighted and excited!
I often dream of a policeman.

Jahmeel Stevenson, Grade 4
Evergreen Elementary School

Love

Love is red.
It smells like sweet candy.
It look like red roses are all around you.
It tastes like fresh cookies coming right out of the oven.
It sounds like waves coming upon the shore.
Love feels like someone is always by your side.

Maggie Preston, Grade 6
St Rose of Lima School

Summer

S ummer is the best time of the year that most of us have fun.
U nresisting things you can't even resist to do.
M any places you can go to have a great time.
M ake sure you already list the things you would do.
E arn some of your summertime to see the sunset sky.
R un away to all the exciting, unresisting, and fun places.

Selena Romero, Grade 6
Thomas Jefferson Middle School

What Is Life?

Life is like Wheel of Fortune
'round and 'round it goes,
where it stops, nobody knows

Life is like a magic eight ball
always searching for the right way to go

Life is like the rolling hills
it has it's ups and downs

Life is like an apple
sometimes sweet, sometimes sour
and sometimes bruised and rotten

Life is like a broken record
At times repetitive and boring

Life is like a jigsaw puzzle
it's up to you to piece everything together

Life is like a journal.
every day is a new clean page

To me, life has so many meanings.

Betsy Wilt, Grade 5
Salt Brook Elementary School

Valentine's Day
Flying hearts are moving through town.
Secret admirers lurk around.
Candy hearts I really do LOVE!
Cupid is watching from above.

The candy is so very sweet!
There is someone I can't wait to meet.
Love is certainly in the air!
Boys can't wait to show girls they care.
Allison Alfonso, Grade 4
St Mary's School

Halloween
One Halloween night
I had quite a fright
So I ran right outside
To get some help
I screamed and I hollered
But no one heard my yelp
I then saw a witch
On a bright white kite
That was one scary night!
Kalena Seaman, Grade 4
Springfield Elementary School

A Person I Admire
Denise
Caring, helpful
Swimming, shopping, stitching
Takes care of me when I am sick.
Mom
Sam Dowling, Grade 5
Ridgeway Elementary School

Baseball
Crack!
The echo of the ball,
Connecting with the bat,
That's your signal to move your feet.
Don't hold back.
Give it all you've got,
Sometimes you lose,
But sometimes you don't.
Rain or shine,
Snow or hail,
If you give it your all,
You will never fail

The throw,
The catch,
He's safe, he's out.
But whatever you do,
Give it your all
Because this is baseball
Kevin Galasso, Grade 5
Tamaques Elementary School

Dear My Friend...
I was always friendless and sad with a soft, but depressing face
My nightmares were endless and mad always in a gloomy, dark place

Every day was wasted away for I could not even smile
Each night I would pray and pray for joy and happiness on the cold tile

But then you reached out to me and became my first friend
I no longer had to hurriedly flee from the sneers others would send

You've given me a reason to exist and not waste my time to pray
And now I will eagerly persist on living and not fade away

Darkness had surrounded me in my memories, in my past
But now I'm happy as can be a joy that will surely last

And even though you're way up high I'm living on just for you
I'm making sure you're not to sigh because I was feeling sad and blue

I'll never forget what you had done for me…just one smile had changed my will
So I'll try my best to be in glee even after the sun hides behind the hill

I'm sure we'll be together one day once again, talking together
And in the sun's gallant ray you'll see two friends together forever
Chloe Chan, Grade 6
Indian Hill Elementary School

The Great Season
The morning mist dribbles off the thinnest blades of grass,
Bare trees begin to bloom,
With tiny buds that smell wonderful and so pleasant.
The azure sky seems so clear with the cotton white puffy clouds,
With a tangerine orange sun makes you shout aloud,
Spring is here.
Warm swift breezes can lift a feather,
Everything is perfect but sometimes not the weather
But somehow it turns out so nice,
The light, gentle showers sprinkle down from a world unknown.
Go outside let it soak you,
Let it become you,
Breathe in the perfumed air,
And you will become spring's slave.
It only comes once a year.

Allie Schwetje, Grade 5
Tamaques Elementary School

When I'm at the Mall...
…I think about money, credit cards and shopping bags too.
…I remember how much I love it — maybe you do too.
…I see and smell the food court, filled with people and delicious food.
…I think about how much I like to shop at *Limited Too*.
…I get so excited buying clothes at every store.
…I want to shop until the day is no more.
…I know I'll be exhausted when I get home.
…I think about staying awake and trying on my new clothes.
Gabriella Micciche, Grade 4
Long Memorial Elementary School

Spring!

Spring is here, oh joy!
You can go play with your friend.
You can start gardening.
Don't put too much water.
You can play baseball, football, basketball, or swim.
You can ride your bike in the park.

Joshua Egbelshi, Grade 4
John F Kennedy Elementary School

The Witch Night

Two witches having dinner together.
What a night, they will remember forever.
A candle between them cannot hold them apart.
The dinner has been a work of art.

Aisha Rana, Grade 6
John Hill School

Summer, the Best Season

Summer is the best season,
Because there is no sleet or hail,
You don't need your coats, the heat you can bear,
Summer is hot, there are so many things to do,
Like going in the pool because it's not cool,
Summer is great! Summer is fun,
You can stay outside all day without rain or snow,
Summer is the best season, so come on LET'S GO!!!

Michelle Keane, Grade 4
John F Kennedy Elementary School

Rat-a-Tat

There once was a drummer who played
A rat-a-tat-tat that he made
All day and all night
'Till the midmorning light
Till people shouted "My ears, what a fright!"

Christopher Volk, Grade 6
Fieldstone Middle School

That's No Sham

I hear, "up to the starting line"
Thinking to myself, he's in eighth grade
I have no chance, that's a sham
The gun, it goes off
People passing me halfway through
I have no chance, that's a sham

I feel a sudden urge for speed
Passing by everyone
Feeling like a boy on Christmas morning
Can I make it, third place, second place, first place
I have an aspiration
Close to the finish, I'm off
Running as fast as I can
First place, that's no sham

Matt Michael, Grade 6
Fieldstone Middle School

Bump, Bump My Heart

The ball was placed on the 18
The crowd was screaming
My team was cheering
The goalie was rocking and getting ready
It was debut in the pros
The pressure was on
I looked where to place the ball
Should I go high or low left or right
My mind was made up I'm going to the left corner
Step by step I made it to the ball
I took my kick
The ball was devastated like a crumpled potato chip
The sweat dripped down my face as I watched my shot
Up, up, up
All I heard was a big loud clank
The crossbar denied the shot
I was infuriated, upset and disappointed in myself
I let a good scoring opportunity go to waste
My team was supportive but I was feeling blue
Then it happened I was fouled again in the box
The ball was placed on the 18

Jason Ertrachter, Grade 6
Fieldstone Middle School

Snow

Snow from Mount Fuji
Lots of white flakes fill the sky
There will be no school.

Kevin Chang, Grade 4
Wayside Elementary School

Family

A mother's heart is warm
She helps you with your problems
Comforts you in the middle of the night
After you've had a bad dream

A father will try to help you
But doesn't always know what to say
And always wants your dreams to come true

An older sister helps you with obstacles in life
And is the person you go to when you want a good fight
During that fight you think to yourself "I love you!"

A dog is always listening
When you cry they will lick your face
And let you know it is going to be okay
They make your world a happy place

Family is your lifelong friends
They are there supporting your dreams
They won't forget you,
So never forget your FAMILY!

Mikayla Mulligan, Grade 6
Walter T. Bergen Middle School

Spring
Spring is in the air
Bunnies roaming everywhere
No one knows what's in store
Daffodils, roses, flowers galore
Birds singing as they soar
Snow no more
Laura O'Shea, Grade 5
St Helena School

Hunting
A hungry snake slithers
slowly
with a deadly
hiss it locks
on its prey.

Suddenly
it jumps out
and strangles the prey
injecting venom
swiftly
as the prey falls.

The snake devours
his meal
happily and quickly
the snake leaves
the bones as it slithers away.
Justin Joung, Grade 5
Robert B Jaggard Elementary School

Basketball Is My Favorite Sport
Basketball is my favorite sport
I like the way they dribble
Up and down the court

Basketball is my favorite sport
Even though I am really short
And when we lose I am to blame
I know I slip and fall

And bang my head against the wall
And knock my teammates to the floor
I never shoot, I hardly score
Sometimes I hit the pole
And then completely lose control

The ball bounces off my toes
And hits the ref in the nose
The ref screams a painful howl
And then declares another foul
He gives the other team the ball
They never miss a shot at all
I guess I just love basketball!!!
Rachel Perez, Grade 6
Mother Seton Inter Parochial School

Thanksgiving
I like Thanksgiving
Turkey and stuffing are good
We give thanks to God
Justin Gallo, Grade 4
Holy Family Interparochial School

Parents
Parents,
loving, bossy,
caring, helpful, funny,
great to have,
adults
Margaret Parzyck, Grade 4
Mansfield Township Elementary School

A Buddy in Need
My dog will always chase me,
Chase me all around,
My dog will always lick me,
Just when I'm on the ground.
My dog will keep on running,
Just running all around,
She kept on running into walls,
Now she's Bumper, the Basset Hound.
She is always barking,
Just barking all alone,
Now she is very happy,
Just because she has a home.
Sometimes she is just sleeping,
Just sleeping in her bed,
So when I see her sleeping,
I will pat her on the head.
When she is awake,
Just sitting in her crate,
I will walk on over and open up the gate.
Bumper, the Basset Hound, is great!
Adam Flynn, Grade 5
North Dover Elementary School

Love
It is hard to part when you're in love,
You ask for one last hug.
You fight over the simplest things,
And you wish you had wings.
You realize it has to end,
You never try again.
Lauren Kelly, Grade 5
St Marys School

The Beach
Kids playing in sand
Ocean roaring by the beach
Crabs are scurrying
Hannah Wrocklage, Grade 4
Stonybrook Elementary School

The Cold Against My Cheek
I feel the cold against my cheek
this weather makes me feel so weak
the winter wind bites at my nose
while 'round the bend
St. Nick ho ho ho's
I feel so guilty that I'm fed
and warm and that I have a bed
I feel so guilty to those who are
less fortunate than me
to those who shiver
and have to plea
for food
I wish there was something I could do
but now I'm going home
I am so cold,
my hands are turning blue
I'll warm myself with all my might,
for after all,
St. Nick comes tonight
Madeleine Fawcett, Grade 5
Toll Gate Grammar School

Halloween
On Halloween night
You'll get such a fright
In the middle of the night
By a flickering light
Derion Dyson, Grade 4
Springfield Township School

My Looks Are Different
My looks are different
I wonder why
Can you help me?
Yes, I can
Everybody's looks are different
It's okay
I'll always be there for you anyway
Thank you, thank you.
Sierra Schloesser, Grade 6
The Red Bank Charter School

Sunset
A pure golden light,
Colors the earth skyward.
The silky grass
makes you feel calm.
Your eyes gently close
you catch a glimpse
of the sun's color fading.
The moon takes over
the stars brighten
The crickets sing a lullaby that
sweeps you into a deep slumber.
Andrew Barbiero, Grade 5
Robert B Jaggard Elementary School

Baseball

Baseball is the sport I play
And I can't wait for opening day.
Hitting is my thing
If you listen closely you'll hear a ding.
I love to pitch
And maybe someday it will even make me rich.
Sometimes I get hurt when I slide and steal.
But baseball is the real deal!

Elijah Porrini, Grade 5
Most Holy Redeemer School

Dandy Candy

We are trying to sell you some very good candy,
That's really fine and dandy.
It could be sweet yet sour.
You can chew for more than an hour.
It's only fifteen dollars.
It makes you want to holler.
It has different flavors like blueberry or apple,
It can even taste like your favorite kind of Snapple.
It's called the dandy candy.
Dada da dandy candy. Oh yeah.

Marina Mollica and Jenna Castaldo, Grade 5
Williamstown Middle School

Glancing

I'm gazing down from the sky.
Searching for people in the night.
I can't see anything
But my neighbors,
   The stars

      Shining,
         Glimmering,
            Dancing,

It's almost like they think they're better than me.
The Queen star usually gives me light
People can see me, but not tonight
I can see the Earth but not tonight
I'll keep looking until I find
The light or a lady in the night
I'll keep glancing down from the sky
   until I find you!!

Deanna Garofalo, Grade 6
Christa McAuliffe Middle School

Jealousy

Jealousy is green.
It smells like a rotten egg that won't go away.
It looks like a lion ready to get its prey.
It tastes like sour milk you can't swallow.
It sounds like a screeching bat flying around me.
Jealousy feels like a bee that won't stop stinging me.

Patrick Curry, Grade 6
St Rose of Lima School

Creme Saver

So much depends on a creamy soft Creme Saver
Peeling off the thin wrapper slowly
It swirls of a tornado picking up speed
Symmetrical lines cover its body
Giving off a sweet smell of strawberry vibes
The smell makes your mind think of wallpaper
That is swirling shapes of lines
Inside a strawberry is a tang of sweet juice
That spills into your mouth slowly
Your tongue licks its shapes off
It's a mouth watering Creme Saver

Brittany Zaintz, Grade 4
Pond Road Middle School

My Day in Middle School

Hard to believe I'm finally here
To walk in the hallways everyone's near
Lots of homework, class work too.
Not a lot of friends here when you're new.
Never got a chance to take a break
After you're done writing your hand starts to ache
Having lunch is the best part of the day
To hear the lunch ladies say have it your way
Oh my gosh! The day is almost over
I can't wait to go home in my dad's new Range Rover

Emily Chevalier, Grade 6
Thomas Jefferson Middle School

Spring

The snow has melted, it is warm outside,
   That is how I know spring is here.
The wildflowers are growing in the meadows,
   That is how I know spring is here.
The bees are buzzing in the air, birds are chirping,
   That is how I know spring is here.
The sun shines right upon us and there are no clouds,
   That is how I know spring is here.
Watching the leaves blow all around like dancing ballerinas,
   That is how I know spring is here.
My heart is racing, I am filled with joy, because spring is here.

Caitlin Oroho, Grade 5
Immaculate Conception Regional School

Winter Ice

W inter is near,
I cicles are forming,
N ever go outside,
T ill winter is here.
E verywhere you go it's very cold,
R eefs will freeze when cool air blows.

I 'll love to skate on the solid ice,
C olors will be gone but pure white,
E ven you'll be surprised by all the Winter Ice!

Ranmi Miyazawa, Grade 4
Nellie K Parker Elementary School

The Hockey Game

I was skating
up the ice yelling,
"Danny, here pass, pass."
He yelled back,
"Go to the far post for a tip in."
Instead he passed to Rojas,
who later passed to me.
I said nice pass to Rojas,
and yelled yippee yippee.
Then I took a slap shot
and put it upper shelf.
They both came over saying,
"We won we won."
Now we're in first place:
Number 1.

Connor Bilby, Grade 6
Chatham Middle School

Summer Vacation

We all scream and gleam.
We run like flies as days go by.
And thinking summer lasts forever
But it's now we enjoy the summer.
As we play, laughing and screaming
Under the sun day after day.

Noemi Valdetano, Grade 5
The Red Bank Charter School

My Dog

This is my dog
He is very funny
He hops like a bunny
This is my dog all young and hyper
When I play with him
He gets all excited
This is my dog
I love him
I love him
I really do!

Alexandra Brennan, Grade 5
St Dominic Elementary School

Golda Meir

Happy, sweet
Determined, passionate, resolved
She was so amazing
Courageous

Aviva Weiner, Grade 4
Solomon Schechter Day School

The Joy of Christmas

Waking up early
Hearing the crunch of paper
Hurray! It's Christmas!!

Craig Scheuring, Grade 4
Holy Family Interparochial School

A Girl

A girl that is ugly on the outside
but deep inside
I am sweet and cute
but as you can see
people don't like me.
I say bye and hi to people I know
and they still don't like the way I look.
When I see them every day I know they talk about me.
I cry on the inside.
A girl
A girl that is sweet and cute on the inside.
I'm in the sixth grade and I don't care what people say about me.

Lidia Rempart, Grade 6
George Washington Elementary School

Family

F ull of laughter and joy.
A lways there by your side.
M oments that sometimes you can't share with anyone else but them.
I n your heart whether they're next to you or far away.
L ovable to you in all ways.
Y ou can't possibly forget them because they are so special and they are yours!

Tal Ben-Avraham, Grade 4
Solomon Schechter Day School

When I See Him Face to Face

When I die, I will be buried in a cemetery for an eternity.
Soon, I will see him face to face. My heart will be filled with joy and grace.
I can't imagine those times, when he finally opens my eyes.
It will be a beautiful place, when I finally see him face to face.

Rebeca Campos, Grade 6
Woodlynne School

I Am

I am an athlete and the oldest of four.
I wonder what my brother will look like when he is older.
I hear basketballs bouncing.
I see the Liberty basketball team play.
I want a frog for a pet.
I am an athlete and the oldest of four.

I pretend that I am a player on the New York Liberty team.
I feel happy when I play basketball.
I touch a basketball every day.
I worry about ghosts.
I cry when I get hurt.
I am an athlete and the oldest of four.

I understand that the Liberty basketball team does not always win.
I say that the Yankees rule.
I dream that the Yankees will win.
I try to be good to my family.
I hope that I am pretty when I am grown up.
I am athletic and the oldest of four.

Michelle Toto, Grade 4
Edward H Bryan Elementary School

Joyful Catch

The batter takes his wooden bat.
Then takes off his red cap.
He puts on his blue helmet.
He then walks to the plate.
He aims for the back gate.
Strike one…
Strike two already…
He swings hard
And the ball flies like it has wings.
A player who stared in awe,
Saw where the ball would land.
He sprinted and dove and caught the ball.
The fielding team beat them all.
They jumped
And screamed
With joy.

Timothy Stroever, Grade 5
Tamaques Elementary School

What Am I?

I fly and soar through the air.
I'm in a hurry so I have no time to spare.
Sometimes when there are storms I'm delayed.
So I might need to fly the next day.

In the morning I'm as noisy as can be.
But at night I'm as quiet as a buzzing bee.
After I fly away, I come back in a few hours.
What am I?

(Airplane)

Gabriela Murillo, Grade 4
Christ the Teacher School

Being a Butterfly

If I were a butterfly,
I'd spread my vibrant wings out wide.
I'd take a giant leap and flutter, soar
into the deep blue sky.

I'd flip, I'd sparkle, I'd twirl,
and dance through the whistling air.
I'd jump, I'd fly, and brighten up the sky.

I'd look down below me
and see a village of pretty flowers.
The colors would excite me
and I'd dip down and take a relaxing nap.

Once I'd awaken, I'd zip into the bright sky.
My wings would follow me,
keeping me up high.
Then I'd float, flutter, fly,
throughout the sky.

Kristen Arnold, Grade 4
Sicomac Elementary School

Fairs

Fairs are fun to go to.
And have fun rides to go on.
I love to go on fast rides because they are cool.
Baby rides aren't that fun.
But now that I'm older,
I can go on the big rides.
Those are even faster and more fun!

Amanda Dolan, Grade 4
John F Kennedy Elementary School

How Do I Describe My Best Friend…

M y age (11)
A thletic
R ight almost every time
Y es, she is amazing!!!

B eautiful, smart, blonde
E verything you want in a friend
R eally polite
K nows a lot
O h my gosh if you met her you'd love her!!!

Haley Durning, Grade 5
Roosevelt Elementary School

Remember*

I remember…when we went swimming
And went on boat rides
And went hunting and played games together
Or when we went on walks
And how you wouldn't stop running after the birds
And how protective you were.

I never wanted you to die.

Nelson White, Grade 6
Little Egg Harbor Intermediate School
*Dedicated to my dog Shadow

What Is Red?

Red is a stop sign telling you not to go.
Red is Santa Claus ho, ho, ho.
Red is the fire that warms you up.
Red is your juice in a big red cup.
Red is the sadness when you do something bad.
Red is the sunburn you wish you never had.
Red is the fish you eat at dinner.
Red is the ribbon you get from being a winner.
Red is the tongue you have in your mouth.
Red is an apple you eat at your house.
Red is a guitar you play with great glee.
Red is a spider you yell when you see.
Red is the bricks you have in your wall.
Red is the blood you get when you fall.
Red is the fox you see on your lawn.
Red is the flowers you give to your mom.

Matt Carlo, Grade 4
Lincroft Elementary School

Spring Is...

Spring is cool
Spring is fun
Spring is for everyone
Spring is nice
Spring is rain
Spring is a day in the drain
Spring is running
Spring is playing
Spring is doing anything
Spring is cleaning
Spring is leading
Spring is really running out!

Ashley T. Stehr, Grade 6
Gilmore J Fisher Middle School

I Love the Spring!

Many trees have bloomed,
I love the spring.
The birds have been groomed,
I love this thing!

Small chicks are clucking
I love to play.
The horses are bucking,
I'll play all day.

Today it's raining,
Can't wait to go outside.
I keep complaining,
Put the rain aside.

Taylor Daly, Grade 4
Stonybrook Elementary School

Joey

Joey
Skinny, funny
Loves my family
Smart, dangerous, trustworthy, cool
Brother

Robert Greenzweig, Grade 6
Central Middle School

Springtime

S unflowers growing higher and higher.
P ut on light clothes
R uler of the seasons
I t's lots of people's favorite time of year
N o bees yet, but they're coming.
G reat weather for playing outside
T hink of all the beautiful flowers.
I f only it was spring all-year-round.
M ajor fun
E veryone's energy unfolds.

Yael Schwarzman, Grade 4
Solomon Schechter Day School

Halloween

It's dark and scary
No one talks
I see spiders that walk
And monsters like stalks
Halloween is a great party
It should be every Friday

Jake Mikhailik, Grade 4
Springfield Township School

Beautiful Mermaid

There once lived a girl
With a house made of pearls

She went to a school
That was taught in a pool

She had a nice tail
Made of millions of scales

Her scales glowed in sun and shade
She was a beautiful mermaid.

Gilvary Pierre, Grade 6
Fieldstone Middle School

My Brother

My special friend came from my mother,
My special friend I do not smother.
My special friend is my little brother!
A special friend, I hope to get another.

Kelsey Plant, Grade 5
Winslow Township School No 6

Poetry

Poetry
rhyming stories
listening, telling, writing
lost in a differing world
Stories
funny, sad
telling, laughing, giggling
in a magical place
Books
poetry, fiction
listening, loving, giggling
always a different subject
School
classes, teachers
learning, playing, writing
going every single weekday
Homework
every day
doing, helping, learning
doing without a choice
Done!

Sammie Lemmer, Grade 4
Solomon Schechter Day School

Flag

Waves like a hand
Waving goodbye
Floats like there is no gravity
Representing everything
We stand for

Lenny Smith, Grade 6
Cherry Hill Elementary School

Cat

Cat
Playful, funny
Meow, stretch, scratch
Sleepy, loving, cuddly, mischievous
Adorable

Adriana Christine Dragan, Grade 4
Mansfield Township Elementary School

Desk

Solid object
Classroom
Square, seat, table
Desk

John Pearson, Grade 6
Central Middle School

Fall

Warm blankets, black cats,
trick or treat, ghouls, goblins, cold
windy, football games

Gabrielle Jarvis, Grade 4
Franklin Park Elementary School

The Raging Brothers

The moon
Mysteriously makes menacing light
Like a flickering lantern

The sun's anger rages
When he is replaced
By the menacing moon

The moon's gaze
Is like an arrow
Launching electricity in kids' veins

Tyler Gray, Grade 6
Little Egg Harbor Intermediate School

The Frog

There once was a a man from Hog,
Who thought he ate a frog.
He went to the bay,
In the middle of the day,
Then he ate a log.

Amanda Thomson, Grade 4
Mansfield Township Elementary School

Spring Is Near

Hurrah, Hurrah spring is finally near.
I can't wait to buy my dirt bike gear.
My mom says the one I have is way too small.
If I ride now without one I'll get hurt if I fall.
I'm not sure what kind I'll pick it out.
Whatever it is I'm sure I won't pout.
Maybe yellow or black with flames on it.
Whatever I pick I know it will fit.
As soon as I get it I'll put it on.
Then I'll jump on my bike and I'll be gone.

Kyle Barber, Grade 5
Immaculate Conception Regional School

Spring Arrives

Spring arrives with warmth and smiles
And renews the Earth complete
Flowers are blooming all around
With lovely fragrances so sweet

As bees buzz around tulips and roses
Their bodies act as a pollen collector
All around the great flowers
They search around for nectar

Birds singing beautiful tones
All through the spring day
The melody of their songs soothe us
They will chase your blues away

Nicholas Nugent, Grade 4
Old York Elementary School

The Final Game

The final day is here,
the last game of the season.
My team is excited,
and also very nervous.
We started the game,
with the jump of a ball.

We start out slowly,
and not strong at all.
The opponents are beating us
all down the court.
Then the coach puts me in,
and I start to kick in.
I dribble down the court,
then pass the ball off.
I get the ball back and lay the ball up.
My heart beats fast and slow.
Then we are all tied up,
and I go with the three.
Four seconds left and I throw the ball up.
It falls with a swish,
and I win the game.

Anthony Delzotto, Grade 5
St John's Academy

Beach

The beach is as cool
As the wind on a winter day.
The sand is as light brown
As leaves on a fall day.
The water is as blue as
The sky on a summer day.

Amber Johnson, Grade 6
Lower Alloways Creek Elementary School

Classroom

The blackboard screeching like crows on a summer day.
The pencils tap like a woodpecker in the woods.
The students' backpacks getting thrown in a pile like garbage.
The papers rattling like tree leaves.

Ashley King, Grade 6
Little Egg Harbor Intermediate School

Under the Sea

They talk among themselves
Joyfully as they float
Softly across
The ocean floor

They see fish, crabs
Sharks and seaweed
They talk with the octopus

Telling him
What their travel was like
As they have lunch

Coming back up to the surface
To look at the mixture of ruby and peach
Salmon and aqua sunset
As it slowly
Disappears into the sea

Kylie Corda, Grade 5
Robert B Jaggard Elementary School

Smile

Whenever you smile,
It is like a big ray of SUNSHINE.
Even though you don't know this, I really like you.

Whenever you smile,
You make my life fill up with happiness.
But when you are down, I am like a pile of dry dirt.

Whenever you smile,
You make that pile of dry dirt grow and grow
Into a beautiful field of grass.

That is what your SMILE does to me.
So crack a smile, I'll help you do it.

Andrew Cannon, Grade 6
Academy Street Elementary School

What's in Mrs. Ocampo's Desk?
Five twelve-inch rulers, pens and highlighters galore, only two late slips (we're a good class), a million gifts from her best class (that's us), hand cream, a coffee mug, bent-out paper clips, extra sticky tape to keep our mouths shut (just kidding), folders, paper, staplers and sticky clips, colored pencils, calendars, and lesson plans. Oh, and don't forget Aengus's pet vampire bunny.

Emily Friedlander, Grade 5
Sicomac Elementary School

The Perfect Tree
Every Saturday after Thanksgiving we go get a Christmas tree
Where we go in Sussex County we see animals that are wild and free
My dad is careful so he drives slow
Even though it's sunny it feels like below zero
In the barn we say hello to the animals, there is no snake,
They're as friendly as an old friend's handshake

When we cut the tree down it falls very slowly
But before that, in the field, my sister and I put on a show with many irrelevant things going on boringly
After the tree is cut down we get it wrapped
We usually get a tall, wide, straight tree with a bottom that's snapped
When we're in the car we pass a frozen river and make a bet
That we can't take a picture by the glowing sunset
Afterwards, in the car, my sister is very obnoxious
So I sit away from her because my car is spacious

Rory Vanderberg, Grade 6
Fieldstone Middle School

Springtime
When spring comes, it makes me want to feel the grass on my feet, the wind blowing through my hair, a cool breeze hitting me with rapid speed. What a wondrous feel. No more snowflakes so white and no more frostbite but wonderful colors of pink, red, blue, and yellow. Picking daisies, doing somersaults, and climbing trees. Oh what a great feel. I can't wait for spring!

Nawal Abbasi, Grade 4
Apple Montessori School

Monkeys
Monkeys come in different shapes and sizes. Some are cute some are ugly. Some are kind and some are mean. Of course many monkeys are playful, but sadly some are lazy. They are brown, black or maybe tan. Some say black monkeys are cool. Do you think that? And when people don't like brown monkeys I frown. And a tan monkey liked a man. Do you like monkeys?
I do!

Emily Gonzalez, Grade 5
Paul W Carleton Elementary School

Red Wolf
T he red wolves have weights ranging from 40 to 90 pounds
H abitats for the red wolves are disappearing
E ven the wild red wolves are threatened by man

R ed wolves have several coat colors to help them hide (cinnamon red, gray, and black).
E very red wolf has massive jaw muscles.
D ens are located in sand dunes.

W olves have 42 teeth.
O nce farmers hated and feared them because they often ate the sheep, cows, or horses.
L ength of these mammals is 55-65 inches long.
F ossils up to 750,000 years old, indicate that these red wolves may be close relatives to a primitive ancestor of the North American canids (having wolf-like features).

Zak Saylor, Grade 4
Franklin Township Elementary School

My Hero

Chris is my hero
He helps me in dance
Through good times and bad
He always is happy
If I struggle he tells me to think
Of all I have done
And to have some fun
He always is willing
To share a helping hand,
Chris makes me feel more confident
Dancing in front of people
Making me feel like a star
Or someone famous
When I am feeling bad
He makes me glad
Chris says to dance as if no one were watching
And I take that in mind,
Chris is very kind
And he is special to me
As you can plainly see!

Brianna Hicks, Grade 5
North Dover Elementary School

Sports

Sports
fun, hard
kicking, hitting, sweating
feeling cool while winning
coaching, running, sliding
happy, excited
Baseball

Daniel Lapka, Grade 4
Perth Amboy Catholic Intermediate School

Beach

Sparkling water in the ocean
Dolphins jumping in a smooth motion
Surfing and playing in the sand
You can think of it as a dreamland

Burying your friend's feet in the sand
Which she thinks is quite grand
Throwing the Frisbees around the beach
It might go in the ocean, what a big reach!

Colorful kites flying high in the sky
Soaring through it looking like a firefly
In relaxation, you give a big sigh
For its beauty could make you cry

Up to your ear, you hold a seashell
Listen to the song it wants to tell
Listening to crashing waves in this
Enchanting flow of water like a kiss

Megan Fernandez, Grade 5
Old York Elementary School

Dreams

The rare day has come for me
to dare someone to do something that they have already done.
In my dreams I see a deer
but not to fear —
it's only a dream
on things that are not real,
but sometimes they seem real.
Once I saw a Moray Eel
in the Pacific Ocean —
It's only a dream.
Outside there was an accident,
the car door was torn off.
I had to do something,
so I called the cops.
The driver was drunk,
and he was locked up —
It's only a dream.
I saw a slam dunk contest, too —
It's only a dream.
And that is all, my good friend,
thanks for listening to my poem.

John Lovett, Grade 5
Roosevelt Elementary School

Spring

S is for sports that people play a lot in the spring!
P is for practice which makes perfect!
R is for rain that comes down in April!
I is for inside with the air conditioning on!
N is for new because everything in spring is new!
G is for great and I hope you have a great spring!

Raymond Jazikoff, Grade 4
John F Kennedy Elementary School

Dogs

I would like a dog because it would play and run.
I would like to play with it in the sun.
We would play all day and play all night.
Boy, that would be a real sight.
Maybe it would cost a lot.
If I get one, I would call him Spot.

Kevin Kellaher, Grade 4
St Rose of Lima School

Spring

Spring has come,
winter's shade has left the sun,
the birds will chirp and the children will run.

The world will be green
as the squirrels will be lean after their hibernation.

The cold will be done,
for spring has come!

Alex MacDonald, Grade 6
Gilmore J Fisher Middle School

Spring

During spring,
The birds come back and start to sing.
I see birds fly,
High in the sky,
Spring is a beautiful thing!
Kevin Beck, Grade 5
St Helena School

My Special Place

I'm aggravated
I need to get out
I go to my special place
Watchung Stables
I ride my favorite horse,
Hobo
As I ride him around the ring
slowly I cool off
unwind and relax
let the horse do anything
he wants.
Over time
I close my eyes
and trust the horse —
drop the stirrups
drop the reins
and just sit in the saddle.
Brenna Madera, Grade 5
Salt Brook Elementary School

Homework

I would rather go to bed
Than doing the thing I dread.
"Homework, homework, homework,"
my parents would always say.
No, no, no, no way.
My parents keep on saying it to me.
It sounds like a buzzing bee.
I wish we didn't have homework
And we only had "playwork."
Alex Pinto, Grade 4
Mansfield Township Elementary School

My Mom

My mom is nice,
though she hates ice,
but gives awesome advice.
She is great,
and has a mate,
they go on many dates.
We make her mad,
when we are bad.
But she loves flowers
and has lots of power.
!!!I love my mom!!!
Lara Espinosa, Grade 4
Rev George Brown Memorial School

Spring

Spring
is here
with flowers
and good showers
rain
Iman Abdel-Malek, Grade 4
Franklin Park Elementary School

My Kitty Tigger

My orange cat named Tigger
His eyes sometimes get bigger
He loves to sit in boxes
He's very afraid of foxes
He can't climb trees
And loves to chase bees
He likes to sniff flowers
And he can play for hours!
Carly Wilkins, Grade 6
Springfield Township School

Trees

Trees live in the woods.
Trees are tall, fat and wide.
The branches have leaves.
When it gets cold the leaves fall.
Zachery Loffredo, Grade 5
Springfield Township School

My Favorite Place

If you like mountains and valleys
And the bright hot sun,
I'll tell you about a special place
Where you can have a lot of fun

You can ride your bike in the park
Late at night when it is dark
You can hunt for snakes and lizards too
But be very careful or one may bite you

There are video arcades
And lots of neon lights
And the light from the stars
Brightens up the night

Take a trip to the dam
Or jump in the pool
It can get real hot
So you want to stay cool

I know what you're thinking
This place is outrageous
But you'll have lots of fun
In a place called Las Vegas
Michael Pappas, Grade 5
Ocean Avenue Elementary School

Drowsy Catnip

Soft, purring cat
Lightly sleeping on the couch
Warm and adorable
Nicole Grupp, Grade 5
Mansfield Township Elementary School

Sweet Mean Kitten

There once was a sweet little kitten
Whose small little name was Mitten
I loved her so
And I think you know
Be careful or you may get bitten
Casandra Damsgaard, Grade 5
Springfield Township School

My Baby Brother

Baby binkie
Baby bed
He sure does like it when he's fed
Baby good
Baby bad
He whines and cries when sad
I love him dearly
So very much
He makes me happy by his touch
Baby, baby
You're a cutie baby
Baby, baby
I love you baby
Nicolette Pizzigoni, Grade 4
Our Lady of Mount Virgin School

The Softball Field

Sunny blue skies
on the softball field
the ball flies
across the dirt field

running the bases
I made it to third
smiles with funny faces
as I slid into home

my teammates gather
and everyone cheers
winning doesn't matter
we're just having fun
Krista Lyons, Grade 5
Ocean Avenue Elementary School

Spring

A flower blooming
It is a sunny spring day
A cool breeze passes by
David Fernandez, Grade 4
Number 15 Elementary School

Big Fat Meany

I don't want to go to school no more,
because there's a big fat meany at the door,
He will grab you by the shirt,
Make you eat some dirt,
That's why I don't want to go to school no more.

Bobby Lewis, Grade 4
Stonybrook Elementary School

Rainbow

Life makes up a rainbow,
    it is full of different, beautiful colors,
Each one is unique,
    and they all come together to make a rainbow
After a bad day
    the colors make it go away
Always in your dreams they stay
    until another rainy day.
In the future the colors will stay,
    just as our friendship, they will never go away.

Shaina Rooney, Grade 6
Walter T. Bergen Middle School

I Made a Mistake

I went to a barn to ride a horse,
I made a mistake…and fell off the course.

I went to the field to plant some flowers,
I made a mistake…and met Austin Powers.

I went to school to borrow a stool,
I made a mistake…and borrowed a mule.

I went to a house to get a string,
I made a mistake…and got a thing.

I went to space to go to Mars,
I made a mistake…and bought some cars.

I went to the store where people spend,
I made a mistake…and that's the end.

Sammi Rubenstein, Grade 4
Sicomac Elementary School

Green Is Many Things

Green is ice cream and an apple
    and the grass that feels smooth
Green is the taste of salad.
Trees and mold smell green
Being on a roller coaster makes me feel green
Green is the sound of buds and Green Day
Green is a park, Greenland, and Ireland.
St. Patrick's Day is green.
Spring is also green.
Green is a grasshopper.

Kayla Egan, Grade 6
Thorne Middle School

Airplanes

They are always soaring
And roaring
Through the sky

As we cruise through the night,
On our long airplane flight,
I look down to see my house,
As tiny as a mouse

I go to sleep
But, I hear a peep,
I wake with denial
For I see an old man, laughing in the aisle

He put me in a daze
With that smiling, old gaze
That I will remember for the rest of my days

Jack Kalin, Grade 5
Brayton Elementary School

Questioning Nature

What is a flower but a petal of color
What is a tree but a long stick full of branches
What is a piece of grass but a green strand of nature
What is a farm but a field full of new beginnings for plants
What is anything but an object consisting of matter.

Nicole Britton, Grade 6
Monmouth Beach Elementary School

Impelling Precious Time

Tick-tock, tick-tock.
There it stands, upright and sky-scraping,
As its mesmerizing orchid pendulum oscillates
Impelling precious time.

As the sun's rays creep through transparent windows,
It gleams, showing its royal importance.
And its ebony arms revolve
Impelling precious time.

Days, nights, weeks, years — still, it will be on its feet,
Watching the mortal scurry past.
Yet, it will be mirthful doing what it does best
Impelling precious time.

Sometimes, though, it needs to take a breath
Or it will begin to wilt.
But with the strength of just one thrust, it will continue
Impelling precious time.

But, even though it is peaceful and self-ruling,
It is there for a sole purpose.
For even in the harshest condition, it will not rest
Impelling precious time.

Bhavin Gala, Grade 6
Woodglen Middle School

Chores

Dishes in the sink,
Chores really stink,
I'm glad to put that in ink,
That's what I'll always think.
Jeffrey McDaniel, Grade 5
Springfield Township School

I Have a Furry Goofy Friend…

I have a furry goofy friend,
Who snores when he's asleep.
Some people think that to be obnoxious,
But I think that's really sweet.

I have a furry, goofy friend
That you would like to know
He looks very handsome
When he's playing upon the snow.

When he wags his long brown tail
That means that he is happy!
Sometimes he walks so slow
I wish he would make it snappy!
If you're wondering who he is,
I'll tell you it's my dog Buster,
He's fuzzy, warm, and golden brown,
He is the color of some mustard!
Ashley Worthington, Grade 6
Fieldstone Middle School

Winter Wonderland

I wish to walk with you
In a winter wonderland
We will skate on the icy blue
This trip will definitely be grand.

We will ride in a sleigh
And drink a warm delight,
You can come and go as you may
It is a wonderful sight.
Julia Contino, Grade 4
St Joseph School

My Dog Ace

My dog Ace has a cute little face
He has fur all over the place
Ace has rough paws
He has short claws
His fur is yellow
Ace is very mellow
I have no fear
When he is near
He is loyal, loving and
Follows me all over the place
I love my dog Ace
Jenna Mancini, Grade 5
St Joseph School

The Fire

It makes me sad and scared when I think about the fire.
Not because I was in it.
Not because I caused it.
But because my best friends went through it,
and I was not there for him for three days…

I was in Jamaica.
He was in his house.
We lived across the street from each other.
I wish I had been there.
After I heard "fire," and "your friend," I just heard bits and pieces.
I felt dead, and only capable of sadness.
Tears welled up in my eyes.
Then I heard "alive," and everything went snap;
back into focus.
I was six when that happened.
People say my reaction would have been different.
That is wrong.
I have, for two seconds, experienced the worst feeling in the world.
Jesse Lax, Grade 4
Toll Gate Grammar School

My Hero

My dad is my hero as you can plainly see
He will always be there for me
He will help me with anything as hard as it may be
He helps me with sports, homework, and swimming in the sea.
He tries to cheer me up when I am feeling blue
Before I get sick and eventually get the flu.
My dad teaches me new things
He teaches me how to cook, build, and even sing
He teaches me new games like air hockey and pool
I think he's really cool
My dad is my hero because he inspires me
He inspires me to be the best as I can be
No matter how hard I try
He tells me never to cry and to always keep my head up high
He inspires me to be a great athlete and to always compete
He tells me not to worry if my hair isn't neat
When I grow up I want to go to college
My dad always says you cannot get enough knowledge
If in all the world I would have to choose
I would pick my dad and never lose
My dad is my hero, and that is true and with all my heart I love you.
Jackie Vorrasi, Grade 5
North Dover Elementary School

Love

Love is pink.
It smells like chocolate chip cookies baking in an oven.
It looks like sweet bright pink roses all around you in a meadow.
It tastes like delicious chocolate candy.
It sounds like birds chirping.
Love feels like you just have the urge to dance and sing.
Kaleigh Ganter, Grade 6
St Rose of Lima School

Sage My Collie*

S is for her sweet hearted nature.
A is for the attention we gave her.
G is for the gigantic size.
E is for her everlasting devotion.

M is for the most wonderful times we had together.
Y is for you and me.

C is for the chase to retrieve my socks.
O is for her obedience to her family.
L is for her ladylike ways
L is for the love we gave to her.
I is for the intelligent look she had.
E is for the enormous amount of *fur* she had.

In my heart you'll always be, my lovely fuzzy collie.
Sarah Peoples, Grade 6
Assumption School
*Born April 1996, died September 2, 2005

White Snow

As the white gentle snow comes falling down
The sad wolf goes crying to the full harvest moon
You can see the glowing gentle owl
Swooping down to catch a mouse
In the moonlight
You can hear the sound of the cricket
And owl
The gentle breeze hitting
The bare trees
Makes a smooth beautiful sound

Stephen Dranoff, Grade 4
Pond Road Middle School

Kitty in the Window

K itty
I t keeps your house free of mice
T rustful
T otally cute!
Y ou know they're watching you play

I nquisitive
N ice

T he best friend to have
H appiest in spring
E njoys the spring air

W aits for you to come home
I mpatient
N oisy
D affodils and cats make me happy
O utdoor cats
W hite, black, and gray.

Dana McKenna, Grade 4
Hardyston Township Elementary School

It's Spring

This sport is not hard at all.
All you have to do is catch the ball.
It does not matter if you are small or tall.
Just remember not to fall.

You will have a lot of fun.
But you will have to run in the hot hot sun!
Clean your cleats on the mat.
Then pick up the bat and take a whack.

In 1839 this game was made.
The first rule is always the same,
Nine players are needed for the game.
There are spaces between all the bases.
Please don't forget to tie your laces.

Ryan Sweeney, Grade 5
Sacred Heart School

Winter Night

Snow glitters on the frozen ground,
Everything is peaceful not a sound.
Footprints of children and their dogs,
Dotting the snow.
Bushes and trees covered in white,
A moon is the only thing glowing this night.
I leave new tracks in the snow,
As I walk home.

Katherine Mandicz, Grade 6
Great Meadows Regional Middle School

Riches or Disaster

One day, a boy was wondering,
"What will be the result of my life? Riches or disaster?"
So he went off to start an adventure.
What will he find? Riches or disaster?
The boy soon came across a large castle,
What will he find? Riches or disaster?
He saw an open door.
What will he find? Riches or disaster?
He went down a trapdoor.
What will he find? Riches or disaster?
He climbed up a dusty ladder,
What will he find? Riches or disaster?
He saw a golden treasure chest,
What has he found? Riches, not disaster.
If you stick to your goals, you will only find riches.

Jesse Chand, Grade 6
Thomas Jefferson Middle School

Forest of Doom

The rain falls like millions of people crying
Lightning hits as if the whole world strikes with anger
Owls watch you in the old dead trees
Eyes see you in the old shaking bushes

Kyle Robert Booth, Grade 6
Little Egg Harbor Intermediate School

Puppy Dog
Puppy
Cute, fluffy
Wild, playing, sleeping
Laying on the rug
Bark
Sabrina Petrunis, Grade 5
Elizabeth F Moore Elementary School

The Life of Dreams
Although the future looks clear,
you may never hide in fear,
for friends are near.

And yet you look for the meaning,
of all the good,
without a meaning,
it isn't the same.

Friends, family, and fiends,
life is but a dream.
In which you never,
need to look ahead.

The meaning is,
that life is how it comes.
A blow to the right,
a growth-spurt in height,
it's all the same,
it is life, life, life.
Niki Siewerd, Grade 6
Walter T. Bergen Middle School

Snowman
How do you feel when you melt?
Sad is how you just felt.
It is no fun,
Melting in the sun.
But if you can,
The melting will stop if you use the fan.
If it can be
We'll wait to see.
Amber Cline, Grade 5
Folsom Elementary School

The Forest
There are many pines in the forest,
And violets too.
Forests can attract many a tourist,
And logging companies too.
The forest is a place of rest,
Where the birds sing.
But termites can be a pest,
Where they live like a king.
Daniel Tanis, Grade 6
Trinity Christian School

Spring
Spring is here
it's the best time of year.
There are many colors to be found,
and little creatures all around.
Smells of nature in the air
we spend the day without a care.
Darkness falls, the Earth will sleep
the sun will rise without a peep.
Spring is grand!
Charlotte Murphy, Grade 5
St Veronica Elementary School

Say What's on Your Mind
Say it loud,
You know why,
Don't be shy,
Don't lie,
Just say what's on your mind!
Nick Cefali, Grade 4
Meadowbrook Elementary School

I Wish
I wish I was a fairy,
So I could sit on a flower.

I wish I was sugar,
So I would never taste sour.

I wish I was a cub,
So I could play with a bear.

I wish I was a model,
So I could have someone do my hair.

I wish I was a queen,
So I could wear clothes of silk.

I wish I was an Oreo,
So I could always be by milk.

I wish I was a mouse,
So I could always eat cheese.

I wish I was well-mannered,
So I could always say please.
Emily Zimmer, Grade 5
Byram Township Intermediate School

Pots O' Gold
Leprechauns love big pots o' gold
At rainbow's end it's found I'm told
A parade of green
Celebrates St. Patty's theme
The Irish jig is danced so bold
Kenny Hesse Jr., Grade 6
Sacred Heart Elementary School

Blackboard
Every morning
New ideas and possibilities
Are given to me
but then they are gone
at the end of the day
with one swipe
of the eraser
and I am left
Alone
in the dark
with no possibilities
until the next morning comes
along with another day
of a new outfit of words for me to wear
but they will just be swept away
again
until tomorrow.
Betsy Louda, Grade 6
Cherry Hill Elementary School

The Ugly Worm
Once there was an ugly worm.
Who really liked to squirm.
He was such a pain.
He had no brain.
But he had a lot of germs.
Matthew Rubino, Grade 6
Thorne Middle School

Ray
There once was a young boy named Ray,
Who lived really close to the bay.
One day when he went,
He wasn't content.
So he went back home to Momé.
Tijesunimi Oni, Grade 4
West End Memorial Elementary School

Africa
Africa oh, Africa,
where my soul is set loose.

Africa, oh Africa,
where I can run like the wind.

Whenever I feel down or blue
I think up of you.
So suddenly and quickly
I became so happy and true.

So Africa, oh Africa,
never turn old and gray
stay beautiful each and every day!
Jamie Currie, Grade 5
Salt Brook Elementary School

Spring

S omething is outside
P laying with a ray of the sun.
R unning with the wind
I n the lazy afternoon.
N ature is starting to blossom.
G orgeous flowers wake up from their winter slumber.

Elana Steinlauf, Grade 4
Solomon Schechter Day School

Outside Inside

Outside there is snow covering the ground like a blanket.
Inside people are warming their hands by the fire.

Outside people are slipping on the street.
Inside kids are waiting for Santa Claus.

Outside people search for Christmas trees.
Inside you hear the slurp of hot chocolate.

Outside there are lots of snowball fights.
Inside people get ready for bed at night.

Alexander Dockery, Grade 5
Byram Township Intermediate School

Winter in the Woods

Crunch! Crunch!
Walking in the snow
Carefully and quietly
Not missing a step.
Making small tracks,
Not knowing what lurks in the dark at night.
Hardly breathing,
As you feel the wind biting your face
All you see is the snow,
Trees and the stillness of the Earth.
The moon is reflecting upon a frozen lake
Someone is calling you…
You run home
And let the fire warm you.

Christa Principato, Grade 4
Pond Road Middle School

Take the Path You Want to Be

Take the path you want to go
Don't give up, there's a reason you must know:
A kingdom is ready, a throne will be passed
Only if you have confidence
Will it be passed
You dream of a road to an enchanted garden
Then think to yourself: is this the right way?
But you can't just dream and play every day
For hard work and perseverance
Will take you that way.

Hillary Chan, Grade 5
Millstone River School

Remembrance*

I remember…we played games together
And the first time we made brownies
When we all went to New York
Telling each other our secrets
And when I first walked, rode a bike,
and my first word "Mom"
Learning something new
When I needed you, you were there for me

I will always think of you in life or death

Colleen Velez, Grade 6
Little Egg Harbor Intermediate School
*Dedicated to my mother

Flowers

Emotions are like a flower
There are petals of happy and glad
And there are petals of mad and sad
They soak above in the rain
But when winter comes snow gives them pain
Flowers Flowers they give me joy
Flowers Flowers my favorite toy

Thomas Popola, Grade 6
Kawameeh Middle School

Consider This

Think about this, since it happens a lot,
It's a rotten evil plot.
Child trafficking is a serious crime.
And people do it all the time.
Imagine this, being taken away,
"Be quiet! Or else." That's what they'll say.
Threats here and there,
Some other things you can't bare.
Cold nights and hot trafficking trucks.
Yes. The worst luck.
Being sold like a piece of meat.
Getting hurt from your head to your feet.
Crying yourself to sleep,
All night, you only weep.
Don't complain about your parents.
They love you so.
Appreciate them while they're there.
Before they're gone.

Jenny Jaramillo, Grade 6
Thomas Jefferson Middle School

Stuck

Sometimes you feel like you're stuck
Like there is nowhere to go
Just go through a tunnel
And see where it leads
Then follow a road and go to a place
That will take your life where it needs to be

Matthew Leconey, Grade 6
Little Egg Harbor Intermediate School

Birthday
Today is my birthday
Oh how I can't wait
I've been waiting all night, year and day
For today is my birthday
Hip, hip, hooray

Presents and gifts
Money and cards
I have no friends
But family to warm my heart

I wanted a bat
I wanted a ball
I didn't get one single thing
I realized today was June 17th
And my birthday isn't till the 19th
Chrissy Calavano, Grade 5
Ocean Avenue Elementary School

My Eyes
My eyes wander
Like the clouds,
Drifting in the sky,
My eyes stare,
Fixed on a tree,
On a star,
On a cloud.
My eyes are my own,
No one else's but mine.
Your eyes are yours,
Her eyes are hers.
But my eyes,
They are mine.
Julia Meade, Grade 5
Hillview Elementary School

Games
Games,
Games,
Games,
Board, video, entertaining games,
Easy, difficult, challenging games
These are just a few.
Fighting games,
Adventure games,
Action, puzzle, racing games,
Strategy, card, memory games,
Sports games too.
Fantasy games,
Strange games,
Don't forget GameCube games.
Last of all, best of all
I like
All games.
Nick Torre, Grade 5
Ridgeway Elementary School

Patti Mellody
I love your perfume and Herbal Essence scent.
You're citrus flavored gum or blueberry Italian ice
on a hot summer day.
You're coffee ice cream, creamy vanilla fudge,
with whipped cream dancing on top.
Your soft, sandy, silky skin is like Spongebob Squarepants pj's.
You are as pretty as a make-believe princess living in a fairytale castle.
Prettier than a movie star walking down the red carpet.
Your voice is a singer standing behind a microphone.
You are the sunshine every day as it fills my heart with love.
Katie Mellody, Grade 6
Franklin Elementary School

Slave
I am scared and scarred.
I wonder if I'll finish the work in time.
I hear screams of laughter from the masters when they are whipping others.
I see chores that need to be done.
I want my mom and dad.
I am scared and scarred.

I pretend that I am free.
I feel the whip on my back.
I touch the rough cotton that rips my hands up.
I worry about what I would do if I got sick.
I cry all the time.
I am scared and scarred.

I understand that I am useless to white people.
I say the words to the song "The Drinking Gourd."
I dream of being free.
I try to escape but never succeed.
I hope to see my family soon.
I am scared and scarred.
Jennifer Latchford, Grade 5
Mary A Hubbard Elementary School

The Colors of the Sky
The colors of the sky are beautiful as we pass by until night skies fall.
Then we look up at the stars make a wish from our hearts.
Soon it is time to start again with a new day.
The colors of the sky are beautiful as we pass by!
Rhiannon Neal, Grade 5
Belhaven Avenue Middle School

My Dog
His fur is as soft as the petals of a flower,
The amber in his eyes is brighter than gems,
When he looks up at me, I feel happy and sad all at once,
He smells like newly cut grass after rolling in it,
When he walks he bounces happily up and down,
Like a leaf blowing in the wind,
I walk in the door and he wags his tail and barks his same excited bark,
He's the best dog because he's mine!
Marie Czirbik, Grade 6
Franklin Elementary School

Lauren
I am a sensitive and caring girl
I wonder why people hurt animals
I hear my parents talking
I see words in a book
I want to have peace in the world
I am a sensitive and caring girl

I pretend that my stuffed animals have feelings
I feel my soft pillow when I sleep
I touch my mom's hand when I am scared
I worry if I am a good friend
I cry when I miss my pets
I am a sensitive and caring girl

I understand why they made school
I always wish that my dreams come true
I dream that I live in peace
I try to do well in school
I hope everyone in the war comes home safely
I am a sensitive and caring girl

Lauren Snieckus, Grade 4
Meadowbrook Elementary School

Best Friends
A best friend is like a diamond,
You can't find a thousand,
They are rare in their own way,
And seem different every day,
You cannot even bear to stay far away from them,
And the time you get to spend with them you cherish like a gem,
They know the song in your heart,
And the rhythm in your art,
That there is no end of a filmstrip,
To the story of our friendship.

Megan Underwood, Grade 6
Long Branch Middle School

Parents Are a Blanket
Parents are a blanket
Sheltering from the cold
Warm and caring
Filled with love and happiness
Calming at the end of a bad day
Guiding you through life
Relaxing and helpful

Brian Havens, Grade 6
Township of Ocean Intermediate School

Bunny
There once was a bunny named Gunny
Who thought everything was funny
He went on a boat
And bought a goat
Then went back to his wife named Hunny

Brianna Zigrest, Grade 5
St Dominic Elementary School

My Favorite Orange
Orange is a monarch, ready to take flight.
Orange is a sunset, the beginning of night.
Orange is a basketball, candy corn, leaves in the fall.
Orange is a mango, a tangle in my new orange shawl.
Orange is my shoe, dancing to the beat.
Orange is a tiger, softly walking on its feet.
When I bite into an orange, I taste sweet orange juice.
But my favorite orange is the delicious orange fruit!

Linette Reeman, Grade 4
Lincroft Elementary School

Spring Is Here
The wonderful aroma of flowers blooming,
Sunlight that glows and warms the face,
Children playing baseball running base to base.
Birds chirping as their little eggs hatch,
Mosquitos born now it's time to scratch.
Warm spring breezes blowing around,
Kicking up those fall leaves still on the ground.
Bees buzzing searching for honey,
Little animals born looking for mommy.
Kids laughing, playing spring sports,
Eating ice cream while wearing shorts.
Fresh cut grass, I love that smell,
Clean cotton linens my mom will tell.
Big bears awake from a long winter nap,
Hoping to find a tree with a lot of sap.
Spring is for fishing for girls and boys,
Moms and Dads, too, Oh, what joy!
"April showers bring May flowers,"
Watch our gardens grow.
Each seed is watered with care,
As springtime is finally here!

Brittany Day, Grade 5
North Dover Elementary School

Running Free
Horses' spirits run free so do their bodies.
No wrangler or horse whisperer can capture these beasts

The wild horses are running free all over many countries
Once they all lived free but sadly that just couldn't be

They are forever free not even the Cherokee
Can tame these wild beasts they are forever free

Forever free that's the way they want to be
It is so fun to see them run

Forever free on the sandy sea
That's the way I want to be running, running forever free

Running free is the way it should be
Running free forever free

Jessica Vaughan, Grade 6
Lower Alloways Creek Elementary School

Saturday

Never,
I won't open one eye, not even twitch!
I'm still half asleep
My eyes keep closing.
My brain isn't working!
I can't go to school,
It's just too cruel!
What? Saturday?
I'm out to play!

Brandon Rodriguez, Grade 4
Mansfield Township Elementary School

Baseball

Baseball is fun,
When we play it in the sun.

When you play on the field,
Your glove is like a shield.

When you're up at bat,
You try to give the ball a pat.

When you hit a home run,
Your dad screams, "Good job son!"

When your season starts,
You really have to take part,

Baseball is the best,
Better than all the rest.

Ryan Ramiz, Grade 4
St Rose of Lima School

Summer

Summer means swimming
And fun in the sun
Races on the beach
Get ready to run
Water parks
Are where we hang out
No children there
Will give a pout
Kids are happy
That school is over and done
No more homework
We could be number one
Sailing on oceans
Long summer rides
Tanning on the beach
Or touring with guides
School is coming
Once again
We all hope that summer
Will never end!

Alexandra Mahon, Grade 6
Springfield Township School

Fruit

Apples are so sweet,
Watermelon is like a treat.
Pineapple is brightish yellow,
Pears are so mellow.
Blueberries are so blue,
Kiwi is easy to chew.
Bananas are squishy,
Citrus oranges are mushy.
All these fruits I love,
For I know God made them from above.

Alexa Stabile, Grade 4
Christ the Teacher School

Sunshine

The sun shines on the grass,
Flowers bloom,
Winters pass.

Say good-bye to friends you know,
Hail, winter, sleet, and snow.
Say hello to friends of new,
Red, yellow, green and blue.
Let's go down to the sea,
And watch the busy bumble bee.
This will be the most wonderful time,
Just you and me.

Grace Polakoski, Grade 4
Franklin Township Elementary School

Thanksgiving

Happy Thanksgiving!
Gravy on mashed potatoes.
Parades and much more!

Jenny Hubert, Grade 4
Holy Family Interparochial School

Lazy Cats

There once was a cat named Sat,
Who never got off his mat.
He would lay down all day,
And throw his worries away,
Just to talk to his friend Pat.

Ashley Costa, Grade 4
Mansfield Township Elementary School

Puppies

Puppy
Small, cute
Playing, biting, running
House pet, Princess, Bear, Ginger
Scaring, finding, hiding
Kind, fat
Dog

Michael Hubosky, Grade 4
Our Lady of Mount Virgin School

Mom

Tall, funny
Loving, caring, sharing
Responsible is what she is
Bettina

Arista Parillo, Grade 4
Our Lady of Mount Virgin School

My Mirror Image

My Mirror Image
is so sweet,
she looks
exactly like me,
she eats and
sleeps at
the same time
as me,
and what do
you know
she even
goes to the same
school as me,
ooops, I forgot
there is a twist,
for you see she
is my identical
twin.

Maya Moran, Grade 5
Solomon Schechter Day Lower School

The Poem

Poem, poem, I need a poem.
One that is nice and long.
Because for school I owe 'em.
Maybe about a wheel with a prong.

Maybe about a cat with sharp teeth.
Or a dog with a long shiny tail.
Maybe about a guy name Keith.
Maybe about some Ginger Ale.

No, no that can't be right.
I need a poem with heart.
Not just with sprites.
But with good parts.

I need one like Shakespeare's.
Not just any old one.
One that the class would like to hear.
Maybe I could use a pun.

How nice it would be.
To have a poem like that one.
Or maybe, just maybe.
I could use this one.

Ian Daniels, Grade 6
Kings Academy

Fall Thoughts

Trees are colorful
Colorful as can be
With the yellow
Darkness from the shadow of the moon's reflection
Darkness from the sky
Brightness from the moon
In addition, brightness from the owl's eyes.

Jessica Samel, Grade 4
Pond Road Middle School

Soccer

I love soccer,
Kicking the balls,
Getting goals.
It's better than playing with dolls.
We need shorts and soccer shirts.
It's better than wearing tank tops and mini skirts.
You need to pay attention,
Listen to the coach!
Keep watch of the defender.
Keep watch of the approach.

Emilyrose Nowak, Grade 4
St Rose of Lima School

Hurt Kids

Some kids coil in fear,
Due to cruel parents,
Some people kill a kid's loved ones.
Kids cry due to the harm that they're put in.
Kids die every day due to their hurt hearts
They're small and fragile,
Innocent and scared, and yet strong in a way,
Hurting inside,
Kids die.
Kids are strong,
Put them in a loving home where they belong!

Gianna Loffredo, Grade 6
Thomas Jefferson Middle School

Lovely Ladybugs

Ladybugs look like a little half pea.
When they're flying they look so free.
They are often red with black spots.
To see how old they are you have to count their dots.

They eat one of the most harmful insects.
For that they gain the farmers' respect.
Their wings open wide when they fly.
Then they flutter around in the sky.

When you spot them, you can see
They are as pretty as can be.
Ladybugs bring you good luck
So when you see one don't ever duck!

Kayla Lanshe, Grade 5
Sacred Heart School

Winter

I can taste the hot, warm chocolate in my mouth
With marshmallows melting
They really calm me down

I see snowy and glistening land
The land is calm with no animals in sight
Only a lonely snowbird chomps again and again
In the still night

I can hear the white whistling snow
Through my ears
And bells tinkling
It's so perfect…
I hear chirping and more chirping

I feel peaceful and calm
The harsh weather makes me shake
I feel happy and glad
The air is so much fun

Jenna Johnson, Grade 5
Bartle Elementary School

The Rocks

The waves crash onto the ocean rocks.
Those wet, jagged ocean rocks
That sit out in the middle of nowhere
With blue seas all around.
I take one last stare and think,
Why are those rocks there?
And as I walk back to my car I see it.
The rocks have a picture of a wolf and a vulture
Chasing a pirate skull.
I sit there, I think, wow!
So as I walk away
I think what it must be like
To be a head chased by animals.

Evan Bray, Grade 5
Oxford Street Elementary School

Angles

What do you think is difficult?
angles, angles, angles,
doing them is terrible
they will make your brain into tangles!

You have to know what a right angle is
180° is when right angles double
if you don't know, smaller than 90 is acute
then you are in big trouble.

What do you think is difficult?
angles, angles, angles,
doing them is terrible
they will make your brain into tangles!

Courtney Masker, Grade 5
Ocean Avenue Elementary School

Eruption

It gave us mountains,
And also land, this is why
Volcanoes are friends
Stephen Giammona, Grade 6
Robert L Craig Elementary School

So Much Depends Upon

So much depends upon
A piece of chocolate,
So yummy and tasty.

So much depends upon
A little piece of chocolate,
How can you deny it,
Such a poor chocolate bar
Waiting to be eaten.
Nick Bossie, Grade 4
Pond Road Middle School

Loving Pets

Puppy
Cute, soft
Eating, playing, running
Home pet, house bound
Scratching, fighting, running
Rambunctious, wild
Cat
Angelica Neer, Grade 4
Our Lady of Mount Virgin School

Spaghetti

Spaghetti! Spaghetti!
It's long and sometimes round.
When it gets tired,
It limps around.
It likes to be
Twirled and curled
Around a fork.
But never, never, never
Be thrown out!
Christopher Moreira, Grade 4
Christ the Teacher School

Basketball

Three seconds left
The point guard waits for the screen
Fakes left
Goes right
Shoots as time expires
It spins around the rim
Then it goes in
The crowd cheers
Everybody goes crazy
The game is over
Justin Jameson, Grade 6
Gilmore J Fisher Middle School

To My Granddaughter with Love

A girl may be many things to her family,
daughter, a sister, a niece, or a cousin —
but being a granddaughter may be the most fun!
Being a granddaughter means being a member in an exclusive club —
one where the only rule is to be available for unlimited love, attention, and affection.
Perfect love sometimes does not come until the first grandchild.
Never forget that the most powerful force on earth is love.
Tatiana Alyna Mora, Grade 6
Thomas Jefferson Middle School

Reality Regrets

Laughter fallen with unwanted tears fades into understanding
I watched as it silently fell for eternity unserved
I felt the stroke of pain wither down and I heard wind calling its name
Spent in moments sworn in truth but lies cross the boundary
Reaching to grab something slipped away echoing in the shadows
Thought of as unfair to see what's undeserved
Grace defined in a distorted vision its meaning lost along the way
Alone in weeping hours flickering happiness dies
Unknown for grasping reality and saving the things we hate
Brightness dimming in its own heart's favor
Darkness overwhelms the life we once wanted but couldn't reach
And in time it said lies we cannot wonder for truth is what deceives
Keri Potvin, Grade 6
Anna L Klein Elementary School

Football

Football is the king of all sports.
It is a big traffic jam with players running everywhere.
It is the sweet scent of lemon zest.
Every time I walk on the field I taste the tangy lemonade
jolting through my mouth.
A falcon flying as fast as Jesse Owens running track goes through my mind.
I love this sport so much.
Football gives me such a rush.

Eric Steckly, Grade 6
Franklin Elementary School

There's a "Monster" in My Home!

There's a monster in my home and she screams night and day,
There's a monster in my home and she never goes away.
There's a monster in my home and I feel an upcoming pain,
'Cause there's a monster in my home and she's driving me insane!
There's a monster in my home and she messes up my room,
Can someone go get me a broom?
There's a monster in my home and she never leaves my sight,
There's a monster in my home and she wakes me up at night!
There's a monster in my home and she's messy when she eats.
There's a monster in my home and she never cleans her feet!
There's a monster in my home and her skin looks lime green,
There's a monster in my home and she always makes a scene!
There's a monster in my home and she plays lots of tricks and game,
There's a monster in my home that has a name...
"Little Sister" oh I wish she was tame!

Allie Florio, Grade 5
St Rose of Lima School

Silver White Winter

The silver white winters that melt into spring.
The geese that fly with the moon's on their wings.
The kittens that have little white whiskers of steal.
The snowman that makes pocker deals.
The Christmas tree as green as could be.
The Menorah lights up just for me.
The angel shining bright yellow.
May God rest ye merry fellow.

Jacqueline Exebio, Grade 6
Thomas Jefferson Middle School

A Monstrous Storm

I walk through the door
    one bright and sunny day.
I lock up my house,
    and start off to the bay.
But when I get down there,
    I find myself in a Monster's lair.
Black clouds are rumbling,
    the Monster is grumbling,
waiting to swallow me up.
    Bullets of rain come pounding down,
as I start running back into town.
    Wind is sweeping me off my feet,
the Monster has started pelting down sleet.
    With my house looming up in the distance,
the Monster pulls me back with insistence.
    All the world's forces are against me today,
who would have thought this would start at the bay?
    As I slam my front door,
the Monster gives a thunderous roar.
    My tense body starts to relax,
as wind whips and thunder cracks.

Abby MacMillan, Grade 5
Brayton Elementary School

My Best Friends and I

My best friends are always by my side
they help me get up on my feet and glide
without them I would be lost
if I get in trouble, we take the blame together
we are like sisters, and will be forever
we take shopping trips, and have lots of fun
our friendship will never be done
our friendship will last a lifetime!

Francesca Buarne, Grade 6
Our Lady of Mount Virgin School

Searching for Shamrocks

On the hill is where I will be
Searching in batches of three
Each section of the shamrocks looking like a spade
So green almost like a jade
There are no more four leaf clovers left for me.

MaryKaitlyn Nielsen, Grade 6
Long Branch Middle School

My Cousin

Michele is like a sugarplum princess,
Her wavy brown hair is a dark colored oak tree
She has skin like a smooth, pink peach,
and hazelnut eyes the size of the moon.
She is freshly picked flowers that have just bloomed
She's as sweet as the finest chocolate not yet opened
Hyper, hip, and totally cool, she's like a kid
who thinks she can travel the world without any sleep.
That is Michele, the prettiest lady there can be.

Angelica Calderon, Grade 6
Franklin Elementary School

Spring

Spring is beautiful, it makes me scream, and shout!
If it rains during the day, it makes me really pout.
I love having barbecue's. I like my hot dogs with sauerkraut.
I love spring, and there's definitely no doubt!

Mikki Oates, Grade 5
Christ the Teacher School

Love

Love isn't something that you buy.
Love is something that you find.
That only 2 people can share.
Who deeply care about each other.
The way they are always together.
Some may be far at distance but not at heart.
Love is a feeling that you can't even explain
You just know you're going to be together forever!
Love is something so special and amazing.
Sometimes you don't know whether to cry or laugh.
Knowing that you can spend the rest of your life
with that person that you love.
Saying I love you to that special person is one
thing that only you two can share.
That person is never going to let you down and be
there when you need it the most.
Through thick and thin when times can't get any
worse that person is there for you.
So hold on to it tight and it will last forever!

Stephanie Fernandes, Grade 6
Thomas Jefferson Middle School

My Dreams

I often dream of bouncing on a cloud.
And wishing for the fresh air hitting my face.

I think of a ball bouncing
From cloud to cloud.

When I dream I laugh and smile.
In my dreams I feel joyful and calm.

I often dream of bouncing on a cloud.

Brianna Jackson, Grade 4
Evergreen Elementary School

Father

F un to be with
A lways there for you
T he best person in the world
H appiest person in the world
E ven if he's gone he'll still love you
R ight always

Ari Sheps, Grade 5
Hillside Elementary School

Making the Team

She wouldn't believe
That I made the team
I showed her the form
Then she performed
The dance of the moms
It sounded like a bomb
Today is the best
I can never rest
I love softball
Because you don't have to be tall
I'm so glad I made the team
I was like a glowing beam

Kelly Winans, Grade 6
Chatham Middle School

Light Blue

Light blue is like a striking thunder bolt
that leads to a bright blue sky.
One small ink pen
A soft blueberry
A light crayon
Lots of blooming flowers
A windy day
One blue sweater
A busy cloud in the sky
A sour piece of ice
Swooshing water
A closing book
A moving stream
One chewy piece of gum
I like blue

Tande Mungwa, Grade 5
Christ the Teacher School

Puppy

I got a puppy yesterday,
I will never give her away.

We played catch with a ball,
Then I went to the mall.

My puppy is so fun,
We like to play in the sun.

Samantha Aruanno, Grade 4
St Mary's School

Ladybug

L azily flying onto a leaf
A ladybug is a welcome sight
D elighted when it comes to visit
Y ou can hold one in your hand
B ut it will tickle
U sually friendly and sociable
G uest of the moment, flies away.

Allie Lemmer, Grade 4
Solomon Schechter Day School

So Depressed

So lonely, so sad,
I feel neglected,
always being rejected.
So meaningless,
so invisible, so despised
I feel like a kite with no wind.

Christian Irizarry, Grade 5
Durban Avenue Elementary School

When I Am with My Family I…

laugh
annoy Kevin by blocking the TV
go to Nags Head
suck the meat off a buffalo wing
watch Smallville
go to my brother's basketball games
cheat at Monopoly
watch amazing movies like Harry Potter
go to parties at my friend's house
shoot my friends with Nerf guns
play Madden 2006 on the PS2
run races in the street
catch the pigskin
laugh
and do it all over again

Tommy McElgunn, Grade 5
Robert B Jaggard Elementary School

Brace Place

There once was a girl from Brace Place,
Who was always in my face.
It's done with love,
She always wears her gloves,
She tells me to pick up the pace.

Justine Bongiovanni, Grade 4
Mansfield Township Elementary School

A Rich Man

There once was a rich man in Spain,
Who had a gigantic airplane.
One day he got stuck,
So he rode in a truck.
The next day he boarded a train.

Abigail Diaz, Grade 4
West End Memorial Elementary School

Crazy Lady

There once was a lady from jail,
Who used to deliver the mail.
She broke a mail box,
And swallowed a fox,
Then noticed upon her head was a pail.

Jessica Chmiel, Grade 4
Mansfield Township Elementary School

Space Today

It is dark up there
There are astronauts in space
Explore the planets
You float and soar like a bird
It would be fun to go up!

Stephen Adams, Grade 4
Mansfield Township Elementary School

The Beach

The beach is teeming with life
Beneath its waters,
Fish are born, and killed
On the sand,
Crabs, turtles, and gulls
Are born, and die

But,
Then we come along and ruin
The process of life, and destroy
The waters
If we could understand,
If we could help save the residents
Then, we could all be happy

The beach is like life,
Always changing, never the same.

Erich Heinzel, Grade 5
Toll Gate Grammar School

No Onions

Hi Mom, I'm totally hungry.
May I have some rice, please.
Of course you can, Katrice.
Gee, I never thought my mom
would be this nice.
Yum! Yum! Yum!
I then spotted an onion.
My mom said fear factor,
if you eat it I'll give you $10.00.
Deal! Oh fine!
I ate it all up.
Ok now! Where is my $10.00?
Ha! Ha! Ha! said my mom.
April Fools Day!!!

Khadijah Yousufi, Grade 4
Mansfield Township Elementary School

Birds

A beauty to your landscape,
An icebox to your anger,
A relaxation to your senses,
A soothing lullaby to your ears.

Viswesh Swaminathan, Grade 6
Bedminster Township Elementary School

Favorite Place

I walk on the sand alongside the ocean,
The sunrise blasts into a volcanic explosion.

As I walk down the beautiful shore,
Seagulls spread their wings and soar.

Waves crash on the beach and lap the land,
muscles and shells are left in the sand.

The beach is empty — no one in sight,
Birds flutter in the wind like an airborne kite.

The gentle wind blows against my face,
I know this is my favorite place.

William Kashdan, Grade 6
Long Branch Middle School

What Bugs Me

The bully
The bully bothers me during class.
The bully calls me names.
The bully does mean things to me.
The bully talks about me behind my back.
The bully gets me in trouble.
The bully makes me want to scream.
The bully drives me crazy!
The bully distracts me when I'm trying to concentrate.
The bully never leaves me alone.
Will this ever stop?

Rene Mantecon, Grade 5
Community School of Bergen County

Gigi

To fly like an angel,
Dropping good deeds on poor and troubled people.
My name is a comfy, bright blue shag rug.
Yellow, like the beautiful sun,
Full of happiness.
A cloud moving gently across the sky.
My name is an electric guitar,
Full of energy and sound,
Or the sweet smell of lavender swirling in the air.
My name is a wish that everyone could be as happy
As sheep frolicking in a meadow!
My name is Gigi.

Gigi Luciano, Grade 5
Salt Brook Elementary School

Sweet Spring

S pring is finally here!
W eekends hanging out in the sweet outdoors
E nd of icy cold winter.
E verything is starting to blossom.
T alking on the porch on a warm night.

S weeping my feet in the wet spring grass
P laying outside in the yard
R unning through the breezy air
I n spring I smell the fragrance of the flowers
N eighbors playing catch outside
G reat times!

Hannah Walsh, Grade 4
Solomon Schechter Day School

Excuse

What!
No way.
Come on.
Do I have to?
My pencil's stubby,
The eraser isn't working.
My brain's not functioning correctly.
I've got a headache.
The nurse must be waiting!
Oh no!
Time's up!
Aaaaaagh!
F, here I come.
I've got nothing on my paper, but a crazy list of excuses.
You like it?
Oh my gosh,
You do.
Thanks for the compliment.
Would you like to hear some more?

Kelly Quigley, Grade 4
Mansfield Township Elementary School

Butterflies

Butterflies,
Butterflies,
Butterflies,
Beautiful, precious, fluttering butterflies,
Silver, Monarch, Checkered White butterflies,
These are just a few.
Colorful butterflies
Soaring butterflies,
Delicate, glistening, kaleidoscope butterflies,
Quiet, swirling, floating butterflies
Fritally butterflies too.
Magical butterflies,
Unique butterflies,
Last of all, best of all,
I like all butterflies.

Laura Merceron, Grade 5
Ridgeway Elementary School

Peace on Earth

The world is unfair
everyone knows,
    the rich, the poor, and me and you.
There's war not peace,
    that's how the world goes.
But all I'm asking for today
is peace on earth, and peace I pray.
    The world is unfair,
everyone knows,
    but if we all work together,
I know peace grows.

Emily Houwen, Grade 6
St Margaret Regional School

Beautiful Land

Over the glimmering sand
There lies a beautiful land
Where the mermaids roam
I wish it were my home.

The water is deep and blue
The homes are all new
Up the tall mountains
There are beautiful fountains.

Unicorns graze
In a misty haze
The sunset gleams
And the moon sends its soft beams.

I wonder if I may
Live there one glorious day!
Krista Traxinger, Grade 5
Lucy N Holman Elementary School

The Sun

The sun is as yellow as
    my pencil
    scrap paper
    a tulip
    Mac n' Cheese.
The sun is yellow like
    butter
    bananas
    lions
    and apple juice.
The sun is yellow!
Dean Cruz, Grade 4
Number 15 Elementary School

River

See the river flow
Watch it trickle down the rocks
That's why it is cool
Nicholas McCall, Grade 4
Our Lady of Mount Virgin School

Fear

Fear is muddy green.
It smells like old rotten eggs.
It looks like the pale skin of a frightened person.
It tastes like a sour piece of candy.
It sounds like the high pitched squealing of a monkey.
Fear feels like your stomach is turning and twisting and sinking down low.
Michael Matlaga, Grade 6
St Rose of Lima School

Train to a New Life

I am weak and alone
I wonder if I will ever find a loving family
I hear the train's loud whistle
I see sad and hopeless faces
I want someone who will care about me
I am weak and alone

I pretend that I live the life of a king
I feel the hard, moldy cushions
I touch the salty tears that I cry
I cry when I think of my dear, loving parents
I am weak and alone

I understand that taking this train may lead my life into misery
I say that anyone can achieve their dreams
I dream that someday no child will have to go through what I am now
I try to keep my spirits high
I hope that every child has their dream come true
I am weak and alone

Emily Calabria, Grade 5
Mary A Hubbard Elementary School

I Am*

I am a victim of war
I wonder where my father is
I hear the cries of my mother burst in my head
I see my baby sister cry of thirst
I want to see my parents again
I am a victim of war

I pretend that I am a bird who can fly away from danger
I feel scared when I think about my future
I touch the light green quilt that my mother knitted for me
I worry that I will never see my father again
I cry over the grave of my beloved mother
I am a victim of war

I understand that I am all alone, and the guardian of my sister
I say that I must be strong for everyone
I dream of the day my father comes home and hugs me tightly to his waist
I try to think of what my father would do
I hope that one day the brutal war will come to an end
I am a victim of war

Iman Virji, Grade 6
William Annin Middle School
*Dedicated to my English teacher Mrs. Brassil for helping me along the way.

Friendship

Friends are like gum.
They always stick together.
Friends are like a bunch of trees.
They never leave their side.
Friends are like a team.
Because they mostly win.
Friends share dreams of what they want to be.
So they fight for making the dream come true.
Friends are like knights.
They are honest, truthful, and brave.
Friends are like music.
It never ends.
Friendship is like a gardener.
Like the gardener plants a seed.
He takes care of it like water it and give love to it.
Friendship is like the moon and the star,
The sea and the land, the clouds and the sky,
The day from the night, and the rain and the earth.
That is what friendship is.
Also to have friends is worth it.

Eduardo Santizo, Grade 6
Gilmore J Fisher Middle School

Summer

Summer is getting near,
All the children clap and cheer.
The sun is shining oh so bright,
Come outside and fly a kite.
Play every day with your friends,
Before fall comes and summer ends.
And when fall comes, have no fear,
Summer will be back next year.

Philip Wuzzardo, Grade 5
Immaculate Conception Regional School

Snowflake

I'll go through the air,
And fly with the breeze,
I'll land on kids' noses
And make them sneeze.
Oh, the joy it will be
To fly through the air,
Because of the ground,
I cannot bear.
I'll go through the air
And land on a tree.
And when I hit,
I'll let some snow free.
Which will fall
On a house
Or hit a mouse.
Oh, the fun
I would make
If I were a snowflake.

Kyle Bogert, Grade 4
Emma Havens Young Elementary School

The Shoe

Do you know what it's like to be a shoe?
People's feet are in my stomach all day!
They just won't get off!
Those people with smelly socks and feet
Make so much smell I can never eat!
They give me a stomachache.
Sometimes on my back they smash it to the ground!
I hope they don't get gum on my back.
It will stick.
They will have to throw me out!
That is my fear!

Carolina Carvalho, Grade 6
Township of Ocean Intermediate School

An Amazing Rose

I seemed quite shocked
when I saw the rose step out of the ground and walk
I almost fainted
when I heard it talk

A rose and I went on a walk
ask the rose
we were friends
until the weather froze

At the first drop of snow
He said he had to go
I understood
and I cried no

He said we'll see each other again
and we'll soon play
and it's getting late
I'll see you in the spring, just another day.

Whitney Wantong, Grade 4
Benjamin Franklin Elementary School

At Night...

…I look up at the night sky.
…I see billions of stars but only one shooting star.
…I always try to make a wish, but it doesn't come true.
…I made another wish.
…I planned to wake up early to look for it.

Christopher Jacobson, Grade 4
Long Memorial Elementary School

Icky Sticky Yucky Glue

Icky sticky yucky glue,
It's stuck to me,
It's stuck to you.
It's stuck to the wall,
It's stuck to my shoe.
Ah man I hate this sticky glue!

Jennifer Hickok, Grade 5
Sandman Consolidated Elementary School

Animals

A pe, **b** ear, **c** at
D og, **e** lephant
F alcon, **g** iraffe, **h** yena
I guana, **j** aguar
K angaroo, **l** eopard, **m** onkey
N ewt, **o** ctopus
P enguin, **q** uail, **r** abbit
S kunk, **t** urtle
U nicorn, **v** ulture, **w** alrus
X ellent animals, **y** ak,
Z ebra

Erin O'Neill, Grade 4
Katharine D Malone Elementary School

If I Could Fly

If I could fly
I'd touch the sky
I'd fly with the birds
Like a buffalo herd
Way up there
I could dare like a bear
When I look down
I could see everyone on the ground
The secrets that the birds would share
Would be very rare
I'd give them a funny stare with a glare
Being up in the air
Would be a wonderful affair!

Juliana Tobin, Grade 5
Liberty Corner Elementary School

Spring

Spring comes in
Winter goes out
And spring comes in

Flowers start to bloom
Birds start to arrive
And the climate gets warmer

Children come out to play
Leaves start to grow back on trees
And lighter jackets are worn

Spring spring spring
It's finally here

Roma Gandhi, Grade 6
Gilmore J Fisher Middle School

Sunlight

Beautiful, bright sun
A big fireball in the sky
Sun brings light
To Earth.

Monica Giampietro, Grade 4
Mansfield Township Elementary School

Leaves

Orange leaves,
Brown leaves,
Red leaves,
Leaves of the fall
Leaves of Halloween,
Crisp leaves, crunchy leaves,
Leaves as bright as the sun.
The trees are so very dazzling
And colorful in the fall,
Oh, the beauty,
Oh, the joy of leaves in fall.

Emma Hilder, Grade 4
Friends School

Class

C ool place to learn
L earn good ideals
A wesome treats
S uper friends
S illy things

Cody Kazaoka, Grade 5
Elizabeth F Moore Elementary School

Zack and the Tack

There once was a boy named Zack,
Who stepped on a thumb tack.
 He started to cry,
 And yelled out "oh my!"
And then fell into a bike rack.

Andrew Cocciolone, Grade 4
West End Memorial Elementary School

Stonybrook

S o many kids.
T otally cool school.
O f course there are teachers.
N o one is a dud.
Y ou are an E student.
B ut that's not positive.
R emember to read.
O f course all of the teachers are fair.
O bviously this school is great.
K idding, everybody is an E student.

Joe Gravino, Grade 4
Stonybrook Elementary School

Joy

Joy is bright yellow.
It smells like freshly planted flowers.
It looks like a sunny day.
It tastes like a cold banana split.
It sounds like a church chorus.
Joy feels like when you first rode a bike.

Laura Harold, Grade 6
St Rose of Lima School

The Stream

The stream moves swiftly
While taking leaves with it
It doesn't let go

Josh Adelung, Grade 4
Stonybrook Elementary School

Spring

Spring is a season.
It's a season for a reason.
It's really sunny and bright,
And not too cold at night.
Spring, spring has arrived,
Catch a fish, or take a dive.
Flowers bloom,
And summer is soon.

Danielle Caruso, Grade 4
John F Kennedy Elementary School

The Fog

The fog comes.
The fog goes.
It makes me wonder,
Where does it go to.
Where does it come from.
Into the trees,
Into the sky,
High in the mountains,
Deep in the water.
The fog comes,
The fog goes,
But where does it go?

Matthew Scheiner, Grade 4
Pond Road Middle School

Day Dreaming

I sit in class,
And stare at the board,
I'm dozing off,
I'm so very bored.

I open my eyes,
And all I can see,
Are squiggles and lines,
And a bumble bee!

Chocolate apples,
And a candy tree,
All so tasty,
And everything is free!

I hear my name,
I startle and wake,
My teacher is angry,
Oh give me a break.

Ana Maroldi, Grade 4
Stonybrook Elementary School

If I Was a Dog What Would I See?

If I was a dog what would I see?
A bird or a bee what color would these things be?
Would trees still be green and brown,
the color of a muddy ground?

Would flowers still be purple, red, orange and pink,
would water still come out of a sink?
If I was a dog, what would I see?
Would the sky still be blue,
would cows still moo?

Would cats still meow,
and when you get a cut wouldn't you say ow?
If I was a dog what would I see,
a bird or a bee what color would these things be?

Bridget Krupak, Grade 5
St Rose of Lima School

Mother Nature's White Blanket

As Mother Nature shows her care,
Some facts are clearly bare:
Like a sudden great white blaze,
She sends down snowflakes in a craze.

In the winter with its glow,
Many things happen to and fro:
As all the kids rush out to play,
All the parents shovel away.

In the end when the day is done,
Everyone hurries in on the run.
As all the children go and dream,
They're all about winter's wondrous gleam.

Sagar Gupta, Grade 6
Indian Hill Elementary School

Dreams Are a Doorway

Dreams are a doorway
Traveling through a mystic world
Not knowing when to wake up
Stepping into the unknown
Wondering if true
Sleep shows the way to the Dream Doorway

Jacqueline Zuhse, Grade 6
Township of Ocean Intermediate School

Spring

S winging on my swing set is so much fun.
P ushing myself as I go higher and higher.
R ising in the air until I feel like I'm flying.
I can see my whole neighborhood as I go.
N oticing buds blooming in their gardens.
G loriously, I swing until I almost touch the clouds.

Dani Scherl, Grade 4
Solomon Schechter Day School

Fishin' with Grandpa

It was my first fishing trip on the Shinnecock canal
We packed the car
Bought some bait
And Grandpa even managed to drive the car straight
We got to the spot threaded our lines
And cast into the water
First hour no bites
Second hour no bites
I was flustered, sunburned, and bored

I was flustered
Third hour no bites
And then when my eyes were closing
A gust of wind
A splash of water
My brother fell into the water
He swam like a fish
Looked like a crab
And my grandpa and I had to fish him out of the water
When he got out he was devastated he was all soaked and wet
I guess that was the end of our fishing trip
I was flustered, how did my brother fall into the water?

John Ganss, Grade 6
Fieldstone Middle School

Born with the Beat!

I play the drums;
I tap, bang and make some hums.

I tapped in the tub when I was three,
My mom would clap her hands and listen to me.

When I was four, I played the bongos,
When people saw me, they said "He's as good as the pros!"

In the starting of concerts I feel so good,
In front of the parents: there I stood.

Practicing at home and going to band,
Compliments I hear with drumsticks in my hand.

When I grow up I want to be a drum player,
Be so famous I'll meet the mayor!

I thank God for the things I do,
I love my abilities I love them true.

Ashwin Prasanna, Grade 4
Indian Hill Elementary School

Spring Fun

I hate having to sit inside on a beautiful day,
But I love looking out in the yard for a place to play!
It is boring to sit inside in a very mope-like way,
But it will be fun to go outside today!

Taylor Donato, Grade 4
John F Kennedy Elementary School

Baseball

The green grass, the bright lights, the smell of leather. No rain tonight. Great baseball weather!
The sound of the bat. Ping! The popping of the mitt. Ouch!
The fans in their uniforms, the umps in blue. The kids looking like Jeter, Damon or A-rod. Strike two!
A smash off the fence. The bases clear. Team confidence builds. Oh, dear!
An attempted steal, a slide in the dirt. Cotton candy, hotdogs and soda. Oh no, mustard on my shirt!
A close call at the plate, the manager doesn't agree. He's out to argue. A melee!
The ump throws him out, as fans start to boo. Who needs an ump like you?
Down by one in the bottom of the ninth, up comes A-rod, crushes one real nice.
The tying run comes home, the stage is set. The pitcher, really upset.
Now comes Jeter, pressure and all, hits one the other way, 400 feet, off the wall!
The fans on their feet, delirious with joy, screaming and yelling with hope — just one more boys!
It comes down to this, all tied in the ninth, Damon at back, heck, it's almost eleven on a school night!
The fans hold their breath, all hopes on the line, Damon swings — oh, my, it's gone!

Trevor Mende, Grade 5
St Veronica Elementary School

Troubles

T ry to avoid them, but they always find you.
R emove them, those terrible troubles, is what we try to do.
O ffend you or someone else is an event that may take place.
U nfriendly they will often be, right to your face.
B etray you is what one trouble will do, but another soon comes to stay.
L ife goes in and out of them, every single day.
E veryone doesn't enjoy them, but everyone has a few.
S undown one day you may have none, but sadly tomorrow, you'll have a trouble that's new.

Hanna Anderson, Grade 5
Belhaven Avenue Middle School

If I Were…

If I were red I'd be the color passion, burning in a person's heart.
If I were orange I'd be a basketball, swishing through the net.
If I were yellow I'd be a honeybee, giving life to millions of flowers.
If I were green I'd be neon lights, shining in late-night New York City.
If I were blue I'd be the calming ocean waves.
If I were purple I'd be a radiant violet, standing tall among other flowers.
If I were all of these colors, I'd be a bright rainbow appearing in the cloudless April sky.

Austin Kim, Grade 5
Sicomac Elementary School

Happiness

Happiness is yellow
It smells like a homemade dinner full of your favorite foods
It looks like a starry night with a big, bright moon
It tastes like sugary cookies with sweet candy
It sounds like children cheering as the ice cream truck comes around the corner
Happiness feels like being cuddled up in blankets on a big chair in the middle of winter.

Colleen Dykeman, Grade 6
St Rose of Lima School

What's in a Football Player's Locker?

Thousands of cups (the Solo brand probably), bottles of Gatorade, pictures of his girlfriend, keys to his mansion, clothes covered with dirt and sweat, an away jersey (covered in mud), a practice football, a smaller pair of cleats, five one hundred dollar stray bills, a six year contract, a picture of his shiny new seven million dollar Corvette, ten packs of gum, trophies from the previous Super Bowls, and a team picture.

Joseph Consolino, Grade 5
Sicomac Elementary School

The Sun
There is a fiery ball out of the atmosphere
That heats our large orbiting sphere
It is the sun
The hot, hot sun

It is the largest star
Not like a movie star
It is the sun
The largest star

With temperature of over a hundred thousand degrees
It warms the Earth, oceans, and humanity
It is the sun
The fiery sun

It is also our source of light
To aid our sight
It is the sun
The bright, bright sun

But at the end of the day the sun can't stay
It must retire so it can rise the very next day
The sun
Our faithful friend the sun.

David Medici, Grade 5
St Veronica Elementary School

Spring
Spring looks like a beautiful picture.
It feels like a flower
It tastes like fresh fruit
It smells like red roses
It sounds like butterflies.

Alyssa Velez, Grade 5
Perth Amboy Catholic Intermediate School

Brothers
Brothers,
Brothers,
Brothers,
Slimy, annoying, eavesdropping, brothers
Hilarious, dirty, athletic, brothers
There are just a few
Toxic, brothers

Traitor, brother
Tough, smart, priceless, brothers
Ear piercing, brothers too
Cologne smell, brothers
Gracious brothers
Don't forget helpful brothers
Last of all, best of all,
I like
All brothers

Cassandra Hrusko, Grade 5
Ridgeway Elementary School

Basketball
People who play this sport
some of them may be short.

If you are tall,
you will get the ball.

For each basket that you make,
that is two more points that your team will take.

Every time you use the backboard,
two points will be added to your scoreboard.

Players like to drive the middle,
nothing but net is not a riddle.

As you can plainly see,
this sport is great to me.

Anthony Lozito, Grade 5
St Veronica Elementary School

A Sunny Sunday Morning
I wake up late
In my soft warm bed
As cozy as can be
On a Sunny Sunday Morning
The sun is streaming through my window
And the sounds
Of cheery talking
Are right downstairs
On a Sunny Sunday Morning
I sluggishly walk
Down the stairs
And eat my delicious bagel
Still warm from being made
On a Sunny Sunday Morning
Sunny Sundays cheer me up
They never make me sad
On a Sunny Sunday Morning, I'm glad

Anna Munroe, Grade 5
Salt Brook Elementary School

Horses
Galloping into the dusky black night.
Gazing at the astonishing sight,
I sit bewildered and seduced.
One horse slows to a canter, then a trot.
She changes her gait to a steady walk —
she stops dead in her tracks and stares up at me.
For what seemed to be forever our eyes locked.
There she stood in all her majesty,
her glimmering jeweled eyes fixed on me.
I smiled as she took off —
and left me standing in a dream.

Molly Kirschner, Grade 6
Fieldstone Middle School

Hummingbird

Humming, humming
All day long,
Humming, humming
The same old song
High notes
Low notes
Half notes
Whole notes
Hummingbird, hummingbird
Flying all day long
Humming, humming
The same old song.

Lauren Brill, Grade 4
Friends School

Artists

Artists
Cheerful, energetic
Draws, paints, colors
Healthy, smart, interesting, and happy
Artists

Yashas Kulkarni, Grade 6
Fieldstone Middle School

Afternoon Sunset

On this late
Afternoon
Of this sunny day,
The sun is a light mix
Of red and yellow
As it slowly
Makes its way
Down to the horizon.
A soft, cool breeze
Blows in my face
While
An orchestra
Of robins sing
Their gentle lullaby
As the sky grows
Dark with dusk.
The smell of pine
Fills my nose
As I watch
The sun
Disappear from sight.

Connor Schwartz, Grade 5
Robert B Jaggard Elementary School

Fast Yellow Cheetah

Fast yellow cheetah
With long sturdy legs
Growls loudly in the day

Mark Sloboda, Grade 5
Elizabeth F Moore Elementary School

Penguins

Penguins sliding on their bellies
Always jiggling a lot like jelly
They live where it is very cold
But in pet stores they are not sold.

Tyler Kay, Grade 5
Springfield Township School

The Ocean

The ocean
Gentle waves
Calming, water, surfing
Fun to play in
Sparkling

Anthony Schiavone, Grade 6
Sacred Heart Elementary School

Fred

There once was a small kid named Fred,
Who had a big fat chubby head.
He jumped on his bike,
Which he did not like,
But it's better than going to bed.

Aaron Buckley, Grade 4
West End Memorial Elementary School

Ode to Chocolate Bars

Ode to chocolate bars,
your goodness sends me to the stars,
Ode to chocolate bars,
I'm so hyper I'd run to Mars.
Oh chocolate bars, to you I praise,
I hope your taste always stays
Chocolate bar don't go away
Please, I beg of you to stay.
Now that you have fled,
My hyperness is now dead

Katelyn Degen, Grade 6
Chatham Middle School

Invisible Dog

Invisible dog where can you be
Invisible dog I cannot see
Are you near or are you far
I don't know where you are
Is that a bark I hear
But, I can't see you so now I sit in fear
Invisible dog I miss you so
Invisible dog why did you have to go
I am upset
from sunrise to sunset
I cried and I cried
While I said my last good-bye
Invisible dog now I sit alone
Invisible dog why can't you come home

Christie Luterzo, Grade 6
Thomas Jefferson Middle School

A Lad from Wales

There once was a young lad from Wales
Who excitedly told tall tales.
He made his kin laugh,
While milking a calf.
His humor never ever fails.

Brock Juliano, Grade 4
West End Memorial Elementary School

Food

Food is
the best,
Food is
the greatest,
I like all
foods,
I would like
to learn to cook
some good food,
There is a lot
of food in the world,
My mom is a
good cook.

Ryan Olters, Grade 5
Roosevelt Elementary School

Swimming

Flipturns don't make you drown,
They make you frown.

When a coach says "IM,"
Don't think of instant messaging.

If you're not dyin',
You're not tryin'.

Cathy Song, Grade 6
Bartle Elementary School

The Most Perfect Beach!

Lay with the brown sugar sand
and try to get the most perfect tan!
Put up your rainbow sparkly umbrella.
As you lay out
Your beach chair — pretend to be a
Lifeguard.
Hooray!
Hooray!
Go get a blue ocean swim.
As it sparkles like a diamond crystals
But make sure the sharks don't get you!
Fetch for some lobsters and crabs
and beneath the sea, yell for joy
because you're on the
Most Perfect Beach!

Ky-Asia Hill, Grade 4
Evergreen Elementary School

Dreams

Dreams are awesome images,
Some are good.
Some are bad.
Some of them can make you sad.
In a dream you can do, be, or have anything you want.
You can be a movie star.
An astronaut.
A person that makes popcorn pop.
A millionaire.
The nightmares get you eaten somehow.
You can be eaten by a monster.
A dinosaur.
A lion.
Be trampled by bulls.
Be beaten by trolls.
The possibilities are endless.
Anyway, dreams are just dreams.
But I'm not sure about nightmares.

John Stillwell, Grade 6
Gilmore J Fisher Middle School

My Family

My family is a birthday cake filled with joy and happiness
My dad is the base, taking care of the other parts
My mom is the icing, sweet and delicious
My dog is the center of the cake the part we all love
My family is a birthday celebration when we are all together.

Tyler Breznak, Grade 5
Salt Brook Elementary School

Bio of Uncle Patrick

Uncle Patrick
Loving, caring, intelligent, friendly
Related to Eliza, Franklin, Grandma, and Grandpa
Who cares deeply about his family and girlfriend
Who feels special to be the youngest son of the Lam family
Who needs a job and the perfect wife
Who gives love to everyone
Who fears Eliza
Who would like to see his family more often
Resident of Macau, China

Sheba Yu, Grade 4
Franklin Park Elementary School

Shopping

Whenever I go shopping I am always bopping around,
To find the perfect shirt or shoe.
I could be in Claire's or in Build-a-Bear.
Now and then I'll take a rest,
But then I'll buy that really cute dress.
I could be hopping around looking for a night gown.
I shop 'til I drop looking at tops.
It is now close to noon but I'll be back really soon!

Alexandra Goetz, Grade 5
Most Holy Redeemer School

Anger

Anger is red,
It smells like sulfur.
It looks like a volcano erupting.
It tastes like spicy food.
It sounds like a big boom
Anger feels like your body is going to rocket into space.

Arun Cheeramkuzhiyil, Grade 6
St Rose of Lima School

When Rain Comes Down

When rain comes down.
One might think of rain as a waste of time.
Another might think of rain as tranquil.
Yet another might think of rain as scary.
When rain comes down. When rain comes down.
When rain comes down.
One might think of it as a waste of time.
Another might think of rain as tranquil.
Yet another might think of rain as scary.
When rain comes down. When rain comes down.
When rain comes down.

Christina Stevenson, Grade 6
Bartle Elementary School

Cats

Cats are very majestic.
They are also really sly.
But they fall off the windowsill
With every single try.
Cats will curl up on your lap
If you allow them to.
They're probably nibbling cat food now,
And chasing dogs. Who knew?
You can own a cat right now
Even kittens that are brand new.
Please take good care of your cat.
And don't leave them feeling blue.

Jennifer Dupre, Grade 5
Immaculate Conception Regional School

My Cell Phone

Cell phones, cell phones everywhere
Leave my house without mine…
I wouldn't dare.
I use my cell phone every day.
I never run out of things to say.
My friends and I love to text each other.
I don't even mind getting a text from my mother.
How did your parents do without them as kids?
I would never be able to live as they did.
Cell phone, cell phone you are here to stay.
I always do my best not to get you taken away.
Cell phone oh cell phone you must know.
I really, really do love you so.

Courtney Weite, Grade 6
Thomas Jefferson Middle School

Free!

I'm running,
Running for life,
I'm hiding,
Hiding from searchers,
I'm screaming,
Screaming with pain,
I'm crying,
Crying for those still enslaved,
I'm jumping,
Jumping for joy,
I'm free,

Free from those who can hurt me!
Free!

Alicia Lai, Grade 4
Indian Hill Elementary School

The Fog Mystery

The fog gathers,
From all different places,
Squeezes into New York City,
Silent spies on kids,
Like a secret agent,
Waiting in the dark and shadowy alley
Like a dog waiting for its food.
The children scurry,
Into their apartment
One old man is still standing
Then a black cat dashes by,
Like a ZAP of lightning
The fog moves on.
With the cat,
No one knows,
No one,
What happened to the man?
What happened?

Baljot Ranu, Grade 4
Pond Road Middle School

My Cat

My cat is so mean,
She bites me a lot.
My mom calls her princess,
Even though she is not.

When you give her a treat,
She'll kiss up to you,
With her water and food,
She'll do the same too.

My cat might be nice,
My cat might be rude,
It depends how you treat her,
And also her mood.

Evan Bolling, Grade 5
Central School

Guess Who I Am

I get up at dawn and go to sleep at dusk.
What do I do?
Well, I don't drive, walk, read, or speak like other people do.
I don't type, teach, talk on a talk show, or any other job that you would do.
How am I speaking to you?
Simple I'm inside of you.
Who or what am I?
Keep asking questions before I decide to retire.
What do I look like?
You have to imagine that part for I have no shape or size I know of.
Why can't you see me?
I am in your imagination if you try you can see me.
When was I born?
When you were born when you will die
I shall do it at the same time.
You give up?!
Oh, well I have to also. I am your conscience that lives inside of you.

Sararose Nassani, Grade 5
Salt Brook Elementary School

Conasauga Logperch

C ompletely invisible near algae.
O nly found in Georgia and Tennessee.
N ot found in New Jersey.
A logperch is a migrating creature.
S tones litter the bottom part of the river (which is its habitat).
A bout six inches in length
U sually dwells on the bottom of rivers.
G reat trees surround this sea creature's habitat, giving it shade.
A true fresh water fish.

L ives most of its life in the Conasauga River
O rchids surround its habitat, the river, during summer.
G ranted fast reproduction.
P ercini jenkinsi is its scientific name.
E ndangered due to "habitat loss."
R eports say this fish is not dangerous.
C onasauga Logperches are green and yellow with tiger-like stripes.
H as a pig-like snout.

Morgan Van Saders, Grade 4
Franklin Township Elementary School

Around Easter...

…I put decorations up around my house.
  Some of them are baskets bunnies and eggs.
  One of them is a happy, cheerful, playful mouse.
…Beautiful flowers are growing everywhere.
  I picked some exquisite pink ones to place in my hair.
…I saw some little blue jays try to make a nest.
  Here they'll lay their eggs and raise their young best.
…The warm, crisp, spring air makes me want to lay on the grass
  and gaze at clouds everywhere.
…All of the hibernating animals awake from their sleep.
  I hear birds chirp and peep.

Jenna DiRito, Grade 4
Long Memorial Elementary School

Spring Is…

Spring is when all the birds come back.
All kinds of flowers bloom.
The trees grow with appealing green leaves.
All the blankets of snow are gone.
Oh how I love spring!

Alejandra Velasquez, Grade 4
Evergreen Elementary School

My Street

Hot sunny streets saccades sing as we head for the playground.
Six constant companions.
I run free in a neighborhood full of children.
A clubhouse in the woods by my uncle's old house.
We're in constant motion.

Michaul Williams, Grade 4
Holy Saviour School

Moon

The moon is my neighbor,
He's haunting me,
The moon is a ball of Swiss cheese,
Maybe a man about to sneeze,
The moon goes this way then that,
It is like the ball that hits a baseball bat,
The moon is the sun's neighbor,
Right in her front door,
The moon's from her floor,
She helps him a lot,
She helps him show what he has got,
The moon is a gem,
The moon is the ball-point of a pen,
It sways this way and that,
But in the morning it falls like a bat,
The moon loves to hide,
It hides for several hours behind the sun,
The moon is a neighbor to me.

Kirsten Cave, Grade 4
Woods Road Elementary School

Silent Snowflakes

Snowflakes, snowflakes falling down from the sky;
Drifting down silently to the ground.
Each little snowflake glistening and glittering;
Covering the world like a cool white blanket.
Everywhere you look is a white winter wonderland.
When the snowing stops and the moon peeks out;
Revealing everything in the new, snowy, silent, white world.
All is calm; all is still.
Everyone is snug as a bug in a rug in their warm cozy beds;
Carefully tucked away from the cold.
Then clouds begin to crawl in the sky;
Shielding the world from the moon's penetrating light.
Then, one by one, each sparkling, little snowflake
Silently drifts to the ground.

Stacey Angelbeck, Grade 6
Chatham Middle School

The War of My Heart

All of my days,   I fight and fight,
My world is in turmoil. The war never ends. I will
fight the good fight all the days of my life. My
weapons come from the Lord. The Lord
gives me courage. I attack with the
sword of the spirit. I defend with
the shield of faith. In school
I fight the war. I fight
forever more. Although
I walk through the
Valley of Death,
I am not afraid.
I will fight for
Jesus, my
Great
King!

Alex Croce, Grade 6
Lower Alloways Creek Elementary School

What Is Green

Green is the grass
And the leaves on trees
And sometimes the color
Of leprechaun knees.

Green is the lettuce
Pickles are too
And one of the colors
That's on my shoe.

Green is the elves
Leaves and the trees
Green is the feeling of a
Country breeze.

Jeremy L. Patterson, Grade 5
Sandman Consolidated Elementary School

Being a Birdie

If I were a birdie
I'd tweet to the heavenly skies
And soar in the lovely air.

My breast would shine
Like a diamond evening sky,
And I would swoop down
And feed my precious babies from above.

I would say hello to all the birds
Soaring and swooping through the sky.

All day I would soar
Up and down,
Up and down

Justin Macaluso, Grade 4
Sicomac Elementary School

About Sharks and Dolphins
Dolphins
Colorful, swift
Swimming, comforting, squeaking
Nice, friendly, ferocious, dangerous
Mysterious, grey
Shark
Zachary Condon, Grade 4
Our Lady of Mount Virgin School

Little Sister
Kasey
Cute, energetic
Always annoys me
Lovable, hyper, fun, spoiled
Little sister
Kristy Hart, Grade 6
Central Middle School

Camera
Sees the world
with
one eye
capturing
the outdoor animals
children playing
people strolling
cars driving
s…l…o…w…l…y
in traffic
it turns on/off
zooms in/out
and…
flashes in the
darkness.
In Hyuk Choi, Grade 6
Cherry Hill Elementary School

Winter
It tastes like water
It sounds like kids playing
It smells like cookies baking
It looks like kids sledding
It feels like soft fresh snow
Antonia Nardelli, Grade 4
Main Road Elementary School

Gorgeous White Eagle
Gorgeous White Eagle
Can you fly
Into the sky?
Gorgeous White Eagle
Is your wing broke?
I could have sworn I heard a croak
Gorgeous White Eagle
Marisa Rivera, Grade 5
Springfield Township School

Pollution
We kick our trash,
We bash our trash,
We throw it out the door,
We try to ignore the fact that,
We might have to clean up more
Gregory Jones, Grade 6
Christa McAuliffe Middle School

In the Woods
I am in the woods
To have some fun

I am going owling in the dark
It is late at night in the fog
We are lucky to find a frog
Hiding in the green, green grass
And then an owl
Light and brown
Comes to rest upon the bough

We come back to celebrate its success
It is now time to take a rest
Jake Stephens, Grade 4
Pond Road Middle School

Flower Art
Piece of art for us
Dandelions and roses
They make us happy
Chelsea Cox, Grade 4
Mansfield Township Elementary School

I Want the World to Be Nice
I want a world
where there are no drugs.
I want a world
where children can be safe.
I want a world
where kids can learn.
I want a world
where people read books.
I want a world
where people can get nice things.
That's how I want the world to be.
Jonathan Guallpa, Grade 4
Evergreen Elementary School

Evelyn
Evelyn
Helpful, caring
Cooking, baby-sitting, reading
She is a caregiver to all
Mommy
Samantha Marrero, Grade 5
Ridgeway Elementary School

Grandpa
My grandpa and me
Just dancing around the room
The music playing, the cars honking.
Why did he have to go?

No hair on his head, no hair on mine
We were both as happy as seals
Never wanting it to end
Why did he have to go?

How could he die?
Where did he go?
Does he miss me?
I'll always ask the question,
Why did he have to go?
Samantha Narciso, Grade 5
Salt Brook Elementary School

Christmas
Christmas is for toys,
And children making noise.
Families having fun,
And gifts for everyone.
Christmas trees with lights,
And a star shining bright.
Everyone is jolly,
As Mom decorates with holly.

But let us all remember!
Jesus' birthday is in December.
So fill your Christmas with lots of joy,
And God will bless each girl and boy.
MERRY CHRISTMAS.
Emily Baker, Grade 4
St Joseph's Regional School

Someone I Admire
Colleen
Smart, honest, cool
Shopping, sporty, talking
She will always be there for me
My sister
Sherry Goetz, Grade 5
Ridgeway Elementary School

My Wish
I wish that someone would listen to me.
I wish that I could be someone else.
I wish that I could be like you.
I wish I could do the things you do.
I wish that you loved me.
I wish that I had friends.
I wish for these things.
But I already have them.
Samantha Owens, Grade 6
Community School of Bergen County

My Crazy Day

Every day we do the same routine
Brush our teeth and make ourselves clean

But one crazy day something unusual took place
A rattlesnake on horseback came down my fireplace

I yelled to my mom, who was near by doing housework
"Did you see what came out of the chimney with a jerk?!"

She looked into my eyes and said something I didn't get
"Oh, that's just Clarence our new house pet."

Evan Taylor, Grade 5
Holy Saviour School

If I Were in Charge of the World

If I were in charge of the world I'd cancel
fighting
bad guys
cleaning your room
bad days
and cancer

If I were in charge of the world I'd change
schools into waterparks
homework into friends
brother into sisters
ccd into bowling
and weekdays into weekends

If I were in charge of the world I'd keep
my family
my cell phone
my friends
my computer
and my heart
If I were in charge of the world.

Deena Fuschetto, Grade 5
Salt Brook Elementary School

The Sun Will Shine My Way

Everything that has a beginning has an end.
And everything in this world has an opposite.
Where there's an up there's a down.
Where there's an adult there's a child;
Where there's a left there's a right
And where there's a day there is a night.
We sit and wonder why the things go the way they go.
But that's a question we can't answer,
It's only God that knows.
My heart is torn and broken,
So every night I pray,
That God keep me together,
So that the sun will shine my way.

Ayshia Robinson, Grade 6
Cleveland Elementary School

Ms. McAvoy

Ms. McAvoy likes to teach
She pushes us to reach
To get some better grades and have a little fun
And fits it all in before the school day is done
When school is over
She hops in her Rover
She goes over the bridge
To the street's ridge
Sits to relax
While playing her shiny, new gold sax
Shortly falling asleep
In her dreamy sleep, asleep so deep
To wake her you'll need something louder than a peep
BEEP!
Her alarm goes
She still wants to doze
"It's a new day" she'd proudly say
She could hear her students "Hip Hip Hooray"
She hears driving away

Lindsay Kugel, Grade 5
Auten Road Intermediate School

From School to Summer and Back Again

School is finally over
Can't you hear the cheers?
Summer has arrived
And it's the best time of the year.

Summer brings camping, swimming, fishing
And all the fun of the outdoors.
Going on big, electric boats
Or the small ones with oars.

Then comes September and
School comes around again.
Gathering books and school supplies
summer finally comes to an end.

Brooke Carleen, Grade 6
Allen W Roberts Elementary School

Nature's Sunset

As I watched the sunset bright as can be
with its extraordinary rays of light
I saw the colorful skies above
with the sky colored pink and dark purple

I sat on the fresh dew of the cut green grass
and looked at nature's colorful portrait
I was getting sleepy, and was nervous
that I would not get home before dark

I was sad as I left the beautiful painting of nature,
it was as if the approaching time of dusk
was trying to show off before the moonlight appeared

Joshua Cohen, Grade 5
Laura Donovan Elementary School

Summer
This summer
I will get a hummer
It will climb a mountain
To get to a fountain
We will have dinner
But it won't be a winner
It was for people with bling bling
Not for me the king
Ryan Jones, Grade 5
Our Lady of Mount Virgin School

Life Is Like
Life is like a
big soccer
game,
people working
together to
reach their
goals.
Defenders here
and there
blocking our
shots
and
passes.
Winning and
losing
is the way
of life.
So don't get upset
if something
doesn't go
your way.
Kelly Carroll, Grade 5
Salt Brook Elementary School

Beauty
Life is beautiful
Why do we have so many wars?
Life goes down the drain.
Zachary M. Caldaro, Grade 4
Stonybrook Elementary School

Ice Cream
Ice cream is good, ice cream is sweet
Ice cream is my favorite treat

When the ice cream man comes around
I am the first one to be found

Ice cream melts on hot days
When the sun beats down hot rays

I love ice cream
Danielle DiPasquale, Grade 5
St Veronica Elementary School

The Beach
Walking on the warm, yellow sand, squiggling my feet through each grain
The sound of seagulls squawking in my ear gives me a pounding headache
The waves as rough as sand paper on my hands
The aroma of the food heads me towards the boardwalk
As my bare feet hit the hard wood, they start to hurt,
As I get splinters on go my shoes
As I stuff a hot nice piece of funnel cake into my mouth I start to tingle
It is beginning to be a sweet day
Sara Lowenstein, Grade 6
Allen W Roberts Elementary School

Pets I've Had
How many pets have I had? There was…

Herbie the hermit crab —
Ran away.
Puff the pufferfish —
Got scared — BOOM!
Polly the parrot —
Choked on a cracker.
Isabelle the iguana —
Stayed under the heating lamp way too long!

And my cows —
How I loved my cows —
They got tipped — I never forgave my neighbor for that!
All my pets I love them all!
I just got a rabbit — no, where is he going…don't back up! OUCH!

Maybe pets —
Just aren't for me!
Marissa Earle, Grade 5
Robert B Jaggard Elementary School

Happiness
Happiness is a bright pink.
It smells like the earthy smell of the outdoors.
It looks like a cute little puppy just waiting to be pet.
It tastes like the soft chewy taste of fresh cookies right out of the oven.
It sounds like the wind blowing in your face, and the birds chirping
and singing on a spring morning.
Happiness feels like you have nothing on your mind and you just want to relax.
Kelley Keane, Grade 6
St Rose of Lima School

Inside/Outside
Inside people are making warm and cozy fires.
Outside leaves are falling from the trees.
Inside people in band are making noise louder than thunder.
Outside animals start to hibernate for the chilly winter.
Inside little babies are getting ready for their afternoon naps.
Outside children are playing like little bear cubs.
Inside children in Mrs. Nesnay's class are writing Inside/Outside poems.
Outside children are getting on school buses to go home.
Jordyn Comley and Maggie Michaud, Grade 5
Byram Township Intermediate School

Spring

Sounds like birds singing
Looks like butterflies drifting in the breeze
Tastes like multicolored Easter eggs
Smells like blooming flowers
Feels like grass damp with dew.

Chloe Gustke, Grade 5
Atlantic Christian School

The Ocean's Wave

You stand on the bay listening,
Listening to the ocean's waves.
Soothing, they are.
You feel like you are on a cloud.
Even if there are dark clouds above;
And people all around, you hear nor see anything but the waves.
Suddenly you feel a spray of the ocean.
Soothing again but untasty.
You then fall into the ocean.
All the waves splash up around you.
Laughter is now heard.
You look all around but still see nothing.
Is it the waves that talk?
Is this really the ocean's waves?

Taylor Zaborney, Grade 6
Thorne Middle School

Leaf Lullaby

Sleep, crimson leaf, sleep!
Float quietly into your damp soil bed.
Dream of hovering softly in the cool fall wind.
Sleep, ivory leaf, sleep!

Gordon Winarick, Grade 5
Belhaven Avenue Middle School

Just a Kid

I'm just a kid,
Guess what I did.
I did something bad,
To make Mom and Dad mad.
I took out their jeans,
And dressed like a teen.
I went in the kitchen there was a big boom,
I got my mom scared and hid in her room.
I do confess,
I made a big mess.

Olivia Zon, Grade 5
St Marys School

Beautiful Rose

One sunny day in my backyard I saw a beautiful rose.
The smell reminded me of my mother's perfume.
I imagine that it tastes like sour patch.
It feels so soft that I could take a nap on it.
When I see it, it reminds me of peace and quiet.

Anthony Ruiz, Grade 6
Community School of Bergen County

Roller Blading

Roller Blading
Roller blading can be fun
You go faster than when you run
As you practice you will be good
Soon you will be grinding your box of wood
The more you skate and practice tricks
Soon you'll be jumping staircases of bricks

Kyle Antonucci, Grade 6
Springfield Township School

Passion for Fastpitch Softball

As I walk with confidence to the pitcher's mound
tied game, 2 outs, you can't hear a sound.

As I warm up, the batter is checking me out
she steps up to the plate, fastball I think, no doubt.

My heart beats fast as I wind up and release
the ball perfect pitch, 1 strike is all I saw.

As the crowd starts to cheer, 2 more is all I need
another fast ball I fired right down the middle indeed.

"Strike two!' Yells the umpire, the crowd up on their feet
everyone is screaming my name, I cannot be beat.

Winding up fast and wild the ball comes in so slow
change-up; strike three the only way to go.

The energy and screams of excitement were so loud
that's why I love to do fastpitch and make my team so proud

Morgan DiVello, Grade 4
Assumption School

Time

My watch is ticking,
Yet I don't have time.
My pencil's moving yet I having nothing to write.
My clothes are washed but I have nothing to wear.
I can't bear, I am scared.

Everything is moving so fast
I can't keep myself
On the right track.
Without you I can be wrong
And I can be right, but I don't understand.
Understand why I can't live without you.
I can't live without you.

My world is spinning yet I'm still here
My phone is ringing, but I can't hear.
Without you I don't know how to deal.
How to deal…shed a tear.

Madison Dorn, Grade 5
Liberty Corner Elementary School

My Pants

When I'm playing soccer,
I rush to kick the ball,
but since I'm wearing white pants,
I stain them as I fall.

I want to be an athlete,
but every time I play,
I'm always wearing white pants,
and stain them every day.

My mom should get me green pants,
red, black or blue,
so I can be an athlete,
and beat the pants off you!

Arielle Kaplan, Grade 5
Solomon Schechter Day Lower School

Best Friends

My best friends are always there for me.
We all work together just like a team.

Even if we're in a fight.
We work it out by night.

My best friends are sometimes crazy.
My best friends can also be lazy.

Amanda Keator, Grade 4
St Mary's School

In a Wood

There is a girl from a wood
Who always said, "you should"
No one disagreed
To this atrocious deed
Not even the wise men in the wood

Then someone said, "I will not!
I should leave you here to rot
I'll spare you today
But next time, nay
I'll send you away on a yacht"

From then on that girl was subdued
She was never in a superior mood
She became camera shy
And never told lies
For she didn't want to be barbecued

The people in the wood were relieved
Until someone came from South Kariv
She always said, "you must"
The people were nonplused
They hoped she'd go back to South Kariv

Deborah Pomeranz, Grade 4
Solomon Schechter Day School

Whooshing Wind

Whoosh, whoosh the wind blows
the wind talks as I talk back
we dance wildly.

Giulia Smith, Grade 4
Stonybrook Elementary School

Fluffy Cloud

Life is like a fluffy cloud,
Floating in the sky.
Oh so many challenges,
Always passing by.

The cloud is very soft and fluffy,
Just like a marshmallow.
Or maybe like a dream,
When you're sleeping on your pillow.

The cloud is very delicate,
Like a newborn baby.
Or maybe like a dandelion,
Or a sensitive young lady.

In the future you'll turn into a cloud,
Floating in the breeze.
Let those challenges fly right by,
And you can do whatever you please!

Alicia Rueda, Grade 6
Walter T. Bergen Middle School

Jet Fast

I see a jet in the sky.
It's flying so fast and so high.
Maybe I can fly with you.
We can fly to Timbuktu.
Maybe we can fly so fast.
Fly back right into the past.

Alex Robbins, Grade 5
St Veronica Elementary School

My Cousin Julia

My cousin Julia
She is sweet
Kind
Cute and cuddly,
Very beautiful.
She makes me laugh
Because of her funny
Words
Goo goo!
Gaa gaa!
Can you guess
How old she is?
Just one precious year old
Oh! My cousin Julia…

Jaime Iacono, Grade 4
Ridge Ranch Elementary School

Would You Believe…

Spring looks,
Fresh new make-up,
A perfect dress,
Your best hair ever,
The love of your life,
The Perfect Prom!

Amanda Haas, Grade 6
Robert L Craig Elementary School

My Magic Net

I roam round the quiet valley

Take out my magic net
Hoping to catch something magical

I close my eyes
Swoop my net

Open my eyes, feel something soft

Pull it out
Open the cloud

There is what I hoped
An end to racism

Isabelle Reynolds, Grade 5
Salt Brook Elementary School

Next to the Beautiful Sunset

In a land there is a lake,
Crystal Spring Lake.
I see the wonderful ocean side blue,
Far away there is a bird.
Chirping heavenly,
It is near nighttime,
And the birds are going into their nests.
Then I turn to my left,
And I am next to
The beautiful sunset.

Briana Carr, Grade 5
Hillside Elementary School

Pink: The Color That I Love

Pink, a special time and place
Pink, breast cancer awareness
Pink, twinkles in the night
Pink, Princess Specialty
Pink, oh so extraordinary
Pink, my heart beating
Pink, kindness towards friends
Pink, My love My compassion
My dreams My hopes My family
My life

Lauren Waldman, Grade 5
Belhaven Avenue Middle School

Mother Earth

M other Earth, her planet abundant with life.
O ver her wide expanse of ocean, graceful birds ride
T he wind that she blows. Even
H er waters are alive. Fish glide through the water,
E ver glistening and looking like the birds. On her lands, plants
R each up to touch her vast blue sky. The graceful birds fly,

E ach with
A different cawing
R hythm to sing.
T his is Mother Earth,
H er large planet ever shining like a brilliant blue star.

Eli Zuckerman, Grade 6
Community School of Bergen County

Dancer, Dancer

Dancer, dancer up on stage,
People clapping, smiling, and cheering for you.
Up there gliding and floating,
Thinking how much you worked to get to this day.
Dancer, dancer on your toes,
Your skirt flowing with your movements.
As the light shines on you,
You look like a fairy in the clouds.
As you bow and blow a kiss,
You think to yourself,
"This is what I want to do."

Tamryn Mistretta, Grade 5
Zion Lutheran School

Who Am I?

I am loving, respectful, and honest.
I wonder what career I will choose when I am older.
I hear bulldozers in my backyard.
I see my puppy every day.
I want to be a doctor when I grow up.
I am loving, respectful, and honest.

I pretend I am a professional singer.
I feel my dog's wet tongue on my face in the morning.
I touch the spoon while I'm eating my cereal.
I worry that somebody in my family will get hurt.
I cry when somebody hurts my feelings.
I am loving, respectful, and honest.

I understand that people have feelings.
I say, "It is better to see the glass half full."
I dream that I will become a doctor.
I try to do my best in school.
I hope that I will learn to do hip-hop.
I am loving, respectful, and honest.

I am Melissa Sherman.

Melissa Sherman, Grade 5
Sicomac Elementary School

A Guinea Pig's Own

When the house is warm and the food is hot,
The guinea pig cries forget me not,
Then a family may clean their home
Only to forget a guinea pig's own
Hungry and cold, a pig feels no love,
Nor tries to continue loving his masters above.
Excepting to be hugged and a snack at night,
Now there is nothing to do but bite.

Unclean, unloved, a pig's life means not,
Like a child play thing, it is simply forgot.
But warning to all who turn their ear,
Let the curse of the guinea pig fear.

Morgan Scott, Grade 5
Williamstown Middle School

Nice Spring

Spring is nice with all the fun and laughs.
Come with me and you will see.
Go to the park and take a walk.
Run if you want.
You will have a blast.
When it rains, it's fun to play outside.
So enjoy spring while it lasts,
Because spring is going too fast.

Robert Adams, Grade 4
John F Kennedy Elementary School

What Teachers Are

Teachers are everywhere I need them to be,
In schools, on playgrounds, and in my thoughts,
Some have nasty attitudes when they talk to you,
And others very pleasing,
Teachers act like computers; complicated and complex,
but understanding,
They don't just say $2+2=4$
They have fun showing you different ways to look at learning,
Helping children is their job; teaching is their job,
But most important being a great role model is their job,
No matter how stuck you are, in math or in language
they will always be with you in the back of your mind,
If he is a boy teacher or she is a girl teacher
they will always be there for you,
And it all pays off for you in the end.

Brianne, Grade 5
Tamaques Elementary School

Easter

What a wonderful day
The Easter Bunny is on his way
He leaves treats and goodies for us to find
While the thought of summer is in my mind
Pastel colors and beautiful flowers
Are all you see during spring hours

Erin Lay, Grade 6
Great Meadows Regional Middle School

Useless Things
A vacuum without a hose
A piano without keys
A person without a nose
Knobby without knees

A baby without diapers
A plant without water
A windshield without wipers
A son without a daughter

A Mike without Myers
Sports without scooters
A store without buyers
Monitors without computers
Joshua Summers, Grade 5
St Veronica Elementary School

Summer Is Almost Here
I love summer!
Summer is fun.
No more winter breezes.
It is all fun in the sun!
I play in the pool.
The pool is quite cool.
In summer, I am free of school.
Emma Sprigle, Grade 4
John F Kennedy Elementary School

Oceanside
White foam on top of blue
salty fish hooks
the swish of waves
the mist hit my face
water with a salty taste
I'm in paradise
Joshua Joseph Yaede, Grade 6
Little Egg Harbor Intermediate School

Fire
Burning, sizzling, crackling, roaring,
The fire burned as the rain was pouring.
As I put a log on the flame,
The fire was almost tame.
When we put marshmallows to roast,
I like to gobble them up the most.
Away from the sheer bitterness,
I lie down as the fire continues to hiss.
Brian Evans, Grade 6
Fieldstone Middle School

The Brook
Flowing gently down
Fish swimming quickly downstream
Beautiful river
Ronda Zughbi, Grade 4
Number 15 Elementary School

Outside Inside
Outside laying on the hammock in the peaceful snow.
Inside reading books by the warm fireplace.

Outside making happy snowmen with long carrots.
Inside decorating the Christmas tree with a glass of eggnog.

Outside sledding in the white Christmas snow.
Inside the smell of roasting chestnuts as sweet as snow.

Outside shoveling the snow and putting up Christmas decorations.
Inside waiting for Santa Claus on beautiful Christmas Eve.
Madelyn Dilley, Grade 5
Byram Township Intermediate School

This World
When someone loves you, you feel welcomed into the world.
When someone doesn't, you feel thrown out.
There are so many times when we float around looking for a friend.
But somehow someone seems to always have all the joy.
They don't.
We all have our bad days.
Nobody's perfect.
Sometimes you get pushed around because the people that push you
around aren't perfect.
Sometimes we all feel like we are better than someone else
but that's just part of not being perfect.
Even being really kind isn't being perfect.
No matter how hard you try you can't be perfect.
That's just part of being in this sad unperfect world.
Sivan Rosenthal, Grade 6
Bartle Elementary School

The Nightmare
Splash! I have fallen into the endless sea
Crashing waves and the dark night is the last thing I see
As I open my eyes I see my mother's face, staring gently down at me.
Caitlin Cavanagh, Grade 6
Allen W Roberts Elementary School

Easter Peace
Two days before Easter, we load up the van.
Driving for nine hours is always our plan.
When we finally get to my grandparents' home,
They are surprised to see that they are no longer alone.

The day before Easter is spent planning and baking.
The excitement of Easter is ours for the taking.
But Easter isn't only about receiving toys.
It's for celebrating the life of Jesus in girls and boys.

We dress up for Mass to celebrate Jesus' gift of peace.
For all he has done, he gives life a new lease.
The peace of Jesus means nothing can separate us from his love.
I know he is watching and loving us from above.
Eric Wagner, Grade 6
Sacred Heart School

Ballet Star

She gracefully went upon her toe,
listening to the music of the piccolo.
Gripping the bar as hard as she could,
trying not to fall, but she probably would.
The song finally came to an end.
Trying not to let her leg bend,
she carefully let go of the bar.
She balanced and felt like a ballet star.

Courtney Chernin, Grade 6
Fieldstone Middle School

Happiness

Happiness is yellow
It smells like fresh steamy pizza
It looks like a big, yellow smiley face
It tastes like sweet and sugary cotton candy
It sounds like kids playing in a park
Happiness feels like when you get your first pet

Kelsey Skinner, Grade 6
St Rose of Lima School

The Flying Penguins

Watching the flying penguins,
high in the night sky.

Hear their beating wings flapping like playing drums.
Feel their cold fur. Brrrrrrrrrr.

See them sketching skyward,
while one falls behind.

Watch them float away,
while one falls behind.

Hear their lonely sigh,
While they say goodbye to the south and say hello
to the north.

Samir Ramadani, Grade 4
Lincoln Park Elementary School

Home Run

Through the blue summer skies,
The small baseball flies.
As the runner rounds first,
You can tell he's the worst.
When he sprinted for second,
Everyone was stunned,
'Cause we knew it was all or none.
When the ball was thrown it looked like a bird,
The unsuspected runner darted around third.
The throw was simply great,
No one knew there would be a play at the plate.
Who thought it could be done,
But the worst player just hit a home run.

Bryan Prohaska, Grade 6
Our Lady of Mount Virgin School

Shooting Stars

Lebron James is always moving up and down the court
He can dunk perfectly because he's tall, not short

Vince Carter is a basketball player who always shoots the ball
Sometimes never passes when his teammates call

Michael Jordan had to retire. He's one of the best
He used to be better than all the others…now he's taking a rest

Nate Robinson won the dunk competition this very year
He's always dunking in his games and never has any fear

Harsharan Kaur, Grade 6
Thomas Jefferson Middle School

We the People

We the people,
The only people,
We share this land, at least we try.
With war and hate we won't get anywhere,
With love and hope we can get somewhere.
We the people, the only people,
A population in the millions.
We have beliefs of the known,
We have beliefs of the unknown.
We the people,
The only people
We will share everywhere!
(I hope!)

Asheley Buchwalter, Grade 5
Winslow Township School No 6

Winston

Winston, my dog.
Whose eyes flame when he barks
Who sings a song when he sees another dog.
Who gets excited when he gets food.
Who steals pizza off the table,
    or even out of your hand.
Yeah, he's really rude,
He's a rip-roaring dude.

Who runs in our back yard,
And makes sparks fly out into the air
He's so fast that a car isn't faster than him.
Who chews our pant legs,
    and my dad's glasses.
Yeah he's really rude,
He's a rip-roaring dude.

Who makes everyone mad
But even though he's bad,
He makes everyone laugh.
Winston, my dog.

Julia Derco, Grade 5
Central School

My Life as a Sneaker

I'm tired of being in the mud
I'm tired of that disgusting smell
I'm tired of being kicked off
I'm tired of getting things stuck in me
I'm tired of getting lost somewhere
Nicole Rodriguez, Grade 6
Thorne Middle School

Dark Days

I see dark days.
When the rain falls, I feel weary.
When the sun shines, I feel cheery.
But really I change with the weather.
I feel like a sweater
Being worn every day.
I feel like I'm being
Put out, shot down.
I can't be myself.
I can't walk by myself.
I feel like I'm controlled
When I'm around other people;
But it's different it's called friendship,
Where no one can control you.
You be yourself; if they don't like you,
That's too bad.
That's not a friend;
That's someone who likes you
When you pretend
But that's not who I am.
I am a friend.
Gabriella Negreiros, Grade 6
Bartle Elementary School

Fall

Apples in the orchard,
Pumpkins in the patch,
This wonderful season is back.

Drinking apple cider,
Baking apple pie,
I smell it in the kitchen,
As I walk on by.

Jumping in the piles,
Raking up the leaves,
Oh, I just don't want this season,
Ever to leave!
Heather DiLorenzo, Grade 4
Meadowbrook Elementary School

Awakening

Big, brown, and content
The bear awaits summer's dawn
Until then, he sleeps.
Monica Fechter, Grade 6
Robert L Craig Elementary School

Stars

Stars in the sky,
Dancing with the moon way up high,
The colors are bold and bright,
Shining brilliantly in the night,
Twirling and dancing the colors spin,
Like light bouncing off a metal tin,
The shimmery colors start to die off,
And rest on a mountain loft,
Sinking down hiding from the light,
Just waiting,
Just waiting,
For the soft peaceful night.
Elana Segal, Grade 6
Bartle Elementary School

Being a Waterfall

If I were a waterfall I'd spill,
stream down the shiny rocks,
and wait in line again.

My cold blue skin would dash
right back down like a hunting fox.

I'd feel like I was on a roller-coaster,
a never-ending river raft ride.

The smooth surface picks me up
as the current rushes again.
Danielle Grossman, Grade 4
Sicomac Elementary School

Red Pandas

Looking like a red raccoon,
running through the trees.

A little red panda looking about,
trying to find bamboo leaves.

Also munching on red, juicy berries,
right off the bush's branch.

With their red striped tail,
and whiskers on their nose.

Small red pandas, all red and white,
eat and travel all day and night.
Emily Schider, Grade 4
Lincoln Park Elementary School

My Dog Teddy

I love my dog, Teddy
Even though he chews on the doll, Betty
And he gets it all wetty.
Joshua Stark, Grade 5
Springfield Township School

My First Day of Gymnastics

Sensational, delightful
Sour, spicy, delicious
Flip, swing, swish, twist
Beam, bars, floor
Wonderful, sweet
Challenging
Lindsey Lawrence, Grade 4
Mansfield Township Elementary School

Time to Let Go

Miss Iacocca is sweet
She is exciting to meet
She's like a little butterfly…

I came to her class and loved it there
So I did what I had to do.

So I could go as far as I could
and now good bye Miss Iacocca's class.
Melissa Arevalo, Grade 4
Evergreen Elementary School

The Sunset

Beautiful sunset
On a warm summer evening
It is so lovely
Sydney Pezzulo, Grade 4
Mansfield Township Elementary School

The Bloom

After a long time of
Lingering through
Fall and winter
Greeting hello
To all the other flowers
Hiding as a fragile bud
Spring is here and
I'm stretching my petals and
Yawning in the meadow
My beauty is breathtaking
With lush colors and
Lovely fragrance
Butterflies dancing around my petals
Nectar is what I possess
The drink of passion
Dina Roowala, Grade 6
Cherry Hill Elementary School

Responsibility

Doing the work
And taking the blame.
Helping another from day to day.
Supporting your family in every way.
These are responsibilities for today.
Erin Ouellette, Grade 6
Springfield Township School

Who Is She?

There she sits,
On a bench,
Wearing dark clothing.

I don't know who she is,
Or what she's doing.

I try not to stare,
But I have never seen anything like this before.

She looks at me,
I suddenly turn,
Like a dog feeling bad.

For I am interested,
But still unsure.

Kaitlyn Cyran, Grade 5
Bedminster Township Elementary School

A Different World

When I got in the plane to come here,
from Argentina I remember it was not near.
Leaving my country, my country home,
I came here and knew none.
I knew a little English, could not understand,
but didn't give up, up I stand.
I learned the language by the time,
but I'll never forget the family of mine.
I'll go back to Argentina to visit them,
family and friends, I'll always remember 'em.

Melina Galinski, Grade 6
Franklin Elementary School

Winter

Crispy snowflakes everywhere
Go outside without a care
Tickling your nose, brings you a chill
Don't be a soldier standing still

Twirl around and fall on the snow
Now is the time when grass does not grow
First drooping, then turning yellow
Not like them, you're a happy fellow

The world is completely white now
Change back to green? I don't know how
Let's go back inside, where it's warm
Outside is a swirling snowstorm

You want to hear something cool?
Mom said, "Today there is no school."
Yes, it is a closed school day
Winter is here, "HOORAY! HOORAY!"

Laurel Meng, Grade 4
Old York Elementary School

The Forest

Trees are always having whispered conversations
Animals are sneaking around in the bushes
The darkness is hushed and calm
Yet still thunderous and deafening
Yet people still go to the forest
They join in the lively chat
Smiling with the trees
They scream at the top of their lungs
Along with the trees

Brandi Hein, Grade 6
Little Egg Harbor Intermediate School

An Amazing Game

Will I choose a 9 iron today,
Or maybe I should pick a 5?
Come up for the backswing, descend for the down stroke,
Blow the ball right out of range.
I finally locate the hole,
It's an extraordinary feeling.
I take out my putter,
Getting ready to succeed.
I prepare for the putt,
Got to make the break, got to get it right.
I know I can succeed
Because it dropped in the hole!
I get up with great feeling,
My fans are all cheering,
Because I have won.
I love this game!

Andrew Dougert, Grade 5
Tamaques Elementary School

Best Friends Forever

My best friends are really great,
but sometimes they're very late.
They're always cool and funny,
I'm happy when it's rainy or sunny.
If we put our minds together I know we'll go far,
so my best friends are great and you know who you are!
So you know my friends are the greatest,
even thought they're the latest!

Katrina Pollare, Grade 4
St Mary's School

Friends

F unny when you are blue.
R ely on them to pull you through.
I n friends we have a stronger bond than anyone.
E ating junk food with them is fun.
N ever let you down.
D epend on them to make you smile.
S tick with you in hard times.

Yes there is nothing sweeter than the company of friends.

Meghan Dougherty, Grade 5
Belhaven Avenue Middle School

My Cat Holly

Holly is not very jolly
She is only friendly to me
To other people and cats
She will hiss and scratch
But for me she'll cuddle and purr
If you try to pet her
She'll fluff up her fur
And then she will growl grrr
She never bites
Although she might
So you'd better watch out…
If you come to my house
She is Siamese
And she only loves me
Victoria Catherine Edwards, Grade 6
Little Egg Harbor Intermediate School

The Halloween Rules

Halloween is coming soon.
The dead will rise at new moon.

I can't wait to trick or treat,
Numbers of candy can't be beat.

I love Halloween it's a holiday.
I can't wait for Halloween Day!

Time to turn the lights out,
So everyone can scream and shout.
Joshua Queiro, Grade 5
Byram Township Intermediate School

Live Freely

Get out of bed.
Wake up energized,
Finding your purpose.
Put good into good morning.
Who says you can't move through
The day like the breeze?
Treat yourself well every day.
Yajahira Alvarez, Grade 6
Robert L Craig Elementary School

Summer

I love the summer seasons.
Having no school is the reason.

I get to go to the pool,
and chill with my friends and act cool.

I like to eat juicy peaches
while I tan on the sandy beaches.

Summer is so fantastic!
Amanda Perez, Grade 4
St Rose of Lima School

Through the Years of Beading*

I've always loved making beaded necklaces.
When I was little I would sit down and string beads on a necklace.
One by one
When I was little it didn't matter if the beads didn't fit right.
When I was little some beads made the string fray a little bit.
When I was little it didn't matter,
I would still put them on my necklace.

Now I acknowledge that some beads aren't what is best for my necklace.
Now a bead can make the other beads look dull.
Now one bead can ruin the harmony of the necklace.

Now that I'm older, I aspire to find the special beads.
Now that I'm older I like to find the beads that make my necklace shine.
Now that I'm older those special beads make my necklace the best it can be.
Now that I'm older finding that one special bead is like winning a medal.
Now that I'm older finding that one bead makes me feel great.
Carly Avezzano, Grade 6
Fieldstone Middle School
*Friends are beads and I am the necklace.

The Puma

T his creature's territory has been eliminated through extensive
deforestation (removing trees).
H ave well-developed whiskers and large eyes.
E lk, bighorn, and sheep are eaten by the puma.

P umas are unspotted and have a black tip on their tail.
U sually, the puma's diet consists of eating mainly deer.
M ountain lion (another name for puma) would also be found in
parts of British Columbia, western Alberta, and Canada.
A n average-sized female puma is about 5 feet long and weighs 90 pounds.
Rachael DeTore, Grade 4
Franklin Township Elementary School

Why Do You Treat Me Like You Do?

Have you ever lived a day in someone else's life?
A day when you felt all their pain and witnessed all their strife
Have you ever been stung, by bee after bee?
Or fallen off your bike so badly the blood gushed from your knee?
Have you ever been attacked by a great big swarm of bugs,
Or watched your older brother suffer from an overdose of drugs?
If you've never witnessed any of this, why do you treat me like you do?
I mean, what did I ever do that's so harmful to you?
Why is it that every time you see me walking down the hall,
You have to stick your foot out and guarantee I fall.
And how come you steal my glasses and stomp on them until they break?
I mean, where in my own life did I ever make a mistake?
How come you proceed into calling me nasty names?
I guess I'll never understand why you think it's fun and games.
Why is being accepted so tough?
Why are teenage years so rough?
Why do you laugh at all my dreams? When I've never said a word to you.
So, once again I repeat myself…why do you treat me like you do?
Nevon Kipperman, Grade 6
Tenafly Middle School

If I Were an American Flag

If I were an American flag,
I'd sway in the cool, swift breeze.
I'd watch the ruby red stripes go back and forth
Like an army running side by side.
I'd be proud of the people who pledge to me and respect me.

Dominick Muccilo, Grade 4
Sicomac Elementary School

I Want a World

I want a world
Where people eat healthy
I want a world
Where there is no poverty
I want a world
Where kids are grateful
I want a world
Where diseases do not exist
I want a world!
I want a world!

Kyle Brookens, Grade 4
Evergreen Elementary School

Space

When you look up high
Into the night sky

You see beautiful stars
And occasionally you can see Mars

When you look up high you'll always hope
That you see something through your telescope

The planets are free
They flow around like the sea

Stars are flying in the night sky
You're waiting for a shooting star to come by

Then you can wish with all your might
That you'll see something amazing tonight

Meghan McCaffrey, Grade 5
St Rose of Lima School

I Want a World…

I want a world
when money is everywhere!
I want a world
when everywhere you turn mosquitos are not there!
I want a world
when kids actually act more young!
I want a world
when everybody acts like God's son.

I want that world!

Sheldon Brown, Grade 4
Evergreen Elementary School

The Things in the Night Sky

There is a blackness that isn't quite blackness,
That's more of a deep navy blue,
In which the moon and the stars shine bright
As well as white and true.

The man in the moon beams down on me,
Though part of him is obscured by a tree.

The stars twinkle down as if to say,
"You have done quite well today,
Now let peaceful slumber take you away."

Rosie Wilkin, Grade 5
Community Park School

Soccer

When you're at a soccer field,
You feel the intensity with no yield,
The fans are cheering very loud,
They sound as loud as a crowd,
When the ref blows the whistle,
We all go off as fast as missiles,
When the ball flies through the air,
There is nothing in its way not even a hair,
When the game is all done,
There is no argument, it's said and done,
This is played around the world,
That is where soccer is a dreamworld!

Grant Jurkowich, Grade 4
Woods Road Elementary School

The Cheetah

The cheetah who prances all around,
the cheetah who climbs trees,
the cheetah who is quick and sure,
who is lovely and sly like many animals may be,
but just to warn you…
if you see a cheetah…be careful…
what they say or do
Or he will have breakfast with you!!!

Caroline Carr, Grade 4
Sundance School

My Favorite Sport

I love basketball
It's like smelling a flower
The sound of the swish
is like doing a dive into a crystal clear pool
The basketball is as orange as a sunset
on a summer evening
When I'm not playing
the sound of the sneakers squeaking on the court
is like a cry of the court
calling me to play.

Brian Seeber, Grade 6
Cherry Hill Elementary School

Nighttime

The moon gleams
Off the ocean surface.

The stars shine like
The glory in someone's eyes.

The day puts on its nightgown
And goes to sleep.

Sara Casparian, Grade 4
Community Park School

Racist

Why do
people have
to be
racist?
Why can't just
be who they
are,
it doesn't
matter what color
they are
what matters is
What's on the inside.
Can you imagine if
everybody was pink
yellow or green,
we'd all look pretty ridiculous
if you know what I mean.
So let's all
get along
and stop being racist.

Sarah Stofan, Grade 6
Mother Seton Inter Parochial School

Winter Wood

In the winter wood I see
The snow falling one by one.
I hear the wind pushing against the trees
I feel the snow
Rushing in my face
As it melts on my tongue.
I could smell the scent
Of the air as the wind
Rushes to your mind.
I could taste the white snow
As if it was a big sugar stick.
I could see the trees
Shaking in the wind
As the leaves fall off
One
By
One.

Andrew Santoro, Grade 4
Pond Road Middle School

Roller Skate

I wanted to roller skate
It was almost half past eight
It was a blast until I crashed
I broke my leg and wore a cast

Bailey Bruno, Grade 4
Katharine D Malone Elementary School

Fear

In the dark
Cold breath on your neck
Fear
Spiders in your face
Snakes on your neck
Fear
Behind your door
Under your bed
Fear
A dark shadow following
Dark shadows under you as you swim
Fear
Gruesome, gory thoughts
Incurable illnesses
Fear
In your closet
In your bathroom
Fear
This is only mine
What is your fear?

Richie Johnson, Grade 6
Fieldstone Middle School

Paper

Fold me, draw me, do what you will.
But don't cut me!
Make something from me, instead
There's so much of me around.

Sometimes I'm colorful,
Sometimes I'm blank.
Now remember not to make me mad,
For I could give you a bad paper cut!

Julie Park, Grade 4
Christ the Teacher School

Drum Beats

It started long ago
With an empty oatmeal box
That I tapped with my fingers
And found it really rocks!

Ba-da-bum, rat-a-tat
Fast or slow, soft or loud
Playing with my drumsticks
Puts me on a cloud!

Tommy Ventura, Grade 6
Fieldstone Middle School

Imagination

Your imagination
Can take you anywhere…

Your imagination
Can run wild…

Your imagination
Is a source of creativity…

Your imagination
Is yours to keep…

Your imagination
Can never run out.

Taylor Cuenca, Grade 5
Roosevelt Elementary School

Mom/Dad

Mom
Female, agreeable
Cleans, cooks, washing
Parent, produce, originate, sire
Works, reads, eats
Man, strong
Dad

Carla Arizaga, Grade 4
St Joseph School

Winter Lantern

Snow
So cold
Beautiful
Shines very bright
White

Meghna Vamburkar, Grade 4
Franklin Park Elementary School

Green

Green is the forest
Green is the trees
Green is the leaves
Green is the grass
Green is the moss
Green is nature

Sean Enman, Grade 6
Christa McAuliffe Middle School

My Guitar

Music
Great sound
Picking, playing
It takes you away.
Guitar

Michelle Moreno, Grade 4
Number 15 Elementary School

Prophets

P rophets preached the word of God and
R ejoiced in His name as
O ur Lord and Savior.
P rophets brought God's word of
H ope and promise to the people. They
E ncouraged true worship of God, which comes from
T he heart of people.
S imply, in God's name they spoke.

Bryan Fondufe, Grade 6
St Joseph's School

Sweet Summertime

As the flowery springtime fades away,
And the summertime blossoms in,
The sun shines bright on a summer day
And all of our joys begin.

The blackberries grow on a bramble bush,
And reveal ripe, sweet tastes to us all,
We climb to the branch of the maple lush,
So strong, so old, and so tall.

The breeze sings a song on the crisp blue lake,
And the grass grows towering high,
As we skip through the meadow on a summer day,
We feel like birds in the sky.

The butterflies dance in the warm fresh air,
Music sings from the golden chime,
Nothing could be sweeter now,
Than the bliss, sweet summertime.

Gwendolyn Morris, Grade 5
St Veronica Elementary School

Why Do You Cry?

Why do you cry?
Is it because you're shy?
Do you mind me asking why?
Please oh please just tell me why?
Sometimes I cry when others exclude me
And when they push me and don't say excuse me.
Is that why you cry?
Please oh please just tell me why?

Jennifer Ramos, Grade 5
The Red Bank Charter School

Happiness

Happiness is yellow.
It smells like a sugary candy store.
It looks like a sunset on a hot summer day.
It tastes like sweet frosted cupcakes.
It sounds like laughter spilling through the room.
Happiness feels like butterflies tickling my stomach.

Victoria Petrozziello, Grade 6
St Rose of Lima School

Icicle

Water dripping, dripping, freezing,
Icicle melting, melting,
     gone.
Next snow falls and
     water drip, drip, freezes.
Extending itself with
     each drip and freeze.
The icicle drips, melts,
     melts,
      melts,
     gone.

Isaac Yassky, Grade 4
Community Park School

My Dog Bandit

I have a dog, his name is Bandit.
When I let him out, he runs quite rampant.

He likes biscuits and bacon, too.
If you shake him, he might bark and bite at you.

He's like a brother with fur and a long nose.
Even though he's not close to smelling like a rose.

Actually, he's not like a brother, he IS one.
He and I are like the moon and the sun.

The sun makes it light,
The moon makes it night.
I am the moon, he is the sun.
I am the butter, he is the bun.

Why, do you ask? Because he is the one.
The one that makes me happy and makes me have fun.

Brandon Bischer, Grade 5
Immaculate Conception Regional School

The Ruby Red Leaves

The ruby red leaves soon
  know their short lives
   will peacefully end.
They will soon slowly descend
  from the enormous tree.
   The deliberate whisper of the wind
slowly tells the crimson red leaves
  to calmly flutter to the ground.
   The heavenly leaves quickly fade
as they harmoniously travel down
  to the snowy terrain.
   As the descend, the leaves observe
all the marvelous branches of the giant oak tree.
  The last leaf struggles to hang on.
   The leaf finally cascades
onto the smooth gentle ground.

Tal Bass, Grade 5
Lyncrest Elementary School

My Family

My family is a first place ribbon, proud bold and first place in my heart.
My dad is a computer, knowing so many things, but still open to learn new information.
My mom is a flower garden, so many different fragrances.
So many parts in her life,
a mother, a wife, a friend, a medical researcher
My sister is a wind-up toy. So hyper and energetic.
But after a while she wears me down.
And I, I am a dove, a symbol of comfort, kindness, peace, and serenity.
My family is the world, different in some ways
but the same in others, strict but reasonable,
firm but calm. Yep that's my family.
And I wouldn't trade them for all the treasures in the world.

Aditi Padmanabhan, Grade 5
Salt Brook Elementary School

The Moon's Ways

The glistening spirit of the moon shining on a gravel path
Being big and round it takes more time for the moon to glide across the midnight sky
The sun always comes to awaken the moon from its deep sleep to tell it morning has come!

Erin Corbett, Grade 6
Little Egg Harbor Intermediate School

What's in the Snack Cabinet?

Crackers, cookies, candy from two years ago,
granola bars, gummy bears, candy canes from last Christmas,
popcorn (we need a lot of that), chips (for my dad when he's watching the football game),
lots and lots of junk food, goldfish and cartoon fruit snacks smiling at me.

Claire Scavone, Grade 5
Sicomac Elementary School

No Tears or Crying, Time to Be Tough

It was the worst day of my life…
It all started with a twist and a turn and then I realized I was other people's concern
To my surprise it was right in front of my eyes
People cared about me…

It was Friday, a warm, sun-splashed day period 5 gym, my time to play
Soccer is what I wanted to play most so that is what I chose
Someone stole the ball from me! Sprinting back to retreat it
A sharp pain surged through my left leg I looked down to see
My knee cap on the left side of my leg
It happened too fast a split second at the most
The pain was excruciating but, I hung tough even though the pain was very rough
The pain was not abating, it was only getting worse I felt so flustered that I was ready to burst!
Everyone was whispering and staring at me but then came Mr. Boyle to save me!
Then I lost feeling in my leg I couldn't move
Mr. Boyle just sat there grasping my hand he knew it hurt so much that I couldn't even stand
The ride to the hospital was only 5 minutes but, it felt like a trek climbing up a mountain
On the stretcher I heard my friends crying in the background
It was the worst day of my life…

It all started with a twist and a turn and then I realized I was other people's concern
To my surprise, it was right in front of my eyes
People cared about me…

Emily Villafranco, Grade 6
Fieldstone Middle School

Beauty Bird

Buzzing or humming,
Through the air,
Backward and forward,
Here and there,
I drink nectar from flowers,
Very tiny, hard to see,
People think I'm a buzzing bee,
Lilacs, tulips, sunflowers too!
I'm not out on the ocean blue,
Beauty Bird is my name,
Humming is how I get my fame.
Bigger birds try to eat me,
But I'm swifter than a bumble bee.
People leave me sugarwater to drink,
Just to see my glistening body that's sleek,
Buzzing or humming,
Through the air,
Backward and forward,
Here and there.

Alexis Holiday, Grade 6
The Red Bank Charter School

Crayons

I have a pack of crayons
It comes with only eight
Yellow, purple, blue, brown, black, orange, green, red
And when I take them out to color
I smell the smell of wax
Straight out of the Crayola factory
Ooo it smells so yucky
I look at the crayon and I love how they're always sharp
Just ready for me to color
My drawings come out great.

Chelsea Todisco, Grade 6
Thomas Jefferson Middle School

The Summer's Day

The flowers insult you with their beauty
The trees seem to astound you in their dominate height
The grass is like an ocean swaying in the gentle breeze
But like a dark knife it comes and it's all over again

Tristan Scott Nino, Grade 6
Little Egg Harbor Intermediate School

Spring Has Sprung

The time has come when the days are bright and long
The buds are popping with beautiful flowers;
The birds are chirping;
The butterflies are fluttering by;
And the bees are busy buzzing by.

While laying in the tall, green grass,
I look upon the sky so clear;
And I know that spring is finally here!

Ashley Jones, Grade 6
Christa McAuliffe Middle School

Spring Is Coming

Spring is coming! Spring is coming!
Aren't you glad it's here?

Spring is coming! Spring is coming!
Is your birthday in the spring?

Spring is coming! Spring is coming!
I can't wait until my birthday's here!

Spring is coming! Spring is coming!
My locker can't wait until no more jackets!

Spring is coming! Spring is coming!
I can't wait until the grass turns green!

Spring is coming! Spring is coming!
I can't wait until the cherry blossoms blossom!

Spring is coming! Spring is coming!
Spring showers are here!

Emily Ung, Grade 6
Gilmore J Fisher Middle School

Music

Music is something that makes you enjoy
bad music can lead to make you annoy
rap, pop, rock, and hip hop
one of the songs that I like is "Candy Shop"
it makes you jump, sing, scream, and shout
there's no doubt of it that's what it's all about
music has hip rhythm and cool beats
it makes you jump off the ground and on to your feet.

Shaheera Kazmi, Grade 6
Gilmore J Fisher Middle School

Jaguar

People call me a Jaguar.
Running through the vegetational forest
I roar as I take down my prey.
I sniff fresh air
And attack the wailing animal.
I feast on my prey which is now my dinner.

Adam Gradl, Grade 6
The Red Bank Charter School

Spring Outside

O utdoors is where I run and play
U sually I go higher and higher pumping on the swing
T rying to reach the sky where the birds fly
S taying outside is what I love to do
I nviting friends to play tag in my backyard
D ancing on my lawn pretending it's a stage
E veryone joins me in celebrating spring.

Jamie Desser, Grade 4
Solomon Schechter Day School

Penguins
Penguins
Like to slide
On slippery ice
All the time
Because it's fun.
Michael O'Brien, Grade 5
Sicomac Elementary School

Football
Football
contact, challenging
sprinting, kicking, catching
lets me play with my friends
Favorite Sport
Jake Joseph, Grade 4
Mansfield Township Elementary School

Fennec Foxes
Hearing sounds afar and near
Digging to and fro
In the North African desert sun
Your sandy fur's aglow
The fennec fox is an unusual thing
With ears so tall and wide
The playful fennec fox kit
Leaps about with pride
Known to exist by very few
It is entirely their loss
It shows the cute creature committee
Who is the cutest boss
Majestically it slumbers
Dreaming about today
Outside under the star filled sky
In the fennec fox way
Jessica Lowe, Grade 6
Chatham Middle School

Will Be with Me
An air-flight
To your 'Home'
Leaves me feeling
So alone.
A blown kiss
From the door.
All of that
Is a memory to adore.
The times we've
Shared together
Will last with me
Forever and forever.
The last moment
Of us like this
Will be with me.
Will be with me always.
Victoria Levchenko, Grade 6
Christa McAuliffe Middle School

My Sports
I love to play all sports
They're all the best to me
It really doesn't matter
If I only compete in three
I'll play hard 'til the end
In whatever sport I choose
When it comes time to dream
It doesn't matter whether I win or lose
I'm hoping one day
That I'll make the team
Which will greatly build my self-esteem
Ryan McGowan, Grade 6
Springfield Township School

Cat
Active cat
In the living room
Hair, small, and active
Cat
Kayla Wyatt, Grade 6
Central Middle School

Malibu Drive
I live on a nice street,
With lots of friends and neighbors,
Everyone is so kind and sweet,
On my street.
BellaRosa Preziosi, Grade 4
Holy Saviour School

Work?
i'm realy bad at spelling
even worse at cooking stew

I cant bee a theacher
Ill sai 4 x 4 is 2

I'm know good at math
so an acontents not mi choice

kno way am i a sergeant
cause I don't have aloud voice

I whant to be a runer
but i always scrape my kneez

I gueess i'll bee an actore
And I'l practice lines whith ease
oh no
I nocked oveer all the vases
from on mi desk
So i'll think of whate to be
while i ridde mi bike the best
Haley Needle, Grade 5
Solomon Schechter Day Lower School

The Wind
The weather outside is roaring.
The trees are waving, "Hi."
Lights are flickering
Wind sounds like a howling coyote.
The sky is releasing its anger.
The rain is skipping.
The smoky clouds are racing by.
Christopher Carlos, Grade 5
Cherry Hill Elementary School

Snow
As children laugh and play,
Their parents gently say,
"Oh no we hate snow!"
Our parents shovel and throw the snow,
But don't they know,
The more they shovel,
The more it will snow.
James Maryanski, Grade 4
St Peter Elementary School

Christmas
Christmas is in the air,
Bows and ribbons in my hair.
Presents under the tree,
How lucky it is to be me!
Fallon Quigley, Grade 4
St Mary's School

My Cat
My cat is so fat
That she can just barely run
Even if she tried hard
Nathaniel Capone, Grade 4
Franklin Township Elementary School

Nature's Wonders
Stealthy snake slithering slyly
Amongst the tall, velvety grass

Ravenous rabbit running rapidly
Its deep black eyes gleaming
Pure as glass

Stunning swan sailing swiftly
Across the sparkling pond

Busy bees bustling
Around the sweet flowers
Collecting nectar

And Me,
Watching nature's magic
Dance before my eyes.
Divya Ramesh, Grade 6
Thomas R Grover Middle School

Think

Life is something you must fulfill
Like your dreams
Dreams will take you places you want to be
Dreams may decide your future
But…it rests in your hands
Try your hardest and you will achieve
Your most wanted dreams
Life is something you must take care of.

Life, your dreams,
THINK.

Lena Halverson, Grade 6
Walter T. Bergen Middle School

To Remember…

I remember the Loud
Loud Loud
crying when my baby brother
was born.
All wrapped in a baby blue
soft
blanket. I had
never seen such small feet in
my life!
This is what I love to
Remember!

Kayla Colon, Grade 4
Evergreen Elementary School

My Mom and Me

Me and my mom
My mom and me
We are so happy together
As you can see.
I like to dance
She likes to prance
I like to sing
She likes to flash her bling, blings.
I like hip hop
And she likes to shop, shop
Me and my mom
My mom and me
We are so happy together, as you can see.

Zina Sinicropi, Grade 6
Hehnly Elementary School

The Stars

The stars are bright.
They shine at night
You have to go to sleep.
But we just want one last peep.
I open my eyes,
And say, "Good-bye."

Sarah-Ann Storino, Grade 6
Immaculate Conception Regional School

Green

Green is the color of a frog
green is the color of the grass.
Green is the color of the trees.
Green is the name of a band,
green is a star fruit.

Devon Bush, Grade 4
Hardyston Township Elementary School

The Seasons

Winter is when the snow falls down.
The sparkly snow covers the ground.
Let's build a snowman in the snow.
Bundle up before you go.
Spring is the time with the last sign of snow.
Spring is the time when the flowers grow.
The rain comes and goes.
Watering the flowers get out the hose.
Summer is the season when it is really, really hot.
In the summer I go swimming a lot.
School is out and it's time to play.
The bright sun is shining all day.
Fall is when the weather gets cool.
It's time to go back to school and close the summer pool.
The leaves fall off the trees.
Now we can have fun in the leaves.
The seasons are great, I love them all.
I love winter, spring, summer and fall!
All the seasons come to an end.
Then, they start all over again.

Colleen Donegan, Grade 5
St Rose of Lima School

The Little Teddy Bear

There was a little teddy bear,
Who was old and raggedy but did not care,
His little girl took him everywhere.
He had only one eye,
A button nose and a cute little tie.
When his little girl left him he cried, "But why?"
He got thrown in a box,
With stinky old socks.
So he sat alone and cold,
Smelling the musty smell of mold,
Hoping he is not to be sold.
He wished that the little girl would come back,
But then his hope began to slack.
Then one day he found himself tumbling into a large sack.
He wondered what was going on,
Then he was dumped onto a bright green lawn
Where he saw a little girl named Dawn.
She picked him up and held him tight
And said I want this one Daddy, all right?
That little bear realized something that night,
He had a new friend that made his life bright.

Andrea Veneziale, Grade 6
Springfield Township School

Springtime
It is spring.
It is time for the birds to sing.
Spring is fun.
I can play in the sun.
I can play with my friends
And the laughs never end.
Spring is the best.
You won't need your sweater vest.
Spring is here.
It is the best time of the year.
Dakota Sabbatino, Grade 4
Apple Montessori School

The Sky
The sky is peaceful,
It seems so lonely and still
Just look up and see
Skies were made for you and me
For us to share forever.
Keila Rivera, Grade 5
Springfield Township School

The Horrible Day
I had a horrible day,
My teacher has a lot to say.
I didn't have a good time,
It was worse than the taste of lime.

There is a boy in school,
Everyone thinks he's cool.
He never listens to directions,
That's why he gets detentions.

My teacher is very kind,
Some kids say it is hard to find.
He is also really nice,
I don't think his heart is ice.

I have a best friend,
Our friendship will never end.
Until the next day,
That's what Lauren always says.

I hope I will have,
A better day tomorrow
Or else I will,
Be deep with sorrow.
Brooke Boykas, Grade 4
Stonybrook Elementary School

A Cloud Cry
Rain jumps from the sky
Clouds throw a loud thunder fit
And cry raindrops
Alexandria Jacobia, Grade 4
Stonybrook Elementary School

Birds in the Silent Tree
The dark shadows of the blue jays in morning sky,
The silent tree begins to rise.
More and more blue jays begin to crowd and the silent tree is now no more.
For as the bright-lit moon begins to come the silent tree is again once more.
Nathan Babore, Grade 5
Sandman Consolidated Elementary School

Sometimes
Sometimes I feel like an inch big
But everyone around me is as big as a tree
Like no one can see me
No one can care
But I will grow old faster than you think
I will look back to my childhood
And I hope I will laugh
For everyone big and small should have a chance
A chance to be loved
A chance to have hope
To live their life the way they want
For everyone is different in one special way
For maybe one day we will all be the same
For maybe one day no one will have to hang their head in shame
They will not be teased or taunted
We will all be the same
Casey Kohut, Grade 5
Parkway Elementary School

Melannie's Marvelous Monkeys
Marvelous monkeys make merriment on many musical instruments
Their melodious sounds are meaningful only to mindless monkeys
Mankind may mouth, NO PLEASE!
Mayhem made by muttering musical monkeys man sees.
Marvelous music, make me more please!
But muddled mess makes men drop to their knees!
"That hullabaloo must move to a zoo!"
"Taking their musical instruments too!"
Mangoes in this example are not marvelous fruit we may eat,
But, "man goes" is something we do with our feet.
When we meet Melannie's monkeys playing instruments in the streets,
More meaningful and moving are the soles of our feet!
Melannie Fields, Grade 6
Trinity Christian School

Inside/Outside
Inside mothers bake cookies with dough as sweet as sugar.
Outside people are driving from store to store.
Inside teachers repeat themselves like recorders until the children understand.
Outside snow starts to come like diamonds falling from the sky.
Inside children are reading stories by the fire.
Outside kids wait for the bus as eagerly as squirrels collecting nuts.
Inside students race to their classes like ants chasing a crumb.
Outside it is so cold that if people were water, they'd freeze.
Inside kids ask if they can go play in the snow, until their parents go mad.
Outside people keep putting up Christmas lights until the whole town is lit up.
Reilly Boyle and Kenny Costa, Grade 5
Byram Township Intermediate School

ADT

What if one day a robber broke in?
If a robber broke in he'd really win!
He'd steal al of my games and toys!
From my sister's Elmo to my two Game Boys!
He might even take my Game Cube too!
If he did my mom would shout woohoo!
But if he went upstairs he'd find,
So much jewelry, it looked like a gold mine!
But when he goes for a better look,
ADT will go off, and he'll be booked!
He may try to run and leave the house,
But those police are as quiet as a mouse!
They'd intercept!
They'd put up a roadblock!
Those law enforcers really rock!
He'd wish he'd never tried to steal from me,
For I myself have ADT!

Ezequiel Dávila, Grade 6
Gilmore J Fisher Middle School

Gone

Losing a parent is very sad
You feel like you can't go on
You want to cry, you want to shout
You can't sleep, you flip about
You think, and think, and think some more
You say why wasn't I there I could have cared
She was sick, she was old
I could have loved her
But now she's gone
Not coming back
I will not forget her

Michelle Potocki, Grade 5
Robert L Craig Elementary School

Spring Is Here

S ports are fun to play.
P lay time is fun in spring.
R abbits are fun and cute.
I love it when spring comes!
N ight gets shorter when summer is coming.
G etting closer to summer…

T oads are hopping out of the pond.
I hope summer comes soon.
M ost of the days are filled with fun.
E aster is almost here.

Michael Rongione, Grade 4
St Mary's School

Sometimes

Sometimes there are days where I feel like a nobody.
Sometimes there are days where I feel like a somebody.
Yet in the end I turn out to be like everybody.

Cynthia Vicioso, Grade 6
Robert L Craig Elementary School

Seasons

Winter is when there is a lot of snow
Kids sled down a hill
In their backyard
While their brother is watching from the window sill

Spring brings budding leaves
Baby birds hatch, grass grows
Kids play outside
And flowers begin to show

Summer is always very hot
It always makes you want to jump in the pool
Put on a bathing suit and bring a towel
Because pool water is always cool

Fall is when school starts
Leaves falling down
Kids running to school
And squirrels running on the ground

Kelly Mulvaney, Grade 4
St Mary's School

The Writer

Inspiration is the key
To the door of your fantasies
Writing is certainly what you adore
Thinking of ways to do plenty more

Songs, dreams, and even books
Help you get a better look
At finding the key that is entirely true
And unlocking the door that is right for you

Yes, you're a writer, a poet, an artist
These are the jobs that make you the smartest
Thinking of ideas and writing them down
Trying to fit in each verb, adjective, and noun

Once you've found that special key
The one that leads you straight to victory
You'll know exactly where you belong
And this method of thinking will never be wrong

Anna Lynch, Grade 6
Indian Hill Elementary School

Friends

F riends are so important.
R emember your first friend
I nside your heart you have a best friend.
E ven when you get in fights you're still best friends.
N ever let them down.
D own in the dumps your friends are
S ure to care.

Jessa Hughes, Grade 4
Middle Township Elementary School #2

Stars

Stars are everywhere.
Summer, fall, winter, and spring.
Stars make me want to sing.

Stars only come out when it's dark.
They're as beautiful as lights.
They are such a pretty sight.

Stars are always there.
You can look up at them at anytime.
There are always more than nine.
Amy DiPasquale, Grade 5
St Veronica Elementary School

Birthday Memories

Memories of my birthday…
The scene was in the afternoon
with my family
on my 6th birthday.
I was so into my cake,
I forgot about my presents
Mom said,
"Open your gifts after the cake."
I could not wait!
I took one and opened it.
My jaw dropped
as I saw a remote control car
I already had and
I couldn't hide
my disappointment.
Erik Macarico, Grade 5
Durban Avenue Elementary School

Winter

We play in the snow
The wind will blow
We throw snowballs
Then we all fall
We have hot tea
It tastes good to me
Winter is fun
We wait for the sun
Marisa Pazar, Grade 5
Our Lady of Mount Virgin School

Cars

My car will be a king.
Cars are good and useful things.
Cars are like kings of the road.
Cars are really like people.
If you put oil in, the car eats it.
If you put gasoline in, it drinks it.
Those are cars!!
Ruben DeAlmeida, Grade 6
Kawameeh Middle School

Spring

Spring is near,
Spring is bright.
Spring is clear,
And spring is in sight.

Spring is the light,
Spring is calm.
Spring has much might,
When birds sing their song.

Spring has many flowers,
Thanks to the showers.
Spring is the best,
Of all the rest.
Vishal Aggarwal, Grade 6
Apple Montessori School

Santa

Santa is fat
He hates his hat
He likes to be free
But we don't see
He likes to eat cheese
He also likes peas
I leave him out Swiss
And a Hershey's kiss
I hope I get a toy
That will be a joy
Ryan Rue, Grade 4
Springfield Township School

Spring

Spring is very fun.
Spring is when the flowers come.
Springtime is the best.

Spring is warm and cold.
Spring makes trees come back to life.
Spring is also rainy.
Ashley Willis, Grade 4
St Mary's School

Cassie the Cantaloupe

Zip, zap, zoom,
Zack the zookeeper
Has gone to Zathura.
Bing, bang, boom,
Brian went to the bookstore,
He couldn't find his favorite books,
So he blasted back to Belgium.
Cling, clang, clap
Cassie the cantaloupe,
Has gone to Canada
To collect all of the aluminum cans.
Jonathan Sung, Grade 6
The Red Bank Charter School

Wild

As a black stallion rides
through the sunset.
Men with beards try to
capture
the beautiful beast
but the
peaceful horse will not stop
because it was meant for
the wild!
As it rides into the sunset
not a sound is heard
As a legend is born!
The bearded men
walk home they know
they have been beaten.
As the joyous day
ENDS!
Thomas Capraro, Grade 5
Robert B Jaggard Elementary School

All About Spring

Sunny days, laughing away,
A boy and a girl playing in the park
Oh how warm and sweet,
They are having a treat
Playing soccer but using a disc
While they are having fun,
They get blasted by a watergun
Oh what fun in the hot sun.
Luis Santos, Grade 4
St Joseph School

Nature

I've never smelled the air so fresh
on this beautiful spring day
I'm walking through the woods alone
but I know I'll make my way

I've camped in these woods
ever since I was small
these kids I know, from back home
would rather go to the mall
but that's not for me, I love the outdoors

I'm twelve years old
and I've never been so happy
I'm feeling the maple trees
and now my hands are all sappy

I love it out here
it is so natural, so real
and all I've ever wanted
is to, feel the way I feel
Melissa Rau, Grade 6
Robert L Craig Elementary School

What I'm Like

I'm like a butterfly who spreads my wings out to fly
I'm like a sun who brightens up your smile
Like a lion that has a lot of courage
With my mightiness I will flourish
I'm like the green sea who gives you the breeze
Oh! What a beautiful sea to see
I'm like the jungle, but not just any jungle
The nice and humble jungle
I'm like a puppy with big sorrow eyes
But sometimes my eyes can be lies
I'm like the rain and you hate when I come,
But let it rain, let it rain just some
I'm like a teacher, really nice when you get to know me,
But just don't bug me
But still I'm like a butterfly who spreads my wings out to fly
I'm like a sun who will always brighten up your smile

Oneika McBean, Grade 6
Gilmore J Fisher Middle School

Games

Every day I play a game.
Some might think that is lame.
There are games that take you through a maze.
There are games where music is a big craze.
Monopoly lets you buy a motel.
However, to win, you need a hotel.
Sometimes I play bingo.
This has its own lingo.
Whichever game, that I choose
Sometimes, I am bound to lose.

Daniel Nargiso, Grade 5
Most Holy Redeemer School

Peaceful

Peaceful is lavender like petunias
Peaceful like quaint, quiet libraries
Peaceful is a soft, fluffy pillow under my head
It is like freshly baked chocolate cake
Peaceful is a thick, frosty milkshake
quenching my thirst

Taylor Martin, Grade 6
Franklin Elementary School

The Letter

I wrote a letter to say hi
and put it into a mailbox nearby.
I wrote it at night between sunset and daylight.
I used my notebook to jot it all down.
My handwriting is the best in town.
I wrote it in the hideout by the fireplace.
I can't write more
because this homework
is staring me in the face.

John Keough, Grade 5
Holy Saviour School

Alissa

A thletic girl
L ives in the woods
I n love with little animals
S he has a satisfying appetite for knowledge
S andy beaches are the place for her
A sks lots of questions when she meets someone new

G oes to Brazil very often
O utstanding in spelling
U nder control most of the time
V ery helpful
E verything she has she's thankful for
I ndigo is one of her favorite colors
A very fun person to be around

Alissa Gouveia, Grade 4
Franklin Township Elementary School

The Spa

No noise to be heard.
The echo when someone speaks.
Warm oil getting poured on their bodies.
A professional massaging soft and slow.
The sweetness of candy that is fresh and new.
The juice from a strawberry dropping in your mouth.
The aroma of roses that just got picked out of a garden.
The whiff of chocolate chip cookies fresh out of the oven.
At first I was as nervous as a cat being chased by a dog.
Soon, feeling like a brightly polished, sparkling diamond.

Shaia Sanders, Grade 6
Franklin Elementary School

Buzz…

Bees Bees
Beautiful Beeeees!
Most people HATE them
But only because when they're being smacked
Around by fly swatters, they tend to have to sting.
I am a bee. I make honey for you.
Please don't hate me just because I sting you.
HERE I'll make a deal with you.
If you don't try to get rid of me.
I won't sting you and I'll keep making that honey for you.

Kelly Tomas, Grade 6
Kawameeh Middle School

Someone I Know

Someone I know isn't mean to me.
Someone I know gave a piece of their heart to me.
Someone I know lives near me.
Someone I know hangs out with me.
Someone I know will always think of me.
Someone I know laughs, cries, and sings with me.
Who is that someone I know?
I'm sure you would like to know…

Monica Matozzi, Grade 6
Franklin Elementary School

Ocean

Graceful ocean waves
Fish and creatures all around
Clear blue reflection
Megan Doherty, Grade 4
Our Lady of Mount Virgin School

Baby Bro

To my little bro, I'm a role model,
He still drinks out of a bottle.
He's just learned to walk.
Now he's learning to talk.
He's growing up at full throttle.
Daethyn Blount, Grade 6
Long Branch Middle School

I Know I Do

Don't you hear
those crispy multicolored leaves
fall to the dry cold ground?
What about those high piled leaves
we'd do anything to jump into?
Can't you feel that breezy air
being blown on your soft skin?
Don't you just want to become
that crumpled up leaf
and swiftly descend
from that maple tree
standing so tall and firm?
I know I do.
Chloe Laniado, Grade 5
Lyncrest Elementary School

Winter in the Woods

With the feeling of cold air
I see creatures
Stirring around the woods
An owl is glaring down at me
With its bright green eyes
I turn around to hear
The crunching sound
Coming from beyond
A deer is walking
To find a warm place
To sleep and get through the night
I look up at the midnight sky
No more birds flying high
All the birds cuddled up in their nests
In a deep sleep
Dreaming about the morning sun
I feel snow running down my back
It is cold and stinging
It is starting to snow
A new snow
More is born
Julia Kardos, Grade 4
Pond Road Middle School

"C" with Reprimands

I worked with industrious efforts like a lion searching for its prey.
I still got a "C"
That test meant a lot to me
It was my life ticket to success
I let it slip right under me, it led me to stress

I get home
My mom looks at it
She fainted right in front of me, after she had a fit
I felt like someone punched me right in my stomach, it hurt I admit
My dad sees it, my trouble intensifies like a lit fireplace getting stronger with every log
He reprimands me the worst he has ever done, it almost made me cry

Finally I'm in bed, free at last
Peace and quiet around me, this day went really fast
If that happens again who knows what will happen to me
All I know is that I tried my best
That is all what matters, now let me get to rest
Anthony Iannetta, Grade 6
Fieldstone Middle School

Trees

Trees are things that change with the world.
In the wind its clawing arms beckon us to come sit next to it
When it is raining I hide under it for protection
Its leaves provide an umbrella that directs the water away
When it snows I run to it for warmth
Its swaying limbs hug me and keep me safe
Its apples are its sweet tooth and tastes like honey on my lips
I love to explore its jungle of leaves and peak my head into the clouds
And when the day is over I look out my window and I feel like my tree
Is looking right back at me, waiting for the first peek of dawn.
Luke Heisinger, Grade 6
Allen W Roberts Elementary School

Tick Tock Time

Hello, goodbye, my, doesn't time fly?
I can't wait for time to abate!
Sometimes time just isn't long enough to achieve great things
I'm addicted to life and living with great friends that stick by your side.
Time is like a roller coaster and you need to enjoy the ride.
Life is emotional and you just need to deal
Why is time so short?

Why do we only have so many years to live and love?
I want to fly forever as a dove
Only enough time to make one choice,
No second chances, not one at all
I feel like exploding with all this frustration
So little time with so much to do
I want to be a firefighter or a policeman
We only have a little time to choose
Hello, goodbye, my, doesn't time fly?
Mia Moose, Grade 6
Fieldstone Middle School

Blackness

I feel my hand buried under the warming sand
My feet resting in the water's white foam
I sit there waiting for the wave to ride up and splash me
In my head I can see a clear picture of my surroundings
But when I open my eyes…
Everything is pitch black
From my blindness
Danielle Villa, Grade 4
Ridge Ranch Elementary School

Easter

E aster is always at my house.
A ll the family comes together
S ome of the eggs never get found.
T hen the family sits down to dinner
E veryone gets something to take home
R ight around seven is when the party ends,
everyone goes home, and we just relax
Braelyn Adamson, Grade 6
Robert L Craig Elementary School

Summer

The warm has passed and the hot kicks in!
Now time to keep ourselves cool.
Time to go for a vacation, or go to the beach.
Summer is the hottest season in the world!
After all that cold now the blacktop feels warm.
Julian Armstrong, Grade 4
Evergreen Elementary School

Being a Waterfall

If I were a waterfall, I'd cascade down the mountainside
And whisper to the trees.
My royal personality would welcome the smiling sunshine.

I'd laugh with the sun and cry with the moon.
My lonely, thoughtful depths would bubble at first light.
I'd be referred to in the forest as your highness.

My silver-drenched hair reflects the brilliant azure sky.
At night, I'd look down the plunging indigo-stained hills
I'd call my haven.
Rachel Horowitz, Grade 4
Sicomac Elementary School

A Perspective on War

As the titans clash,
the earth becomes the endless battlefield
As one falls,
the moon becomes the beacon of peace once more
Winds will shout in glee
while clouds will cry in anguish
Victory is taken with grace,
the loss never forgotten
Margot Lin Hultz, Grade 6
Little Egg Harbor Intermediate School

Depression

Depression is blue.
It smells like a musty attic.
It looks like a person trapped in a house,
crying by the windowsill.
It tastes like all of the sour and rotten foods
in the refrigerator —
thrown together as a meal.
It sounds like the silence of space.
Depression feels like being trapped
in an endless void
of misery and woe.
Matthew Puchalski, Grade 6
St. Rose of Lima School

Numbers

What have I got? I've got a lot!

One wonderful self
Two loving parents
Three favorite sports: tennis, swimming, and basketball
Four pairs of sneakers to wear
Five comfy beds to sleep in
Six favorite colors: blue, green, yellow, red, orange, and purple
Seven series of books I'm reading
Eight stylin' outfits to show off
Nine years old
Ten friends: Brittney, Gabby, Cydney, Kayla,
Sheba, Imani, Iman, Taylor, Sienna, and Lexus.
Alexandra Leigh Brown, Grade 4
Franklin Park Elementary School

Birds

Birds, birds, birds
Their soft chirp in the morning
It's very peaceful
Especially when you wake up in the morning
Birds, birds, birds
Emma Bunce, Grade 5
Springfield Township School

Alaska's Beauty

Passersby pause to admire,
Alaska's beauty.
It has mountains and lakes of its own.
It is a captured picture,
That will turn you around from all your problems.
It may even take your breath away,
By how each piece of nature is placed,
There are animals such as bears and moose,
Which will bring you even closer to this state.
Just face that you want to go,
So step in a plane, and go fly over the rocky mountains,
For a magnificent view!
Lindsey Holzinger, Grade 6
Chatham Middle School

Mayhem

...pared,
...orn,
...evoured.
...n fries broiled
and get crispy.
Buttered rice
is eaten in one gulp.
Burgers darken
and get blanketed with cheese.
Chicken legs get smothered
with barbecue sauce.
"What do you know,
I ate it all."

Evan Hearn, Grade 5
Robert B Jaggard Elementary School

Loving Spring

Spring
Birds sing
Robins lay eggs
Butterflies fly
Warm

Domonique Thorne, Grade 4
Franklin Park Elementary School

Life

The meaning of life
Is nothing you would believe
It is beautiful

Kim Novak, Grade 4
Stonybrook Elementary School

At the Park

When I was young at the park
I would go with my friends after school.
We loved to swing and try to get to
the top of the monkey bars.

When I was young at the park
I'd beg my mom for ice cream
from the ice cream truck.
Sometimes the ice cream fell off
the stick onto the ground.

When I was young at the park
I would run around and get
all hot and sweaty.
My face would turn bright red.

When I was young at the park
I had to say goodbye to my friends
until I saw them again.
The next time we were together
at the park.

Katelyn Sissick, Grade 5
Central School

Holidays

My favorite holiday is Christmas,
I love it because of St. Nicholas.

Valentine's Day has a lot of hearts,
I love it because of the sweet tarts.

Thanksgiving has a lot of turkey,
I'd rather eat that instead of beef jerky.

Easter is in the Spring,
With it comes the birds that sing.

Halloween is really sweet,
I love it for all its treats.

Tricia Florio, Grade 4
St Rose of Lima School

I Hear the Jungle Singing

I hear the jungle singing
I hear the monkeys swinging

I hear the cheetah running
I hear the poachers gunning

I hear the toucan cawing
I hear the leopard clawing

I hear the snake biting
I hear the gorillas fighting

I hear the parrot yelling
I hear the tiger compelling

I hear the slow sloth clinging
I hear the jungle singing

Alexander Roll, Grade 4
Sicomac Elementary School

Life's a Beach

Soulful and sinking
Between little toes
Sat on beach thinking
The way blue waves grow

Sweet peaceful feeling
Each blissful child gets
Blue oceans healing
I can't leave, not yet

White seagulls roam
Soaring through skies
Sounding like a poem
As we say goodbyes

Melissa Bandstra, Grade 6
Woodcliff Middle School

Summer

Rain or shine I like to play,
Did you know I play all day?
I play all day and play all night,
Even though there is no light.

With the sun bright,
A gigantic light,
It guides my way,
Through the summer day.

At night I watch the moon,
It comes up too soon,
After that I get fed,
And then I go to bed.

I had a very good day,
And I know I love to play,
But after I get fed,
I have to go to bed,
And end a very good day.

Katlyn Alexander, Grade 4
Stonybrook Elementary School

Summer

Summer is the hottest
Season of them all
Summer is the best season
Better than the fall

I love to play outside
Play outside in the sun
In the summer
I have tons of fun.

Ryan Flohr, Grade 5
St Veronica Elementary School

Vacations

North Carolina
Beach, peaceful
Swimming, running, playing
Sand, water, seagrass
Walking, reading, running
Beautiful, noisy
South Carolina

Alayne Mahler, Grade 6
John Hill School

My Grandparents

My grandparents are not on Earth
They watch me from above
Only Grandpop was here for my birth
Now they both look down with love
I still have other grandparents here
I love them all so very dear!

Marlena Buonasorte, Grade 5
Belhaven Avenue Middle School

The Wave

The wave of wonder
always under brightly lit candles of hope
washed away with misery of greed and overconfidence
but a burning fire will not burn out
if you believe in yourself

Lakshmi Iyengar, Grade 4
Indian Hill Elementary School

Spring

Spring looks like colorful flowers everywhere.
It feels like peace all around the whole wide world.
It tastes like all types of cotton candy.
It smells like fresh pie.
It sounds like birds chirping in the sky.

Sebastian Casas, Grade 5
Perth Amboy Catholic Intermediate School

Summer Lemonade

In the summer, I sit in the shade.
Sipping and slurping lemonade.
The taste, how bold.
The ice, so cold.
My lips shut so tight.
That's how I like my lemonade.
I think it tastes just right.
I also love a glass at night.
Whether it's Country Time or Minute Maid,
I still love lemonade.

John "Jack" Zuber, Grade 4
St Rose of Lima School

Harry Potter: The Wizard Hero!

"The boy who lived," he was,
He did stop "you-know-who,"
And this was all because,
His mother's love was true.
Harry was his name,
One heard all over the place,
And he had lots of fame,
All magic folk knew his face.
A lot of magic he learned,
And when "you-know-who" was near,
He knew it, for his scar burned,
But he did not feel fear.
The Sorcerer's Stone he found,
That Voldemort wanted to take,
And he knew a Parseltongue sound,
Of Slytherin's gigantic snake.
That Sirius Black he saved,
He used the Patronus charm,
And the Triwizard Tasks he had not craved,
Got Voldemort blood from his arm.
Now Harry must win, or shadow will fall.

Varun Kambhampati, Grade 4
Indian Hill Elementary School

Ode to My Brother

I see a reflection in every glance
Through you I seem to get another chance
I see your personality every day
You try to make me smile and laugh in any way
The way you have grown is just unbelievable
In every moment you are different as you are conceivable
You are like no one I have ever met
For this I will never regret
You have taught me to love and learn
As you entered my life a great deal I did earn

Dylan Parker, Grade 6
Chatham Middle School

Colors

Red is the color of a dachshund's silky hair.
Blue is the color of the ocean and all of its waves.
Yellow is the color of the bright rays that shine upon us.
Orange is the color of tangerines.
Black is the color of night sky.
Gray is the color of an old man's hair.

Andrew Kristofick, Grade 5
Sicomac Elementary School

Friends

F un games they play with you every day.
R eturn your things when they are lost.
I ncomplete without them.
E ternal friendship for life.
N ever let you down on anything.
D o always help you out on tough situations.
S tand up for each other always.

Nick Slusher, Grade 5
Belhaven Avenue Middle School

Mrs. N.

Mrs. N. is really nice
        Like sugar and spice
            Every time I see
                her I'll say, "Hey,
                Mrs. N. You're
                    sugar and spice
                        and always nice
                    like a best teacher ever!"

Dahlia Fioretti, Grade 5
Roosevelt Elementary School

Happiness

Happiness is pink.
It smells like chocolate chip cookies in the oven.
It looks like flowers blooming in spring.
It tastes like a chocolate fudge sundae.
It sounds like laughter spreading throughout the room.
Happiness feels like nothing can go wrong,
        and all you can do is smile.

Micala Demchak, Grade 6
St Rose of Lima School

Without a Day of Snow

Without snow
There will be
No December
There is no day off
For the kids to play
It has rained, rained,
And rained but not
Even a drop of
Snow!

Donald Martin, Grade 6
The Red Bank Charter School

If I Were a Teddy Bear

If I were a teddy bear,
I'd give out hugs to anyone in sight.
My fuzzy paws would clap songs of joy
Like a little baby's hands.
I'd pounce from cushion to cushion
And never get tired of it.
Wherever you go, you can find me there
Because I'm never letting go.
When you throw me out,
You'll always be in my memories
And I'll always be in yours.

Meredith Hayden, Grade 4
Sicomac Elementary School

The Beach

At the beach
I see the waves
Crashing against the jetty
Sea gulls in the sky cry
I love the beach.

Paige Venta, Grade 4
Wayside Elementary School

I Wish…

I wish I were a credit card,
so I could spend and spend.

I wish I were a teddy bear,
so I could always be someone's friend.

I wish I were an astronaut,
so I could float in space.

I wish I were a magic carpet,
so I could levitate.

I wish I were a star,
so I could shine all night.

I wish I were an only child,
so with my sisters, I would never fight.

Alexis Wheeler, Grade 5
Byram Township Intermediate School

Water's Whisper

Can you hear it?
Can you hear the ocean speak to you?
It whispers a secret.
Feel the gentle breeze flow through your long silky hair.
Feel the water against your skin.
Dive in as if the world were empty with only you and your thoughts.
As you go under the surface, the voice gets louder,
Hear the voice calling for you.
Listen hard…
The voice drifts away,
Rise to the surface when everything is silent,
That's when you hear the water's whisper.

Emma Lysek, Grade 5
Tamaques Elementary School

If I Were…

If I were green I'd be a lucky four-leaf clover swaying in the sun.
If I were orange I'd be a bouncing basketball about to go through the net.
If I were purple I'd be a juicy grape waiting to be eaten.
If I were pink I'd be the color of the sky at sunset.
If I were red I'd be a blazing fire warming the room.
If I were yellow I'd be the warm sand under someone's feet on the beach.
If I were blue I'd be the tumbling waves in the deep ocean.
If I were brown I'd be delicious milk chocolate melting in someone's mouth.
If I were black I'd be a stormy cloud dropping rain.
If I were ALL these colors I'd be the colors of a peaceful world!

Erin Borst, Grade 5
Sicomac Elementary School

Spring Is Here!

Flowers blooming, spring is here!
Birds are chirping, Easter is near!
Green leaves are starting to grow
As the nice breeze begins to blow

Can't wait to go Easter egg hunting,
And hear those sweet birds singing.
To find things like chocolate and other surprises.
Find quarters, dimes, and other prizes!

Spring is great and full of fun.
As the sun sets another day is done!
When the sun creeps through your window to awake you
Birds chirping, bunnies hopping, squirrels climbing as they do.

And as you walk out the door you feel spring is not near
But it is here!
It's here! It's here! For all to see!
You found it! You found it! The springtime key.

What key do you say? The key that comes on that March 21st day.
What a sight to see! People walking, people jogging, children going out to play.
What great fun! Well it's time for me to play
On this wonderful springtime day.

Victoria Arena, Grade 4
St Mary's School

Sailing on the Sea
As we were sailing,
Sailing on the sea,
The pure, brilliant white sails
Were billowing freely in the breeze.
The water was as beautiful and clear
As the salty breeze blowing by,
As we were sailing,
Sailing on the sea.
I could hear the sound of the waves,
Crashing wildly against the boat,
As we were sailing,
Sailing on the sea.
We would constantly wonder,
Why does the world seem so peaceful here, so silent?
As we were sailing,
Sailing on the sea.
We were away from all of the obstacles, the difficulties to come,
As we were sailing,
Sailing on the sea,
We were free.

Tori Ortega, Grade 5
Salt Brook Elementary School

I'm in Love
I'm in love with a girl who's so so sweet.
I wonder will she be my treat?
Or will she treat me wrong and not do me right.
I wonder will I take her out tonight?
Is she really my love?
Or is she one of the above…
I wonder am I really in love?
Some say no, some say yes.
But, I can care less.
What do you think?
Should I let my love drain down the sink?
I'm in love with a girl —
Am I really?

Najawun Shields, Grade 6
Cleveland Elementary School

With These Hands
With these hands
I learned to turn the first pages of a book
That opened up many mysteries in my life.

With these hands
I learned how to write my first story that was magical
And had happiness on every page.

With these hands
I learned many challenges
And have and will have
Happy times
With These Hands.

Cara Esposito, Grade 5
Salt Brook Elementary School

A Blanket*
Inside
a child sleeps,
while the moon's long,
sensitive fingers start to
weave a blanket. The trees
snuggle down and almost tip
over — while every blade of grass
curls up for a midnight doze. The
bushes simply drape the blanket over
themselves — like a cape. The blanket does
not make friends with the river — so the wind
just freezes the river and then the blanket covers
the ice. The sky had an orange tint from the streetlights'
reflection. Inside the child still sleeps, for all of this was quiet.

Chloe Patrick, Grade 4
Friends School
*Inspired by Alice Wilkins

Ode to Family
Oh family, oh family.
Thank you for taking me everywhere
You cook me dinner and clean up after me.
Oh family, oh family thank you
for playing with me when I am lonely
Oh family, oh parents thank you
for paying for all the things I want
And all of the clothes I have.
Oh family oh family
Thank you for all the things you let me do
Oh family thank you for everything

Derek Singer, Grade 5
Salt Brook Elementary School

Spring
Spring is a wonderful wondrous sight.
The sun is out,
And the flowers will sprout.
There will be a gleaming sun,
As bright as can be.
A glowing ray will come upon our beautiful earth.
So the best of Earth can be seen.

Harsh Patel, Grade 4
John F Kennedy Elementary School

Keep a Smile on Your Face
Keep a smile on your face to brighten someone's day,
Plant a smile on the ground for people to pass day by day
Soon someone will pick that smile up,
and turn their awful frown upside down
So keep a smile on your face to brighten someone's day,
Plant a smile on the ground for people to pass day by day.
No one likes a glaring face, just change it to a smile…
and never, ever let it go

Katherine Nydegger, Grade 5
Salt Brook Elementary School

The Last Day of School
The feeling of freedom
the feeling of glee,
the last day of school,
gets the best of me!
The last day is the funnest of all,
no homework, no teachers,
a time to go to the mall.
It tastes like sweet chocolate,
it smells like fresh air,
it's the last day of school,
and I don't have any other care!
Melissa Samaroo, Grade 6
Franklin Elementary School

Sunset
The colors
Of the sunset
Fill my day
With purples,
Reds,
Oranges,
And yellows.
It's like
A miracle!
The huge star
Shines on me
As the sun
Goes down
For a long
Night's sleep.
Nidhi Desai, Grade 5
Robert B Jaggard Elementary School

Spirits
I believe there are spirits in the air
They will help you get by
They must really care
These wonderful creatures really try

Spirits come in different ways
You never know how
They'll be there for all your days
They're so great, they should take a bow

I trust them for their help
These spirits are so kind
They probably are even there for kelp
These spirits do not mind

I believe there are spirits in the air
They will help you get by
They must really care
These wonderful creatures really try
Lillie Capone, Grade 6
Gilmore J Fisher Middle School

Ocean
A horizon of blue
The musky clams
Loud crashing water
Sprays of salt
A new beginning
Courtney Gill, Grade 6
Little Egg Harbor Intermediate School

Homework, You Say?
I forgot what to do.
I left it at school.
Don't have enough time.
I'm too busy playing.
I need lots of help.
My pencil just broke.
I'm much too tired.
I must go to bed.
Homework you say?
Maybe some other day.
Bo Smith, Grade 4
Mansfield Township Elementary School

Frogs
Amphibian
Slimy, green
Jumps on lilies
Cool, exquisite
Frog
Jessica Morfin, Grade 5
Paul W Carleton Elementary School

Tears
When you are sad and cry,
Catch your teardrops.
It is like holding a tiny ocean
In your hand.
Matthew Regan, Grade 4
Wayside Elementary School

I Want a World
I want a world
where there'll be peace
people would be free

I want a world
where people would care
people would learn to share

I want a world
where blind eyes would be able to see
as far as the wind can blow!

Now do you see?
This is how the world should be
Kiana Hackshaw, Grade 4
Evergreen Elementary School

Yu Gi Oh
My favorite thing is Yu Gi Oh.
I like the game and I like the show.
I always play the game.
The duel is never the same.
My favorite card is Wildedge.
To play it often is my pledge
Monsters on the field
You better have a shield
The strongest card is a must
In it I must have a lot of trust
The God Emperor cards win it all
Who is the next one to make the call?
The duel is on, come take your turn
And how to lose, you will learn!
Nick Maida, Grade 6
Gilmore J Fisher Middle School

Flowers
Flower, colorful
Beautiful, tiny, gorgeous
Makes my day happy
Seda Bektas, Grade 4
Mansfield Township Elementary School

I Can't Take Out Trash
Forget it!
I'm laying down.
I'm tired.
I'm sick.
My favorite show is on.
I've got a headache.
I'm sleeping.
You've got 2 legs.
My legs hurt.
I can't see straight.
My neck is stiff.
What? Where?
You'll take me on a trip?
To where?
Chuck-E-Cheese?
All right, hold on!
Ben Wainwright, Grade 4
Mansfield Township Elementary School

Snow
Snow is white,
It is really, really bright,
Touch it you get a chill,
Then you get ill,
Go out in the snow and play,
The come inside, sit and lay,
By the fireside you stay,
Dreaming the night away!!
Brianne Lechner, Grade 6
Great Meadows Regional Middle School

Snowboarding

Snowboarding
It's just me
My board
The unmarked, untouched terrain
Nothing else goes through my mind but…"GO"
Moving swiftly through the freshly powdered snow

Advancing so rapidly
Seeing everything as a blur
Soaring so high
Until I'm towering over everything
I have an epidemic
Like becoming an addict
Yes, an addiction
Snowboarding

John Tonelli, Grade 6
Fieldstone Middle School

Friends

F riends will always make you feel happy when you're sad.
R eaching out whenever you are in need.
I ncomplete without your friends.
E verlasting friendship will always be with us.
N ever say anything bad about you behind your back.
D oing fun things together on the weekend.
S taying up all night with each other.

Alexis Wagner, Grade 5
Belhaven Avenue Middle School

Ebony*

I remember we played ball together and you gave it back to me
And when I locked you in my room because you bothered me
When you would roll around and get the carpet dirty
And when we took you for walks and you wouldn't move
Until the day you went to the doctors and got put to sleep
You were our favorite pet in the world
Now you're gone and not coming back
I love you.

Krista Bailey Logue, Grade 6
Little Egg Harbor Intermediate School
*Dedicated to my dog Ebony

Rainbow Girl

R ed is for the love I give
O range is for the energy I use to live
Y ellow is for the surprise in my eyes
G reen is the earth's color that keeps me alive
B lue is the color of the infinite sky
   Where my dreams drift way up high
I ndigo is the color of the beautiful waters,
   The size of my heart for you and the others
V iolet's my favorite because it keeps me me
   Which is who I'll always be.

Sian Scott, Grade 5
Tamaques Elementary School

My Dream

I often dream of being a policeman
And wishing to be the best policeman in the world
I think of being really tall and helping people
And when I dream I chase people that are bad
I feel happy…
I often dream of being a policeman

Pedro Morales, Grade 4
Evergreen Elementary School

My View of Winter

The snow falls gracefully from the sky to the ground,
These crystals are magnified to anything that can be found.

I stare in awe at the midnight sky,
Amazed that something so pure came from the world so high.

I presume to gaze upon this view,
The snowflakes sparkle like the morning dew.

Sleds fly up and down a bleach-white hill,
The air is frigid with a cold winter chill.

Most folks prefer to stay inside and sip hot tea,
While small children play in the snow with glee.

People are bundled up like eskimos beneath their coats,
They shiver and shriek as snow gently floats.

This scenery is sure to be here next winter time,
So be sure to remember this wonderland rhyme.

Jacqueline Kuczinski, Grade 6
Indian Hill Elementary School

Life

Life
Is a journey
That holds chains of opportunities
Just grab on
And hold on
Enjoy the ride
For you never know where it may take you
Life is a journey
That hurls you through the air
Leaving you dangling in the wind
And you grab on to the stars
For dear life
But you keep holding on
Because you know it's not the end
Life is a journey
A magical call from the sun and moon
It triggers new beginnings
Life is a journey
Of its very own
That shall never cease

Bhargavi Ganesh, Grade 6
Thomas R Grover Middle School

I Can't Take Out the Recyclables
No way!
I'm not doing it.
It's too heavy
The smell is awful.
Why can't you do it?
You're the parent of the house.
Jeez!
I'm too tired.
I woke up at 2:00 am.
Mark kicked me in the shin.
What's that?
I don't have to do it.
The trash man is gone?
I'm not doing it next week either!
Kevin McGillen, Grade 4
Mansfield Township Elementary School

Sycamore Tree
S low hard thought
Y early growing
C autiously developing gnarled limbs
A top lies a treasure of verdant life
M aking the world around minuscule
O bserving, watching
R emembering perspectives of lives
E ntrust your dreams into its deep roots
Dominic Noviello, Grade 6
Long Branch Middle School

Everything You Could Imagine
Fall is here,
the acorns are falling.
Fall is here,
the leaves are wet and moldy.
Fall is here,
the raking is becoming a pain.
Fall is here,
the treats are delightful
and frightful
costumes, witches, goblins,
and everything you could imagine.
Gino Lipuma, Grade 5
Durban Avenue Elementary School

Sand
Smooth. Soft.
Slithering between my toes.
It lies upon my feet like a sheet.
Soft, smooth and oh so gentle.
I love the sand.
I love the sand.
How it greets me every day,
I look forward to the next and the next
Waiting for it to come out and play.
Jillian Ostek, Grade 6
Christa McAuliffe Middle School

My Inspiration
My sister is my inspiration
She helps me up when I stumble in life
And inspires me to pursue and follow my dreams wherever they may take me
She's been a big part of my life
Since the day I was born
And has already reserved a special spot in my heart
She's intelligent and humorous
And caring to her family and friends
My sister is very adventurous at home
And especially on vacations
When I'm with her my creativity sparks
And my imagination dreams
Her bubbly and spunky personality helps her to make new friends
And keep her old ones
She tells me to have confidence
And to step in rhythm with my own heart
I love her for many things, but most of all for who she is
She's very athletic, and plays lots of sports
But she's also determined and hard working
I really love her a lot
She's my hero, inspiration, and idol, who I will always love, need, and look up to!
Christina Gerew, Grade 5
North Dover Elementary School

Fear
Fear is black.
It smells like someone smoking like a chimney in your face.
It looks like a poisonous snake biting a human.
It tastes like a stale potato chip dipped in rotten sour cream.
It sounds like a person screaming for help.
Fear feels like you do not have any life left and you are falling forever.
Drew Ballester, Grade 6
St Rose of Lima School

Jolly Old Christmas
What do I love about Christmas?
I love presents, family, and tree lighting
Everything is peaceful and there is no fighting
My mom is very impartial with the gifts she gets for my brother and me

The snow is as white as a shiny white pearl
On Christmas Eve I am the only girl
The best part about Christmas is family
If you are not good then you get coal
So, you better have a good soul

My little cousin has an aspiration to see Santa
It is nice to see family this time of year
When we get a present we all cheer
We all drink hot chocolate
Then we all sing a Christmas song
On Christmas we always play ping pong
That is what I love about Christmas
Nicole Hoogland, Grade 6
Fieldstone Middle School

Shopping

Shopping can be so much fun
You never want to say you're done.
Going to buy clothes, shoes, and toys
Is never fun when you bring along boys
You tell your mom you're gonna buy a Coke
The next thing you knew you're going broke
See a cute outfit then go to try it on
The next thing you know the line's a mile long
Shopping can be so much fun
You never want to say you're done

Nicole Fowler, Grade 6
Gilmore J Fisher Middle School

Spring Flowers

Beautiful flowers in spring,
There are tulips, petunias, and lilies,
Beautiful colors such as red, yellow, and purple.
Smell as pleasant as fresh-baked cookies out of the oven.
Fabulous, and welcoming,
Grown in the most beautiful places.
Like peaceful gardens, and calming meadows,
Spring flowers are like a vacation to your eyes.

Amanda Nardone, Grade 4
Lincoln Park Elementary School

Confusion

Confusion is gray.
It smells like a sour and sweet smell mixed.
It looks like a twisting of all different colors.
It tastes like fruit and meat mixed.
Confusion sounds like one drowsy note on the piano nonstop.
It feels like your head spinning around in a giant whirlpool.

Jordan Yuro, Grade 6
St Rose of Lima School

I Am?

I am a great cheerleader and cute.
I wonder if we will make it to Disney again?
I hear cheers underwater.
I see a mermaid wearing our uniforms.
I want to win nationals.
I am a great cheerleader and cute.
I pretend I am a flyer.
I feel a cheer angel.
I touch a cloud that is a cheerleader.
I worry about people falling from stunts.
I cry when I get hurt.
I am a great cheerleader and cute.
I understand why we came in 4th in nationals.
I say I am a national champ.
I dream of becoming an all-star cheerleader.
I try to be the loudest on my team.
I hope that we will win regional and go to nationals.
I am a great cheerleader and cute.

Jessica Hutchinson, Grade 5
Laura Donovan Elementary School

Springtime

S cented smell in the air.
P eaceful sounds of birds.
R ain showers feel fresh and new.
I see flowers blooming too.
N ew life has come for birds and flowers.
G lowing sun (sometimes) shines.
T icking clocks waiting for the showers to stop.
I ce has melted from the winter.
M other nature colors this pastel season.
E veryone loves spring.

Leor Wasser, Grade 4
Solomon Schechter Day School

Weeping Willow

The weeping willow's branches droop,
Drooping, drooping, falling down to the ground,
Its lonely cry flows through the sky,
Light green leaves hanging down,
Hanging down to the ground,
Decorations for the earth.

What the weeping willow wants,
No one knows,
It weeps to the ground,
Not to the sky,
God made him that way.

You plant a seed,
And watch it grow,
The weeping willow forms,
It grows to enormous size,
You use it for shade.

For years it will weep,
Until it dies,
The sadness in the bark,
The sadness in the heart,
The sadness in the weeping willow tree.

Rosemary Lombardi, Grade 4
Lincoln Park Elementary School

Ashley

Athletic, exciting, joyful
Sister of Zachary
Who loves softball, cheerleading, and shopping
Who feels excited about poetry
Who needs support, love, and laughter
Who gives love, effort, and support
Who fears bugs, the dark, and strangers
Who'd like to see Grams
Who dreams of being a teacher
A student of Mrs. Rudinsky
Ash

Ashley Sheppard, Grade 4
Mansfield Township Elementary School

Lion
Hair around its neck
The lion looks for its prey
King of the Jungle
Helena Adams, Grade 6
St Augustine Regional School

Tip, Tap
Tip tap, tip tap
Goes a student's pencil.
Spit spat, spit spat
Goes an artist's stencil.
Kristina Lapira, Grade 4
Mansfield Township Elementary School

Fire
F laming hands
I ntolerably burning
R eaping fire
E xtremely hot
Tyler Marlette, Grade 5
Elizabeth F Moore Elementary School

Cards
Cards are so beautiful,
you must have some cards.
Because if you don't have any,
it will be like you lived on Mars.

Cards are so great,
they make you have fun.
Might have a hand of 5,
and end up with a hand of 1.

Cards are so wonderful,
they're so cool.
Like I said if you don't have any
you're a fool.
Devon Green, Grade 6
Gilmore J Fisher Middle School

Sun and Shadows
Sun low in the west
Moon floating up in the east
Flowers in shadows
Abbas Elfaki, Grade 6
Bartle Elementary School

Lexy
Pets, pets I love them so.
At five, I wanted one you know.
Now, Lexy is the dog I love so much.
She likes to play and walk and such.
I play with her all the time.
I'm so glad she's really mine.
Kyle Fischer, Grade 4
St Rose of Lima School

Mom
There once was a mom named Jean
Who never ever was mean.
She always made rice,
She was very nice,
And would make a very good queen.
Jamie Isaacs, Grade 4
Sicomac Elementary School

Fusion
Light
Bright, sunny
Shining, warming, burning
Light and dark fuse
Fading, dimming, blackening
Dull, shadowy
Dark
Adam Jutte, Grade 5
Community School of Bergen County

Friends
F riends stick together forever
R eal friends don't leave each other
I is for team
E veryone is friends
N ever give up on friends
D o things to help your friends
S tay together no matter what
Darrin Corbin, Grade 6
Bartle Elementary School

Swimming
I'm on the block,
let's start the race,
Soon I will win
and take first place!
Madalyn Anagnou, Grade 4
Middle Township Elementary School #2

The Land of Make Believe
Take my hand,
As we go to a faraway land
Your heart will leap for joy
Go see the magic show
The circus and more
Come along with me to the food festival
Or even the petting zoo
Whatever you choose you will desire
Go see the juggler
Or the man that eats fire
When it's time to go
You will always know
To come to a place with
Magical wonders
Kallan Murray, Grade 6
Chatham Middle School

James
J ust a loony
A crazy kid
M ad when he loses
E mpty mind
S occer player
Stewart Girdwood, Grade 5
Roosevelt Elementary School

The Trees in the Spring
When the wind blows by
You feel this very cold chill
But you like it so.
Shayna Argenziano, Grade 4
Stonybrook Elementary School

NASCAR
Two cars racing to the finish line.
There comes number nine.
The driver's name is Dave.
He is so brave.
Abanobe Salib, Grade 6
John Hill School

Lightning
L ight of yellow
I ncredible scene
G one crazy
H owever, it makes a bad storm
T oo terrible
N o one likes it
I t is real bad
N ot very cool
G one mad
Sal Gaetano, Grade 4
Main Road Elementary School

The Unicorn
Unicorns run away
As people come, as people stay
But underneath an apple tree
A Unicorn sang to me
So now I really do believe
You and I can help today
Just close your eyes and say "O.K."
Then maybe you and I can see
The moonlit night and apple tree
Were a Unicorn sang to me
Sydney Nolan, Grade 4
Alpine School

winds divine
out in the cold day
the winds divine are flying
like ferocious hawks
Mark Chung, Grade 5
Cherry Hill Elementary School

I Wish

I wish I were a monkey,
So I could swing in the trees.

I wish I were a bird,
So I could fly in the breeze.

I wish I were a chicken,
So I could eat all day.

I wish I were a millionaire,
So I could pay my way.

I wish I were a butterfly,
So I could fly around.

I wish I were a hummingbird,
So I could almost never touch the ground.

Kaitlyn Clark, Grade 5
Byram Township Intermediate School

A Moment in Time

Standing on the beach looking at the sun,
And I see the colors as they start to run.
Much better than light much better than dark,
As I start to lay down I hear a harp.
Beautiful music that's what I hear,
Closing my eyes to what is near.
The sun is gone I must get home,
So now I will not be alone.

Rebecca Marfil, Grade 6
The Great Commission Christian Academy

Snow Days

No school, hot cocoa, snow all around
Friends and sleigh riding is where you're bound
As soon as you hear that lovely horn go off
You won't have to fake that you have a cough
Build a snowman at such a fast pace
But hope that a snowball doesn't hit you in the face
So wear your pajamas inside out
'Cause snow days are what winter's all about

Mary Berko, Grade 5
Roosevelt Elementary School

Mom

Mom
You are very loving, very protective, nice, and funny.
Cares deeply about our family and friends.
Who feels happy when I get a good grade.
Who needs love and affection.
Who gives love and support
Who fears for me.
Who would like to see her mom more often.

Sharon Lody Abed, Grade 4
Franklin Park Elementary School

I Wish, I Wonder

I wish I could fly.
I wish I could be the sky.
I wish I was tall.
Would I hit my head on a tree branch?
I wish I could be the smartest in the world.
Could I get too smart?
I wish I could be famous
I wonder how it would be.
I wish I could be a teacher.
Can I reach out to the kids
and teach them that they must do their homework?
    I wish I wonder.

Shevon McPherson, Grade 4
Evergreen Elementary School

Evil Bed

I'm not going to bed, there are spikes in it.
Don't show me to my room
I'll be there in a minute.
What? 30 minutes went by?
But it's only eight forrr…daylight savings??
But I…(yawn)
No!
That wasn't a yawn it was a big breath
so I won't go to bed.
I'm not even slleeeeeeeee…
What?!
I will never go to…(yawn)

Ryan Galik, Grade 4
Mansfield Township Elementary School

Who Am I?

I am artistic, smart, and outgoing.
I wonder what I will be in the future.
I hear the sound of birds in the trees.
I see the beauty of nature all around me.
I want to enjoy myself every minute.
I am artistic, smart, and outgoing.

I pretend I'm a wonderful artist.
I feel great when I get good grades.
I touch my keyboard while doing my homework.
I worry about my little brother.
I cry when I am called a nasty name.
I am artistic, smart, and outgoing.

I understand that life's not perfect.
I say "Treat others the way you want to be treated."
I dream of being an artist.
I try to get great grades in class.
I hope to travel the world.
I am artistic, smart, and outgoing.

I am Steven Gonzalez

Steven Gonzalez, Grade 5
Sicomac Elementary School

Some Winter Fun

The sun showers the earth in sunlight, and awakens all the tiny people that live upon it.
The snow covered house sits upon a banquet of fluffy snow.
The flying snow falls from the lightly lit sky.
The furry, little animals awaken from their long nights rest.
A small, stray dog runs after a skimpy, little mouse running as fast as he can.
The bright sun is rising faster and faster!
The moon sits in the lit sky, waiting for the sun to set once more.

Brett Barnes, Grade 5
Sandman Consolidated Elementary School

The Song

It pulses with the sunset's glare, the song of hope with no despair.
It dances with the crashing waves, I know it's me it chooses to save.
It ripples with the crispy air, it traps me in a dreamy stare.
It travels around me, then meets my gaze, then leaves me in a dreamy haze.
It blows with the sand beneath my feet, it enters my mind, it touches my soul, and it has yet just one goal.
It jumps with the dolphins, they sing its song. They know the melody, they've been singing it so long.
It tells me to forget about doubts or worries, because what is the point of life if you live it in a hurry.
Ancient beauty breathes this song, it's pure, it's lived so long.
It holds wisdom of age, it never trembles, it never sways.
The song enters me one last time, sings its last enchanting rhyme.
I know I can hear it, I know why it was meant for me to see, the answer is…it lives in me.

Sarah Wolfe, Grade 6
William Davies Middle School

Family of Dancing Snowmen

The family of dancing snowmen are dancing wildly.
The tall leafless tree branches surround them.
Snow is not falling but is twinkling in bundles on the ground.
Puffs of smoke come from the brick red chimney.
One lonesome snowman is cheering the family on while they dance.
I wonder, will the family of dancing snowmen do an excellent dance and become famous?

Sabrina Temple, Grade 5
Sandman Consolidated Elementary School

The Red Sled

The sparkling church bells fill the town with sound.
The waking people get ready for a whole new day.
The children groan like lions as they leap out to the red sled and ride down the hill to the church.
The children's footprints lay in the snow as the kids sit quietly in the church.
The snow runs down swiftly as ever.
The children wait still as a tree, for what seems like forever to leap into the snow.
And the red sled sits in the snow and waits for the children to jump into its seats and ride off up the hill to the house for some cocoa and cookies.

Austin Mitchell, Grade 5
Sandman Consolidated Elementary School

Peacefulness

Peacefulness is lavender
It smells like sugary blue cotton candy
It looks like a colorful sunset over a calm blue ocean
It tastes like cold vanilla ice cream running down my throat
It sounds like the waves crashing on the shore and the seagulls overhead
Peacefulness feels like the grainy sand in between my toes and the cool water of the ocean

Kelly Wall, Grade 6
St Rose of Lima School

I Am From…
I am from rice and beans
Mixed with non-fried pork

I am from calm and peaceful Highland Park

I am from my hardworking ancestors
Who were also slaves

I am from my grandma's special fried chicken

But mostly I am from the great game of football
That the male side of my family
Plays from generation to generation

Melshawn Taylor, Grade 5
Bartle Elementary School

Spring
Spring is fun,
Spring is cool,
Spring's where you spend time in your pool,
Spring is awesome,
Spring is great,
Spring takes away your anger and hate,
Spring is coming,
Spring is near,
So let's all give one big cheer!

Mike Olano, Grade 4
John F Kennedy Elementary School

Wishing to See My Friend in Santo Domingo
I go to the port,
I see the ship,
Dreaming of the bluefish,
Wishing I could get on the ship.

I see the ship,
Wanting to visit the Dominican Republic,
Wishing I could get on the ship,
Smelling the cooking of the ship's kitchen.

Wanting to visit the Dominican Republic,
Blackbirds making noise,
Smelling the cooking of the ship's kitchen,
Wishing to see my friend in Santo Domingo.

Blackbirds making noise,
Thinking of my friend makes me happy,
Wishing to see my friend in Santo Domingo,
Blue sky moves.

Thinking of my friend makes me happy,
Dreaming of the bluefish,
Blue sky moves,
I go to the port.

Arely Atenco, Grade 5
Lanning Square Elementary School

The Most Influential Woman in My Life
Christine
Generous, sweet
Crafting, coaching, reading
Loves my sister and me a lot
Mommy

Cassie Mellea, Grade 5
Ridgeway Elementary School

Friendship
Friendship is a rope.
Three strands, three friends
Pulled in different directions
Ever lasting
Twisting with different stories
Laughing and crying till one dies

Kaitlin Carr, Grade 6
Township of Ocean Intermediate School

Hatred
Hatred is black.
It smells like thin, musty air.
It looks like grinding teeth.
It tastes like dirt and smoke.
It sounds like screams in your head.
Hatred feels like fire and smoke in your soul.

Tyler Shiovitz, Grade 6
St Rose of Lima School

The Sun
God's flashlight ignites the early morning.
And shines his light toward all nine planets.
The world becomes just like a dark forest,
As he slightly falls behind the sky.

So many light years away
He still shines on us with brightness.
He is the center of our galaxy,
High up in the atmosphere.

When the sun gets frightened
He hides behind the clouds.
When he gets angry,
A storm will come your way!

He brightly incandescence the sky
With his 4.5 million degrees.
This giant flaming fireball
Can blind you with one look.

But this great nuclear reaction
Will not last forever
One day his flames will die
And the planets will cease to exist.

Tyler Hoffman, Grade 6
Woodglen Middle School

Fisher Spirit

Fisher spirit fly high
Fisher spirit don't die

Having spirit isn't easy as pie
So please just try

Having spirit is great
Having spirit is something to appreciate

So Fisher spirit fly so high
And please Fisher spirit don't die
Ashlee Ingram, Grade 6
Gilmore J Fisher Middle School

Sandy

In the shadows it grows
It is feared
It is waiting for a victim
Ah ha! *A chew toy*!
Squeak!
"Good Sandy!"
It's my dog
James Chadwell, Grade 4
Toll Gate Grammar School

Cheese

Cheese
moldy cheese
eating moldy cheese
worst cheese I ever tasted
limburger.
Robert O'Gara, Grade 6
Fieldstone Middle School

A Very Windy Day

The wind is blowing
The rain is showering
The trees are dancing with the wind.
The wind is pushing
The rain is pouring
The leafless trees are bending
For it is a beastly windy day.
Jamie Woods, Grade 5
Cherry Hill Elementary School

Me

My name is Tiara the Dancer.
I like to prance and dance.
I learn a lot of steps,
but I'm not that good at it.
I *love* the audience watching me.
I feel like I'm famous!
It's so fun and I love it!
Tiara Maysonet, Grade 6
Roosevelt Elementary School

Beware Beware

The lights are off
The door is closed

Beware Beware

The clock strikes twelve
The cat yells

Beware Beware

The moon is full
The wolves are out

Beware Beware
Samantha Krupa, Grade 6
Kawameeh Middle School

Summer

Every day we wake
Every night we sleep
Every day we play
Every day no homework
Every day is hot
No matter the day…
I love summer
Cody Kohut, Grade 6
Gilmore J Fisher Middle School

Taking Out the Garbage Stinks

I hate it.
It makes me crumble.
It hurts my back.
It stinks.
I get a headache.
It makes me throw up.
I touch icky things.
I can't stand the weather,
It is so cold outside!
William Steven Miccio, Grade 4
Mansfield Township Elementary School

Halloween

Halloween is scary green,
Pumpkins glowing very bright at night,
You get to eat if you trick-or-treat,

Black cats on scary doormats,
The moon glowing bright,
Black bats at night,
Scarecrows staring at you,

Bats and owls looking straight at you,
If you see scary green,
Then you know it's Halloween!
Ann Ciancia, Grade 4
Friends School

A Tall Man

I saw a man who was really tall,
He looked like he was going to fall.
Soon he ran across the hall,
Trying to enter the mall.
He stole a doll and broke a wall,
The cops caught him using a ball.
Warren Crasta, Grade 5
St Marys School

Trash Talk

The trash is really stinky,
the bin, it's way too small.
I won't take out the garbage,
so don't even try to call.
I'm busy eating sushi,
I'm bathing in the sun,
I'm watching my favorite TV show,
And *that's* a lot more fun.
It takes too long to get there,
I'll measure if I can.
I'm putting on my sneakers.
No! Here I go again.
This poem's really horrible,
I'll put it in the trash.
Fine, I'll take out the garbage
BUT I'LL EXPECT SOME CASH!!!
Tyler Sapp, Grade 4
Mansfield Township Elementary School

Star

S o know there's a star
T onight in the light
A s the light shines
R oads are clear
so the star can show its light.
Amanda Ohrn, Grade 5
Ocean Avenue Elementary School

Family Fun

My dad and I like to play ball,
Usually in the fall.

Sometimes I pitch to him,
Then we take a swim.

After that we have lunch,
With a really loud crunch.

My sister joins the fun,
For dinner we have burgers on a bun.

My mom makes the food,
In a really good mood.
Daniel Poracky, Grade 4
St Mary's School

Singing
Singing was just what I adored.
I stood there with my fingers shaking and trembling.
"Ohhhhhhhhhh…"
And the notes flew away.
They started out lame, but ended up mighty.
I sang in the light morning and in the dark night.
It was All City Chorus that was frightening.
The room was as large as twenty elephants.
But not big enough to overcome my strong confidence.
"Ahhhhhhhhhhhhhhhhhhh…"
I still sang my heart out.
And it sure was worth it.
I made it to All City Chorus and now I'm jumping with glee.
My dream had come true.
Maybe yours will too.
Just a couple more steps to becoming a Hilary Duff.
I admire singing!
Hannah Painter, Grade 5
Tamaques Elementary School

Judo
Judo
Challenging, fast
Throwing, holding, flipping
A painful, exciting competition
Kicking, turning, pushing
Courageous, calm
Master
Cristina Felicetta, Grade 4
Perth Amboy Catholic Intermediate School

Friends in Their Selfless Black Hole
Friends are people that stick by your side
True friends do not talk behind your back
Real friends are there to make you happy
I think I am living in an artificial world
Everywhere I turn, friends are making fun
of their own friends
I wish it were only pretend
Maria Rivadeneira, Grade 6
Thomas Jefferson Middle School

Fireworks
Boom! A flame of red!
Bam! A flash of green filled the sky.
Bursts of colors appeared before my eyes.
My heart was beating as if there were no tomorrow.
A burst of golden flowers shot out.
A burst of blue came outwards.
What a sight before my eyes!
Fireworks,
Fireworks,
What a time it was!
Catherine Poggioli, Grade 4
Connecticut Farms Elementary School

Saint Nick
Now the darkness arises.
The cold wind drifts in with no surprises.

The children are fast asleep.
Saint Nick is here, roaming the sky deep.

Up and down the red brick chimneys
and across the vast sky he flees.

Children rise awake
hoping Santa ate their cookies and cake.

Leaving presents under the tree on the cold winter night,
he sets off the roof to continue his flight.
Esther Hwang, Grade 6
Fieldstone Middle School

Wrestling
Wrestling is fun because I am great at it.
When I was little I wrestled for just a year.
Wrestling, wrestling, wrestling is good exercise.
Wrestling is very wonderful and awesome.
I pin everyone so I could win.
I am a good wrestler.
Courtney E. Allocco, Grade 4
John F Kennedy Elementary School

The Living Room Lamp
A lonely object
bearing a sleek black color,
it contains five arms coming out of the top of its body
like a stem with five petals.
It sits in the corner of the room waiting forever patiently,
for someone to go over and turn the knob,
so it can happily share its brilliant light,
giving the person the gift of light,
letting the person see his surroundings.
It sits by itself most of the day
and is very worn out at night.
It never complains about being turned on too roughly
or getting hit too hard.
But it understands that it was made for this,
and with that knowledge,
it puts on the best face
even for the worst happenings.
Derek Liu, Grade 5
Indian Hill Elementary School

My Pogo Stick
My pogo stick is my friend till the very end.
It's yellow and black and it will never talk back.
I feel high, free, tall and lean.
I touch the sky with my hand that's free.
That's my friend, Po-Go and me.
Thomas Fischer, Grade 4
St Peter Elementary School

Winter

Winter feeling of snow
Harsh weather
Happy but then ungrateful awhile later

Winter tastes of snow
Boiling, creamy hot cocoa
Steaming, hot soup

Winter sights of snow
Colored leaves
Icicles
White pellets falling to the ground

Winter sounds of snow
Crunch-crunch
Harsh winds
Shivers of yourself

Winter

Daniel Siegel, Grade 5
Bartle Elementary School

Snow

S nowflakes running down my face.
N othing is more
O utstanding to play in.
W onderful!

Danielle McCann, Grade 4
Middle Township Elementary School #2

Grandpa Bill

Hair as white as sea foam
Skin as wrinkly as a prune
Laying in his bed
In his lonely room

Grandpa Bill
Watching baseball
His own sport
The dream he lived
Now alive in Cooperstown, NY

Grandpa Bill
Quiet as a mouse
Never could be arouse
Waiting for a fate
That wouldn't come late

Grandpa Bill
Could have passed in World War II
He decided to live on
Now he is a legend

Grandpa Bill
Emily Acerra, Grade 6
Monmouth Beach Elementary School

Dreams

Dreams make you believe what seems to be true to you.
You may be dreaming of a bike or dog that may be new.

You may be dreaming of boys or girls,
or a dog that twirls.

You could be dreaming of what you think God looks like,
or maybe even you scored the winning goal in a soccer game and you're psyched.

Dreaming is what makes you believe,
so you can achieve.

Dreaming is what tells you who you are,
and you know what, you're a star.

Madison Dunn, Grade 4
St Rose of Lima School

Susan Springer

Susan
Fast, energetic, clever, annoying
Sister of Brook
Love of ice cream, puppies, and martial arts
Who feels happy when I'm with my family,
Sad when a family member dies,
And thrilled when a new person comes into my family
Who needs a loving family, friends, and pets
Who gives friendship, love, and kindness
Who fears cats, spiders, and sicknesses
Who would like to buy a horse, meet my sister and birth parents,
And live in Florida
Resident of Wyckoff on Briarwood Drive
Springer

Susan Springer, Grade 4
Sicomac Elementary School

If I Were in Charge of the World

I'd cancel
Stupid fights that make no sense at all.
Bullies who take your lunch money and who think they rule the world.
School lunches where meatballs bounce and taste even worse.
Nasty comments that hurt inside you will remember most of all.
War that doesn't do much good only hurts the heart.

If I were in charge of the world,
I'd change
Junk food to fruit that tastes so good,
Hate into love for millions of years or maybe forever,
Enemies into friends for all to have good laughs that will never end.

If I were in charge of the world
I'd keep
Families that will stay together to be there for each other,
People to believe in us and to forgive us no matter what we do.
If I were in charge of the world.

Suzie Gargiulo, Grade 5
Salt Brook Elementary School

Mystery of Past

What's past is past some might say,
Perhaps the mysteries will be solved one day.
There have been many a mystery,
That occurred throughout history.
But if there were no mysteries in past,
Interest in it would be lost very fast.
Everything would have an explanation,
Our town, our country, and even our nation.
Life would not be very fun,
Because every question would be answered and done.
Everyone would know all,
And our civilization would fall.

Ryan Randall, Grade 6
Our Lady of Mount Virgin School

Best Friends

B est friends 'til the end
E asy to tell your friends stuff
S o nice to see your friends
T elling secrets with your friends is fun.

F riends are fun to be around
R ight away you're happy to see your friends.
I t's nice to see your friends happy.
E asy to help your friends out
N ice to chill with your friends
D own in the dumps they have my back!

Alyssa Sullivan, Grade 4
Middle Township Elementary School #2

Day at the Beach

The hot fierce particles of sand stab my feet
as I tiptoe to the shore.

The sun's beams deny my sight
as I try to glare anxiously into the sky.

Seagulls' chirps sing gentle graceful sounds
to my ear.

The water, ever so clear, looks into my eyes
and greets me with its crash on the shore.

The beauty and glory of this sight that nature created
is just as magnificent as any artist's work.

Katelyn Ann Glebocki, Grade 6
Little Egg Harbor Intermediate School

Shamrock Street

My street is a beautiful street.
It has great neighbors.
But it has trees, bushes, and a lot more stuff.
There are some beautiful backyards.
I like my street because it has everything.

Allison Conley, Grade 4
Holy Saviour School

Nature Is Fun!!!

I looked at the sky.
I saw the birds fly.

I laid on the grass and looked at the trees.
I stood up onto my knees.

The wind made a noise like a shush.
Suddenly I fell into a bush.

Then I stood up on my feet.
Playing outside can't be beat!

Colleen Burke, Grade 4
St Mary's School

A Paradise Day

When the sun shines on that last summer day
I can smell the ocean water
And hear sounds of birds in flight
Sitting in a chair above the warm soft sand
Dreaming of memories, already long passed
Forgetting my troubles
'Cause they're too hard to ponder
With shades over my eyes
And a nice cool breeze
I drift off in thought
And think to myself
I can't wait till that
Paradise Day

Carolyn S. Daly, Grade 6
Mother Seton Inter Parochial School

The Farm

The farm is fun,
It is where the animals run.
In the fields, vegetables grow,
While the farmers sow and mow.
Eggs, butter, milk, and chicken,
Come from the farm, and we find them in a kitchen.
This is where my dreams come true,
I hope your dreams come true, too.
Why do I love the farm,
Because it has a lot of charm.

Cassidy Coulombe, Grade 4
St Rose of Lima School

Mountains

Mountains are glorious,
High soaring — victorious,
Climb one and you shall see,
Many of God's great handiworks,
But the greatest of all His handiworks are the mountains,
Wherein the Lord doth dwell,
Who made all things.

Stephen Morrison, Grade 6
Trinity Christian School

Nature Musical
Birds are singing
Some trees are playing discos
Deer and bears dancing
Ryan Nees, Grade 4
Stonybrook Elementary School

Trees
Swaying in the wind
Losing green color in fall
Showing new colors
Treetops touching the blue sky
Home to many animals
Bryce Chase, Grade 6
Springfield Township School

Today
Wake up jolly,
Read out loud.
Paint a picture,
Feel so proud.
Go to school,
Write a song.
Have some lunch,
Play along.
Go home now,
Whisper a tune.
Say goodnight to the moon.
Amber Czesnolowicz, Grade 4
Lincroft Elementary School

Buddy, My Best Friend
B est friend
U nforgettable
D og of mine
D oesn't ever fight with me
Y ou are fun

B est dog ever
O nly dog for me
Y ou can't resist him
Andrew Winkleman, Grade 5
Our Lady of Mount Virgin School

Summer Days
Remember that time
When you were playing
Outside with your friend
You felt the hot blazing sun
You started to swelter
You saw your friend
Running towards you
And you played together
In the heat of the day
That was summer.
Giana DiRese, Grade 4
Edward H Bryan Elementary School

On My Birthday…
…I got a big present.
…I wondered what it was.
…we finally got to open the gifts.
…I was so excited.
…I finally opened the big one.
…there was a stereo and candy.
…It was a good birthday for me.
Randy Piacentini, Grade 4
Long Memorial Elementary School

Poem
Poem is a sweet word,
Music to my ears
It takes thought to write a poem
Many, many, thoughts
You must write with feeling,
With a turn, with tone
From the heart
Not the head
Concentrate, concentrate.
Madeleine Gene, Grade 5
Liberty Corner Elementary School

Thank God for Spring!
Collecting spring flowers
Takes up all the hours.
When you're having fun
Playing in the sun.

In spring the birds come out
You always want to shout,
Hear the birds sing
And thank God for spring!!
Emily Carrigy, Grade 5
St Veronica Elementary School

I Want a World
I want a world
where children play.
I want a world
with homes for everyone.
I want a world
with no drugs.
I want a world
where money grows on trees.
I want a world
with fair chances for immigrants.

P	G	M	T	W
l	i	e	h	o
e	v		i	r
a	e		s	l
s				d!
e				

Carolina Cordero, Grade 4
Evergreen Elementary School

Fear
Fear is black.
It smells like sweat.
It looks like a pale white face.
It tastes like sour milk.
It sounds like heavy breathing.
Fear feels like goose bumps and chills.
Victoria Freeman, Grade 6
St Rose of Lima School

I Want a World…
I want a world with
no violence
I want a world where there's
more silence
I want a world where
we can play all night
I want a world where there's
no suicide
I want a world where it's just
so peaceful
and I just sit and pray
for that day
to pass by.
Mi'Quanah Johnson Fagg, Grade 4
Evergreen Elementary School

When the Wind Blows
When the wind blows at a perfect speed,
When the trees dance the waltz
When the bushes swirl in a perfect circle
You may hear the voice
The voice of peace and tranquility
But the party can only last so long.
The world is back
And the wind is gone.
Tess Erickson, Grade 6
Bartle Elementary School

Spring
Flower beds bloom
And empty classrooms
Children swimming
Red birds singing
Hotter days
And fun always
Oh, spring is here
And winter is in rear
Everything is perfect
With strawberries unpicked
Sparkling lakes untouched
Kites being clutched
No way can there be
Any season more bouncy
Than spring
Agatha Winiarski, Grade 6
Jefferson Township Middle School

Football

I like football. I can play all day.
I play in my yard, until the sun goes away.
Eleven men play defense,
Eleven play offense.
Coaches teach the team,
While refs judge and scream.
Fans go nuts when their team scores,
You hear a lot of noise and roars.
Football is the greatest sport,
I like it better than running on a court.

Michael Fiorino, Grade 4
St Rose of Lima School

Spring Is…

Spring is…
the time when flowers open up like the sun
Spring is…
the time when bees Buzzz!
and make honey
Spring is…
the time when people sweat
like raining tear drops —
Drip! Drip!
Drop! Drop!
That's what spring is to me!

Steven Tiban, Grade 4
Evergreen Elementary School

Beach Days

Waking up on a warm, sunny day,
With nothing or no one standing in your way.
Walking to the beach,
While hearing all the seagulls squeak.

The ocean water;
Clear as can be.
You can see all of the fish,
Swimming around in the sea.

The sound of the wave hitting the shore,
Is a calming sensation that I just adore.
The sounds of the seagulls chirping in the air,
Is a fact that if you look up in the sky; they will be there.

The feeling of sand between my toes,
And the tropical breeze against my face.
Lets me know that here anything goes,
When life takes you to this beautiful place.

Here on this lovely beach,
With ocean water only a couple feet out of your reach.
I want to stay here forever,
And for me, that would be very clever.

Brianna Gardner, Grade 6
Allen W Roberts Elementary School

Horses

Horses are beautiful
Horses are kind
You have to watch them
Because of their mind.
    A girl is a filly
    A boy is a colt.
    Sometimes there are
    More girls than boys
    That's not my fault!
Wild horses run free
While others stay in the sun
They are all the same
But they still have fun.
    Foals are wonderful babies
    Still they need care
    A horse named Summer is having one
    That will fill my heart with air.
Now we have to go
Pepper says good-bye,
We will always talk another time
Please Pepper, don't cry!

Erica Vieira, Grade 6
Immaculate Conception Regional School

Valentine's Day Love!

Cupid shot me in my spine
Now I feel it in the air, hearts all over
This is the day I can say I love you!
The day when every girl and boy, man and woman
Can express their feelings freely without being shy
Roses, candy, cards, gifts, and love are given
Just three words that mean I Love You
can send a smile and a tingle in the
heart from coast to coast, country to country,
face to face!
Show emotion to someone special…
And love will set you free
Cupid shot me in the heart
So now we are not apart.

Stephanie Valentine, Grade 6
Kawameeh Middle School

That Feeling About Spring

There's just that feeling about spring
When you wake up in the morning
That refreshing breeze that you feel upon your face
Those wonderful sun showers during the day
The feeling that the sun is never going to fade away

Those thoughts of picnics on red checkered blankets
The feeling of magic in the air
You look around and see
That you're not the only one thinking
The feeling of spring will never fade away

Nicole Mennona, Grade 6
St Veronica Elementary School

Tito

There once was a man named Tito,
Who sometimes used a cool big bow.
 He was in the Army,
 And he hated Barney.
So Barney became his new foe.
Jason Medina, Grade 4
West End Memorial Elementary School

Friends

I have many friends
Our friendship never ends
We giggle and talk
Sometimes we just take a walk
We sit under the sun
While we have some fun
We eat our ice cream
While we SCREAM
It's time to say good bye
We ask each other why
Tomorrow will be another day
Will meet at the Y.M.C.A.
Natalie Castello, Grade 5
Our Lady of Mount Virgin School

Sunset to Sunrise

Sunset is…
A bright flashing,
color of orange,
going *down* in the,
ground.
'Till it be tomorrow.

Sunrise is…
Bright colors of orange and red,
coming *up* to give,
us warmth,
and stay,
'Till it be dusk.
Nada Mohamed-Aly, Grade 4
Evergreen Elementary School

Dinosaurs

Have you ever thought
What dinosaurs think of you
We look like small ants to them
We look like tiny appetizers too.
He wants to know why I'd be scared
of those big sharp teeth he's got
His roar can blow you right away
Across two parking lots
So it's a good thing
That dinosaurs aren't around anymore
Or they'd pull of your roofs
And cave in your floors
Richie Ferrazzano, Grade 6
Thomas Jefferson Middle School

All Will Come Through

Life has been rough around the world
Natural disasters are causing pain
Wars on terror and destruction threaten the future
But the world will come through, the world will come through.
Innocent lives are taken each second
Soldiers at war are killed in action
Children suffer and die of hunger
The souls of people are taken by cancer
But the world will come through, the world will come through.
A child grieves as she witnesses her house burning,
She pictures herself living on the streets.
But she will come through, she will come through.
The disasters of our nation are forged and will not be forgotten,
The people that had suffered are scarred.
From the heartbreaking fall of the Twin Towers to Hurricane Katrina,
There would still be pain in the heart and soul of America.
But our nation will come through, we will come through.
From all that is said, all will come through.
All will come through as long as there is hope and faith
In the souls of people for a better tomorrow.
From hope and faith, there may be such entity as peace.
Jessie Trespeses, Grade 6
Springfield Township School

Waiting

Sitting on a damp hollow log in a snowy meadow I stare at the wan winter sky.
Watching each snowflake sink soundlessly into the quiet meadow.
I wait as the storm slowly creeps closer.
Smelling the gray smoke coming from the distant chimneys, I wait for spring.
Colin MacGregor, Grade 5
Lyncrest Elementary School

The Dreamer

I'll fly above the mountains, then I'll dance across the sea.
And then I'll have a lovely conversation, with the spirit of a tree.

I'll make the clouds rumble, with my fastly beating drum.
But I still need some lightning, could you try to come?

When it came to my dreaming, my grandma encouraged me,
She said that life is far too short, to not spend it happily.

But when it came to my dreaming, my mom is on a different stool.
"Why don't you stop dreaming, and focus on school?"

They said that I dreamed too much, and I supposed that it was true,
They said, "Instead of dreaming, why don't you get out there and do?"

So I went out into the cold, boring world and became quite a successful girl,
I had some ups and a lot of downs, I had to be serious, could not fool around.

But when I'm alone, in my mind's eye,
Above the mountains, this girl can still fly.
Teresa Frenzel, Grade 5
Lafayette Elementary School

Catching Dreams

Looking out the window on a bright and sunny day,
Seeing all the dreams that are floating away,
Coming in the window and leaving out the door,
I wonder how they found their way
I wonder how they found their way,
I wonder and I wonder some more

Tara Franzoni, Grade 4
Pond Road Middle School

On Horseback

On horseback, the whole world seems to change
Mainly as you're walking across the open range
The trees look greener the sky looks bluer
Even the blades of grass look newer
And when you're in that state of peace
You never want the moment to cease
So you canter away to a perfect spot
Where commotion, perplexity and clamor is naught
When the sun goes down it's hard to deny
That soon it will be time to say goodbye
So you mount back up and ride off again
For soon you will be back in your state of Zen.

Samantha Reinis, Grade 6
Springfield Township School

The World War II Memorial

People looking up and down,
People looking all around.
Sadness has filled the air,
People crying everywhere.
People quiet, not even a peep,
People quiet, not even a beep.
The only noise is the waterfall,
Other than that, no one talks at all.

It makes me feel very sad,
But no one there is ever mad.
When I look at the statues, I know I'm protected,
And that thought I have, I never forget it.
The stars represent people who died,
And when I've looked there, I've cried.
After we've been there for a while,
We leave and I turn back and smile.

Ashley Addvensky, Grade 5
Roberge Elementary School

Friends

F riendly to you no matter what.
R eally happy every day.
I nvolved in what you say.
E ncouraging when you think you can't do something.
N ew surprises every day for you.
D own to earth when you feel bad.
S uper at keeping secrets when you tell them one.

Valerie Byron, Grade 5
Belhaven Avenue Middle School

Being a Sailboat

If I were a sailboat
I would sit at the harbor
tied to a pole,
waiting to be set into the sea

Then my sail would spread out
and flutter in the wind
as if I were a butterfly soaring in the air
with no cares in life

I'd bob up and down,
up and down
in the rippling sea

Seagulls soaring,
looking for a bite to eat;
pelicans gulping fish by the dozen
in their built-in net

I could sail the seven seas 'til my sail was sore
I could see so many things from A to Z…
if only I were a sailboat!

Anna Convery, Grade 4
Sicomac Elementary School

A Snowstorm Is Coming

I crept down the stairs one dark night
To see a joyous sight
I raced to the TV and turned it on.
The weatherman announced,
"There will be no school tomorrow
Snow will be covering the lawn."
I screamed real low,
So my parents would not wake,
Since I was in the living room below
When I ran up to my bed, I whispered,
"A snowstorm is coming 7 feet tall,
A snowstorm is coming taller than a wall,
A snowstorm is coming as high as the sky,
A snowstorm is coming really, really high"
The next day as I awoke,
I ran to my window to see what I spoke,
And there it was, my dream day,
You guessed right
I shouted out a big hurray!!

Jenna Kuhn, Grade 4
Sunnymead Elementary School

Games

Games are rated with stars and letters
They show which games are worse and better.
Some cheat codes are great, some are lame
They usually help you beat the game!

Joshua Quintana, Grade 5
Robert L Craig Elementary School

Water

Water is beautiful
Water is blue
Whether in an ocean or a sea
Or a puddle or lake
Water is amazing

Water helps fish survive
Water supports crabs and lobsters
Water is the home of jellyfish
Water keeps creatures alive

Water is what we drink
It's what we swim in
Water makes us clean
When we add some soap
We use water to save lives
When we put out fires
I've talked about water so much
I think I'll get some now
Gregory Monteleone, Grade 6
Our Lady of Mount Virgin School

Colors

Orange is like the sun
Purple is all about fun

Red is like raspberries
Blue likes blueberries

Yellow is like a smiling face
Black is as good as an ace

Pink is like sweet candy
Tan is all about getting sandy

Brown is the color of my hair
White is the color of a hare
Cristina Sulzer, Grade 5
St Dominic Elementary School

Spring Fever

S inging birds on the wires.
P eople having picnics.
R abbits frolicking in the meadows.
I ridescent colored skies
N oisy woodpeckers in the trees,
G raveyards growing into gardens.

F lowers sprouting from the soil.
E ccentric smelling flora
V icious weather, I think not.
E veryone playing outside,
R ushing to the door of fun.
Eyal Kleiman, Grade 4
Solomon Schechter Day School

Work

Work work
I work all day
When I come home
I want to play
Work work
All the time
Why can't I do something else,
Why can't I rhyme
It's boring doing work all day
So please help me,
Please help me pray
So I won't have to do
My work all day.
Nathaniel Young, Grade 5
Roosevelt Elementary School

Kelly

Having a name like mine is a little tough,
People call you Miss Belly.
Things like that hurt me,
In the end, I love the name Kelly!
The name means I am very smart,
Yet, sometimes I'm dumber than jelly.
And every day my life is good,
Because my name is Kelly!
Kelly Mae Brown, Grade 4
Rev George Brown Memorial School

Summer

Summer is freedom,
A time that only comes once a year,
Summer is a time to play,
A fun two months appear,
Summer is a time to cheer,
Every day you wake up and smile.
Michael DiMaulo, Grade 6
Cherry Hill Elementary School

Snow Angel

Easy to make,
On the white fluffy snow,
Moving your arms like wings.
But you forget about her,
Going in for a cup of hot cocoa.

She takes a feathery breath,
More fragile than a heart,
Tries out her wings.

Flying silently away, away.
Skimming like the faintest handwriting,
Over icy lakes and untouched meadows,
Where the cattle graze in summer,
Only to return the next day.
Michelle Chen, Grade 5
Laura Donovan Elementary School

Little Puppy

Puppy
Soft, tiny
Playing, jumping, running
You are so cute and cuddly.
Golden Retriever
Caitlin Doherty, Grade 4
Our Lady of Mount Virgin School

Pink

What is pink?
Pink is a rose,
A grapefruit,
A flamingo's feather,
A heart,
Pink is wild,
Pink is gentle,
It's sweet
Yet sour
Pink is a calm day,
The color of the sky
During a sunset,
Pink is the music of rock,
A squeaky, little pig,
Let's not forget bubble gum,
Pink is the smell of
Cherry blossoms blooming
In the spring…
Kristen Kieffer, Grade 5
Paul W Carleton Elementary School

Baseball

Baseball season time is here.
All the kids start to cheer.
I once hit a ball,
all the way to the wall.
This was one good year.
Arthur Cummins, Grade 4
St Mary's School

The Flea

The flea flew onto a tree.
He thought to become a bee.
It was so strange.
It was deranged.
He thought if only I were a bee.
Elijah Gisleson, Grade 5
The Red Bank Charter School

Life

L ong
I nvigorating
F antastic
E nlightening.
Herschel Jordan, Grade 5
Robert L Craig Elementary School

Winter Breeze

Here I am in the winter breeze.
I have a jacket so I do not freeze.
Winter has come and we've just begun
To feel the cold, and not the sun.
To make a snowball, it's easy as 1, 2, 3.
But when you make it, try not to throw it at me.
As the cold wind comes in
It feels rough on my skin.
I shiver and I shake
In my boots, my feet quake.
There's a big hill up ahead
I sure wish I had a sled.
The best part is I get to have fun
But it is not in the hot summer sun.

Eric M. Goodmok, Grade 4
Assumption School

Water

Water, water in a fountain, water in a hose
Water, water, very fast; in a stream it flows

Water, water in the pipes, always very near
Water is the greatest thing that's happened to us here

Water has many purposes, it can clean and heal and quench
Water can be lots of fun if you want to be drenched

We need water to stay alive, animals need it too
Water, water for us on Earth is nothing very new.

Liam McCarthy, Grade 5
St John's Academy

Ice Cream

I t's luscious
C old
E verybody likes it!

C rispy toppings
R ed, white, and blue sprinkles
E vening dessert
A perfect spring snack
M any flavors!

Allison Smith, Grade 4
Hardyston Township Elementary School

Sick/Healthy

Sick
misery, anguish,
kills, hurts, burns,
North Pole, South Pole, America, Australia,
helps, heals, resolves,
flourishing, blooming,
Healthy

Yogeswari Medepalli, Grade 4
Christ the Teacher School

Clouds

Every day when I walk by;
I sit on the hills and look at the sky.

When I look up at a cloud;
I look up and laugh out loud.

Clouds are different in lots of ways,
As I see them, these short days.

As I see these clouds go by;
I see a diamond in the sky.

Clouds are cool, and full of wonder;
Oh no, it just began to thunder.

Walking in the rain isn't such a pain;
It's insane how much water goes down the drain.

Lexie Hay, Grade 5
St Joseph Grade School

Butterflies in January

Butterflies here
Butterflies there
Butterflies everywhere
When they fly in the sky looking for food everywhere.
It's too early for butterflies.
When it's cold butterflies are migrating somewhere warm.
Butterflies have stripes or even swirls.
Butterflies add color to our world.

Brianna Burrello, Grade 5
St Joseph School

Snowy Day

Look at the four, puffy snowmen having a snowball fight,
With a black puppy keeping score,
There is snow on the ground, but will there be more?

There is a soft squirrel and a cute puppy making snowballs
As soft as powder for friends,
Just until their snowball fight ends.

Over there, on a bench, is a well-dressed snowman in black,
Petting an adorable orange cat's back.

Now that our day has come to an end,
Come back tomorrow, but bring a friend.

Lauren Hoagland, Grade 5
Sandman Consolidated Elementary School

Vents

Whish, whish go the vents.
I can't get it out of my head, it makes no sense.
I can't hear my teacher,
Living up there must be some creature!

Amarpreet Kaur, Grade 4
Mansfield Township Elementary School

Summer Days
It is a beautiful day.
It is time to play.
Have some fun
on this very special day.
It only comes once a year.
So let's yell, "Hurray!"
Now as the sun goes down
for the whole town
Don't have such sorrow
There is always tomorrow.
Vikkie Valenta, Grade 6
Bartle Elementary School

Ted
There once was a bear named Ted,
who happened to fall on his head.
His head made a thump.
He got a big bump,
and then his bump turned red.
Stephanie Sudziarski, Grade 4
St Mary's School

I Wish…
I wish I was a butterfly,
So I could fly so high.

I wish I was a cheerleader,
So I could cheer with pride.

I wish I was a president,
So I could help the poor.

I wish I was a millionaire,
So I could have ten floors.

I wish I was a polar bear,
So I could roam so free.

I wish I was Santa Claus,
So I could share with glee.
Nicole Castelluccio, Grade 5
Byram Township Intermediate School

Snowstorm
I remember
the stinging cold,
the gray sky,
the snow plunging down
all around me.

Trees still —
as the snow blasts around them
Taking in ragged breaths of frigid air.
I hiked through the wicked snowstorm
Roxanne Lee, Grade 4
Evergreen Elementary School

My Dreams
In my dreams I am an artist, using paints, pens, and chalk I'm the smartest.
Or sometimes I am a vet, meeting animals like dogs, cats, and a pet.
And to relax I'm on a beach, with sand, and shells but I will not teach,
Hearing the sound of the ocean, makes me put on more suntan lotion,
I hear the dolphins talking, when I'm on the boardwalk walking,
As we get on a ride, I scream and yell as we glide.
Sometimes, I'm by the pool, being very cool,
Or drinking lemonade, in the shade,
Maybe even having fun, or in the sun.
With my skis, can I go please?
With snow in my eyes, I'm sure to win a prize.
Even with my friends dancing. Or playing or laughing.
Amanda Hughes, Grade 5
Most Holy Redeemer School

Nature
Have you ever stopped to think about nature?
Have you ever wondered what's on the outside world?
Have you ever thought about how beavers cut down over 100 trees,
Or how ducks look so peaceful swimming on the surface?
Like a leaf gliding on the surface of a lake,
but underneath they're paddling like the wind.
Our world is made up of nature.
There wouldn't be a world without nature.
Even your backyard is nature.
Instead of thinking of work or school,
take time to think about what's around you!
NATURE!
Linda Pluhar, Grade 6
St Veronica Elementary School

Stuck
I am on stage, in the light, the glowing light that is bright.
I am playing Dorothy in the forest, on opening night.
As I stare into the light, I forget my lines and forget what they sound like.
I feel like a stray cub, lost and confused,
Not knowing anything at all, I mused.

The light is as bright as the sun, blinding me so I can't see.
The light is now agitating me.
It seems as the light is challenging me.
I must be candid with my co-actors,
"Help me!" I whisper,
"I forgot!"
"Lions and tigers," the Tin Man snorted obnoxiously.
"Thank you," I murmur quietly.

"I have trekked all this way and now we will get frostbite!
Lions and tigers and bears, oh my!" I recite.
Everybody laughs joyfully.
I smile into the white light,
It is now my friend.
I am on stage in the light,
The bright, white glowing light.
Amanda Eisenberg, Grade 6
Fieldstone Middle School

Your Wedding Day

Pick a dress that fits you right
and imagine yourself dancing all night.

Find the flowers that are white and pink,
and believe me, they'll look better than you think.

Pick a cake that looks tasty,
but don't eat it too hastily.

Pick a tuxedo that will fit your man right,
and imagine him dancing with you all night.

Make your hair as pretty as can be,
and put a veil in it that will look pretty.

I hope your day goes fine
and everything looks divine!

Laura Fowler, Grade 5
St Rose of Lima School

School

Sometimes school could be cool,
But it could be real cruel.
Once in a while we laugh and play,
But usually we work all day.
Teachers could be nice by giving you advice.
Just to let you know,
Behind teachers friendly smiles,
Is evilness that goes on for miles.

Elyssa Magee, Grade 5
Roosevelt Elementary School

Lost

Running, running, running
Can't find my way
It's getting dark, hard to see
Then I sit down, not knowing what to do
Should I keep running or should I sleep
I got up and started running again
I lay down and went to sleep
When I woke up I wondered where I was
I sat up and looked around
I was in my room in my bed
With my mom's voice telling me it's time for school

Luke Smith, Grade 4
Toll Gate Grammar School

Dancing

Dancing in the sun is fun,
I like dancing on the run when I'm done.
Dancing is what I love to do,
Being on stage running and jumping too.
Dancing is my life long passion,
I can't wait to wear this year's fashion.

Candice Corbin, Grade 6
Gilmore J Fisher Middle School

Jumping

I like jumping on the trampoline
It is fun
It feels like you're flying up into the sun
I feel free, like an eagle soarin' high,
Way up there in the sky
I can do back flips and front flips with the greatest of ease
It feels so good to be jumpin' with a little breeze
In spring I bounce on the trampoline,
It feels nice
Not like in winter when it's as cold as ice
Oh gotta go, 'cause daylight's almost over,
I'm gonna leave with a wave over my shoulder.

Marley Ghizzone, Grade 6
Our Lady of Mount Virgin School

Basketball

Basketball is my favorite sport,
I dribble up and down the court.
The ball bounces off my toes,
It hit my teammate in the nose.
He said it hurt a lot,
But he grabbed the ball and made his shot.
The game was close till the end,
Then I passed the ball to my friend.
He shot the ball across the gym,
To our surprise, he made it in.
We won the game, which was great!
The score was twenty to eight.

Vincent Paolo, Grade 5
St Veronica Elementary School

Mr. Golden Sun

Mr. Golden Sun
Shines down on me
Mr. Golden Sun
Is so bright like a light
Mr. Golden Sun
Is hot like a boiling pot
Mr. Golden Sun
Brightens up a new day
Mr. Golden Sun
Makes everyone have a smile on his or her face
Mr. Golden Sun
Is so wonderful to have each and every day

Michelle Player, Grade 6
St Veronica Elementary School

The Man from Albuquerque

There once was a man from Albuquerque
Who was addicted to hot turkey jerky
He went to the store,
But they had no more,
So he just went berserky!

Timothy Jones, Grade 5
Springfield Township School

Skating

S kating is fun.
K eeps you entertained.
A lways have fun.
T he hard tricks.
E ncore skating!

Christopher Aguiar, Grade 6
Roosevelt Elementary School

Birds

Birds sing through the day
sailing through the sapphire sky
soft feathers gliding

Rachel Maryash, Grade 4
Sicomac Elementary School

Helicopters

The beautiful maple helicopters
Brown and whitish
Falling slowly onto the ground
Where kids try to catch them.
The soft and crinkly helicopters
On the quiet maple tree.

Dashmeet Sahi, Grade 6
Thomas R Grover Middle School

The Earth

The Earth
Loved from birth
Being walked on
Being talked on.
From Adam and Eve
To robots and machines.
Through generations and generations
Trying to keep me clean
But I'm dying slowly
From pollution and evolution
The Earth, the Earth
Our wonderful Earth!!

Nicole Ceballos, Grade 6
Thomas Jefferson Middle School

Halloween Night

Dressing yourself up,
From your toe to your top,
Whether it's made or it's bought,
You're being something that you're not.
You could be a witch or a ghost,
Or a fancy queen with the most.
Excited as you go door to door,
Knowing you'll get more and more.
Haunted houses are made for fun,
But sometimes you just have to run.
It's fun playing outside in the fall,
But Halloween fun is the best of all!

Danielle Rizzo, Grade 4
Kennedy Elementary School

What I See

Look into the mirror and tell me
what you see
It's all brand new and peaceful
You left my sight once
and you came right back
So don't leave me anymore
PLEASE

Tiffany Wilson, Grade 6
Little Egg Harbor Intermediate School

The Dance

Take a step, a twirl, a spin
then take a bow, look up
and then you're in another world
filled with your imagination.

You're in a beautiful ball gown
with pearls that gracefully fill your neck
and then you look down, turn around
and everyone's clapping for you.

But then you think,
what did I do?
All I did was take a step, a twirl
and into another world!

Gabrielle Rosolia, Grade 5
St Rose of Lima School

Celestial

Elegant moonlight
The graceful lunar sparkles
Throughout the night sky

Tashmeen Rouf, Grade 6
Thomas Jefferson Middle School

Basketball

I say it's really fun.
Inside or under the sun.

Dribbling, passing, shooting hard.
When on defense, playing guard.

Staying focused or laughing out loud,
winning games makes my team proud.

On the benches or on the courts.
Different plays, different sorts.

Screaming, yelling, cheering us on.
High-fives, hugs, until we're all gone.

So it's great, can't you see?
Loving it is the key!

Casey Nicol, Grade 6
Fieldstone Middle School

A Monster in My Closet

There's a monster in my closet
The closet in my room
The closet with the mop
And the dust pan and the broom
He's really very scary
He's green with purple eyes
He has blue and yellow polka dots
And I think he even flies
I named him "Scary Boo"
Because he gives me such a fright
My parents have to come and save me
In the middle of the night
One night I was really scared
But when I felt a little better
I looked in the closet and
The monster was a sweater

Julia Giambastiani, Grade 5
St John's Academy

Dreams

On a Saturday night
When I fall asleep
I dream of many things
It could be a robot that says beep beep
Or a picture that sings
But on one Saturday night
I had a very strange dream
Everything was normal
It's how life should seem
I didn't want to have this
Happen at all
I had to change this dream
It's like there's a wall
But wait one second
There is something wrong
I think I'm awake
It's morning's dawn

Jack Baisley, Grade 5
Indian Hill Elementary School

Winter

On a beautiful winter night
The northern lights shine bright
A pleasant sight to remember
Kids ice skate on frozen lakes
Dogs sliding across the slippery lake

Cayleen Maria Rizo, Grade 4
Sunnymead Elementary School

Pine Street

On Pine Street we play all day
On Pine Street we never lay
On Pine Street when the kids come out
No one can possibly be left out

Kelly Breslin, Grade 4
Holy Saviour School

I Want a World

I want a world where people do not have to pay for school.
I want a world without violence, a world without noise.
I want a world with people that don't go to jail.
I want a world where people love to learn.

I want a world…
I want a world…
I want a world…

Dontel Carmen, Grade 4
Evergreen Elementary School

You Can Never Find a Better Spot

Super sunny
Super hot
You can never find a better spot
Than the beach
This is the best place to get a tan
But don't get attacked by the sandman

Take a swim in the ocean
But don't forget your suntan lotion
It's like a day at the spa
This is not a sham
It seems like a really good plan
To go and sit on the beach

Do nothing but relax
There are so many facts
Sit on a blanket swim in the ocean
Some people think the beach is addicting
You can do anything
Super sunny super hot you can never find a better spot

Kristen Guzman, Grade 6
Fieldstone Middle School

Allen Iverson

Allen Iverson
He's the best
He outdoes all the rest
Throwing hoops is his game
Allen Iverson is his name
Iverson is the player for me
On the Sixers he's number 3
In all of basketball
A.I. is the best of all

Kayla Dagostino, Grade 5
Immaculate Conception Regional School

Gymnastics

I like gymnastics when it's challenging
Now we will take off with a very big spring
Then we will try the balance beam
If I do fall I will scream

Cassie Lynch, Grade 4
Katharine D Malone Elementary School

When I Think About Ice Cream…

…I see the ice cream truck.
…my green eyes gleam.
…everything is great!
…I think of chocolate chip mint.
…I imagine hot summer days.
…I see my ice cream dripping down the side of the cone.
…It makes me hungry.

Angela Calasso, Grade 4
Long Memorial Elementary School

Blue

Blue is the color of the ocean
the thing we may have all swam in.

Blue is something you can't live without
it's the feeling we all have at times

For without blue there would be no sadness.

Blue can by anything,
mean anything, say anything

Yet the one thing blue has a problem with.

The one thing we all treasure…
Happiness.

Jawann McBeth, Grade 6
Gilmore J Fisher Middle School

Understanding the Meaning of Poetry!

My paper finds my pen
My words come from my heart
I put them both together
and create a work of art.

I can tell you why I'm happy
I can explain why I'm in tears
I can tell you all my dreams
and also describe my fears.

For all the words that rhyme
which mostly end in "e"
I can spend a lifetime
on writing poetry.

I think for just a little
but then a little more
sometimes I think I'm right
but yet I'm not so sure!

My thoughts can keep me writing
I would never want to stop
I could keep on going
until my pen just drops!

Kayla Paladino, Grade 6
Thomas Jefferson Middle School

The Days of the Seasons

Today it's spring.
Tomorrow it's fall.
Yesterday it was winter,
And summer has not come.
Today it is like spring.
Today it is warm.
Yesterday it was freezing.
Tomorrow it's just like fall.
All you need is a light coat.
Yesterday it was just like winter,
As cold as an ice cube.
Summer has not come,
But when it does,
It will be hot,
And the ocean
Will be warm and beautiful.

Nichole Mosher, Grade 6
Lower Alloways Creek Elementary School

Sister

Someone who loves you
Is kind to you
Someone who helps you
The one who comforts you when you're down
Eternally there for you
Recognizes you for who you are

Caroline Rottkamp, Grade 6
Immaculate Conception Regional School

A True Friend...

A True Friend,
A true friend is always by your side
In the good and the bad
A true friend picks you up when you fall
A true friend can cheer you up when you're feeling blue
A true friend guides you when you lose your way
A true friend wipes your tears when you cry
A true friend loves you no matter what
A true friend always has a listening ear
A true friend is always the hope you need
A true friend shares the good and bad times
A true friend is willing to lay down their life for you

Feba Samji, Grade 6
St Joseph's School

My Dad

My dad is rad
We play sports together
But he is never bad
And he never gets sad
But sometimes gets mad
He is usually glad
I love my dad

Stephanie Wager, Grade 5
Immaculate Conception Regional School

Love

L ove is magical, love is true,
   love is what I feel for you,
O n a boat or in a car it doesn't matter where you are,
   I want to hug you, kiss you, love you too,
   and that's how I feel about you.
V alentine's Day is special too.
   that's when you say, "I love you!"
   It doesn't matter when or where,
   but that you want to have it fair.
E verybody says I love you,
   even if they don't want to.
   Love is something that you feel
   that's what makes life real!

Lea Salei, Grade 4
Solomon Schechter Day School

Rain and Thunder

What is the point of rain?
When it rains I go insane,
Because I cannot play with my Great Dane.
When I hear that thump I shiver all over.
The windows in my house start to blur.

What is the point of thunder?
When it thunders little kids get scared all over.
Why I wonder?
It is only a sound.
It is like the world is shaking all around.

Carlee Ray, Grade 6
Trinity Christian School

Spring

Spring
Colorful flowers
Skating, running, jogging
Bees buzzing in my ear
Spring

Jayson Cabrera, Grade 5
Perth Amboy Catholic Intermediate School

I Am

I am brave and funny
I am as sweet as a bunny
I am a soccer star
I am one who sets my goals very far
I am as smart as a whip
I am not clumsy, so I don't usually trip
I am a good reader
I am therefore a good achiever
I am a shimmer in the sky
I am someone who will make you want to fly
I am a person who loves the beach
I am one who likes to teach
I am me

Kelsey Ryan, Grade 5
Laura Donovan Elementary School

Football

F un and really exciting!!!
O n the field it's great to score a touchdown!!!
O ne chance to show the coach how good you are!!!
T he best play is always the pass plays!!!
B est position is tight end!!!
A ll comes down to the last play of the drive!!!
L ook at the crowd when you get a touchdown!!!
L ike the sport because it is amazing!!!

Matt Riviere, Grade 6
Allen W Roberts Elementary School

Come with Me

Come with me and we'll stare
at the pearl white clouds floating
in the sky.
Come with me and we'll shout
and turn while playing a game of tag.
Come with me and we'll search
for scaly fish in the freezing cold
water of the ocean as it refreshes us.
Come with me and we'll trace, draw and color
on rainbow colored paper while
we exchange our feelings.
Come with me and we'll cuddle together
with a handmade blanket covering us
and keeping us together.
Come with me and we'll tuck in bed and
kiss goodnight and get ready for another
long exciting day.

Veronica Zega, Grade 4
Lincroft Elementary School

Championship

Have you ever been to the championship
You think you can't be any more nervous
Versus the undefeated team
Dribbling down the court
Looking for a pass
With only 5 seconds left
You see your teammate in the corner
Down by 3, he shoots and he scores
Now you're in overtime
Another chance to take home the win
You must concentrate
And don't think this is over
The battle has just begun
20 seconds left to show them who's boss
50 to 50 this is a close game
You must score right now.
The crowd at the edge of their seats
You shoot to win
Yes, it goes in
You just won the championship
Your coach supporting you the whole way.

Heithem Odeh, Grade 6
Thomas Jefferson Middle School

Barbara

B eautiful person!
A ctive in everything!
R espectable and reliable!
B est friends with Elizabeth and MANY more!
A thletic in sports!
R eally loves her friends!
A dorable in every way!

Barbara Bogado, Grade 4
Franklin Township Elementary School

Personality

I'm not her or him or they or we
I've got my own personality!
I've got my own room, my own clothes and family
I've got my own personality!
People try to change me and I don't know why
It's like they rip it out from inside
And when I wake up, my personality is gone
And I act like someone I'm not
Someone I wished of being
Someone I'm not!
Someone I wanted to be
Someone I'm not!
I think of how I am
And how I'm being now
And it's totally not me
Over the days that I haven't had my personality
I figured out that everyone has their own personality
And that's what makes us special

Nia Mahoney, Grade 4
Gregory Elementary School

Last Goodbyes

I am in pain and slowly dying
I wonder how I can help my family survive this imprisonment
I hear heaven calling
I see a bright light from the holy place up there
I want to see my children one last time
I am in pain and slowly dying

I pretend to get up but I am too weak
I feel the coldness rush over my body
I touch my child's cheek
I worry how my children will survive
I cry because I know I am dying
I am in pain and slowly dying

I understand my time is slowly coming
I say to my children, they will always be in my heart
I dream my people will be freed
I try to relax and die peacefully
I hope I will be free in heaven
I am in pain and slowly dying

Neil Forrester, Grade 5
Mary A Hubbard Elementary School

Dog

I know a dog named Chip.
Now and then he does a flip.
Chip lives in a dog house.
He made a friend who was a mouse.
Manny Betancur, Grade 6
John Hill School

Sadness

I'm drowning in deep sorrowful grief
I'm losing myself slipping beneath
My hand reaches out but nothing's there
All I can grasp is cold, thin air

I pull my hand in near my broken heart
Where empty feelings decided to start
As I look up from this position
I see a faint smiling disposition

Even though my old dog is dead
She's still in my heart, still in my head
I'll remember all the good times we had
But right now I'm still really sad
Dana Smith, Grade 5
Old York Elementary School

Summer

Summer is the season of fun,
playing with your friends in the sun.
No school at this time of year,
but don't worry it's still here.
You can go on vacation,
and have a celebration.
Having fun with family and friends,
acting like it is the end.
Swimming in the pool for one last time,
leaving summer will be no crime.
Next year's summer will be the best
hoping it's better than the rest.
I'm going to miss this summer,
getting cold is a big bummer.
Summer has gone by so fast,
summer vacation will never last.
Tara Brett, Grade 6
Our Lady of Mount Virgin School

Bees

Buzz, buzz, goes a bee,
I can't wait to see the bee fly.
It will fly into the sky.
Bee, do you see me?
I see you.
You like flowers.
I do, too.
Buzzing, buzzing, bee.
Giselle Kertis, Grade 5
St Joseph School

Spotlight

To be in the spotlight.
What is it like?
What does it take?
Who does it take?
Drowning in old memories.
Hiding in old glories.
Trying to come out of your shell but frightened by the spotlight.
You used to be a star.
But now your just a fading memory.
The paparazzi ate you up and spit you right out.
Never thinking twice, never looking both ways.
Always trying to be what you used to be.
But never doing enough.
To be in the spotlight is a fading memory.

David Holden, Grade 5
Hillside Elementary School

Woodland Dance

Fields of glistening rubies, sapphires, diamonds and more,
sparkling in the morning dew.
With the birds chirping in the morning rays,
and the gleaming daffodils bright and cheery on a foggy morning.

While in the shadows of the shade,
moving slyly in the luscious bushes spiraling through the branches,
in a single bound the dance was in the treetops,
leaping and twisting in the full canopy of branches,
and newly sprouted leaves of afternoon.
With a flick of a bushy tail, the shadows were gone and the afternoon was awake.

Eyes like the last sparkling stars in the evening sky
peering through the branches of a lilac bush.
A sweet-smelling, purple lilac in her munching mouth,
and her crumbly leaf-colored pelt and white bushy tail.
With long steady legs she and her wobbly legged fawn
leaped into the wilderness.

The woodland scents dwindled,
while the summer's sparkling light kissed Mother Nature,
And the dancing jewel said good night,
crying colorful rays into the rainbow sea, high above the woodland creatures.

Kathleen Mai, Grade 6
Woodglen Middle School

A Nature Rainbow

If I were red I'd be a spotted ladybug crawling up a rock.
If I were orange I'd be a fluttering monarch landing on a flower.
If I were yellow I'd be a buzzing bee busy 'bout my work.
If I were green I'd be a frog lying on a lily pad.
If I were blue I'd be a sky that gazes down on all the creatures.
If I were purple I'd be a sunset over the ocean on a summer afternoon.
If I were pink I'd be a rose growing in a planter's pot.
If I were all these colors I'd be a nature rainbow.
Katherine Pappalardo, Grade 5
Sicomac Elementary School

Mailing a Letter

Mailing a letter is really quite easy,
it's something you do almost all of the time,
don't wait 'til sunset
just do it in the daylight.
So you go to your hideout
and look at a map,
to find out where the post office is at.
Go to the one that's right nearby,
put your letter in and say goodbye.

Emily Parker, Grade 5
Holy Saviour School

The Bout of the Dueling Dragons

The bout of the dueling dragons
Was a catastrophic sight
Two beasts of immense power
Setting earth alight
These horrors wouldn't rest,
Until one was announced the best.

The final hour of the world,
Was wasted with blue flames being hurled
At the dragons
Still dueling as neither will
Diminish their pride as
An obliterator.

Flames crashed
Dragons clashed
In the bout of the dueling dragons.

Daniel Dougherty, Grade 5
Tamaques Elementary School

A Ride of All Rides

When I was a boy
About knee high
I rode on a ride
A big ride

The ride was tall
It went very high
I thought I would fall
But instead I touched the sky

It twisted and turned
My stomach was fluttering
My eyes burned
And I was stuttering

When the ride was over
I was so glad
I would pay all I had
To never ride that ride again

Andrew Breslin, Grade 6
Lower Alloways Creek Elementary School

What Is Blue?

Blue is the color of the sky,
Blue is the color of cotton candy,
Blue is the color of my eyes,
Blue is the color of part of the American flag,
Blue is the color of the ocean,
Blue is the color of New England,
Blue is the color of a Bluebird,
    That's what blue is!

Sonny Brancaccio, Grade 4
Hardyston Township Elementary School

The Stars

You can see the stars from many places,
    They shine down on people's faces.

They shine so brightly in the sky,
When you look up you see them passing by.

When you see them fall you make a wish,
    You might wish for a new pet fish.

They form pictures in space,
They look like things that you can trace.

Lucas Voli, Grade 4
Huber Street No 3 Elementary School

Punting Zone

I was at the punting zone when…
I kicked the ball.
I felt it hit my cleat.
All my team heard BAM.
I smelled sweat when it went down my face.
It hit the ground.
YEAH, we all cheered!

Michael Allen, Grade 4
Franklin Township Elementary School

DeQuahn

D Q is what they call me.
E xcellent at all Xbox games.
Q uick runner.
U ltimate video game player.
A wesome at paintball.
H alo 1 and 2 are two of my favorite video games.
N umber one at basketball.

DeQuahn Jones, Grade 4
Franklin Township Elementary School

Strange Friends

There once were some mopey green frogs,
Who had some strange friends that were hogs.
    All day they did weep,
    For their dear friends, sheep,
Who got lost in the thick, gray fog.

Taylor Moore, Grade 4
West End Memorial Elementary School

Dogs
Dogs are crazy and smell like a daisy
But sometimes they get lazy

Dogs are cute big or small
They come to you when you call

Dogs love to chew bones
They even love ice cream cones

Dogs love you no matter what you do
They always try to please you

I love dogs!!!
Stephanie Santora, Grade 5
St Veronica Elementary School

My Walk Home
Flowers blooming
Birds singing
Trees budding
My walk home

Light clothes
Heavy bag
Tired feet
My walk home

People coming
People going
Figures moving
My walk home

I see it now
I'm almost there
The path is clear
Now I'm home
Jennifer Litzinger, Grade 6
Sampson G Smith Intermediate School

Oh Halloween
On Halloween night
I get quite a fright
There are Cyclops with one eye
One came up to me and I said "Bye"
I saw monsters in black
So I turned my back
There were ogres and elves
And cows with bells
Kids say "Trick or Treat"
But all they see are little feet
Now this night is done
So I must say, "Good night, hon."
Jenna Ferrell, Grade 4
Springfield Township School

A Good Night's Sleep
The comfortable pillows upon my bed
Is where I can rest my head.
Where I dream all night
To make sure the bed bugs don't bite
I could stay there 'till I am dead.
Julie Sheridan, Grade 6
Community School of Bergen County

Under the Bed
I hear the loud screech of my sis
out of the blue

The scream made me jump really high
yes, it's true

A chill from the toe to neck
made me go and see

When I went to see
I saw why she screamed

A frightened girl hiding under the sheets
shaking like crazy

A pair of glowing eyes under the bed
not looking happy
Joey Gibli, Grade 4
Solomon Schechter Day School

Me
I think you don't know me
You think that you do
When everybody loves me
You think you love me too
It's the game of popular
It's the game of cool
If you think that you know me,
Do you think that I'm cruel?

My mind is messed,
My heart depressed
These words all come from me.
Me the one that's popular,
Me the one that's cool.
If this is the person she turned me into,
I know why you hate school.
Jayne DeRogatis, Grade 5
Liberty Corner Elementary School

Tish the Fish
I have a fish named Tish
She lives in a dish
She wants to be set free
Just like you and me
Shelby Evans, Grade 6
John Hill School

Today
Jump out of bed.
Turn on your light.
Eat some breakfast.
Be happy and bright,
Smile real big.
Giggle a joke.
Play with a friend.
Drink some Coke.
Dance to a song.
Sing a tune,
Go to bed,
Make a wish on the moon.
Brianna Haspel, Grade 4
Lincroft Elementary School

Spring
Snow is melting.
Spring is here!
The birds are chirping.
Flowers blooming.
Green grass growing.
People laughing.
This is my favorite time of year.
Irene Song, Grade 4
Apple Montessori School

Grizzly Bear
There once was a great grizzly bear
And he was born without any hair
He knew he was bald
And became quite appalled
when people would stop and stare
Sam Demirjian, Grade 5
St Helena School

The Sleepy Cat
Is it fun to be a cat?
Yes, you can sleep on a mat,
Or you can nap on the bed.
But oops, you bumped your head.
Now you are ready to fight.
I have to watch out before you bite.
How could it be,
That he would try to bite me.
Joshua Stippick, Grade 4
Folsom Elementary School

Happy
Happy
Fun, joy
Laughing, smiling, grinning
Having a nice day,
Be happy!!
Samuel A. Henick, Grade 4
Solomon Schechter Day School

Betrayal Is…
Betrayal is something friends should not pursue.
Betrayal is dishonest, unfaithful, and untrue.

Betrayal is when you go back on your word,
In my opinion it's rather absurd.

A person who betrays, will not be cared for,
And your popularity level will certainly not soar.

Do not have pity on a person who has betrayed,
Because they really have disobeyed.

But it is okay to forgive an act of betraying,
Because everyone does bad things.
Joseph McKenna, Grade 5
Sicomac Elementary School

Trees
Trees sway in the wind
as it blows and blows it goes
through orange leaves
Zach Fogg, Grade 6
Lower Alloways Creek Elementary School

Apples
Apples, apples, they grow on trees,
In the winter they would freeze.
Apples, apples, they grow on trees,
In the spring the flowers bud and attract the bees.
Apples, apples, they grow on trees,
In the summer they swing with the breeze.
Apples, apples, they grow on trees,
In the fall they get eaten by ME!
Megan Kaulfers, Grade 5
St Joseph School

Alexandra
Running as fast as can be
from one place to another
finding a cure for cancer
so everyone can do everything they want to do.
Beginning to get tired,
I start bouncing with every bounce
being a speck of joy in my journey.
Stopping to rest,
I turn into a piano
with every key being pressed
becoming a new masterpiece to one's ear.
As I find that cure for cancer
I turn red,
confident,
strong,
and never giving up.
My name is Alexandra.
Alexandra Esposito, Grade 5
Salt Brook Elementary School

The Desert
The Desert,
Shining bright and shining gold
With sand dunes that are new and old.

Miles of sand north, south, west and east
With the continuous rise and set of the sun.

Our water's running low and we will never know
When our journey will end.

We're riding on luck, good fortune,
And hope to lead us out of the Desert.

So many grains you can't even count
And tiresome camels you have to mount.

As long as the sea and just as wide
Is the place we call the Desert.
Sean Carey, Grade 5
St John's Academy

The Sea
The sea has calm waves and roaring waves.
Seagulls flying, squawking near the ocean.
The sand slithering on my feet,
and colorful seashells on the sand.
Sandcastle high and straight,
People swimming and having fun in the sea.
Sitting on the sand, looking at the sunset,
and the beautiful sea.
Alice Chong, Grade 5
Christ the Teacher School

Listen
Howl like the wild wolf
Roar like the mighty lion
Soar like the proud eagle
Gallop like the untamed horse
Glide through the water like a silver dolphin
Splash like a killer whale.
Listen to the music of nature.
Melody Ting, Grade 4
Princeton School

Thunder
A roaring scream and a scary sob.
These are the sounds of thunder.
A quick blaze of light moving through the sky.
This is the look of thunder.
Burning, fiery, smoldering —
these are the smells of thunder.
Sound, smell and sight —
oh, the power of thunder!
Navin Raj, Grade 6
Fieldstone Middle School

In My Magical Net
In my magical net I grasp the six members of my family
I capture the loving people who put a roof over my head, dinner on the table,
and cheer me up when I'm sad
I catch the people who play with me, the people who drive me places
and celebrate my birthdays. Without these six people I don't know what would happen.
Nobody to talk to, nobody to laugh with,
and nobody to share a Thanksgiving feast with.
These six people keep me from freezing in the winter.
They keep my heart from breaking as well as keeping my body from slicing apart.
There would be no meaning in life without my family.
There would be no Mother's Day or Father's Day.
There would be no ones smiling face to look forward to seeing after school.
My family is what keeps me. I love them and I always will!

Mike Felezzola, Grade 5
Salt Brook Elementary School

What's in My Mom's Pocketbook?
A wallet, a cell phone charger, a whip (just kidding), a cell phone, a pen (a blue one I think), mints, lipstick, oodles and oodles of crumpled receipts, old gum (maybe even moldy), a crayon or two, CDs, some piece of a board game (how did that get in there?) an iPod (it's silver), a miniature dictionary, a piece of tape, and a glue stick (just in case).

Meredith Papera, Grade 5
Sicomac Elementary School

The Messy Room!
Is this my room you say? But do I have to clean it today?
Because my room looks like a horror movie, and there are ants swimming in my Jacuzzi,
The stinky socks are on the ground, or is it just me spinning around?
Is this my room or house? Or is it just that filthy mouse?
With all of the clothes hanging on the wall, and all the toys running down the hall,
When you step in the house you will say "Ouch," and because there are toys all over the couch, you will also say "Ouch,"
Because my underwear is taking over my TV, they are telling me,
To clean my room right this moment, or else this house will need a big improvement,
Because there is a huge wolf spider hanging in my closet, now it is eating my monthly deposit,
There are monkeys hanging on my roof, then there will be a big poof,
Because not only is this my room, but when it falls I will need a bigger broom!
So from starting from this day on, my filthy room will be rather gone,
But I am not cleaning it at all, because I am heading straight to the mall!

Sonal Agarwal, Grade 4
Stony Brook Elementary School

Breast Cancer
B ringing terrifying news to hundreds of families every day.
R ight now a family is discovering that a member of their family has this disease.
E very day hundreds of women die because of this horrible disease.
A ll women in the world are scared to get breast cancer.
S pending months in chemotherapy
T hinking that today might be the last day.

C onstantly people with this disease need treatment.
A ccompanying women through this test is the best you can do to support them.
N o woman should go through this torture.
C ertain people don't understand the consequences of this disease so please inform yourself.
E xam yourself at least twice a month so the number of deaths will decrease.
R especting and supporting the breast cancer association can save another life.

Sara Jaramillo, Grade 6
Thomas Jefferson Middle School

Soccer

S occer is my favorite sport
O bviously I sign up for it every year
C urving is hard because you could slide and fall down.
C ourage is all you need to be goalie.
E veryone can play soccer if they try,
R unning fast as offense.

Jacob Naim, Grade 4
Solomon Schechter Day School

Dad

He is cooler than Carlito.
He is kinder than a puppy.
He is more sly than a fox.
He is nicer than a baby bunny.
He is hotter than lava.
He is stronger than the world's strongest man.
He is my dad.

Connor Hall, Grade 6
Thorne Middle School

I Am Sad and Scared

I am sad and scared
I wonder if I will see my family again
I hear the happy spiritual songs that are sang
I want to be free

I pretend to be free
I feel scared of what will happen if I escape
I touch the tears on my face
I worry about my family
I cry very often
I am sad and scared

I understand why they hurt me
I say "I want to be FREE!"
I dream of escaping
I try to think of happy things
I hope I will be free
I am sad and scared

Lauren Myer, Grade 5
Mary A Hubbard Elementary School

Vets and Pets

Vets, pets, pets, vets, the vets take care of the pets,
or do the pets take care of the vets?
You drop them off and leave them there,
when you don't know what's going on in there.
The vets take care of the pets you assume
but now the pets are in charge!
So that's the story, now you know,
to always stay and watch the show
Because when there's only one vet in the room,
there could be some trouble happening soon!

Anton Ferraro, Grade 4
Stonybrook Elementary School

I Am

I am athletic and funny
I wonder if I'll become a pro-snowboarder
I hear the board gliding across the snow
I see myself going down the mountain
I want a pro's snowboard
I am athletic and funny

I pretend I'm REALLY good at snowboarding
I feel that I'm good at it
I touch the snow with the board and do a 360°
I worry about hitting a tree
I never cry
I am athletic and funny

I understand that I am good at snowboarding
I say that I can do it
I dream that I am a pro
I try to do a 540°
I hope I will become a pro
I am athletic and funny

Chris Barnish, Grade 6
John Hill School

Twin

Twin
Always my friend
Helps me with my homework
Caring, loving, sharing, helping
Best friend

Emily Hicks, Grade 4
Katharine D Malone Elementary School

The Ocean

Fish
Colorful, shiny
Calming, searching, swimming
Slow, mammal, cold-blooded, huge
Biting, eating, sneaking
Scary, fierce
Shark

Brooke Prohaska, Grade 4
Our Lady of Mount Virgin School

The Classroom

The classroom is a place of peace
A place to learn I'm sure
Then again there are the little things that drive us all insane
The squeak of a chair
The rattle of a desk
The tick of a clock
Nails on a blackboard
A classroom is like life
You learns to deal with all the little annoyances inside
The Classroom

Murf Butler, Grade 5
Toll Gate Grammar School

My Dogs

One of my dogs is a mutt.
He has a big gut.
He goes outside,
Mostly to hide.
He runs and plays,
All his days.
He never follows one rule.
He's a big fool.
My other dog is merrier,
He's a Boston Terrier.
He's black and white,
He likes to bite.
His collar is red.
He loves to go on a sled.
He's very small,
He has a big ball.
The first one's name is Apollo,
The other, Troy
They're both boys.
They're special to me,
Even if their bite stings like a bee.

Peter Stankiewicz, Grade 5
Most Holy Redeemer School

Fall

The crisp red leaves crunch
when I walk on the cold ground
in the cool forest.

Neha Hinduja, Grade 4
Franklin Park Elementary School

Beautiful

An
everlasting desert
of
numerous dandelions
rising
near the highway
Scarlet
red rubies
glisten
in the sun
Dashing
multicolored
rainbows
arise after
a ruthless thunderstorm
Rich
coated treats
dazzle
hungry men
in wonderful delight

The world is made of beauty

Davis Rohrer, Grade 5
Robert B Jaggard Elementary School

Book Life

Life is like a book,
You have to read every page.

You have to concentrate on every word,
To understand the event.

A book comes in chapters,
Event by event.

You may sometimes get tired,
And have to leave a bookmark.

You may have to go to sleep,
When it gets very dark.

You may be surprised,
On what you have heard or seen.

At least it will be,
In your wonderful dream.

Emil Sadikoski, Grade 6
Walter T. Bergen Middle School

A Puppy

Puppy do you feel lucky,
When you eat a guppy?
You must enjoy to play,
When you find a guppy under the hay.
Or would you zoom
To your room,
To play with me,
And your soft squeaky key.

Brandi Veneziale, Grade 4
Folsom Elementary School

Water

Water flows nicely
Not to disturb the beauty
Water helps all life

Katie VonSchalscha, Grade 4
Stonybrook Elementary School

Basketball

B ack on the court
A lways practicing
S wishes through the hoop
K nowing I would make the shot
E dging on your seat
T hrough the hoop
B utter fingers
A ll you can think about is winning
L ong game and ready to go home
L ose or win it's so much fun!!

Felicia Apito, Grade 6
Central Middle School

I Wish

I wish I was a rock star,
So I could be well-known.

I wish I was a scientist,
So I could make a clone.

I wish I was an explorer,
So I could find great treasure.

I wish I was a piece of cake,
So I could bring others pleasure.

I wish I was a watch,
So I could tell the time.

I wish I was a police officer,
So I could help fight crime.

Liam Baglivo, Grade 5
Byram Township Intermediate School

Moonlight

Moonlight
It shows no fright
Moonlight
It strengthens your might
Moonlight
It shines on the sea
Moonlight
Your soul feels free
Moonlight
It protects my friends
Moonlight
Its light never ends
Moonlight
It shows something new
Moonlight
It shows seedlings with dew
Moonlight
It soon goes away
Moonlight
It escapes before day

Billy Andersen, Grade 5
St Veronica Elementary School

Spring

Spring is fun,
Spring is near.
Spring is filled,
With baby deer.

Spring is fun,
Spring is cool.
Soon we'll be,
in the pool.

Lawrence Yetman, Grade 4
St Mary's School

A Raindrop

Dripping off the tips of fresh, green leaves
Down to the grassy damp ground
I trace a raindrop's path on a window
With my fingertip swirling around

What fun it must be for a raindrop
To go wherever it would please
Dangling from the rooftops
Or talking to the trees

For if I were a raindrop
I'd surely travel the world
Seeing all the lovely things
No matter how far I've twirled

Taryn Pochon, Grade 5
Old York Elementary School

Kites

Kites are dancing way up high,
Dancing in the deep blue sky.

Spring is finally awake
When the kites give the city a slight shake.

Kites make shapes as they fly by,
Making pictures in the sky.

The wind is blowing round and round,
Blowing without a single sound.

From the kites, the city can tell
That spring is here and fun as well!

Paige Halas, Grade 5
Apple Montessori School

A Day at the Zoo

I went to the zoo to see a monkey,
But all I saw was an elephant with a big long trunky,
I went out over to the lion's cage.
I saw a lion of an old old age,
Next, I saw a tiger with teeth so long and white,
He looked at me and smiled, what a frightening sight,
As I left the zoo the animals roared and cried,
I waved, I'll come back, I'll try.

Amy Krumenacker, Grade 5
Most Holy Redeemer School

Spring

S mell the sweetness in the air
P urple flowers blooming
R obins singing beautiful songs
I nsects crawling around the park
N ow the warm sun shines
G reen grass growing in the meadows.

Noa Hockstein, Grade 4
Solomon Schechter Day School of Bergen County

My First Show

My first show, I was so excited!
All the music and lights, I just couldn't hide it.
People looking all around,
Tickets falling to the ground.
When we got in the theater I held my breath,
Waiting to find out what happened next.
The lights went dim and the music started,
My heart raced when the curtains parted.
I waited to see the people come out;
To see them singing all about.
When it was over, all I could do
Was sing the songs. Wouldn't you?

Samantha Pace, Grade 6
St Veronica Elementary School

Down by the Brook Where the Little Fish Swim

Down by the brooks where the little fish swim,
A cute little fishy tried to win.
But he made himself into a yummy lure,
So a pelican swooped and took his score.

Down by the brook where the little fish swim,
A second little fishy had a simple whim.
He bravely decided to compete,
Making another meal for the pelican to eat.

Down by the brook where the little fish swim,
There was a smarter little fishy who could not swim.
He flip-flopped in the water, creating a splash,
And when he got back in, he gave a big thrash.

Down by the brook where the little fish swim,
The pelican saw and gave a big grin.
He dove down deep and missed the fish,
Hitting his head on an old, sharp, broken dish.

Down by the brook where the little fish swim,
The water was peaceful, and not grim.
The fish were not eaten,
And best of all, the pelican was beaten.

Jennifer René Alford, Grade 6
Great Meadows Regional Middle School

My Name

Kyle
It means integrity, trust and kindness.
It is 12.
It is like a dark plum.
It is the memory of my father,
Who taught me perseverance and respect,
When he raised his family.
My name is Kyle.
It means I believe in not giving up and always being respectful.

Kyle Oksten, Grade 5
Williamstown Middle School

Horses

H ave fun riding them
O h, so cuddly!!
R iding them is so exciting!
S o soft
E nthusiastic
S ometimes surprising!

Julia O'Brien, Grade 4
Main Road Elementary School

Fantasy Follies

Werewolves and vampires
Creatures of badness
Banshees and harpies
Bringers of sadness

Unicorns and phoenixes
Bring happiness and joy
Elves, fairies, pixies
They might annoy

Trolls and ogres
Ugly creatures
Dragons and mermaids
Have beautiful features

Satyrs and fauns
Followers of Pan
Minotaurs are
Part bull, part man

The Loch Ness Monster and the kraken
Creatures of the seas
Nymphs live in
Lakes, ponds, and trees

Dan Delmonaco, Grade 5
St Helena School

A Funny Bunny

I once had a bunny,
He looked kind of funny,
I named him Sunny,
And he wasn't really funny
And he was my buddy
I will never forget Sunny the bunny.

Wayne Johnson, Grade 4
Stonybrook Elementary School

Sunflowers Blooming

S unflowers blooming.
P acking picnics.
R unning, playing, having fun.
I nside or out still beautiful.
N obody stays inside.
G rabbing some sun.

James McCartney, Grade 6
Bartle Elementary School

If I Were a Cough Drop

If I were a cough drop I would be small and sticky.
I would be red and cherry-flavored.
I would be a friend to all the other raspberry cough drops in the bag.
I would be made at the Luden's factory.
I'd smell nice to all the kids.
I'd help every boy and girl.
I would die every day and then come back to life.
My wrapper is my skin.
And the words on my skin are like small cuts.

Dina Rosenski, Grade 4
Sicomac Elementary School

Snowfall

"Pow"
As the snowball forces me down I sink into the snow
The glittering chill of the snow settles on my face
I plot my revenge as I continuously roll a snowball
Too bulky to even hold
Snow tickles my face and dissolves in my mouth
I sprint inside to get a scarf, carrot, chocolate chips, and M&M's
My snowman turns out horrible, but I don't care
I create snow angels and sled through the freezing air
A snowball bursts in from nowhere and pushes me down
I struggle to get up, but then fall down again laughing
I hear winter birds chirping
As they spread their pure white wings open
I see white powder falling from the sky
I smell the aroma of hot chocolate coming from my house
I feel the warmth of my jacket and the frosty tingle of the snow

Clara Smith, Grade 5
Tamaques Elementary School

Rust

Rust oh rust! Oh how can it be,
Blind as a bat that I couldn't see,
That rust could get me, the red ribbon of glory,
The ribbon of second place, and this is the beginning of my story,

I presented my tri board, oh so tall,
With my report, results and all,
And the judges came to take a look,
Then dashed to the bleachers to write in their book,
The day went fast like a leaping leopard,
Evening arrived and with my family by my side,
I waited for the winners to be called,
A kid walked by and looked appalled,
The moment came, I WON I WON!
I never knew winning could be so much fun!
I felt like a super star ace!
But I know that it was by God's grace,
That I was awarded second place,
And my family rewarded me with a Dunkin Donuts trip…
Rust oh rust! You are real hip!
Now pass my latte so I can have a sip!

Zachary Barden, Grade 5
St Veronica Elementary School

Life in the City

I live in a city
People treat it like it's their room
Everything nice is ugly
As the darkness spreads
The city turns ugly
While the blue turns black
And the people feel cold
Then they die
While we cry and say good bye
Everybody that's good
Gets treated bad
Everybody that's bad
Gets treated good
I'd like to help
But I'm the only one in this city feeling pity
I feel
But I think
Not believe
The room needs to be clean
Good luck

Chris Fernandez, Grade 6
Mother Seton Inter Parochial School

A Friend

Someone who brightens and lightens your day.
Friends make you feel all is ok.
They come when you need them or just to have fun.
When we have a sleepover we'll stay up till one.
Friends are a treasure the old and the new,
Good friends are a gift from God to you!

Colleen Pitt, Grade 4
St Peter Elementary School

Green

Green is the water, splashing in the ocean,
Green are the leaves rustling in the trees,
Green is the grass, which gives the fields motion,
Green are the stems, pollinated by bees,
Green is the color of a football field in spring,
Green is the feeling of clearing away dust,
Green is the smell summer will bring,
Green is life that grows around us.

Myungjin (Daniel) Ro, Grade 5
Sicomac Elementary School

Dancing

Dancing
Wonderful, glamorous
Twirling, spinning, jumping
Assume elegant dance positions
Gliding, sliding, blazing
Beautiful, enchanting
Ballet

Evelyn Skelly, Grade 4
Perth Amboy Catholic Intermediate School

My Fun in the Sun

I love to have fun in the sun,
Riding waves on my boogie board
It doesn't matter if the tide is high or low,
The waves make me go.

I like to play in the sand,
Sometimes it is hot, and sometimes it is cool,
It's much more fun than being in a pool,
This is how I have fun in the sun!

Kelsey Brown, Grade 4
St Peter Elementary School

George Washington

G reat man
E xtraordinary troops
O n April 30, 1789 George Washington became President
R ested at Valley Forge
G eorge Washington was very thoughtful
E veryone likes George Washington

W ashington was a patriot
A nd fought for freedom
S aid kind things to others (except opponents)
H is Vice President was John Adams
I say he was a great President
N ot a mean person
G eneral of the Continental Army
T old the truth
O nly president who didn't live in the White House
N ever missed a meeting in Congress

Richard Stryker, Grade 4
St Mary's School

Cape May

When I am here I am replenished
All my bad thoughts drift away
When the sun sets I feel relaxed
All I want to do is lay in the cool sand
The soft waves bring joy to me
I never want to leave
As I lay in the tropical sun I feel warm
I could lose myself in all the pleasure
When I swim, in the water I feel renewed
My body, like a seashell
All I can hear is the waves
Gently rolling on the shore
Sometimes I hear the ocean speaking
It says, "Stay longer no need to rush"
the starfish and crabs tickle my feet
As the seagulls soar above
I feel as if I will stay forever in this paradise
But I know it is not true
When the day is over I am not upset
For I have yet another day in Cape May

Caitlen Perniciaro, Grade 5
St Helena School

Family Reunion

My family members happily together
The sweet laughter of my little cousins
Old memories, never to be forgotten
Joyous and content
The aroma of family recipes
This will be everlasting in my memory

Willa Davis, Grade 6
Long Branch Middle School

The Net

When I shoot the ball,
it feels like I'm six feet tall.

When I'm running up the court,
it feels like I'm playing a different sport.

When you hear the ball go "swish,"
it feels like you're being kissed.

If it goes in,
you already win!

Royell Woods, Grade 6
Franklin Elementary School

Thomas Hughes

There once was a boy named Tom.
While playing hockey he is calm.
He loves to play hockey.
I'm sure he is lucky.
Watch out N.H.L. here comes Tom.

Thomas Hughes, Grade 6
Fieldstone Middle School

Night

The darkest light
the prettiest sky
when I see the farthest star
I lie under stars
until the morning light.

Stephanie Jimenez Tavarez, Grade 5
Roosevelt Elementary School

What Really Is a Dream?

What really is a dream?
And will it make you scream?
Will they happen soon?
Maybe once in a blue moon?

Will they make you smile?
Are they worthwhile?
Can they make your personality beam?
What really is a dream?

Colette Durante, Grade 4
St Mary's School

Friends

F orgive you if you made a mistake.
R ely on you when they need your help.
I nvite you to parties or events.
E ven give you help on homework.
N ever let you down.
D o you big favors.
S eem to be the best thing you ever got.

Tommy Robbins, Grade 5
Belhaven Avenue Middle School

Vermont Sunrise

I sit on the bed looking outside,
When a golden-pink mix pours
Into the sky and dyes the clouds orange.
I watch the rays come over the hill.
As they rise, I wonder about how the sun
Makes life so peaceful at dawn and dusk.

Emma Jane Cohen, Grade 4
Community Park School

Bird Watching

I see a bird, flying away
It looks so free this early day

It makes a soothing, chirping sound
As I watch it land on the ground

Birds are happy, peaceful and free
I love to bird watch as you see

Nicole DiLeo, Grade 5
St Dominic Elementary School

I Hear the Cave Singing

I hear the cave singing
I hear the water dinging
I hear the stalagmites dripping
I hear the bats gripping
I hear the headlight switching
I hear the explorer itching
I hear the water rushing
I hear the man shushing
I hear the fish splashing
I hear the rocks bashing
I hear the scientists achieving
I hear them finally leaving

Ben Stern, Grade 4
Sicomac Elementary School

Basketball Is Fun

basketball
fun, jump
dribbling, shooting, running
have to run a lot
bball

James Bridda, Grade 4
St Mary's School

Perfect

Those celebrities in the TV screen
They look so flawless
With their perfect teeth
Perfect hair
Perfect everything.
And those people in the books,
The good guys,
They always win
And the bad guys lose.
But I know.
I know what they're hiding.
It's not like that in real life.
Life is not perfect.

Lilach Brownstein, Grade 6
Bartle Elementary School

Spring

On the twenty-first,
Flowers start to burst.
The birds are singing,
And the wind is ringing.
Birds begin to fly,
High into the sky.
The sun gets stronger,
And the days get longer.

Dominique Otiepka, Grade 4
St Joseph School

Friends Forever

People say friends come and go,
But I certainly don't think so.

Friends will cry with you,
Friends will smile with you.

They are always there,
Even when you think they don't care.

Friends know all about you,
And still love you.

Friends stick together,
Always and forever.

Emily Burke, Grade 6
Fieldstone Middle School

Dog

Dog
soft, fluffy
barks, cries, hides
cheerful, peppy, adorable
Dog

Jenna Seco, Grade 6
Fieldstone Middle School

Flowers All Around Me

Flowers, oh flowers,
all around me.
There are green ones and red ones,
they are even on a tree.
There are also white ones and yellow ones,
even orange flowers.
But there is one thing about them,
they're all around me.

Salvatore Manétto, Grade 4
St Rose of Lima School

Soccer Rules!

S is for soccer, the sport that rules!
O is for on my soccer team we have the best players.
C is for come on! Hustle! That's what my coach says.
C is for come join the team!
E is for entertaining, that's what soccer is.
R is for Rockets, that's the name of my team!

Inan Sikel, Grade 4
John F Kennedy Elementary School

Summer

Summer, taking a dip in the clear blue pool
Summer, having three months off from school.

Summer, the vacations, the parties, the friends
Summer, I wish it would never have to end.

Summer, long days and warm, clear nights
Summer, little fire flies that fly high and bright

Summer, did you know I wrote this poem for a reason?
I wrote it because you're my favorite season.

Stephanie Galea, Grade 5
St John's Academy

The Day of the Test

It's the day of the test
I'm tired because I couldn't get any rest
I was worrying about this test
There are 20 questions
And I'm shooting for at least 90 percent

It's one day later
And the teacher is handing back the tests
I didn't get mine back yet
I'm waiting and as flustered as George Bush about to talk
To the whole U.S. on national television

I finally get it back and look
It's a 100
Inside of me was a bomb ready to explode with joy
This grade was no sham
I did my best and can't wait 'til the next

Mark Cieslak, Grade 6
Fieldstone Middle School

A Wrestling God

Rey Mysterio is a wrestling wonder
When he hits you, it feels like thunder
His forty masks add to his fame
His wrestling moves add power to his name
If you have to fight him, he will put you six feet under!!!

Nicholas Coco, Grade 5
Our Lady of Mount Virgin School

Spring

Spring is here so come have fun
Spring is here everyone
Come out and play
Spring is here and I wish to say
Spring was here every day.

Nicole Rodriguez, Grade 4
The Great Commission Christian Academy

A Day in the Snow

The
Snow
Stacked
Up a foot
High against
The door makes
You feel like going
Out in the blistering winds.
When you are out there your face
Feels all tingly from the snow slapping
Against it. When you're under a tree and the snow
Falls down your back and you shiver while
It slowly and sometimes painfully
Drips down your back. After
Falling off your snowboard
Coming down a hill
Your arm feels
sore and some-
times
Bro-
ken

Philip Szalczinger, Grade 6
Immaculate Conception Regional School

Hide and Seek

Oh, how I love the game of hide and seek
I hope the seeker doesn't peek.
No telling what the seeker will find,
a person, a pet, maybe a gold mine.
How suspenseful it is to sit and wait,
to wait, and wait, and wait, and wait
Until at some point eventually,
the seeker finds, and shouts yippee!
But when you decide to play again,
who will be the seeker then?

Ezequiel Dávila, Grade 6
Gilmore J Fisher Middle School

Softball

Softball season
is finally here.
I can't wait to play
and hear the fans cheer.

When I get up to bat
it's so much fun.
This year I hope
I hit a homerun.

I may be pitched
and I think I'll do good.
I've been practicing
as my dad said I should.

I love playing
and all the new friends I meet.
The best part is when we win
we all get a treat.

Softball season
is the best time of all,
So grab your glove
and let's PLAY BALL!!!

Nicole Derise, Grade 5
Ocean Avenue Elementary School

Spring

The sun is shining,
As the flowers wave in the breeze.
The children are all out playing,
And they all seem pleased.
No one is unhappy
There's not a reason to frown.
On this nice spring day,
Everyone is happy; no one is down.

Susan Pizza, Grade 5
St Joseph School

Tropical Island

Beautiful sandy beaches
Sand between my toes
Crystal clear blue water
I forget all of my woes

Palm trees swaying in the wind
Sailboats drifting in the sea
Suntan lotion and ice cold drinks
I am so glad you are here with me

Swimming with the tropical fish
You are always looking for treasure
Being here with my whole family…
It is always a pleasure!

Kristen Nuzzolese, Grade 5
St Veronica Elementary School

My Puppy

My puppy Max is my best friend, you'll see,
He always looks up to me, and yelps when he needs me,
He cheers me up with a big wet lick, and makes me mad when he chews on sticks,
We play fetch in the park, and lay together in the dark,
A loyal friend, I know!
That is why I love him so!

Michael McMullen, Grade 4
Assumption School

Manhunt at Night

Cold shivers running down my back.
Amazingly large clouds covering the moon so it was dark as coal.
The neighbors were counting.
The rest of us were biting our nails and pulling out hair from our head.
I started sprinting to my hiding place.
I see it!
It is in the bushes.
Just enough space to fit my body.
Nobody could see me.
I dive into it because I hear footsteps coming toward me.
My stomach is doing a hundred flip-flops.
I get lower in my hiding place.
The person passes.
I come out of my hiding place.
I feel a hand on my shoulder.
I'm caught!

Sarah Leahy, Grade 5
Tamaques Elementary School

The Three Little Pigs and the Big Bad Wolf

There once lived some pigs
three I think but that doesn't matter
Anyway when they set out on their own
They were warned about the big bad wolf

One pig made his house of bricks
where he got the bricks from that doesn't matter

One made a house of sticks
but who knows where he got the sticks from but that doesn't matter

One pig wasn't very smart
making his house out of sweet smelling flowers

One day came the big bad wolf
Looking at the pig houses
he knew they would go down easily

But with all his hugging and puffing
none of the houses fell down
This must have been a very weak wolf
as for the pigs, well you know
they lived happily ever after.

Joe F. Flanagan, Grade 5
Salt Brook Elementary School

I Am

I am talented and funny
I wonder if I will ever make the baseball team
I hear God telling me YES
I see me running the bases after making a good hit
To actually do something important in my life
I am talented and funny

I pretend like I am on a Broadway stage singing my heart out
I feel my heart pounding, sounding like it is clapping for me
I feel my hand touch everyone else's as they leave the theater
I worry I will never make my dream come true
I cry just thinking about it
I am talented and funny

I understand this is a once in a lifetime opportunity
I say to God, "PLEASE help me"
I try to think positive
I hope I am right
I am talented and funny

Anthony Evans, Grade 6
John Hill School

What Is Green?

Green is a fern,
green is the grass.
Green is the leaves on an oak tree.
Green is an apple,
a pine tree.
Green is a new car
clean and polished.
Green is half of the world!

Dustin Guillemin, Grade 4
Hardyston Township Elementary School

Homework

Industriously working all day in school.
Working day and night.
No time to hang out and be cool.
Reading, writing, and arithmetic are the basic bore.
Ugh, what a chore.
All this work is like an endless climb.
I never seem to have enough time.
The lists on the Internet are there every day.
The list is too long today.
Homework is a daily pain, boring, and everlasting.

Oh, how I miss the summer.
My last swim in the pool.
Thinking about it makes me drool.
It is hard learning all the countries' names.
Let me be candid I miss my video games.
ABC and 123
It is all work to me.

James Russo, Grade 6
Fieldstone Middle School

What Is Gray?

Gray is a big, baby elephant,
It's the color of my grandma's curls.
Gray is the skin of a mole,
It's the dust on some old pearls.

Gray is a color a wolf can be,
It's a really small mouse.
Gray is lint behind a dryer,
It's the ashes of a fallen apart house.

Gray is the color of storm clouds,
It's the color of your hair when you're old.
Gray is the color of a computer mouse,
It's the color of your breath when it's cold.

Gray is the feeling when you're scared,
It's sometimes the color of a ceiling.
Gray is the color a marble can be,
It's the color of something that's peeling.

Courtney Conrad, Grade 5
Sandman Consolidated Elementary School

Spring Is Here!

Spring is the season when the flowers spring up singing!
The trees reach so high that they almost touch the sky!
The ladybugs and butterflies rejoice with the sun!
Spring is here everybody cheer!!

Brenna Carrigy, Grade 6
St Veronica Elementary School

My Skinny Locker

My locker is really skinny…
Like the pasta linguini.
I do not like my skinny messy locker.
I see it every day.
But…I use it anyway.
My locker is really mini.
My locker is really funky.
It is the color of a monkey
I intensify the limit of getting there.

I wish I could say goodbye.
I think you all know why.
I want to say goodbye.
Maybe in July.
I guess it's just the beginning of a new hi.
I wish it were shiny.
I wish I had the say…
Maybe possibly to…
Have the authority to change it every day.

My friends say it's messy Jessi.
I say don't pick on me…
Let me be with my skinny messy funky mini LOCKER!

Jessica McFarlane, Grade 6
Fieldstone Middle School

Draw
D ream
R ainbow
A rt
W onderful
Chris DiPisa, Grade 5
Ocean Avenue Elementary School

Spring
Spring is here,
Spring is there,
I want to plant flowers
Everywhere.

It's not that simple
To grow flowers,
Because when I did it
It took me hours.

I planted lilies
Tulips and a rose.
After that I had to
Water them with a hose.

Soon later
The sun came out
And the flowers
Started to grow.
Julia Topor, Grade 5
St Joseph School

I Made a Mistake
I went to the park to see a duck,
I made a mistake…and sat on a puck.

I went to the zoo to see a moose,
I made a mistake…and got a goose.

I went to the gym to get some miles,
I made a mistake…and got a tile.

I went to the store to get a mop,
I made a mistake…and found a cop.

I went to L.A. to see a band,
I made a mistake…and saw a man.

I went to my room to get a book,
I made a mistake…and found a hook.

I went to the moon to get a spoon,
I made a mistake…and found a dune.

I went to the show to see my friend,
I made a mistake…and found the end.
Andrew Hartophilis, Grade 4
Sicomac Elementary School

Blooming
B eautiful, fragrant, colorful flowers,
L ife bursting out of the ground.
O rigin of this sunny season,
O bviously we all love spring.
M any bees sipping the nectar;
I nviting flowers welcome them.
N ever a flower without beauty,
G oing to the garden to look at them.
Shira Yellin, Grade 4
Solomon Schechter Day School

My First Day of School
My first day of school was a blast
I broke my leg and got a cast
I ran too fast
In full blast
Into fiberglass
Megan Helmig, Grade 6
Chatham Middle School

Being an Eagle
If I were an eagle
I'd be defiant,
soaring in the lovely sapphire sky,
waiting for my prey to arrive.

My divine wings flapping,
catching a glimpse of the green carpet,
awaiting every human.

My firm spine
allowing me to be dauntless,
I'd be invincible,
when I had to hunt.

My pointy beak
pecking at little things,
dominating whenever I pleased,
gliding in the air,
being arrogant.
Caroline Chagares, Grade 4
Sicomac Elementary School

The In Crowd
The kids in the in crowd,
they feel so very proud.
They think they're in the cool clique,
yet to me that seems like a trick.
They think they're so smart,
but do they have a loving heart.
But always in the end,
be the great friend.
Jacklyn Churchill, Grade 6
St Veronica Elementary School

Springtime
The rabbits are coming out.
It is still very cold.
And I'm numb from running 'bout.
It should be warm I've been told.

March is a time for fun.
It is when flowers bloom.
You can play in the sun.
March will be over soon.

The sky is always blue.
The grass is turning green.
I hope you like March too!
The tree buds are to be seen.
Taylor Zaleski, Grade 4
St Mary's School

Sports
Sports are so fun,
When you play them in the sun.

When you score a basket or a goal,
You feel the happiness in your soul.

When the different seasons start,
You have to really want to take a part.

Basketball is the best,
Better than all the rest.
Gianni Cucciniello, Grade 4
St Rose of Lima School

Music Rocks
M any
U nbelievable
S ongs
I
C an't

R esist
O ver and over again
C raving for some more
K inds are bad
S ome are great!

I love music!
Ann Claire Macalintal, Grade 5
Robert L Craig Elementary School

Fishing
Fishing on the deep blue sea,
There is no place I would rather be,
I love reeling in big fish,
It is my one and only wish.
Colin Fitzpatrick, Grade 5
Springfield Township School

Summer, Yay!

Summer makes the greatest year
Walking on all those boardwalk piers
Swimming in the pools are fun
Summer has the brightest sun.
Hopefully it's not that far
Vacation of catching fireflies in jars.
It's not winter, spring or fall,
Summer is a favorite to all!
I wish it really couldn't end
There's more time to play with friends.
Waking up to see it's bright,
Me and my sister can never fight.
You may sometimes see a bee
I really hope it doesn't sting me!
Knowing you don't have to wake up for school
That part is really cool
You can stay up very late
And sleeping in feels really great!
But soon enough, summer will end.
And we'll all have to go to school again!

Amber McGonegal, Grade 5
Roosevelt School

Our New Destiny

We sailed the ocean blue
To seek our new destiny of life.
Day by day we hoped to find the
promised land, America.
Then the glorious words came
"Land Ho."

Jessica Williams, Grade 6
Township of Ocean Intermediate School

I Am

I am athletic and quiet
I wonder how my grades are
I hear my conscience telling me to study
I see the world in my hands
I want my own money
I am athletic and quiet

I pretend I'm rich
I feel ghost-like
I touch my inner soul
I worry about my parents
I cry when someone important to me walks out of my life
I am athletic and quiet

I understand I can't always get what I want
I say what I believe in
I dream about my future
I try hard in school
I hope my future is successful
I am athletic and quiet

Steph Charette, Grade 6
John Hill School

Flowers

Flowers, flowers everywhere,
this is the poem I'd like to share.
Walking through the garden it's so much fun,
underneath the yellow bright sun.
Smell the hot pink rose,
it tickles your barefoot toes.
The aromas of flowers fill the air,
and that was the poem I wanted to share.

Christina Holl, Grade 5
St Veronica Elementary School

Hate or Love

I hate the way you talk to me,
how you go on and say nice things about me.

If it's my hair or my eyes,
don't say goodbye.

I hate your cute smile and your face,
not a disgrace, just me and you.

Will you ever say the way you feel?
I hope you do.

But most importantly,
I love the way I "hate" you.

Alicia Pagan, Grade 6
John Hill School

Summer

Summer is fun, summer is great,
the ocean, the pool, the board walk, a clam bake!
Bathing suits, surf boards, all the gear,
the ocean, the pool, a vacation is near!
The soft sand in my toes,
soft as a voice on the fourth of a July.
Family and friends in the sun,
they laugh, they talk and have lots of fun.
The summer is fun, the summer is great,
see you in June, don't be late!

Katie Cappola, Grade 5
Liberty Corner Elementary School

I Will Not Clean My Room

It is clean!
It does not smell.
The dust bunnies like it here.
You can see a little bit of my floor,
My dog is sleeping on my floor right now.
I can find everything in here, SEE!
My friends don't mind it,
I'll pay you to clean it,
I just won't do it.

Corrine Ann Pine, Grade 4
Mansfield Township Elementary School

Summer

It must be summer,
'Cause it's getting funner,
So, go out on a day,
You could even play!

There is no school,
That is so cool,
No spelling, science, even math,
You don't even have to take a bath!

Shane Park, Grade 4
Stonybrook Elementary School

Indiana

I is for independent
N is for neat
D is for dancer
I is for intelligent
A is for active
N is for nice
A is for artistic

Indiana Ross, Grade 5
Robert L Craig Elementary School

Basketball

You don't need to be tall
To play basketball

It is so much fun
Just like playing in the sun

You can shoot and score
And keep hoping for more

I love to play this sport
Especially on a beautiful wood court

This is a really fun game
And BASKETBALL is its name!

Chrissy Mascarelli, Grade 6
Fieldstone Middle School

Summer

Summer is fun. Summer is great.
It's a time I don't hate.
Summer is just for laying in the sun.
It's a time to play and have fun.
Summer is a time to hit the beach,
To make sand castles every week.
It's time to say, "Hurray,"
For not staying in school all day.
Summer is a time to play with friends,
And to stay up all night on weekends.
Summer I wish would last all year,
So all my friends would always be near.

Connor Fecso, Grade 4
St Rose of Lima School

What Is Black?

Black is the color of shadows, it engulfs the menacing night,
It's an opaque color, and it can bring much fright.

Galloping through the night, can be a ghastly black horse,
Tearing through the air, with a great amount of force.

It's death's true color, a storm's favorite one,
Pen ink is mostly black, the color pushes away the sun.

A spinel jewel can be black, a dark raven's mother,
A diamond jewel can be black, it takes over most other colors.

Black may be a falcon, black could be a cat,
Black is a deep hole, and black can be a rat.

Black is the mouth of a cave, a haunted house's dead end,
Clarinets are usually black, it's quite a sinister blend!

The color of an ash, a color to detest,
The true thing about this color though, is that is seeps through the rest!

Liam Munz, Grade 5
Sandman Consolidated Elementary School

My Hero, My Mom

My mom is like a warrior,
Who protects me, like a lion protects her cubs.
She is my hero.
My mom has always been by my side,
Singing like beautiful wind chimes when I was a child,
Tucking me in at night. My mom is the greatest.
She helps me with my homework.
She even takes care of three cats.
My mom takes care of them and feeds them.
She takes care of three dogs and three horses.
My mom takes me to horseback riding every Tuesday.
She also loves and cares for our dogs
And that is why all our animals love her so much.
Mom you are my hero, my guardian angel.
You protect me and love me.
I hope to grow up and be just like you,
Because you can do anything, and you are the sweetest person ever.
Mom, you care for kids of three, have a job,
You are and will always be a hero to me.
Mom, you are the best person I know in the whole world.
I love you, Mom, and you are my hero!

Brooke De John, Grade 5
North Dover Elementary School

Elements in Action

Fire is as mean as an older brother when his little brother annoys him
Wind is as gentle as God
Ice goes away for spring
Rock is as hard as a human fist
Water plays tag with the shore

William Alexander Hart, Grade 6
Little Egg Harbor Intermediate School

Night

As the bright morning
Begins to fade,
Into the dark night
It is as if the morning sun goes to sleep
And the silent moon wakes.
For the cold night closes in
So we are forced to go away to our warm beds.

Nicholas Douglass, Grade 5
Sandman Consolidated Elementary School

D-Man

My dad is my hero
And I love him so
But when he pushes me
I go go go
When I'm down and gloomy
And feeling very sad
My dad cheers me up
And makes me feel so glad
I love basketball
And so does my dad
I think his team is great
He thinks they're bad
He was playing Rahway
In the State Championship
They unfortunately lost
But the game was a hit
My dad's 50th party was very cool
But I felt bad, because I beat him at pool
My dad is awesome
He cares for three
He's the best thing that has ever happened to me!

Kody Fenchel, Grade 5
North Dover Elementary School

Life

Life is a dream, that we all hold.
Some have been found some are unknown.

Life is a breeze, in the air.
That swirls around, without any care.

Life is our future, will be seen.
It will be clear, and it will be clean.

Life is a gift, given from above.
Brought to you by your family, smothered with love.

Life is a mystery, that cannot be solved.
It grows larger and longer, and slowly evolves.

Then life slowly grows older, without a purpose.
It gently moves away; it vanishes, into a vast, cold world.

Christina Haywood, Grade 6
Walter T. Bergen Middle School

The Ugly Trolls

Three ugly trolls, big and dumb
Saw Bilbo Baggins, forest from
But when the hobbit tried to steal
They grabbed him, made him loudly squeal!

Three ugly trolls, big and dumb
Thought, "What to do with this piece of scum?
Let him free, or cook alive?"
One troll preferred to let him thrive.

Three ugly trolls, big and dumb
Called each other "fool" and "bum"
Till Gandalf came and proceeded to
Continue to make the trolls argue.

Three ugly trolls, big and dumb
Fought until they all got numb
For they had brawled around the clock
And, come the dawn, they turned to rock.

Katie Little, Grade 6
Indian Hill Elementary School

My Magical Net

I hold my net with nothing in it
as I run, still holding it up high
I see a butterfly fluttering by
and I capture it so it can forever be peaceful

With my magic net I run to the park
I spot a puppy tied to a tree, crying
with all the sympathy my heart can hold
I put it in my net so it can be in paradise

With my magic net I go to the fields
and see a bright red rose swaying in the wind
gently so I don't ruin the beauty
I pick it up and place it in my net
now it will have enough rain and sun to live

With my magic net I walk home
I think of all the memories with my family
I capture every happy memory
so I can hold and look at them
for the rest of my life

Erin DiGuglielmo, Grade 5
Salt Brook Elementary School

Fear

Fear is gray.
It smells like dead fish in the ocean.
It looks like a robber breaking into your house.
It tastes like poison.
It sounds like a window shattering.
Fear feels like falling off the biggest cliff in the world…

Danielle Matteo, Grade 6
St Rose of Lima School

Cleaning the Table

I can't clean the table.
My fingers ache.
I have stomach viruses.
My head feels like a rake.
I don't feel up to it.
I can't take this anymore.
Please just leave me alone.
Before I start a loud tome.
I don't feel like doing it.
But maybe I'll try a little bit.
Hey this isn't that bad.
Now, I don't feel that mad.

Amanda Frappolli, Grade 4
Mansfield Township Elementary School

Shopping

I like to go shopping.
I buy lots of clothes.
I like to buy shoes,
All different colors inside.
Some are rainbow, red, and blue.
I like to buy coats,
All furry inside.
I like to buy funky shirts,
Some yellow some blue.
Shopping is a dream come true.

Kirby George, Grade 4
St Rose of Lima School

I Admire Billy Joel

I admire Billy Joel.
I love Billy Joel's music.
One you start listening to it,
You can't stop!
When you play it on the piano,
You can't stop!
When you sing it,
You can't stop!
I like how most of his lyrics rhyme.
His songs have really good melodies.
When I grow up,
I want to write music like Billy Joel.

Luciano Minetti, Grade 4
Christ the Teacher School

Day and Night

Kids play in the day
and sleep in the night
Kids love to play video games
and bike outside
Kids dream of having lots of fun
the next day.

Joshua Levy, Grade 5
Community School of Bergen County

My Life as a Chalkboard

I hate getting written on.
Most of the time people stare at me.
It is fun being cleaned.
The bad part is that I can't move.
Lucky for me I get to learn for free.

Douglas Cardoza, Grade 6
Thorne Middle School

Felines

Felines
Lovely things
Jumping, lying, meowing
Dancing with much grace
Beauties

Madelaine Doherty, Grade 6
Sacred Heart Elementary School

Rollerblade

I can do 360's
I think the halfpipe is nifty
Watch how high I fly
I do very cool tricks in the sky
The trees go by in a flash
I hope I don't crash

Peter Pravata, Grade 6
Fieldstone Middle School

Spring

Spring
Sunny, warm
Boating, hitting, dribbling
Playing sports are fun
Lacrosse

Lauren Kubler, Grade 4
Meadowbrook Elementary School

This Halloween

This Halloween
each time I went to a doorstep,
memories came to me.
At one house there were
tombstones in the ground.
At another house they
were throwing a birthday party,
so no candy.
At the end of that night,
my friends and I
counted our candy
like bank tellers.
We talked about it
many times after that,
but it was never as
sweet as holding
that candy in our hands.

Stojan Goranovic, Grade 5
Durban Avenue Elementary School

Friendship

We shop 'til we drop
And tell each other secrets.
We sleep over at each other's house
To party all night long!!

Rachael Purdy, Grade 4
Middle Township Elementary School #2

Puppy/Slime

Puppy
playful, active
charming, barking, sleeping, outrageous,
friendly, yucky, messy, grass, sticky,
oozing, disgusting, mushy,
Slime.

Jaquanay Macklin, Grade 4
Mansfield Township Elementary School

Moon Dreams

Moon dreams about clouds
Moon dreams about stars
Moon remembers planets.
Moon moves like a slow snail
Moon is the promise of hope.
Moon vacations the Earth
Moon is a sign of peace.

Leanne Manna, Grade 4
Pond Road Middle School

New York

I hear the people running fast
I hear breaking glass

I hear the sirens ringing
I hear the kids swinging

I hear a lady getting robbed
I hear people losing their jobs

I hear a plane crashing
I hear people dashing

I hear the cops yelling
I hear the vendors selling

I hear the cars speeding
I hear the pedestrians proceeding

I hear the kids bouncing balls
I hear the people in the malls

I hear the yellow taxi
I hear America, I am free!

Danny Rakow, Grade 4
Sicomac Elementary School

Old Man Frank

There once was an old man named Frank,
Who worked and worked til he stank.
But when he came home,
He didn't answer the phone,
And now he's in trouble with the bank.

Patrick Carver, Grade 4
Mansfield Township Elementary School

Cat

There once was a cat,
He ate my pet bat.
Then he ate a mouse,
He tried to eat my house.
What do you think about that?

Joseph Pellicone, Grade 4
St Mary's School

Fairy Tale

F lying through the night they sprinkle magic fairy dust.
A ll of the fairies are beautiful.
I n Neverland is where you see them most.
R ight by your side when you need one.
Y ou can only know the magic of fairies if you believe.

Alexa Zito, Grade 5
Assumption School

Foxes

Foxes,
Foxes,
Foxes,
Fennec, Red, Sahara foxes,
Nasty, adorable, sly, foxes
These are just a few
Intelligent foxes,
Small-minded foxes,
Interactive, aggressive, shy foxes,
Carmel color, white, jet black foxes,
Captive foxes too,
Newborn foxes,
Frail old foxes,
Don't forget extinct foxes

Last of all, best of all
I love
All foxes!

Cassandra Grod, Grade 5
Ridgeway Elementary School

Love

Love is a rope.
It stays together.
When it is cut.
It falls apart.
Love is no more.

Gordon Jamieson, Grade 6
Township of Ocean Intermediate School

Winter in the Woods

As I crunched through the snow,
The crisp pine smell filled my nose.
Pine trees swayed in the blowing wind,
Sunrise returned the sky blush pink
With the clouds forming plushy pillows.

Whoo, Whoo, and Whoo,
My voice called out,
Slowly responding, an owl whooped.
He silently made a perch for himself
On a huge grandmom oak.
Those golden eyes glistened at me.
The gold rays in his eyes shined so bright,
Just like the heavenly sun,
Forever and ever.

Julia Perhacs, Grade 4
Pond Road Middle School

The March of the Penguins

We are marching
Tired, hungry, but together.
It is frigid, icy, and barren
Here in the Antarctic.
Headed to where our mothers gave birth.
Headed to where we will give birth.

Plunged into ice and snow —
Marching through blizzards and storms,
But we are still together huddled and warm.

Some of us will die along the way,
Some of us will live.
Will our babies survive?
Some of them will.

I, the Emperor Penguin,
Must lead my colony.
We are tired, hungry, but together.

Suveer Bhatia, Grade 4
Community Park School

Time Traveling

I woke up one morning in my old shaggy bed,
I saw a bright tunnel that appeared beet red,
I jumped into it to see what was inside,
Other people would say it was a lie,
I ended up being in a dinosaur park,
Let me tell you those dinosaurs really can bark,
Then I leaped back into the present,
There my ears felt a little more pleasant,
I saw a flying car over my head,
Then I realized it was a dream and I was still in bed.

Deanna Fatigato, Grade 5
St Veronica Elementary School

Statue of Gold

There once was a statue of gold,
That soon became covered in mold.
    The King cleaned it up,
    With maple syrup,
And now it is sticky and old.
Joshua Wells, Grade 4
West End Memorial Elementary School

Spring Flowers

Flowers
All different kinds
They are so beautiful
Every day flowers spring from buds
Carnation
Alexis Huguenel, Grade 4
Katharine D Malone Elementary School

Spring Is Truly Here

Whistling softly now…
Swirling, spinning through the trees…
Spring breeze is blowing.

Beautiful weather…
Bright, lively, wonderful days…
Spring sun is shining.

Rainbow of colors…
Different but always the same…
Spring flowers have grown.

Noisy, yet so calm…
Rainy, yet so very nice…
Spring is truly here!
Kathleen Davin, Grade 4
St Mary's School

Spring Has Sprung

S alamanders crawl next to the water.
P retty flowers bloom in the sun.
R aindrops fall quickly from the sky.
I nch worms roam in the soft ground.
N ightingales fly gracefully in the sky.
G rasshoppers hop in the green grass.
Liat Kugelmass, Grade 4
Solomon Schechter Day School

One Wish

One wish,
Just one,
Oh I know,
I'll wish I could have a bubble
big enough for me to fit in!
It could bring me up above the clouds!
Maybe I'll wish for it, right now!
Samantha Smith, Grade 4
St Peter Elementary School

School

Teachers, classrooms, chalkboards, and quizzes.
Projects and due dates.
So much to remember.
The capital of New Hampshire is Concord.
8 times 4 is 32.
Math, reading, writing and language.
Social studies, science, along with spelling.
Many rules to follow.
1. No talking.
2. Respect everyone.
3. Listen carefully to all instructions.
You don't hear much noise until recess and lunch where we all play.
It isn't much fun that I must say.
But I still have to go every day.

Sarah Hearon, Grade 5
Tamaques Elementary School

Shane Myer

Shane
Messy, caring, nice, and little
Brother of Brandon
Lover of pasta, dogs, and eating
Who feels happy when playing with my dog,
Sad when punished, and annoyed when bothered by my brother
Who needs family, more time to study, and to improve my reading
Who gives money and food to the poor, gifts, love
Who fears the dark, staying alone, and mushrooms
Who would like to swim with sharks, train dogs, and go to Australia
Resident of Wyckoff on Lynch Place
Myer

Shane Myer, Grade 4
Sicomac Elementary School

It's My Mom We're Talking About!

My mom is as helping as the North Star to help you find your way home.
I am addicted to her.
She is always there for me no matter what the problem is.
She is so industrious in everything it scares me.
This is her job and she won't quit.
She has been there through the hardest and the easiest.
"We'll get through it I promise," she always says.
I finally think I know we will because it's my mom we're talking about!

But it's hard when she wants me there for her.
To see that tear drop down from her graceful eye.
It's just too hard,
Sometimes I just want to cry.
But I know we'll still get through it,
Because it's my mom we're talking about.
When I get hurt inside and out, she's there.
So Mom thank you for being there when I need you most.

My mom is as helping as the North Star to help me find my way home!
Sarah Elmiry, Grade 6
Fieldstone Middle School

Paine

There was once a smart boy named Paine,
Who had an enormous brain,
   His grades were the same,
   A's just came and came.
'Til later he went insane.

Ivan Olvera, Grade 4
West End Memorial Elementary School

My Fantasy

Come in, my child, and you will see,
The wonders of my glorious fantasy,
Where war is abolished and light never ends.
The fox and the rabbit will always be friends.

My fantasy, my fantasy, is my place alone.
The flowers have bloomed and the rivers have flown.
It's quiet, it's peaceful, no troubles are there,
Except when bad people come into my lair.

A shot rings out, a woman cries,
I see it before my very eyes.
My home has been tattered, and ripped, and torn.
I drop to my knees and begin to mourn.

My fantasy's gone; I have no place to go.
New seeds in my life are what I must sow.
I never thought fantasies could be destroyed.
But then again, emotions were never toys.

Amy Russo, Grade 6
Sampson G Smith Intermediate School

I Made a Mistake

I went in my room to look for a ball,
I made a mistake…and was in a hall.

I went to the bathroom to comb my hair,
I made a mistake…and found a papa bear.

I went with my parents to find a house,
I made a mistake…and found a mouse.

I went to Florida to see the balloons,
I made a mistake…and was on the moon.

I went to school to learn some math,
I made a mistake…and ate 89 hats.

I went to the circus to see the clown,
I made a mistake…and found a noun.

I went to the store to buy some foam,
I made a mistake…and wrote this poem.

Kristen Gilbride, Grade 4
Sicomac Elementary School

The Fast Lane

Speeding around a wild banked track,
trying to stay at the front of the pack.
Going at speeds at about 183,
tinkering with the car to see what it may be.
Leading the pack on the final lap,
is a real honor if you're not a sap.
Celebrating for the win by a margin of 2,
in victory lane with your crew and you!

Brian Dolph, Grade 6
Franklin Elementary School

Wind

Smashing, crashing everywhere.
Flying here, and flying there.
Twirling, swirling, making whirling turns.
Blowing, slowing around the trees.
Even picking up the fallen leaves.

Michelle Marie Pendas, Grade 4
Christ the Teacher School

Winter

Winter is the time to play in the snow
We have snowball fights you know
When it is time to go inside
We have hot cocoa with the fireplace by our side
The next day in the morning we hope it will be snowing.

Justin Thomas Licciardello, Grade 5
Indian Hill Elementary School

The Rush to Win

Click clack clack WHAM!
I feel a rush of energy as I hit the ball into the goal
Biting my new rubber mouth guard in concentration.
The field calls me,
"Come play, I need to be broken in."
I yearn to be on that field.

The field is a meadow of freedom.
Leaving me to have fun
And to be competitive.
Being defense is tough
Dodging balls from all angles
Zooming at me like comets passing through the Milky Way.

Offense has lots of responsibility
Running all around the field
You get tired easily.
Forgetting about the many rules
I make a 360 degree turn
And the referee yells out, "Obstruction, seven, green!"

Dribbling, I sprint as fast as I can
Trying to beat my guard to the goal.
I score, and hear the crowd's thunderous applause.

Courtney Gnash, Grade 6
Woodglen Middle School

My Friend

My friend is cool
I go with her to school.
We go to the bay.
And she would always say,

Let's go on the sand.
We can tan.
Then let's go in the bay
As we drift away.

Cortney Hanson, Grade 5
Our Lady of Mount Virgin School

My Beach House

I am going to my beach house,
It is where I like to play.
I am going to my beach house,
where a week feels like a day.

My beach house is by the ocean,
Where the ice cream man comes to sell,
His ice cream vanilla or chocolate,
Both of them are swell.

My beach house is my favorite place,
Because of all the sights I see.
I hope when I come back next year,
My beach house will remember me.

Carrie Schroeder, Grade 5
St John's Academy

I Used to, But Now…

I used to have two grandparents
but now I have none

I used to have light skin
but now it's darker

I used to like the color purple
but now I like the color blue

I used to be short
but now I'm taller

I used to have one mom
now I have two

I used to have fifty cousins
now I have fifty one.

I used to have one hundred friends
but now I only have ten.

I used to crawl
but now I walk.

Meah Jones, Grade 4
Franklin Park Elementary School

Spring's Things

Flowers
Elegant plants
Growing, blossoming, sprouting
Rainbows blooming on grass
Stationary

Rain
Heavenly showers
Refreshing, drenching, cleansing
Tears of angels' weeping
Purifier

Birds
Tranquil souls
Flying, darting, crooning
Swimming in the sky
Angels

Caterpillars
Unusual creatures
Wiggling, inching, transforming
Harmless little legged snakes
Crawlers

Amanda Kontor, Grade 6
Sacred Heart Elementary School

I Can't Do My Homework

I forgot it.
Kitty ate it.
It's Friday.
We don't have any pencils.
I have other things to do.
I'm busy!
What about my chores?
What?!?
It's Sunday already?!?
What?
Bedtime?
But my teacher is going to be furious!
Oh well.

Kara Chamberlin, Grade 4
Mansfield Township Elementary School

My Little Green Friend

My odd green buddy
Is dirty and covered with muddy.
He's always eating glue,
And is chewing my shoe.
And oddly this is nothing new.
He speaks Chinese.
And has many fleas.
He's an alien how about, you?

Michael Marinaro, Grade 5
Most Holy Redeemer School

My Brother

My brother is mean.
My brother is tall.
But when he's nice
he wants to play ball.

My brother has
a lot of friends
and he collects
tons of pens.

My brother inspires me,
oh, so much.
But if I tell him
he'll give me a punch.

So I'll keep quiet
and shut my mouth
So he won't punch me
all the way south!

Shana Hayes, Grade 5
Roosevelt Elementary School

Winter

The wind stings my cheeks
I'm afraid to go outside
I want to stay warm.

Abigail Wilson, Grade 4
Wayside Elementary School

The Grand Rainforest

Blazing golden sun
Birds singing to heaven light
Woosh! Wind wrestling down.

Anna Rulli, Grade 4
West End Memorial Elementary School

My Messy Room

There's posters all over the wall,
Be careful not to fall.
Clothes wrestling on the bed,
The hamster is dead.
You can't see the door,
You can't even see the floor.
My sock is in the fish bowl,
My bowling ball doesn't roll.
You can't bend,
And that is the end!

Taylor Donnellan, Grade 4
Woods Road Elementary School

Rain

Rain comes quick and loud,
And you know when it's coming
So look up and see.

Jennifer Cooney, Grade 6
Robert L Craig Elementary School

Winter's Wonder
Winter's wonder is the snow,
Who doesn't like it I'd like to know.
It's so cold out I'm gonna freeze,
Then when I thaw I start to sneeze.
Then when I get my hot cocoa,
There's so much sugar I go loco.
Then when it starts to get warm out,
I get so mad I start to shout.
A blanket of snow would really be nice,
With the buckets and buckets and buckets of ice.
Oh why, oh why, can't it always be snowy,
I would love it from my head to my toey.
But even though now I am an old grandfather,
I still think about snow, but why do I bother?
Because ever since I was a boy,
I've always loved snow, the greatest joy.

Anthony Vitagliano, Grade 4
Friends School

Happiness
Happiness is bright yellow.
It smells like sweet flowers in the spring.
It looks like a cute puppy playing in the grass
or a small baby smiling at you.
It sounds like the laughter of some little
kids playing together and having fun.
Happiness feels like a cold ice cream sundae
on a hot summer day at the beach.

Kayla Dunn, Grade 6
St Rose of Lima School

The Sun
The sun rises in the morning shining so bright
it's yellow, orange, and even red.
It makes us warm in the day.
At the end it makes a sunset.
Then the sun leaves, but not forever.
It will come again the next day.
At the night it brings its friends.
The moon and stars to bright the night again.

Julio Rivas, Grade 4
Mother Seton Inter Parochial School

My Friends
My friend Madi is really funny,
Sometimes when I'm with her, she hops like a bunny.
My other friend Hayley is really nice,
Did I mention she hates mice!
My good friend Geena loves to play,
And she loves the month of May!
My friend Casey is really cool,
When you get to know her, you'll see she is a soccer fool!
Having friends is greater than ever,
And I really love being together!

Keri Kiernan, Grade 4
St Rose of Lima School

Virginia Avenue
It's not in the state of the same name.
It has four houses that look the same.
You can hear the traffic throughout the night.
Even though there is not one traffic light.
From the deli to the pretzel store
On my street you'll be hungry no more.

Alana Colontonio, Grade 4
Holy Saviour School

The Heart of the Horse
The heart of the wind
Rushing by
Your soul aflutter
Your heart bouncing through the clouds
Her mane thrashing through the wind
Her tail prancing over the hills
Her legs bending and twisting through the steady gallop
She is tired but she won't give up
She is a horse
And I am a spirit
And we are one

Emily Smith, Grade 5
Bedminster Township Elementary School

Serenity
Serenity is blue
It smells like an aroma of freshly baked cookies
It looks like a sun setting on a beach
It tastes like a yummy piece of chocolate
melting in my mouth
It sounds like the sea water washing up on the shore
Serenity feels like a soothing massage at a day spa
after a hard day of working

Justine Galang, Grade 6
St Rose of Lima School

Forever Free
Lovely tan meets snowy white,
Please do not run in fright.

Small black hooves,
Cloven it moves,
Running fast away from wolves.

Large doe eyes filled with bright light,
The little ones never leave its sight.

Grassy green meadows shaped round, like a bowl,
All these things, they make me whole.

Sleek and swift it starts to bound,
For it is free, running across the ground.

Jessica Nardolillo, Grade 6
Hardyston Middle School

The Blue in Between

Every day the clouds in the sky make our imaginations go wild, but what about in between the clouds?
The river rushing down the bluffs; the women hanging up her sheets on a breezy day;
You may not, but I see the blue in between.
The fair face of a child, eyes full of pain; a young boy and his sailboat;
You may not, but I see the blue in between the scene of a party;
A quilt that reminds you of the one your grandma made you when you were young.
You may not, but I see the blue in between.

Tatiana Fulmer, Grade 6
Gilmore J Fisher Middle School

Snow Day

Today I woke up to a perfect, white blanket of snow.
The enormous smile on my face meant school was cancelled!
The snowflakes falling from the sky were as immense as marshmallows.
I hurried outside to build a couple of friendly snowmen to guard my beautiful snow covered house.
When I came in from the bitter cold I had hot cocoa in front of a blazing fire.
Snow days are like getting all A's on your report card!

Mike Foster, Grade 5
Sandman Consolidated Elementary School

If I Were...

If I were red I'd be anger being expressed on someone's face, or I'd be a cherry waiting to be eaten.
If I were orange, I'd be the color of a goldfish swimming happily in its bowl.
If I were yellow, I'd be the sun or a star shining down to Earth, or a buttercup blossoming in the spring.
If I were green, I'd be the grass in the vast forest, or the stem of a beautiful flower, sprouting up from the ground.
If I were pink, I'd be a lollipop at the fair, or a breathtaking tulip in the meadow.
If I were all of these colors, I'd be a rainbow shining beautifully in the spring sky.

Ariana Sedaghat, Grade 5
Sicomac Elementary School

Family

The best things in life are important, like your parents, and your grandparents, and brother and sister.
In a way, this is what you call a good luck charm, this is what keeps you out of trouble. They may yell and scream at you, but personally, they're all you have. A lot of kids think parents are here to keep us like this forever, but they're not, they're here to protect us. A lot of us think that grandparents are here to pinch our cheeks, but they're not. A lot of us think brothers and sisters are only here to annoy us, but they're not. They are just like your friends except they love and cherish you more. You may say they're the worst people in the world, but they're the best in yours.

Nazirah Wilson, Grade 5
Tamaques Elementary School

It Should Be #1 and Not #2

I never really wondered,
Why is the number 2 on the really good pencils.
It doesn't make me think too much.
I always hear that the #2 pencils are the best.
The one precise lead that the computers can read clearly.
It really bothers me now, like a flea bothering a dog.

It should be #1 on the pencil and not the #2, because it is the BEST!
But I guess I have no authority to change, explain, or complain to the pencil company about my problem.
I don't have the largest aspire to know why it is the #2.
I guess it's just the way it should be.
I acquire many of these "number 2" pencils.
But I still don't know why it must be the number 2.

Chelsea Chung, Grade 6
Fieldstone Middle School

Love

Love is pink
It smells like a lovely sweet perfume
It looks like candy on a shelf you want to taste
and help yourself
It tastes like a box of sweet, tasty, truffles
It sounds like the chirping of birds in the spring
Love feels like you're on top of the world

Casey Shea, Grade 6
St Rose of Lima School

Fear

Fear is black.
It smells like a dirty alley.
It looks like something creeping through the shadows.
It tastes like stale Halloween candy.
It sounds like someone screaming.
Fear feels like your heart beating out of control
and your whole body becoming numb.

Tommy Mergenthaler, Grade 6
St Rose of Lima School

I Admire Mom

I always admire my mom.
She teaches me how to cook and
How to clean the house.
Sometimes she gives me good reasons to do something.

She's always on my side when I get in trouble.
Now, when I grow up,
I'm going to do all the things my mom has done for me.
I'll always love her no matter what.
When she's upset, I'll always cheer her up!

Angelique Matesic, Grade 4
Christ the Teacher School

A Special Place

My special place is the old farm,
with the slowly moving river,
to the old wooden barns,
with cows mooing happily as they chew on the tall green grass,
which is a beautiful green grasshopper color,
with hints of brown and black,
The rolling fields with the tall weeds blowing,
and the wind singing songs of joy,
The sweet silence, and then,
the old red truck starts in the distance,
Its roaring engine scares the cattle to the pastures,
The truck's rumbling sounds are sweet and sorrowful
bringing back old memories of joy,
with the barn's creaking broken boards swaying in the wind,
as if in a dance,
the never ending dance of life...

Hannah Black, Grade 5
Salt Brook Elementary School

A Day at the Beach

Sunlight reflects on foamy ocean
Bluish waves glitter like stars
Salty water rushes with motion
Nature's beauty untouched, unmarred

Feet sinking into soft grainy sand
Ocean breezes hastily blow
Vivid shells run slowly through my hands
Jump in the glistening sea as it flows

Rushing water is cold and deep
But the feeling remains calm and serene
On warm blankets, babes tranquilly sleep
Comforted by hushed, peaceful dreams

Cian Barron, Grade 6
Woodcliff Middle School

Missing My "Toof"

I can't eat an apple,
I can't chew gum.
Something bad has happened
And now I feel dumb.
I was messing around
On my play set roof,
One bad step
And now I'm missing a toof!

Alex Miller, Grade 6
Immaculate Conception Regional School

Molly Makes Marvelous Muffins

Molly makes marvelous mint mulberry muffins
Molly mashes many mulberries for muffins in March

On Monday mornings Molly makes many muffins for
munchkins to munch on

Molly made millions of money from her marvelous
mint mulberry muffins

Miranda Leone, Grade 5
Springfield Township School

Here Comes Spring

Oh the wonderful things about spring
It makes my ears ring to hear the birds sing
When there is wind during the day,
It makes all the leaves sway.
What do you do when the sky is blue?
There are many things to do.
Don't be a grouch
And get off the couch.
Go out and play.
Have a great day.
Hurray, hurray,
It's spring today.

Brandon Ozbalik, Grade 4
John F Kennedy Elementary School

Wind in My Hair

I will be
　So happy and free
Riding my bike
　By the deep blue sea

I look up at the clouds
　Under the sun
I will smell a hundred flowers
　And not pick one

What more can I ask
　The heavens and stars
I want nothing more
　Than to ride by the shore

To look at the ocean
　And breathe in its air
To feel like I am flying
　The Wind in My Hair
Alexandra Cirra, Grade 5
Liberty Corner Elementary School

Dogs

Puppies
Cute, precious, nice
Playing, chewing, eating
Play with people all day and night
Cockers
Steven Hand, Grade 4
Middle Township Elementary School #2

The Dream

On a cold sparkling night
While I drink my hot chocolate
I watch the snowflakes fall
Against my window pane
And upon the frosty ground.

I feel tired so I climb the stairs
To my cozy bedroom.
Slowly I close my eyes and fall asleep.
Soon a penguin appears.
The penguin invites me
To a party at midnight.

Through the blizzard I go
Wearing an overcoat
Feeling warm as a polar bear.
I go to the party —
Then I follow the penguin home.
I wake up in the morn
And discover my dream.
Kai Iwamoto, Grade 4
Community Park School

Colors

White you see everywhere
Brown is the color of a bear.

Blue you see on my jeans
Yellow makes you want to scream.

Orange is the color of a peak
Purple I wear every week.

Green is the color of the grass
Gold is not like the color Brass.

Pink is my favorite color on the earth
Red is the color of my aunt Birth

What do colors do?
Shawna Ingraham, Grade 5
St Dominic Elementary School

A Hurt Dove

A dove if hurt,
to some is useless.
But to me,
a gift of life to care for,
a bird of peace,
a light of hope.
For some, if hurt and found,
a useless thing an insignificant bird.
But not to me I see something that has
a chance to fly to the sky again.
Katlyn Garcia, Grade 5
Durban Avenue Elementary School

Halloween

Skeletons are clanging
And bones are hanging
This night is very weird
I think I might want to grow a beard!
Melissa Lancaster, Grade 4
Springfield Township School

Life

Always turns on you
Don't know what will happen next
Living to the max.
Samuel Porter, Grade 6
Thomas Jefferson Middle School

Mom

Gina
young, slim
goes to work
loving, funny, laughing, working
Mom
Kristen Ford, Grade 6
Central Middle School

Old Dog

There once was a jolly old dog,
Who adored the rain and the fog.
　In bad weather he'd dance,
　He'd wiggle and prance.
Then away with the sun he would jog.
Sharvae Pollitt, Grade 4
West End Memorial Elementary School

Spring

When spring comes
it's like a dove.

The dove flies over all
with a fabulous call.

The call sweeps over the flowers
with its tremendous powers.

The flowers sing
"IT'S SPRING"
Mackenzie Mooney, Grade 4
Apple Montessori School

Snow

The whiteness,
The brightness of snow
That can't be beat.
Children in the snow,
Playing
Snowmen, snowballs, snowforts,
Sledding in the snow
Take a seat
No school
No homework,
This is all a treat.
The joy that kids love to play in.
Nicole Chillemi, Grade 4
Friends School

Oak Tree

Once I saw an oak tree
Then it spoke to me

"I am getting very old
I need a friend who is very bold
You probably do not understand
Because you're a young man."

I was staring at him with a scare
And my face was turning bare
I never left him from then on
Until the day that I was gone.
Tyler Batesko, Grade 6
Briarcliff Middle School

Beach Ballerina

One day at the beach I saw a dolphin.
It was a dandy dolphin.
It was a dandy, dainty dolphin.
It was a dandy, dainty, darling dolphin.
It was a dandy, dainty, darling, dizzy dolphin.
It was a dandy, dainty, darling, dizzy, delicate dolphin.
And it was dancing on the shore!

Nicole Mount, Grade 6
Robert L Craig Elementary School

Lost

Lost, my parents somewhere in the big world
No sister or brother to guide me
As I stare in the ocean on a sunny day,
Feeling empty and completely hollow.

As I look in the clear, blue water
I feel more and more hopeless.
For months trying to find my family,
I give up.
Suddenly, I hear my mother and father calling my name.
And as I turn,
I smile,
Heading to the first family dinner.
Safe at last.

Melanie Hung, Grade 4
Indian Hill Elementary School

Dream

I had to have been a little girl
When the stories gave me dreams.
Dreams so scary that it feels as if
It was really happening to me.
I can feel the pain. I am frightened and hurt.
In my dream I am sad and lonesome
In a deep need of help.
In my dream I become weak.
I lie down and rest my head
On a rock so I can go to sleep.
Before my sleep I say a small prayer.
My prayer goes like this:
"Now I lay me down to sleep
I pray the Lord my soul to keep.
Skies and gardens through the night
Wake me up the morning light."
I wake up and I am safe.

Heather Ramsey, Grade 5
The Red Bank Charter School

Leaf Lullaby

Sleep, soft young yellow leaf, sleep!!
Tip toe quietly into your soft comfortable bed.
Dream of slowly swaying in the wind.
Sleep, yellow leaf, sleep!!

Erin O'Connell, Grade 5
Belhaven Avenue Middle School

Us

I am confused
In a world which I do not know.
Everything is different.
I turn and see nothing but chaos.
What happened to peace,
Love and harmony?
I used to know these things,
But my mind was contaminated
With war and hatred.
Who will save us,
Save us from this disease
That is spreading all around us?
Is it you?
Is it I?
No, it is us.

Anna Poliski, Grade 6
Lower Alloways Creek Elementary School

Belle Prater's Boy

Belle Prater's boy lead a sorrowful life,
His mom disappeared and left him with strife.

Cross-eyed with glasses and hand-me down clothes,
Everyone questions what Woodrow knows.

His mom only left him with a few little clues,
She took some of his clothes, his money and one pair of shoes.

Woodrow moves from Crooked Ridge,
to Coal Stations, VA with his grandparents to live.

After trying to open her father's locked bedroom door,
Gypsy looked in the window and found him dead on the floor.

Out of her anger, Gypsy cut her long blonde hair,
Got the "Dixie Pixie" and made everyone stare.

Cousins and friends, the tree house their secret place,
Gypsy and Woodrow in that "in-between place."

Anthony Feltre, Grade 6
St Augustine of Canterbury School

All About Poland

A summer in Poland is so cool.
First of all, I slide down the golden sand dunes.
Making Polish food is great.
Pierogies and other foods make my tummy rumble!
Finally, I ride my grandpa's black motorcycle.
Vroom, Vroom.
I go off with the wind!

Vroom, Vroom, Vroom!

Claudia Maria Moskal, Grade 4
Lincoln Park Elementary School

Skiing

S kiing down a steep slope
K ids racing behind me
I want to get to the finish
I n first
N o kid is
G oing to top my speed

Chris McClintock, Grade 5
Belhaven Avenue Middle School

Lacrosse

Lacrosse
Rough sport
Spectators cheering loudly
Catching, hitting, shooting, scoring
Baggataway

Andrew Boman, Grade 6
Fieldstone Middle School

Apes

Apes
Apes
Apes
Hairy, muscular, fearsome apes
Weak, strong, gargantuan apes
These are jut a few
Lounging apes,
Jungle apes,
Black, brown, albino apes,
Sleeping, roaming, tribal apes,
Brilliant apes too
Playful apes,
Scary apes,
Don't forget sign-language apes,
Last of all,
Best of all,
I like all apes!

T. Connor Vail, Grade 5
Ridgeway Elementary School

Springtime

The springtime is coming.
You can hear the birds humming.

The colors are amazing.
Pink! Yellow! White! They're blazing.

The temperatures are cool.
But you can't go in the pool.

As the days grow dark
You can't hear the dogs bark.

When spring is over
You will see a four leaf clover.

Alicia Colón, Grade 5
St Veronica Elementary School

Spring

S inging birds fly around when they hear the spring sound
P eople playing soccer and baseball too bad football is in fall
R unning around the soccer field we have no time to stop or yield
I ndigo, violet, and other colors too under the sky so blue
N everending spring fun playing under the bright yellow sun
G oing home after a great day good thing it is only Saturday

Kevin McClintock, Grade 5
Belhaven Avenue Middle School

Children

Children, children are just so sweet.
You think they are ugly and just so mean.
Do you realize when you look into their eyes that it makes a great disguise?
All our children just make our hearts flow.
Our hearts feel good when we know our kids are true.
We don't have to beat them just teach them.
My heart and your heart is put together.
When your kids are mad just leave them alone for a little while.
If you knew how we felt and if they knew how you felt,
Maybe our family and that child too could come with us.
This is how I knew that we should be children forever together.

Cierra Martin, Grade 6
George Washington Elementary School

A Good Day

A good day is fun in the sun,
and no school.
A good day is laughing with friends,
and no school
A good day is riding a bike to a friend's house,
and no school.
A good day is finally beating your brother's video game score,
and no school.
A good day is shooting hoops and making almost every shot,
and no school.
A good day is going for ice cream on a hot day,
and no school.
A good day is jumping and flipping on a trampoline with the sprinklers on,
and no school.
A good day is turning on the radio and your favorite song is just starting,
and no school.
A good day is enjoying a long summer vacation
and seeing all your friends on the first day of school…
and going to school.

Luke Shuscavage, Grade 6
Our Lady of Mount Virgin School

Spring

S unny skies notify me of spring.
P urple petunias popping up in my yard.
R ainy April showers make the green leaves grow.
I dle moments to watch the changes.
N ewly sprouted flowers look back at me.
G ratefully I gaze at the gorgeous world and breathe in the warm spring air.

Dara Kotek, Grade 4
Solomon Schechter Day School

When I'm Asleep…

…I can't hear a peep.
…everything is quiet.
…things are just the way I like it.
…I have many dreams.
…I can't see the stars gleam.
…sometimes my sister will snore.
…Mom knocks gently on the door.
…I feel as happy as a cat snuggled on a pillow.

Dana Gorab, Grade 4
Long Memorial Elementary School

What Is a Sunset?

A sunset falls at sundown.
A sunset is the passing of the sun below the horizon.

A sunset has many wonderful, beautiful, marvelous colors
Like a mosaic on a museum wall.

A sunset is the most beautiful sight ever.
A sunset tells us when the night begins.

Sunset is the opposite of sunrise.
Whatever goes up must come down.

A sunset is God's creation
Don't you think so?

Jazmin Velasquez, Grade 6
The Great Commission Christian Academy

The Climax

When you're with that special someone
And an exciting event rolls by,
You'll think of the future of your life.
You'll feel that you can cut tension with a knife
When that special event happens o' so fast.
I hope that this will last.
This feels like a dream
It is a moment to be.

Jordan Specchio, Grade 6
Walter T. Bergen Middle School

Spring

Beautiful flowers bloom with color
No flower is the same as the other
Colorful days of blue pink and red
Go outside to plant a flower bed
Spending time outside with your families
With lots of shade under the trees
Grab a cool glass of water
Fathers, mothers, sons and daughters
Go to the park to play with your friends
Every night you're happy when the day ends.

Colleen Magley, Grade 5
St Dominic Elementary School

My Sis

Every day she smells like blossoms.
Her hair feels so soft.
When she sings, it sounds so good
it brings music to my ears,
even when she is out of tune.
She's so beautiful!
Even if we fight, which we do sometimes.
The next day, we're back to being friends again!

Joseph Stabile, Grade 4
Christ the Teacher School

What Is Green?

Green is the color of the grass.
Green is the color of the leaves.
Green is the color of a tree.
Green is the color of a stem.
Green is the color of a flower.
Green is a collar on your shirt.
Green is the color of seaweed.
Green is the color of a chalkboard.

Kristina Cohen, Grade 4
Hardyston Township Elementary School

Irish Dance

I practice and practice
Until I can't feel my toes
Blisters and Band-Aids
That's what it takes
Practice and practice
You start dancing great
When you love to dance as much as I do
All those bumps, bruises, and black and blues
None of it matters when you go home
With that big trophy
Half the size of you
With Irish dance you have to have fun
That's the easiest way to be number one
Dancing is my thing
But not for the trophy
It is my thing
Just for the love of the sport

Corinne Harriet Day, Grade 5
St John's Academy

My Sister

My sister is not mean,
She is a jumping bean!
She plays her Gameboy every day,
And she always wants to go outside to play.
Her favorite word is olé olé!
After school is her favorite time of day.
She is happy when she gets her way!
Lucky for me, I have more than one,
'Cause that means twice the fun!

Tina Pomante, Grade 4
St Peter Elementary School

Softball
Softball
fun, awesome
batting, catching, running
softball is so great
Baseball
Kerry Enright, Grade 4
St Mary's School

Spring Blooms
Spring is finally here,
you don't have to shed a tear.
For the flowers are bright,
it's such a good sight.

The flowers cover the meadow,
in different shades of blue,
I'm getting a clue the summer
is coming too.

No one's in a bad mood
because of all the great food.

Spring is here, so lets all
give a cheer.
Alexa Van Beveren, Grade 6
Franklin Elementary School

The Best Horses
Macho
Calm, yellow
Jogging, sleeping, walking
Halter, saddle, blanket, bridle
Jumping, trotting, eating
Fast, gray
Dunnwhick
Katie Karl, Grade 6
Assumption School

Heaven
Blessings being shed
Fragrance of fresh flowers
The graceful motion of an angel's wings
Soft, sensitive, silence
Sweet sugar in the mist
Heaven is a true destination
Sabrina Nichole Vickery, Grade 6
Little Egg Harbor Intermediate School

Flowers
Flowers
Bud in the spring
Blooming far up and up
Flowers make me sneeze quickly
Violets
Ashley Lesch, Grade 4
Katharine D Malone Elementary School

Sports
Baseball
Fun, cool
Running, batting, stealing
Energetic, functioning, scoring, dribbling
Scoring, shooting, blocking
Nice, easy
Basketball
Darnel Walker, Grade 5
Paul W Carleton Elementary School

Hot Diggity Dogs
Dogs, dogs
we like them
we eat them
dig them up and down
and then we eat them
all over town.

Eat 'em with chili
or sauerkraut
Eat 'em all day
or else I pout.

I eat corn dogs on a stick
no mustard on the side
'cause I like the taste
there's nothing to hide.

Can't get enough hot dogs
I eat 'em all night
I eat 'em all day
just pass some to me
I eat 'em anyway!
Denzel Rucker, Grade 5
Roosevelt Elementary School

Damp Leaves
The delicious essence of damp leaves
drift through the frosty air.
The cool breeze blows in my face.
The savory smell surprises me,
makes me happy,
makes me feel like I am
flying and flowing
in the breezy wind.
I land softly in a pile of soggy leaves.
No matter how hard I try to sit up,
I fall instantly back down
into the moist leaves.
I make the leaves splatter
like a raindrop hitting
the delicate wet ground.
Chloe Branch, Grade 5
Lyncrest Elementary School

A Snowy Day
Snow falls from the sky
Kids are sleigh riding down hills
Snowballs being thrown

But when the snow melts
There is no more sleigh riding
All the fun is gone
William Joyce, Grade 5
St Veronica Elementary School

Jesus
J esus is God's son.
E liminating all evil spirits.
S on of God.
U se prayer if you want to talk to God.
S ee Jesus in your dreams.
Michael Reim, Grade 4
Trinity Christian Academy

A Penguin's Life
Slip, slide, go go ride
Eat, eat, cold cold feet
Waddle, waddle, squabble squabble
Black and white
Just might like
Victoria McDermott, Grade 4
Franklin Township Elementary School

Tree
I look at a tree
It looks at me

It has green eyes
In his afro of leaves

I asked him to please
Stop staring at me

Staring is rude
How could it be

The tree
Keeps staring at me
Tyler Cacoso, Grade 6
Christa McAuliffe Middle School

The Difference
Goldfish
Beautiful, shiny
Playing, swimming, eating
Tank, pet, predator, ocean
Stinging, hunting, floating
Slimy, ugly
Jellyfish
Brianne Pizzigoni, Grade 4
Our Lady of Mount Virgin School

Confusion

Confusion is purple.
It smells like sour milk mixed with eggs.
It looks like a corn maze.
It tastes like something bitter.
It sounds like everyone talking at once.
Confusion feels like the world is spinning.

Krista Lepping, Grade 6
St Rose of Lima School

The Baseball Game

Out at the park for a big game,
    let's hope there is no rain.
First man is up at bat,
Hold on to your baseball hat!

First swing is a strike,
Two more of those and he can take a hike.
He is not a very good batter,
So, soon it will not matter.

He hit it, and he's going for first base,
    Now the pitcher is on his case.
"Oh no," the pitcher threw him out,
He is now sure to scream and shout!

Zachary Kotteles, Grade 5
Sacred Heart School

If I Were the Solar System

If I were the solar system, I'd be full of planets and stars.
My heart would be vast and empty.
I'd be a pal with all the planets.
My brain would be as hot as the sun.
I would have meteors and ships buzzing around me.
I'm always spinning, spinning,
And hearing nothing but the Earth.

Sean Waldron, Grade 4
Sicomac Elementary School

Cain

There once was a young man named Cain,
Who jumped off a really big plane.
    He fell to the ground,
    And hit a big mound.
Now he is in horrible pain.

Jason Cramer, Grade 4
West End Memorial Elementary School

Music Bands

Music bands playing their guitars.
Rock bands in the house of blues.
People cheering for the bands.
DJ's getting new records.
And country bands playing with their hearts.
And country bands playing with their hearts.

Nicholas Ferraro, Grade 4
Pond Road Middle School

Friendship

Friendship is a work of art.
A work of art takes lots of smarts.
Friendship feels like stars in the sky,
Friendship feels like you could fly.
Friendship is like shining shells in the sea.
Some people feel that it's a shopping spree.
Friendship is a jewel to treasure,
From it, I get my greatest pleasure.

Richard Freeman, Grade 4
St Rose of Lima School

Green

Green is grass and leaves
and sometimes makes you sick.
Green is the taste of apples.
Mints and limes smell green.
Being out in the country makes me feel green.
Green is the sound of bugs and leaves.
Green is Scotland, Ireland, and parks.
St. Patrick's Day is green.
Spring is also green.
Green is spearmint.

Mike Coccaro, Grade 6
Thorne Middle School

My Family

My family is like words in a story,
they tell a terrific tale.

My daddy is like my coach
teaching me everything I need to know.

My mommy is sweet, like a chocolate bar
helping me with whatever I have to do.

My sisters are Band-Aids
always helping me every step of the way.

My dog is like a guard
always looking out for me.

Nicole Sanczyk, Grade 5
Salt Brook Elementary School

Baseball

B abe Ruth
A lex Rodriguez
S ammy Sosa
E dgardo Alfonzo
B arry Bonds
A lfonzo Soriano
L ou Gehrig
L uis Ramirez

Tyler Nichols, Grade 4
Hardyston Township Elementary School

Thunder

You cannot see it
but you can hear it
loud clashing noises at night

As it roars
you see the lightning
travel across the sky

People fear it
when they hear
this frightening noise above

It clashes a few more times
for you to realize
that it is only thunder

Ela Cagar, Grade 6
Pioneer Academy of Science

Movies

Movies can be funny,
Movies can be sad,
Movies can be scary,
Movies can be bad,
Movies can be real,
Movies can be fake,
Movies can be anything you like.
If a movie is good,
Sometimes I'll stand and clap.
If a movie is not so good,
I might just take a nap.

Joseph Foley, Grade 4
St Peter Elementary School

The Country I Love

There is a country I love
That is truly unique.
In fact, it's so great,
There is no need for critique.
It frees all the people
Set in chains by their lands,
And when someone needs help,
Everyone gives a hand.
Its people are happy and safe
In their wonderful home,
This is the best place
That they've ever known.
The country I love
Is the best of its kind.
However, it's not
Just a place in my mind.
In fact, it's still here,
To this very day,
For the country I love
Is my U.S.A.

Amanda Osborn, Grade 6
Roosevelt Elementary School

This Test

This test — a trek with only one tool — a pen.
I need to confront my fears of this test.
This test — impossible for anyone with a below-average mind.
I'll try my best.
I studied hard — all night long.
I need to pass, to pass this test.
This test — I need some help!
I want to scream, or shriek, or yell!
I feel like I can't breathe!
This test — I'm rubbing my forehead, my chin — I'm so confused!
I need a lifeline — either that or more time.
This test — a mess.

But wait! Number 4 is B!
Number 7 is D!
Number 12 is C!
This test — now so easy.
This test — how could I have had so much trouble with something so simple?
This test — A+!

Amanda Sablowsky, Grade 6
Fieldstone Middle School

My Hero

My dad is my hero
He makes the world a better place
He cheers me up when I am sad and he takes care of me when I'm sick
My dad fixes all of my problems
No matter what
He is always there to catch me when I fall
He is very intelligent and inspires me to be the best I can be
My dad is always helping me
He teaches me everything that I need to know
He brings a smile wherever he goes
And he always makes me laugh
My dad is always putting my family and me before himself
He is very, very special to me
And very close to my heart
You are my hero Daddy,
And I love you!

Madeleine Joynt, Grade 5
North Dover Elementary School

My Best Friend

I stand in my bedroom in the dark, by myself
Staring at everything around me and looking on my bookshelf
It was a small picture of my best friend, my buddy, my chum,
And when I thought about her I cried and then some
I have dreams of her of all the good times that we have shared, I remember one
Of when she needed me the most, to look at what she had done
But then I remember that painful week when she moved on that day,
And then my vision of her began to fade away.
If only I could go back in time and stop all of this
But it is not possible and now I'm in darkness.

Lisa Rodriguez, Grade 6
Thomas Jefferson Middle School

He Is Crying Again
When the rain hits the roof with a pitter patter,
I know He is crying again.
When the wind blows, He is angry,
And when the rain stops He is fine,
But for now God is crying again.

Sarah Elizabeth Godfrey, Grade 6
Little Egg Harbor Intermediate School

Isabel, Isabel
Isabel met a giant bee,
Isabel saw it in a giant tree.
The bee was so hairy,
Isabel thought the bee was very scary.
Isabel saw the bee's big stinger
Isabel thought the bee was going to sting her.
Isabel, Isabel didn't worry,
Isabel didn't scream or scurry.
Isabel led the bee to a giant bowl of jelly.
Now the bee smells like grape jelly.

Etienne R. Clarke, Grade 6
Thorne Middle School

The Heart and Clock
Thy clock ticks and tocks, and will tock without stop.
Thy heart thumps and bumps from here on out.
Beating, tick, tock, thump! Who is more willing to win?
Thy heart is everlasting, but thy clocks batteries die.
Thy clock dies with. Thy heart's willing love and passion
is thy truth to you.

Karl Rufo, Grade 6
Thomas Jefferson Middle School

Huskies or Shih Tzus?
Huskies helped many,
One time in Nome,
In the Ming Dynasty Shih Tzus didn t help any
This is why Alaska's a Husky's home

Yet, it would be so cool
On a satin pillow
Just sit there and rule
Next to a tree called a willow

It's so hard to choose
Both would rule
They won't win or lose
Diamonds or frosty cool?

For me, it's a tie.
I'm a Husky puppy girl
I don't want to lie
But, wow, I really want a Shih Tzu's pearl!

Gabi Beeferman, Grade 4
Stonybrook Elementary School

Studying
Sometimes it can be lame.
Sometimes it's like giving me a brain.
I think and I think and I think some more.
My brain sizzled all day long.
My head almost fell off from studying so long.

Kyla Granroth, Grade 4
St Peter Elementary School

Winter
The snow is falling and twinkling too,
You can't wear sandals you have to wear boots.

The snow is a blanket on the cold hard ground,
Footprints of animals imprinted on snow are found.

After a long day hot chocolate is the cure,
The taste is sweet and so pure.

I climb in my bed, oh so cozy,
Finally I fall asleep because I'm so drowsy.

Lauren Cronin, Grade 6
Allen W Roberts Elementary School

Green
Green is money it is rough bumpy frogs
Green is the moss on ridged logs.

Green is sneaky leprechauns it's also fresh grass
Green is the color of a shimmering bass.

It is the color of vegetables it is the color of trees
It is even the color of my morning tea.

Green is the color of a glittering Jade
As well as the scales on a beautiful mermaid.

Green is the color of some people's eyes
It's also the wings of a dragonfly.

Green is some moods it's either dull or bright
And it's sometimes the color of Christmas lights.

Lime green, olive green sea green, too
It is also a relative to the color blue.

Leah Obermeier, Grade 5
Sandman Consolidated Elementary School

Depression
Depression is the color dark blue.
It smells like dead flowers.
It looks like a big storm cloud that ruins a bright sunny day.
It tastes like cereal without milk.
It sounds like blues music.
It feels like you just swallowed your heart.

John Holland, Grade 6
St Rose of Lima School

Spring

S pring is flower-growing season
P etals collecting morning dew
R aindrops moistening the soil
I n the spring everything is blooming
N ew plants growing
G ardens showing their colors.

Jason Levy, Grade 4
Solomon Schechter Day School

Moon

Moon dances at night,
light in the peaceful darkness,
one with the night stars.

Julia Abolafia, Grade 4
Meadowbrook Elementary School

Spring

S unny days have come.
P retty butterflies fly around.
R obins burst out in song.
I nch worms slowly creep around.
N ewts roam the grass.
G eese lay their eggs.

Noam Eitan, Grade 4
Solomon Schechter Day School

My Cousin

Oh, my cousin dear
How I wish she was near
She is so far away
Over the ocean gray
Without her I am blue
We stick together just like glue
My life wouldn't be the same
Without me thinking about her name
She shines like a star
I wish she wasn't so far
I love her so dearly
Without her I can't think clearly

Aayushi Agarwal, Grade 5
St Marys School

Paying Attention

Sit there, staring, absentminded.
Teacher calls.
Don't know.
Never thought.
Hand wasn't raised.
Asking, answering.
Wrong.
Second try.
Right.

Jenny Fletcher, Grade 5
Toll Gate Grammar School

Basketball

Playing my sport
Out on the court
Dribbling the ball
Not in the hall
When I make a basket
The crowd makes a racket
It's not racquetball,
It's BASKETBALL!!!

Clara Kinnison, Grade 6
Monmouth Beach Elementary School

My Country

The people the food
What shall I do
When I move away from you
Your style your grace
Always give me faith
But then I had to leave you

Jennifer Edson, Grade 6
Thomas Jefferson Middle School

Santa

He has a great red rat
That has a great red hat
I like the presents under my tree
They are very pretty
One cold, cold night
Santa came to town
In his red old sled
And said "Go to bed."

Melissa Lancaster, Grade 4
Springfield Township School

Islam

Islam, Islam,
I love Islam.
It is the religion Muslim people follow.
In Eid-al-Fitr we have so much fun,
Before we had to fast,
Thank God we are done.
In Eid-al-Adha we play,
Then we are done with the day.
But before we have fun and play
We have to go to the mosque and pray.
All I want to say is I love Islam!

Douha El-Hely, Grade 6
Kawameeh Middle School

Clare's Dare

There once was a girl named Clare.
Who was never afraid of a dare.
When asked to kiss a lion,
She began to start cryin'
She wouldn't complete this dare.

Erin Yetman, Grade 4
St Mary's School

Springtime

Springtime is coming near
And finally today it is here.
Birds are singing,
Kids are swinging,
There is a breeze,
And there are many bees.
Plants are growing,
Water is flowing,
The sun is out,
There is much to shout.
Spring is a sensation,
And best of all there is spring vacation.

Selena Senachai, Grade 6
Springfield Township School

Homework

Sometimes homework is boring.
Sometimes it's really fun!
I only actually like it
When it's completely done.
When it is I feel relieved,
I can go outside and play.
And hang around with my friends
For the rest of the day

Lucy Frezza, Grade 5
Hillside Elementary School

Swimming in My Pool

Swimming in my pool is fun,
See the water splash.
Watch me do a cannonball,
Hear the water crash!

It's always fun to dive and jump,
Inside the swimming pool,
I like to do it with my friends,
They think it's really cool.

Hear the skimmer flapping,
Thump! Thump! Thump!
As the water's flowing,
Pump, pump, pump.

Smell the chlorine's scent,
As it burns my nose.
I can feel the bubbling jets,
They really tickle my toes!

I like swimming,
All day long,
With me and my friends,
We can't go wrong!

Domenic Pontarelli, Grade 4
Assumption School

Looking at the Stars

Looking at the stars is a beautiful sight
To see how they glow and shine in the night.

Looking at the stars is a beautiful sight
As they brighten my room and give me light.

Looking at the stars is a beautiful sight
To see God's glory, power and might.

Looking at the stars is a beautiful sight
How wonderful it is to see them at night.

Eileen Marie Molina, Grade 6
The Great Commission Christian Academy

Life Is Like a Cake

Life is like a cake.
The ingredients are like your choices.
You mix it up right and a great cake you'll have.

Life is like a cake.
Baking the cake is like having self-esteem.
Too much will hurt you.
Too little and you stay flat.
The right amount brings you up.

Life is like a cake.
The icing is like your friends,
With none you're dull.
And the more you have the better you are.
Never can you ever have too many friends.
Life is like a cake!

Robert White, Grade 6
Walter T. Bergen Middle School

Fireflies

Fireflies dancing with gold lighted wings.
Glistening stars make them sing.
You can catch them once only a memory.
The stars vanish from all the sky.

Victoria Holowienka, Grade 6
Immaculate Conception Regional School

My Pet

My pet is not much fun,
I found it on a sandy beach laying out in the sun,
It doesn't need much to eat,
But water and heat,
Its color is gray all over,
And it didn't move when I told it to roll over,
My pet's shape is kind of round,
It isn't scared of anything; not even a bloodhound,
Can you believe my shock?
Have you guessed yet?
MY PET IS A ROCK!

Emely DeJesus, Grade 5
Perth Amboy Catholic Intermediate School

Valentine's Day

Come with me and…
    We'll float joyfully upon the sky
        On a soft fluffy cloud.
Come with me and…
    We'll soar through the sky
        Gracefully as we laugh together.

Come with me and…
    We'll skip through a field
        Of flowers all colored in pink.
Come with me and…
    We'll play like there's no tomorrow
        and sing, dance, and play.

Come with me and…
    We'll sit on the roof top and
        Watch the stars glisten in the moonlight.
Come with me and…
    We'll open our eyes
        To a new world full of imagination.

Come with me and…
    We'll rest our sleepy heads
        On the cozy pillow and have pleasant dreams.

Maria Brucato, Grade 4
Lincroft Elementary School

Spring

No more ice, no more snow,
Plant the seeds and the flowers will grow.
After that the flowers will bloom,
You could pick it and put it in your room.

The birds chirping every day,
Some on the rooftop where they will stay.
Some flying in the sky so bright,
Passing by a bright red kite.

The breeze is so brisk and cool,
Remember, it's too early to go in the pool!
The pool is for a hot season like summer,
Spring is too cold, that's a bummer!

Squirrels play,
Every day,
The leaves covered with dew,
Are good as new.

I like spring, I think it rules,
If you don't like it, you're such a fool,
Because spring brings fun,
To everyone!

Mirei Sakane, Grade 5
Apple Montessori School

Sounds

Trees waving at me
Wolves howling at the bright starry sky
Birds hoot silently
Kate Coppa, Grade 4
Stonybrook Elementary School

Earth

Orbiting in space
Third planet from the sun's rays
Many things to see
Katie McFadden, Grade 4
Sicomac Elementary School

As the Winds Whistle

As the wind whistles to me,
I thought it would be
Like a stallion running free.

And as the sun gleamed,
It seemed
It would shine for eternity

The sky was blue,
As my heart is true.
The trees were above
And beyond the blue seas.

As the deer had a voice so sincere,
Anyone from Heaven could hear.

Ever since time, from the start,
The wind's whistle will be in my heart.
Johanna Perez, Grade 5
Winslow Township School No 6

My Soul

I am lonely and empty.
My heart is a black rose,
Dying, Dying, Dying.

My life is lonely and empty.
I live like a rose,
I seem to be harmless,
But once you touch me,
You get badly hurt.

I have no happiness,
I have no enjoyment.
Sometimes, I hide secrets,
And sometimes I don't.

I am a detective,
Who hides things,
I am a rose.
Reema Shah, Grade 6
Kawameeh Middle School

Spring

Spring is a flowery heaven with plants every color of the rainbow,
Busy bees buzz by my head collecting nectar,
Children laugh and play on the play grounds,
The smell of peaches and blooming flowers tickle your nose,
The taste of freshly baked apple pies take your taste buds on a sweet journey,
The cool spring breeze whizzes by my head making me wish spring would never end.
Kristina Michael-Doyle, Grade 6
Franklin Elementary School

The Calming Summer Rain

It is now dawn
I'm awakened by the rain
I'm in my warm pink pajama pants as a bright pink warming heart
With a bright yellow shirt like the sun it's very warm.

I can hear the tapping of the rain
"drip, drop, drip, drop"
I can feel my dog's wet, cold nose snuggle on to me and I can feel my dog's soft fur.

I'm thinking about my life
I'm now opening the window just a bit
I can hear the wind as it drags the leaves
As I fall back asleep.
The sun rises.
Veronica Cardoso, Grade 5
Bedminster Township Elementary School

Teachers

Teachers are good; teachers are great;
They are the people who more should appreciate.
They teach us our math and reading too,
Without them what would we know or do.
Through all the years from elementary to college,
Every year we gain more knowledge.
The knowledge we gain helps us get jobs to make money,
Without an education we wouldn't have a good job and that wouldn't be funny.
We always try to do good on a test,
Because when we get an A or A+ we think we're the best.
When you turn in a project you have just made,
You really hope it gets a good grade.
Teachers teach us so much we just can't measure,
Some of the lessons we'll always treasure.
Whether they are young or old, male or female they all have one thing in mind,
They want to teach children; teachers are one of a kind!
Morgan Lowrey, Grade 6
Carl W Goetz Middle School

Embarrassment

Embarrassment is pink.
It smells like a rotten banana.
It looks like someone's face as bright as a tomato.
It tastes like sour milk.
It sounds like people laughing at a person for something they did.
It feels like running away and crying your eyes out.
Alexa Basso, Grade 6
St Rose of Lima School

What Is Red?

Red is fire
Red is dark
Red is evil
Red is hot
Red is a cardinal
Red is a color of some people's hair
Red is a nice color
Red is an apple
Red is the 7 stripes on the American flag.

Megan Zeigler, Grade 5
Paul W Carleton Elementary School

My Love

When I think of the pain you've been through
I feel that pounding pressure of not knowing what to do.
Sending her away or having her stay.
Making her go, will make people cry,
But keeping her here is another way to pray
For making sure she is here to stay and never fade away.

Having this feeling is a painful thought.
With her gone we will have the tears
Of missing a loved one,
And the fear of losing someone else.
Just having you two makes me feel complete.
I love you both oh so much but
Losing you is our family's number one fear.

Kristen Galayda, Grade 6
Bartle Elementary School

Seven Ways of Looking at the Ocean

When the ocean is near,
It's like a dragon, roaring,
Protecting me.
The glimmering blue horizon,
Makes the lands meet,
And we are united.
When the sun sinks low,
The ocean is its home,
And all that I see are the ocean and the sky overlapping.
Wandering off onto the sand,
The ocean guides me,
To wherever I shall go.
The bubbling water,
Makes a soothing drink,
For everyone to quench their thirst.
When day comes near,
The ocean is boiling,
With excitement of the people.
Creatures of the sea,
Keep a close, watchful eye,
On their incomers.

Paige Carleen, Grade 6
Allen W Roberts Elementary School

Candy Dream

I had a candy dream.
It was as sweet as a lollipop.
There were tons and tons of pieces of candy.
The candy tasted so good, it was heaven.
But the most candy I had was chocolate,
Tons and tons of chocolate.
But too bad it was a dream and not real.

Gabby Gutleber, Grade 5
Williamstown Middle School

My Special Place

My special place is
A book
A safe haven
When things go wrong
Away from everything
Going on in my house
It relaxes me
When there's commotion going on in my life
I sit in my room and read
Books take me places
Happy places, sad places, and
Magical places
Only if people knew
How it feels
When you get a book
And read all out

Erik W. Wehner, Grade 5
Salt Brook Elementary School

Sky Is Calling

The sky is calling wh-oooo
In the dark, dreary night
The sky is calling pitt-patt
It gives quite a fright
The sky is calling in all different sounds
Who knows what's calling, for there's no sight

Shobhik Chakraborty, Grade 5
Millstone River School

Teachers

Teachers get happy
Teachers get mad
Sometimes even teachers get sad

Teachers teach us math and to subtract and add
They teach writing, reading, and math

Teachers are the best
They look nice in a dress

There's a teacher that teaches math
I like math
It's a blast!

Ivan Martinez, Grade 4
Evergreen Elementary School

Soccer
During soccer you need a ball.
It doesn't matter if you are short or tall.

The team needs a goal keeper.
And the coach needs a sweeper.

You need a boot.
And you need to know how to shoot.

You can score a header.
And you need a defender.
Ricardo Gomes, Grade 5
Most Holy Redeemer School

Spring
Spring
blue skies
butterflies
flowers blooming
birds
Cydney Simon, Grade 4
Franklin Park Elementary School

Cat Tale
There was a cat who's very shy
He really, really wanted to fly
So he made some wings oh my
He was scared I don't deny
He's going to fly to the sky

He jumped up to start his flight
Closer closer got the light
The cat got up from his dive
"Oh this is fun," said he
And he married Angely
Avital Ron, Grade 4
Solomon Schechter Day School

Stars
Star
Bright light
Lit up night
Can see from earth
Except in the day
Patrice Chiaramonte, Grade 4
Katharine D Malone Elementary School

My Guinea Pigs
exciting, motivating
enjoyable, exciting, sweet
growing, eating, jumping, performing
running, scratching, dumping
accomplishment, joy
interesting
Aaron Kelsey, Grade 4
Mansfield Township Elementary School

Sadness
Sadness is blue
It smells like a wet dog
It looks like something is getting hurt
It tastes like water from an ocean
It sounds like a baby crying
Sadness feels like you are all alone
John Osborne, Grade 6
St Rose of Lima School

The Shut Out
On page 153,
There's a bug that I see.
Its death seems like a mystery
With wings so free,
I ask to me,
Why suddenly it did not flee,
Perhaps somehow it did not see
The hand that killed so easily?
Dylan Cahill, Grade 5
Mansfield Township Elementary School

Little Sisters
Little sisters are so bad
Little sisters make me mad!
Little sisters are destructive
And they act so crazy
But sometimes they're just lazy!
I hate it when they always get their way,
It's no fair to me,
And it won't be any day!
Danielle Cox, Grade 5
Winslow Township School No 6

My Street
My street is very nice.
It is as beautiful as can be.
But it would need a little more beauty
at the dumpster especially.
But other parts are nice and bright.
God blessed my street with all His might.
Ebony Andruzzi, Grade 4
Holy Saviour School

Giraffes
A giraffe has four legs,
But doesn't have any pegs.
It eats sixteen to twenty hours a day,
And doesn't eat any hay.
A new born is only six feet tall,
And has to take a four foot fall.
The giraffe has a very long neck,
If one chased me I'd be a wreck!
Carly Todd, Grade 5
Most Holy Redeemer School

Ruby
Green are apples,
Ice cream is white;
Ruby is the color
Of an angry termite.

Black is night,
Orange is soda;
Ruby is the color
Of a red Toyota.

Brown is caramel,
Gum is pink;
Ruby is the color
Of my red ink.
Killian Baldwin, Grade 5
Robert B Jaggard Elementary School

Excitement
Excitement is all around
Like a rushing roller coaster,
A fast and happy feeling!
Julia Delaluz, Grade 4
Wayside Elementary School

Cute Cats
Cats
Cute animals
Run very fast
Nice, smart, loving, tiny
Animals
Alexis Chaparro, Grade 4
Our Lady of Mount Virgin School

Snakes
A slithering snake
Awaits its
prey while
nestled on a
mossy emerald clover.

As he lays
so still and
quiet
he dreams of
a journey
across the
loneliness of desert.

When reaching his final
destination
it kills
its prey
so innocent and tiny
and escapes the midnight forest.
Victoria O'keefe, Grade 5
Robert B Jaggard Elementary School

The Evil Lunch Room of Crazy Town School

Today I enter Crazy Town School,
Feeling pretty confident, but have the chill of the ghoul,
The bell rings, time for lunch to start,
Finally the strong thumping stops in my heart,
As I enter the room, I stare in shock,
There are bullies and bikers and lots of bad talk,
I stand in line as stiff as a rock,
When I get my lunch, it's a sweaty gym sock.

For weeks it goes on, tons of terrible food,
Rotten tomatoes and mystery meat they say has been stewed,
"Action, back on set!"
Oh yeah…did I forget to tell you the best part yet?
I'm an actress!

Alyssa Kinney, Grade 4
Stonybrook Elementary School

A Fun Way to Get Active

Hitting, catching, throwing, sliding.
Watch the ball go through the air, gliding.
Hit the ball, then run to first base.
Hurry! Run faster! Keep up your fast pace!

When the pitcher throws the ball,
Don't drop down and fall!
Just swing with all your might,
And hold on tight!

When you're out on the field,
Your mitt acts like a shield.
If the ball comes near you,
You jump up high and act like you can touch the sky!

Lianna Rubinaccio, Grade 5
Sacred Heart School

A Woman of Love

There was a woman who served those in need
She went around to spread God's wondrous deed
Mother Theresa was her name
For the poor is why she came
She went around with God's grace
Hoping people could see God's face

Brittany Perpepaj, Grade 4
St Joseph School

On My Birthday…

…I get out of bed and jump for glee.
…I go downstairs and have a special breakfast.
…when I open gifts I thank everyone for them.
…I hop and hop like crazy.
…we go outside and I get to decide where we go.
…I might choose the park, movies, or the arcade.
…when the day ends and the moon rises I say,
    "Man! What a great Birthday!"

Justin Byrnes, Grade 4
Long Memorial Elementary School

Spring Is Coming

Spring is coming before you know
    so say good bye to all the snow
Green grass is growing
    red roses are spudding
The sun is rising
    and the clocks will spring ahead
We'll have longer days
    especially the days in May
Baseball season starts
    it goes through April, May, and June
Starting each month with a new moon
    with several holidays to celebrate
As we near spring
    that means school is coming to an end
So we can play outside
    in the nice 70 degree weather
Packing away winter clothes
    is what I'm about to do
So buckle up it's a wild ride
I hope you enjoy the trip

Steven Manela, Grade 5
North Dover Elementary School

Electric Guitar

If you play an electric guitar,
you can go really far.
There won't be any regrets,
as long as you keep your fingers on a couple of frets.
When I play music it makes me happy,
because the electric sound is just so snappy.

Priscilla Bauer, Grade 5
Robert L Craig Elementary School

My Favorite Flower

I love to watch the daffodils
While they're growing on the hill.
It is so much fun
To watch them grow in the sun,
Because, when they're done,
You can pick them and run!

They have the most beautiful trumpet-shaped crowns,
The crowns always reach up;
They never fall down.
The way the crowns reach up
Never makes me frown.

Daffodils always stand straight and proud,
They stand so tall,
They could reach the clouds!
I could watch them for hours and hours,
Because they are my favorite flowers.

Kaitlyn McMillan, Grade 5
Sacred Heart School

Know Yourself

Walk in.
Set your mood with the sun.
The best of everything
Is inside your heart.
Michelle Camacho, Grade 6
Robert L Craig Elementary School

America

A ll the people are free
M en and women you see. The
E agle is our bird
R eally proud as can be.
I can't get over how our
C ountry is treated fairly,
A merica is my home.
Nathan Horvath, Grade 4
Middle Township Elementary School #2

Life Is…

Life is hard sometimes
You never know what is next
Some days are easy
Some days are hard
You just have to let things go
And just keep the flow
And as long as you know
That you may be sad
Tomorrow you might just be glad.
Imani McKelvey, Grade 5
Roosevelt Elementary School

Newborn Foal

As I stretch my legs
and open my eyes.
I see the sun
I am alive
I stand up
and fall down.
But then I stand again.
Then I go hobble
to my mother.
I drink her milk
and then I yawn.
And the day is over.
I lay down
next to my mother.
And then we fall asleep.
Arielle Branco, Grade 6
Cherry Hill Elementary School

Snowflake

Sparkles in your eyes
Glistening in the sun's light
Winter's gold beauty
Joanna Salerno, Grade 4
Sicomac Elementary School

School Writing

We all got assigned to write a poem,
so we all packed our books and headed home.
With empty paper in our backpacks,
and a pencil in our hands,
we were ready to write on demand.

At home I thought and I thought,
but nothing came handy,
not sports, or animals, or even candy.
It was hours, and hours, and still nothing clicked.
The main problem was a topic couldn't be picked.

I looked out the window, still having a blank page,
when I saw kids playing, I was brought to a rage.
This was very unfair, me sitting in this hot room,
while my friends were playing kickball, and watching flowers bloom!
So I picked up my pencil, and ideas came soon!

I couldn't stop writing,
so many thoughts to put down,
as the words raced through my head,
this was a miracle, I was writing a poem.
I can't wait to recite it when my mom comes home.

Ryan Lago, Grade 6
Gilmore J Fisher Middle School

Wood Stork

W hen a fish touches a wood stork's bill, its bill snaps shut in 25 milliseconds!
O n a branch is where it makes a nest.
O ne interesting fact about this bird is it has quick reflexes.
D ull croak is the sound a wood stork makes.

S mall fish is what it likes to eat.
T he newborn usually weighs about 2 ounces.
O n a HOT day, the mother will drizzle water into the baby bird's mouth.
R eally, the wood stork is an endangered animal.
K nows how to fly, but it usually likes to walk.

Rachel Herzer, Grade 4
Franklin Township Elementary School

Disney World

D isney characters to greet you to your trip to Disney World.
I think that Disney World is the best place on Earth to have fun.
S o much amazement and exploration everywhere.
N ever a dull moment through each step you take.
E pcot, Animal Kingdom, MGM, and the Magic Kingdom are parks to enjoy.
Y ou and your family together make it even better.

W onderful shows and fireworks displays over Cinderella's castle are shown every day.
O utrageously good food and snacks.
R ides of many kinds, to give you delight.
L aughs and fun to everyone.
D elight to all on a trip to Disney World.

Arianna Zito, Grade 6
Assumption School

Family

A family will tell you
what's right and wrong.
A family will tell you
how to be strong.
Brothers, sisters, and parents too,
a family will always be there with you.
Life wouldn't be good for me,
if I had no family.
Sisters, brothers, mothers and fathers
all have love for one and each other.
We go to school, we go to play,
and my parents go to work each day.
Families stick together whether they are wealthy or poor,
that is what a family is for.

Katelyn Hummel, Grade 5
St Joseph Grade School

Meaningless

She walks through the large school
she feels so small.
Quietly and softly,
nobody sees her.
Meaningless and left out
Everyone has someone to talk to.
She waits,
she says Hi
but nobody hears her.
Do you feel that way?

Amanda Scallan, Grade 5
Durban Avenue Elementary School

Gardens

G ardening
A pples growing on trees
R ed flowers
D arkness in the night
E ating the stuff grown
N o weeds are allowed to come!
S tuff to be planted and grown.

Kristin VanArsdale, Grade 4
Hardyston Township Elementary School

Foot

I'm a foot.
You know me for walking
I was born small.
I move all over.
My best known friend is the shoes.
I fear stinkiness,
Because it makes me sick.
I love being washed in a bubble bath.
I dream I could be the biggest arcade in the world.

Alexander Kim, Grade 4
Christ the Teacher School

Music

In music types of sounds are very wide
As high and low as the ocean's tide

Music can be really long
And as sweet as a hummingbird's song

There are so many instruments to play
There are some I don't even know how to say

In all music is really cool
It's ever better than a hot day in the pool

Michael Pozo, Grade 5
St Veronica Elementary School

The Wind

The cloud's crying and running away.
The wind sounds like a roller coaster.
The wind is like a monster.
Branches cheering with the crowd.
Trees dancing to the rumbling beat of the wind.
Trees waving like the ocean.
Shingles flapping like they're trying to fly.
Branches flying off like Mother Nature has finally
Let them have their freedom.
Lights flickering like ghosts haunting us.
Wind howling like a wolf that's just seen the moon.
Winds having revenge on us for polluting.
Flags fluttering for freedom.
Wind sounds like elephants stomping on us.
Wind's saying
"We'll be back."

Charlene Lee, Grade 5
Cherry Hill Elementary School

Fred and Ed

There once was a robber named Fred,
Whose new partner in crime was Ed.
They stole ice cream cones,
That their neighbor did own.
But the neighbor found crumbs on his bed.

Jeffrey Hock, Grade 4
West End Memorial Elementary School

Bio

Mom
Loving, caring, hard worker, beautiful
Related to Nancy, Rodney, and Willie
Who cares deeply about me
Who feels comfortable when I am with her
Who needs a break once in a while
Who gives her money for me to play tennis
Who fears for my happiness
Who would like to see me do my best
Resident of Franklin Park, New Jersey

Chental-Song Bembry, Grade 4
Franklin Park Elementary School

The Day I Was Adopted

Nervous, excited
Great, cool, pretty, sweet
Happy tears, clapping, glad, joy
Beautiful, sweetness
Wonderful
Hazel Ryan, Grade 4
Mansfield Township Elementary School

Homeless

While thousands are still asleep
I cry and weep
I sleep in a box
While I have the chicken pox
I roam around the streets for food
Half of it's not even still good
While my clothes are tattered
People act like I don't matter
If people just cared a little more
My heart wouldn't be so torn
Tom Karmel, Grade 6
Chatham Middle School

Grandfather

Grandfather
Intelligent, terrific
Writing, working, trying
A hard working person
Me
Sedara Peacock, Grade 4
Mansfield Township Elementary School

Mike

There once was a guy named Mike,
Who would often fall off his bike.
He got really dirty,
And stood quite unsturdy
Now Mike will always yell "Yikes!"
Kay Crawford, Grade 4
West End Memorial Elementary School

History

I like to learn history,
it is not a mystery.

History is really cool,
I learn it in school.

History is never boring,
so I am never snoring.

History is knowledge,
you will use in college.
Matthew Morin, Grade 4
St Mary's School

Beach

Sitting on a rock
watching the waves roll in
beating up the sand,
squishing the rocks,
burying them,
washing the shells
until the night,
waves will sleep alone
until morning, watching.
Marissa Miuccio, Grade 6
Cherry Hill Elementary School

Andres

A lways is happy
N ever gets defeated
D ifferent from others
R arely dominant
E ntertainer and good spirit
S eems natural
Andres Mota, Grade 6
Fieldstone Middle School

The Silly Monkey

There's a monkey at the zoo
Who loves to eat people's shoes.
As the people walk on by,
You never know if he will say hi.
He loves to hang upside down,
And loves to go around and around
Like I said, He's at the zoo
Watch out he's coming after you.
Sydney Gugel, Grade 5
Most Holy Redeemer School

I Have

I have a sister
She has a blister
My dad is known as mister
And sometimes he whispers
But mostly he yells.

I have a dog named Sunny.
She is as fast as a bunny.
Coconut is my cat,
And he lays on a mat.
Obeton Osgood-Otis, Grade 6
Gilmore J Fisher Middle School

Cary

There once was a girl named Cary,
Who believed in a nighttime fairy.
When she went to sleep,
She heard a small peep,
And the night was very scary.
Maya Hamilton, Grade 4
West End Memorial Elementary School

I Hear the Valleys Singing

I hear the valleys singing
I hear the flowers dinging

I hear the wind blowing
I hear a river flowing

I hear the birds flying
I hear the wolves crying

I hear the grass swaying
I hear everyone playing

I hear the leaves scattering
I hear the branches clattering

I hear bees humming
I hear a storm cloud coming

I hear the lightning clashing
I hear feet quickly dashing
Melanie Psota, Grade 4
Sicomac Elementary School

Teachers

Teachers o' teachers,
Don't know what they'll be.
Some so happy,
Or some with no glee.

Our teacher's so nice,
But sometimes gets mad.
Kids these days,
Can get pretty bad.

She teaches us lessons,
So much we don't know.
Reading some books,
None that are low.

Mrs. Signorelli
Is my dear teacher.
She's loving and caring,
And a huge beacher.
Jill Ashinsky, Grade 6
Allen W Roberts Elementary School

Kobe

Kobe
Fast guard
Penetrating, dribbling, shooting
The fast, running star
The great.
Carlos Arruda, Grade 6
Sacred Heart Elementary School

Boo!

Witches scare me through the night
Ghosts spook me
I have a big fright
Creepy candies
Like eyeballs and ears
I freak out and my mom says,
"What's wrong, dear?"

Katie Barron, Grade 4
Springfield Township School

I Lost Someone Special*

When you lose someone special
It is hard at first and it is not easy to move on
But you should know that someday
It will be your turn to move on

Sometimes you think to yourself
About your life while you walk a dark path

As you walk that violent road of sadness and sorrow
Maybe the death was a good thing
He/She could have been suffering for a long time
It was their time to go

That someone special will always have
A reserved spot in your heart

Kimberly Bradley, Grade 6
St Veronica Elementary School
Dedicated to my aunt who passed away this summer

Veteran's Day — Thank a Soldier

Protecting our country
Protecting our nation
Protecting schools and education
The Marines, the Air Force, the Navy and the Coast Guard too
To people that support by wearing, red, white and blue

The Air Force helps by flying planes
Wow! That takes a lot of brains
The Navy and the Coast Guard protect our sea
To make it safe for you and me
The Marines fight on the ground
Creeping and crawling without a sound

What would we do?
What would we do?
What would we do without you?

Where would we be if you weren't here?
Would we live in constant fear?

Being free and proud
That is our way
We thank you each and every day.

Gregory Vlahakis, Grade 6
Chatham Middle School

A Young Girl from Spain

There once was a young girl from Spain
Who walked to school with her Great Dane;
They returned from school
Jumped into the pool,
And then went for a walk down the lane.

Madison Laske, Grade 4
Mansfield Township Elementary School

Writer of Stories

Writer of stories I am
writer of tales and poetry
but no story shall I now tell
to keep alive the mystery.

We all sit around this fire
watching the flames climb higher and higher
the sky above us shines with stars
the one that shines brightest is Mars.

The moon is waxing, shining bright
in the darkness of the night
the sun has set, it has gone away
to come back again another day.

Each one of us holds inside
a secret that will stay inside
and all of us have been trusted by another
to keep their secret between each other.

Writer of stories I am
writer of tales and poetry
but no story shall I now tell
to keep alive the mystery.

Leah von Essen, Grade 6
Indian Hill Elementary School

I Am From…

I am from a place where cats are lying on the couch
And my great grandma's old rocking chair

I am from a backyard where there is a nice hammock
And a HUGE trampoline

I am from a viola
A big clubhouse underneath my own bed
And seven cats

I am from phrases, phrases like "Yeah, live with it"
Also, "It's not the end of the world."

But mostly I am from a place where cats take over
And rule the house

Maggie Dominick, Grade 5
Bartle Elementary School

Candy

Candy is so sweet and delicious. With its taste that is irresistible to anybody. With its extraordinary smell that you just cannot say no to, whether it's chocolate, gum, lollipops, and anything else you can imagine. There is no limit to what you can make when it comes to candy. Your imagination can go to where you never thought it would go before. Your wildest dreams will come true. Once you take one bite of any candy it feels like you are taking a bite out of Heaven. There is really no word that describes or explains what happens when you take that bite or that lick or anything else. There is nothing that would explain it because you would have to try it first, but there is always one candy that everybody likes the one candy that nobody can live without because it is so good. So whether it is fruity or sticky or anything else you always come back for more. Just because it is candy.

Tiffany Cruz, Grade 6
Chatham Middle School

Let It Snow

Deep in the forest where there are many beautiful trees.
It it snowing right now on those green and white evergreen trees.
There is a joyful snowman waiting to be played with.
As the snow happily dances around.
The beautiful, evergreen trees like to watch the dancing snow land on each branch.
The very delightful snowman likes to be with the snow, but now the snowman says, 'it's time to go!'

Rebecca Hedum, Grade 5
Sandman Consolidated Elementary School

Spring

The smell of spring is a garden of tulips and roses that have just bloomed.
It is like a freshly baked basket of corn bread and a chocolate cake with sweet vanilla frosting.
Spring feels like smooth beach sand tickling in between my toes.
Spring is a beautiful buttercup flower blooming beautifully in the backyard
It is an orchestra playing the beautiful song symphony 9.

Brian Gastaldi, Grade 6
Franklin Elementary School

Injury on the Court

The knee will heal, as my unfortunate spot in the wooden bench will not.
Losing my chance to play in the championship could not be real.
The coaches treated the injury with urgency, even though the injury in my knee was not feeling harsh.
I could not question the main authority now.
Being down in this game and our best player in foul trouble, we were in a deep abyss.
Someone tapped my shoulder.
My coach asked me if I could play, and my answer was retort.

I go in between two offensive players, and as quick as a cat I pounce on the ball and steal it.
Moving the ball I pass it to my teammate.
He shoots and misses.
I am a beast as I rebound the ball and put it in.
Down by three after I hit a jump shot we foul them.
He misses both shots as we rebound the ball and call timeout.

Only thirteen seconds on the clock we inbound the ball.
I quickly leap and receive the ball.
A player pulls a cheap foul on me as I aggravate my knee again.
I pop up like a jack-in-a-box.
At the free throw line I pop the first shot.
Down by two I intentionally miss the second.
I grab the loose ball, turn, and heave a three-pointer.
SWOOSH!

Ross Dember, Grade 6
Fieldstone Middle School

Ordinary Day

The sky is blue the day is gray
The clouds are white and the birds are light
The grass is green and the people are mean
The class is wild and the lunch is mild
The dog is black and the boy lacks
The bell is yellin' and her name is Helen
And that's an ordinary day with Mcmelon

John Blake, Grade 5
St Rose of Lima School

When Nighttime Comes Around

The silver moon holds the sky
Sending a glow to all below
When nighttime comes around
The stars hang high
Where gravity is gone
When nighttime comes around.

Children nestled in their beds
All is calm, not a sound
When nighttime comes around
Waiting for the day to arise,
Their dreams fly higher than the sky
When nighttime comes around.

The trees are majestic beauties
Standing tall and proud
When nighttime comes around
The animals are lulled to sleep
As the branches sway gently in the breeze
When nighttime comes around.

Megan D'Avella, Grade 6
Woodglen Middle School

The Girl Who Placed

I'm getting ready before the race.
I know my time I know my place.

I go to my lane. I get in line.
Should I stretch? Do I have the time?

I'm in the water swimming fast,
gliding, reaching. My opponents I've passed.

The official watches my every move.
I use technique my stroke is smooth.

I touch the wall my race is done.
My teammates are screaming, "You won. You won."

I'm feeling good. There's a smile on my face.
As I hear a kid whisper, "That's the girl who placed."

Christina Sollitto, Grade 5
St John's Academy

Ode to My Basketball Hoop

Oh, basketball hoop. Oh, basketball hoop
I remember the first time I made a basket in you
I was so very proud
But it was the simplest shot.
Today I could make it like pie.
You taught me to dribble.
You taught me to shoot.
All the basics I learned in front of you.
Thank you for your teaching me so very much.
I hope you will never leave my lawn.

David DiBenedetto, Grade 5
Salt Brook Elementary School

Winter Play

Winter is cold.
Winter is bold.
Snow is wet.
But don't fret.
My mom gives us mittens to play in the snow.
So my brother and I can go, go, go.
I go to play with Bill.
Then we race down the hill.
I see wolf and deer prints.
And rabbits that sprint.
We build a snowman pair.
And then some cocoa to share.
The trees are all a glisten
And the animals all around listen.
The wind whistles.
The fire sizzles.
We jump around.
And don't hear a sound.
The day is over.
And we all have a big sleepover.

James Mack, Grade 5
St Veronica Elementary School

I Love Birthday Cake

I love birthday cake
It is great
The cake and frosting are so sweet
They come in yellow, white, and chocolate
The taste goes to my head
It gets on my fingertips and around my mouth

The candles light up a room
It is the best sight
And makes me smile with delight
The decorations are a surprise
Flowers, trees, trucks or balloons

I love birthday cake
It is great
I love birthday cake for goodness sake

Avery Arce, Grade 6
Gilmore J Fisher Middle School

Clouds
Soft and gentle clouds
Higher than Heaven can go
Surrounding the Earth
Louis Rozzo, Grade 4
Sicomac Elementary School

Useless Things
A pen with no ink
A pig that's not pink

The sky that's not blue
A cow that doesn't moo

Pants that are small
Leaves that don't fall

Phones that don't ring
Birds that don't sing

Brains that don't think
Eyes that don't wink

Drums that don't sound
Rain that doesn't pound

No clouds above
People that don't love
Ellen Lou, Grade 4
Sunnymead Elementary School

Friends
A friend is a person you can trust
A person who is always there for you
A person who keeps secrets
A person who is nice
A person who is kind to other people
A person who likes you for who you are
That is what a friend is
Stephanie Toal, Grade 5
St Joseph Grade School

Spring
Ah! It's the season of spring!
Everyone's in a mood to sing.
The spring breeze'll make you relax
Oh, but don't forget the income tax!
April's the time for showers,
For those beautiful garden flowers
The tall trees are dancing,
As if they're romancing
Then it's my favorite month May
And it's time for some baseball play
Spring, spring, spring
I love this season with a zing.
Meehir Shah, Grade 6
Kawameeh Middle School

Fog: Boredom of Life
It blinds the eye,
It bores the soul,
It lurks behind, stops your life,
You stop your Sunday drive,
It makes you wait,
For the mist we call fog we all hate.
Brian Frino, Grade 6
Allen W Roberts Elementary School

Deep Within
Rocks split apart,
Metal against rock,
Rocks screaming, who cares?
Human sweat stinks up the mines,
Work-worn hands plow down endlessly,
Human greed calls for the minerals.
Carl Lin, Grade 6
Bartle Elementary School

Tall Tree
Tall tree,
You shade me from the sun.
You bring me lots of fun.
And when the summer's done…
Delicious apples are to come.
Tall tree
In the fall you give me leaves.
In the winter you look so free.
Springtime you hide me from the breeze.
And when the year is done…
I can't wait till the next year has begun.
Tall tree.
Lena Rawley, Grade 5
Hillside Elementary School

Thanksgiving
T hinking of you.
H aving to give thanks.
A lways helping others.
N ever say no to helping.
K ind people.
S o very good for you.
G ood to others.
I ncredibly awesome.
V ery loving.
I am very nice.
N ice is a thankful thing.
G iving thanks and love.

D on't say anything mean.
A lways care for others.
Y ou better eat up!
Nicolette Hassett, Grade 4
Main Road Elementary School

Ben
There once was a farmer named Ben.
How he always played with his hen.
He hid in the hay
At the end of the day
And was never heard from again.
Ernest Tolson, Grade 4
West End Memorial Elementary School

Sad Feeling
As sad as a butterfly without a home
Crying and crying
Until it starts flying
Away in the fog and the mist.
Emily Lang, Grade 4
Wayside Elementary School

Strawberries
Strawberries are round and delicious.
In some way they are very suspicious.

Their seeds are like tiny eyes,
that look at you like a spy.

Inside them is a sugary and juicy
surprise.

It's almost like a human,
only it's a sweet luscious fruit!
Liana Conticello, Grade 4
Christ the Teacher School

Jill
There was a teacher named Jill
She jumped off a very big hill
She hurt her right leg
and started to beg
for a very large pain pill
Josh Rudin, Grade 4
Solomon Schechter Day School

My Life
As the clouds fly above me,
I look up and think,
When I wake up,
My life will be a skating rink.

I try to dodge obstacles,
Which are difficulties in life,
I try to stay peaceful,
So I will not have strife,
I will be kind and helpful
To animals so they are not rife
This is just a preview
Of my whole entire life.
Brisa Zhu, Grade 4
Indian Hill Elementary School

I Am

Love, kindness, caring
I care very much about my dog and sports
Honesty is very important to me
Kindness is very important to me
Hope is important to me
Loving is a good thing
Yams are bad, but they have a lot of vitamins
Love is wonderful
Relationships are good
Don't be mean
I Am

Elliott Henderson, Grade 6
Little Egg Harbor Intermediate School

Always There

I walked down by the deep blue sea,
And listened to the ocean for one last time,
Saw the waves glisten in the moonlight,
Heard the crash of waves upon the shore.
I waded into the chilling water,
The sand swirling 'round my feet,
Waves rolling and moaning,
Whispering to me, ever so softly
As I stood there for a while,
And let the ocean massage my feet,
Scrunched my toes and felt the shells,
I smelled the salty air and knew
The ocean was there for me.
I started to speak, and then I gushed,
'Til at last there wasn't but a thing in me,
That the ocean did not know.
I stared into the reflection of moonlight,
And I thought I saw, far off in the bay,
A wonderful harmony of peace and life
And then I knew, as I took in the sights
It was the ocean that was always there for me.

Daway Chou-Ren, Grade 6
Indian Hill Elementary School

Inside Outside

Outside the fireworks are bursting into stars,
Inside people are cooling off from the heat.

Outside the salty air flows around us,
Inside we get our beach equipment ready.

Outside we watch the sunset,
Inside we get ready for bed.

Outside the stars shine,
Inside we sleep silently.

Outside the sun rises,
Inside we wake up.

Brittany Southard, Grade 5
Byram Township Intermediate School

What Is Pink?

Pink is the color
Of a Valentine's rose,
The bow in my hair,
My very best clothes.

It is also the color
Of a cancer ribbon,
That belongs to a place,
The Breast Cancer Coalition.

When I think of pink,
I see my friends.
When they're wearing pink,
The fun never ends.

Sleepovers are pink,
Gumballs too.
Lipstick is pink
And a high heeled shoe

Flowers and love,
Will keep me insync,
Only, only,
If it is pink

Meaghan Joyce, Grade 5
Sandman Consolidated Elementary School

Glass Cup

"Smash!"
A glass was knocked off the table,
shattering into a million pieces.
Water flew all over the floor as it broke.
Tiny pieces of the cylinder glass were now all over the floor,
just waiting to be stepped on,
and the water waiting to be slipped on.
The expensive cup was fragile,
and destined to break someday.
"Oops," the three year old exclaimed reluctantly.
The mom came into the kitchen
and swept up the clear, colorless pieces of glass
and the clear water.
She filled up a plastic cup for the toddler.

Michael Aronson, Grade 5
Tamaques Elementary School

Depression

Depression is a deep, deep blue.
It smells like rotten food.
It looks like a dark empty room.
It tastes like poison.
It sounds like everyone in the world moaning at the same time.
It feels like someone pounding you continuously.

Vincent Braccia, Grade 6
St Rose of Lima School

The Forest's Secret

A small stream hides
Deep in the damp woods
Where the water whispers
Like the afternoon breeze
As mossy tree limbs reach out
Over the cool water
Where small water bugs
Dart along the water's surface
Like song birds
Flying to and fro
Across the darkening sky
And it is here
Where as the final rays of sunlight
Peek through the forest canopy
The stream shimmers
In the ever darkening forest.
Casey Sederman, Grade 5
Salt Brook Elementary School

Winter

Shining on the ground
Crystals falling from the sky
Sparkling new wonder
Nicholas Ingenito, Grade 4
Sicomac Elementary School

Sunset

June butterflies
Hover gracefully
Swirling winds
Rush them upward
Screech owl's
Glowing eyes
Peering through trees
Searching for prey
A mother robin
Sings a lullaby
To her beautiful
Yelping newborns
While an orange
Shimmering spirit
Weeps of loneliness
For it is
Fading in a
Sea of blue
Starry evening
Has Come
Keira McGee, Grade 5
Robert B Jaggard Elementary School

Gorillas

Kings of the jungle
coolest of all the mammals
very strong and smart
Cody Melton, Grade 6
Springfield Township School

The Rainbow Song

When do rainbows come around? Tell me loud and clear!
When do rainbows come around? When do they disappear?
Rainbows come for warmth and light, and they go back home at night.
That's when rainbows come around, that's when they disappear.

When do rainbows come around? Tell me with no lie!
When do rainbows come around? To brighten the blue sky.
Rainbows come for hope and love, then they soar up like a dove.
That's when rainbows come around, that's when they disappear.

If you see a rainbow, shout and yell and scream.
When it glows so very bright, you will surely beam.
If you see a rainbow, don't keep it from a friend.
Pass it on to everyone, so this song will never end!

That's when rainbows come around, that's when they disappear.
Julianna Perez, Grade 4
Edward H Bryan Elementary School

A Car's Life

Headlights act as powerful eyes.
Horn cries out an angry snarl.
Wipers clean the tears from his glass face.
He jolts as his four protective arms slam his shoulders and hips.
On board computer controls his conscience.
Getting thirsty for some quenching gas.
Searches for a pair of shoes in the tire shop.
He twitches in pain as the mechanic surgically removes his engine.
Unlike us, someone else puts the junk in his trunk.
Don't get him mad, or you'll set off his alarm!
Sean Haney, Grade 6
Little Egg Harbor Intermediate School

Memorial to Winter

It is spring now, winter's wrath is gone.
But a trace of it is a drift of snow yet little snow remains.

Land is not barren, it's covered with trees.
You listen to the birds and the bees.

Snow can melt, a new season
Has been dealt along with warmth.

The ice is gone, daylight is long. And warm.
We've made it through winter's frigid storm.

Huge, hungry grizzlies are now awake.
A blanket of ice has left the lake.

It soon will be summer, then fall and after that winter's wrath will ring
Throughout the land until it's spring.

It is spring now, winter's wrath has fled.
It is spring now, winter is literally dead.
Louie Howman, Grade 4
Community Park School

What to Wear, What to Wear
What to wear, what to wear
I don't know what to wear there's blue jeans there are T-shirts
There are capris and long shirts
What to wear what to wear please tell me what to wear
I like pink, green, and blue
It is so hard to pick when you are going to school
Please tell me what to wear

Mary Foster, Grade 4
Stonybrook Elementary School

A Fierce Battle
An ultimate amount of bullets flying over my head,
Gunfire and cannons all around me,
The smell of unpleasant sulfur,
The ground vibrating underneath me,
I taste the nauseating gun powder in the air,
The men of "Black Hawk Down" will survive.

Andrew Ashton, Grade 6
Long Branch Middle School

Spring
S prinklers splattering everywhere I go
P laying children ready to run
R ays of sunshine touching their faces
I mpatient flowers waiting to bloom
N apping nature waking up
G ardeners planting spectacular smelling flowers.

Sydney Silverstein, Grade 4
Solomon Schechter Day School

Loving My Family
Our family is great.
Full of surprises.
All happy and fun.
I don't want another one.
We are good together
I don't think it could be better.
I'm going to stop talking about this while I'm ahead.
To let you know I love my mom and dad.
I would go on and on.
But I choose to stop.
I'll tell you this, our family is at the top.

Greshauna Peterson, Grade 6
Gilmore J Fisher Middle School

Spring
S cary rollercoaster.
P retty fast.
R olling good.
I ntentional fall.
N ever ever ride a rollercoaster.
G ood bye.

Travis Ramage, Grade 5
Immaculate Conception Regional School

Light Green
Light green is the color of grass,
a leaf,
a stem of a flower.
The color of your shirt,
a piece of paper,
a chalk board,
a book,
a paintbrush,
a sweater,
some sneakers,
a snake.
Light green is my passion for fashion,
I love light green!

Sloan Toriello, Grade 4
Hardyston Township Elementary School

trying hard
struggling to try hard and to never
give up, but there's a wall that stands
behind me

struggling to try hard and to never
give up your wisdom, but there are trials
and tribulations standing beyond me

struggling to try hard and to never
give up your friends, but walls of enemies
are standing beyond me

trying hard to give up your father
but, there's a wall with love that stands
beyond me

trying hard to give up your mother
but you can't 'cause there isn't any wall
to block you from her love

Samaiah Rollins, Grade 6
Louise A Spencer Elementary School

Dogs
Dogs are a man's best friend
They'll be with you until the end
Some are small, some are large
My friend's dog is named Marge
Some are dirty, some are clean
Some have rabies and act mean
My dog has a blue squeaky toy
When we take her for a walk, she jumps for joy
Some have black hair, some have white
Some wear collars that are tight
When dogs go to the bathroom on the rug
You should never give them a hug
Some are short, some are tall
But I love my dog best of all.

Diane Arlotta, Grade 6
Our Lady of Mount Virgin School

Awake One Night

One winter night
The moon's bright light
kept me awake all night.
The moon's bright glow
on the white snow
flowed through my room's window.
When I closed the shade,
the light started to fade,
but I still couldn't fall asleep.
The sun came up, the moon went down,
my sleepy smile became a frown.
I was up all night
because of the light
of the bright new moon.

Christian Giancarlo, Grade 5
St John's Academy

School Is Sickening

I will not go to school!
I very well refuse.
I don't want to go.
I wish I could choose.
My dog got sick, so did I
My temperature is fine?
How could that be?
I am allergic to pencils
Oh, wait! It's Saturday!
It's funny, I feel better this way.

Ernie Oravsky, Grade 4
Mansfield Township Elementary School

My Street!

The street I live on
Is very fun!
When you visit you
Will always see the sun.
See the sun
So very bright
Our street is a very spectacular sight!
North Princeton Ave.
Is the best!
Will you come over and…
Be my guest?!

Isabella Rodier, Grade 4
Holy Saviour School

Old Man Pat

There was an old man named Pat,
Who loved to eat this and that.
His favorite was cheese,
He'd say "more please,"
And that's why he got really fat.

Morgan Bookholdt, Grade 4
Mansfield Township Elementary School

My Life Is in Ruins

My life is in ruins —
    I gotta look to it
'Cuz my smile ain't cute anymore.
Good times are long past
    No worry —
I'm more serious than sad.
I'm cryin' all night
    Tryin'
To make the world better.
I get ashamed of my eyes
    But I gotta think fast
My life's going right past.
I just cannot believe —
    All my life
I've been on the wrong track.
But now I know
    All this was a test
To see if I could pass.
And be given the chance
    To live my life forever
Then, again, I'd be so sad.

Samah Aldaraghmeh, Grade 6
Academy Street Elementary School

My Special Place

I'm upset, I don't feel good
I go to my special place
I walk into my TV room
and cuddle up in the corner
of the couch and
turn on the TV
I feel warm and cozy
I sit alone
thinking of nothing
helps me get away from all "the noise"
My special place might
not always be the same place
but I will always have one

Alex Kaplan, Grade 5
Salt Brook Elementary School

Tree

A tree standing still,
Right on the hill.
It blows left and right,
That it looks very bright.
It grows and grows very high,
That I will ask why.
It comes in all kinds of colors,
Including some with flowers.
It stays there all days,
And never goes away.
I hope you never die,
Because I would cry all day.

Dorothy Peng, Grade 4
Christ the Teacher School

My New Bunny

One glorious Christmas morning
I woke up and saw
a new baby bunny
in my living room.
His tail was so adorable and fuzzy,
his ears so silky soft,
and his cute little button nose,
twitching at every scent.

Emily Sobeck, Grade 6
Cherry Hill Elementary School

Camp Hoover

I went to Camp Hoover
I am a mover
I made lanyard in arts and crafts
I road rafts
I went in the lake
I baked a good cake
My counselor had pet mules
OH Boy!! Too Many Rules!!

Morgan Mazellan, Grade 5
Our Lady of Mount Virgin School

Spring Is Fun

Spring is fun, it's time to run!
Run and play, play all day!
Days get longer, flower stems stronger!
Gorgeous flowers, long warm hours.
The weather is great, no time to wait!
Let's go outside, for a bike ride!
Spring is fun, spring is fun!

Monica Spooner, Grade 4
John F Kennedy Elementary School

Summer/Winter

Summer
Tangy, peppery
Cheerful, open, colorful
Pleasant, radiant, dull, quiet
Gloomy, colorless, dreary
Bland, stale
Winter

Stephanie Perpepaj, Grade 4
St Joseph School

Kitten

Small, fun
Pouncing, purring, sleeping
Meow. whiskered, playing, killing
Hissing, scratching, taller
Big, old
Cat

Andrew Fenstermacher, Grade 4
Mansfield Township Elementary School

The Drums

Hitting the cymbal with my drum stick
Pounding on the bass drum with a hard kick
Every time I hit the drum I don't forget to count
I like to hit it light at first and then the sound will mount
The drums involve lots of sound
Sound so loud it might shake the ground.

Matthew Bent, Grade 4
St Mary's School

What Is Red?

Red is a black spotted lady bug, fluttering in the sky,
Red is the bright color on the Fourth of July,
Red is the stripes on an American flag,
Red is when you trip and fall when you are playing tag,
Red is leaves everywhere on a breezy fall day,
Red is when you're laying in a stack of hay,
Red is a juicy apple picked fresh from a tree,
Red is when you're on a roller coaster yelling out "Whee!"
Red is a beautiful bouquet of red roses on Mother's Day,
Along with a box of chocolates given in a special way,
Red sounds like the bells on a tambourine,
Red goes very nicely with green,
Red is a beautiful sunset on a lovely summer evening,
Where it is so quiet you can hear yourself breathing,
Red is love on Valentine's Day,
Red is a vacation far far away.

Sagheer Khan, Grade 5
Edgar Middle School

Life of a Storm

A lion roars
A ghost whispers
The trees are scratching the sky, so it weeps
The wind whips the very trees who scraped it
This is the life of a storm.

Meaghan Velten, Grade 5
Cherry Hill Elementary School

Friends

F ollow you when they think there's something wrong.
R ely on you to always watch their back.
I nterrupt you when they are bored.
E ncourage you when you're down.
N eed you when they're hurt.
D o everything you do.
S ometimes have solutions to your problems

Nikki Storr, Grade 5
Belhaven Avenue Middle School

What Is Blue?

B lue is the color of water
L uscious blueberries
U ltimate blue sky
E xcellent blue ocean

Randy Raymond Roof Jr., Grade 4
Hardyston Township Elementary School

Isabella

I am a sweet and loving girl
I wonder why I have such wonderful gifts
I hear tiger's roar on television
I see birds outside on my front lawn
I want to work with tigers in captivity
I am a sweet and loving girl

I pretend I sing on Broadway
I feel my friend's special touch
I touch and pet my parakeets
I worry about my stomach
I cry when I am sick
I am a sweet and loving girl

I understand why I should do things
I always play with my sister
I dream of singing with my friend
I try to do my best
I hope to be a famous singer one day
I am a sweet and loving girl

Isabella Fronte, Grade 4
Meadowbrook Elementary School

My Valentine

It would fill that heart of mine
Just to get a Valentine
Sure I have a man a little bit away
But people don't believe me to this very day.
They say I'm too ugly to find a man
And think it's all a plan,
To attract popular friends
They all think my so-called sham will end.
Since 3rd grade I haven't got a Valentine
Except from that "imaginary" boyfriend of mine
Every other girl who has a boyfriend
Has backpacks of flowers that seem to never end
They say I should drop it
But I just won't stop it
Until they get in into their minds
That he's cute, sweet, and very kind.

Melissa Cannella, Grade 6
Thomas Jefferson Middle School

The Train

If only if only, the conductor sighed
The branches on the trees will grow with pride
If only if only, the train whistle blew
The train traveled fast as the dark shadows grew
If only if only, the passengers know
The weather got cold and it started to snow
If only if only, the train wheels turned
They would be home soon, they learned

Peter Flanagan, Grade 6
St Veronica Elementary School

Evergreen

Evergreen, you're evergreen
Through summer, spring, and fall
Even when, in wintertime
Your branches catch snowfall

Evergreen, so evergreen
Your emerald color bright
The color you behold to me
Is miles beyond delight

Evergreen, 'O Evergreen
You stand so proud and tall
Even though your pine needles
Might seem to you so small

Evergreen you're green and true
Through my windowpane I stare
And I see you — how wondrous
A great tree beyond compare

Evelyn D'Elia, Grade 4
Old York Elementary School

Fred

There once was a guy named Fred
Who had a dog that fled

He ran to the park
All he did was bark

Will he come back to Fred?
Matthew Colvin, Grade 4
St Mary's School

Dad

Dad
Male, strong
Sleeping, playing, cool
Can't beat at anything
Playing, acting, running
Watching, awesome
Handsome
Justin Hellar, Grade 4
Katharine D Malone Elementary School

Santa

Santa is very jolly
He likes to hang up balls of holly.
Santa made a special dolly.
He gave it to a girl named Molly.

Santa made lots of toys.
He made them for the girls and boys.
It makes their hearts fill with joy.
Especially my baby brother Troy.
Daniel Cortes, Grade 4
Springfield Township School

Fantasy Creatures

There are many creatures with names that start with different letters of the alphabet.
For **B** there is the fiery Balrog
For **C** there are smart centaurs and one-eyed cyclops
For **D** there are colorful dragons and rough dwarfs
For **E** there are enchanting elves and tree-like Ents
For **F** there are magical fairies and friendly fawns
For **G** there are colossal giants, sly goblins and naughty gnomes
For **H** there are the housewarming hobbits
For **L** there are the crafty leprechauns.
For **M** there are sea-loving mermaids
For **O** there are the big-as-a-house Oliphaunts and sturdy Orcs
For **P** there are the flying Pegasus, the flaming phoenix and the petite pixies
For **T** there are tricky trolls
For **U** there are the mono horned Unicorn
Finally for **W** there are the wondrous wangs, wise wizards, and weird wulfs.
Rebecca Pocelinko, Grade 6
Trinity Christian School

Summer

School is out, let's all scream and roar!
No more learning about math and the war!
The pool is open, the diving board is fun!
Sometimes we tan under the hot, hot sun!
The ice cream man he comes around!
And when he does you hear the dingy sound!
Going on vacation with family and mates!
Going out to the beach, and out on late night on your roller skates!
Staying up late nights with friends is the best!
Especially when you don't get any rest!
Shayla Sweeney, Grade 5
St Rose of Lima School

Come with Me

Come with me and…
we'll soar through the cool blue sky
with clouds touching our faces as we fly gracefully.

Come with me and…
we'll lay on the warm hot sand at the beach
as we refresh ourselves with water and when we eat sandwiches.

Come with me and…
we'll run into the clear ocean with
the fish fins touching our feet making them tickle.

Come with me and…
we'll laugh our way until we get
back to our house and then get ready for bed.

Come with me and…
we'll share our special memories
together as we read our family album.

Macayla Ferry, Grade 4
Lincroft Elementary School

Bumblebees

B usy bees flying all around
U sually making me petrified.
M aking loud sounds to warn people to get away
B uzzing everywhere
L eaving their hives to gather honey
E asily sting people and make them cry.
B othering people enjoying a day at the park
E very day bees build hives around bushes and trees.
E xcited bees surrounding a meadow of flowers
S ettling in their hives 'til dawn.

Kylie Feldman, Grade 4
Solomon Schechter Day School

Spring

Spring is warm,
Spring is bright,
Spring makes all of the flowers
Grow back to life.

Spring is beautiful,
Spring is the best,
It is better than the rest.

Spring is awesome,
Spring is cool,
Spring makes me want to
Jump right in a swimming pool.

Devin Peterson, Grade 6
Immaculate Conception Regional School

Being a Wave in the Ocean

If I were a wave in the ocean
I'd lift my wings of water
And soar down to the sheet of velvet sand

I would greet the children
As they jumped into my blue shirt

I would lift my head up high
Way above the heavens
Say hello to the angels
Then come back to my fortress of sea

Wind would ripple my hair
God would hit a strike
An amazing beam of light would hit my head
And amaze everyone in sight

Then I would calm down
And look up at the sky
The moon and stars reflect off me
As my waves whisper in the night

Colleen McGuire, Grade 4
Sicomac Elementary School

Grandpa Steve

Caring and loving
As kind as can be
Always looked so happy to me
With a smile on his face,
showed that he was full of grace
You would never know that deep inside
he was suffering with cancer
Eleven days in the hospital
And I guess on that last day he wasn't meant to stay
because he passed away
No one will ever know how sad I was on that day
that they told me my grandfather passed away
I thought there goes my grandpa my best friend 'till this day
I couldn't live without him there's no way
No one as caring or as kind as he
But, it was nice to know he died loving me

Anastasia Murray, Grade 6
Roosevelt Elementary School

My Dad…Friend and Coach

My dad has taught me
All there is to learn about football
I still need to learn a lot more
Though he shows me all the basics
But I'm still missing one more thing
And that is my appreciation
But sometimes when he teaches me
I forget about my concentration
I always know
He still loves me no matter the situation
Even when I win sometimes
I show off like I'm the best
He teaches me to always try my hardest
Always try to win
I love him even if he weren't a coach
Because he is always
My loving and very caring father
But also a very good friend to me
He will always be a part of my life
So here is one way I can brighten his day
By telling you are my dad, friend, and coach

Trevor Signorino, Grade 5
North Dover Elementary School

My Wish

Can I see once more the shining sea?
You know it means the world to me.
At dusk I sit upon the sand.
I patiently wait for something grand.
But as far as I can see, a glimmer, a light.
Maybe just for me.
No, I want all to know how the glow of moonlight thrills me so.
The brilliant stars in a black sky, the ripple of the sea.
Best of all, I love what it does for me.

Robert Lawler, Grade 6
Our Lady of Mount Virgin School

My Many Questions

I have too many questions
Sitting in my head
They are stuck
Trying to come out
Only some of them come out
And are told.
But some
Stay in my head
Waiting for their turn
To be asked.
Why is paper so important?
How do birds fly?
Where is Santa Claus?
Can giants touch the sky?
Questions, Questions, Questions,
Does anyone have the answers?
Rebecca Ahmad, Grade 4
Toll Gate Grammar School

Nelly

There once was a girl named Nelly,
Her big sister's name was Kelly.
    She loved to play ball,
    She made all the calls.
Until a ball hit her big belly.
Sherry Stanek, Grade 4
West End Memorial Elementary School

Someone I Know

She smells like a room filled with roses;
Her hands as soft as the velvet petals;
Love whispers like the soft wind blowing;
Blushing beauty, blooming gently,
sweet sensation, joyful flavors
Jamal Golding, Grade 6
Franklin Elementary School

Nature

The birds are singing
The insects are crawling around
None of them will frown.
Jonathan Brauner, Grade 4
Solomon Schechter Day School

Today

Wake up happy
Jump out of the room
Prance with joy
Watch the flowers bloom

Run inside
Time for bed
Say good night
Rest your head
Erin Walsh, Grade 4
Lincroft Elementary School

Morning Whispers

I can see the bright
Shining sun peeking
Over the horizon,
As the birds start to
chirp loudly,
Waking up the neighbors.
I can smell the pancake syrup
Being sprinkled
Onto steaming breakfasts.
The wind blows fresh air
from outside
In my window…
Morning Whispers
Alison Wolfer, Grade 4
Ridge Ranch Elementary School

The Boogie Board

Crash! A wave comes up behind me,
I kick up from the sand,
I feel nearly weightless,
As my boogie board supports me.
I see a blur of color; I'm going so fast.
I think it was my mom.
I begin to laugh.
Oh boy it's fun, so I get up on my knees.
Then I stand up shaking just a little.
People jump and scream and run away
Even though I will not hurt them.
I feel like I'm flying!
No one can ever bring me down!
I feel free.
I feel myself get slower,
Then I come to a halt.
My ride is done,
It was fun.
Come on, let's do it again.
Alison Simon, Grade 5
Tamaques Elementary School

I Admire My Dad

I admire my dad.
He works all day so very hard.
When he comes home,
He is so tired.
Yet he plays games
With Scott and me.
He even helps me
With my homework.
But most of all,
He tells me that
He loves me.
My dad!!!
Sean Balian, Grade 4
Christ the Teacher School

Fall

Fall is when
all the leaves go down
and you see all the different colors
lying on the ground
Valerio Ceva, Grade 6
Gilmore J Fisher Middle School

Wolves

Hear them howl
A sorrowful tune
See them prowl
Under the moon

Living in a pack
Like a big family
So they won't fight
They have a hierarchy

When they're hunting
As fierce as can be
Catching their prey
That's trying to flee

Wolves are amazing
Smart, sneaky, and sly
That they are majestic
No one can deny
Noah Thomas, Grade 4
Old York Elementary School

The Moon I See

The moon is my neighbor
That I love to see!

The moon is like a pearl
Snow white as you can see.

The moon is like a gem
On a ring of stars.

The moon is like a ball
Being hit by a ring of stars.

The moon is like a doorknob
Waiting to open.

The moon is like a snowflake
Waiting to fall.

The moon is like our earth's shadow
It follows every turn we make.

The moon is like a neighbor
That I love to see!
Raveena Midha, Grade 4
Woods Road Elementary School

Rain

Do you hear it?
On my bed I sit
Watching while the rain goes pitter, patter, pitter
Upon the windowsill, I see it glitter.
Drip, Drop, Drip, Drop
As the rain goes flip, flop
Onto the sidewalk
I'm there, not daring to talk,
Just watching the rain
Glisten upon the windowpane
And as the water drops fall
I seem to hear them call
"Go and help the Earth
To give its glorious rebirth."

Margaret Roche, Grade 4
St Joseph School

If I Were an Owl

If I were an owl,
I'd soar through the night sky.
My wings would feel like a piece of paper
Flowing in the wind.
I would swoop down and get my prey
When the peaceful night is over,
I'd start heading back to my cozy, dark hole
Until night comes again.

Cynthia Brain, Grade 4
Sicomac Elementary School

Helmets: On Pads: On Losing: Off

There are many things that are important to me
But playing sports are addictive you see
I start out the season playing football
I'm very confident I'll get the ball
This isn't a sham it's as plain as I say
Scoring a touchdown would surely make my day

Playing football makes me feel strong
Just like a lumberjack knocking a tree on the lawn
I'm happy, excited, and pumped when the season starts
I feel I play a very big part

When the season ends I feel like I lost my best friend
I can't wait for it all to start up again

Jesse Rosenthal, Grade 6
Fieldstone Middle School

Love

Love is pink.
It smells like fresh cut roses.
It looks like a rainbow of hearts in the sky with a pot of love.
It tastes like ice cream cake.
It sounds like birds singing in the morning dew.
Love feels like the sensation that words can never explain.

Carly Burke, Grade 6
St Rose of Lima School

Rainforest

Rainforest, rainforest
Watered by the sky's tears.
Branches sliced by garden shears.
The floor is alive with bugs a'crawling,
You can hear the birds cawing.
It is alive with life,
Soon it will be still.

Going…
  going…
And before we know it, it is…
      gone.

Dylan Rhile, Grade 4
Middle Township Elementary School #2

Can I?

Can I make life as sweet as chocolate cream,
Can I make life nothing but a dream,
Can all this be possible,
Can I be held responsible?

Can I see the future in the past,
Can I make a moment last,
Or can I make time go fast?

I can see what the future holds,
I can see a heart of gold,
I can see the warmth inside.

I can see your hopes and dreams,
I can see all the seams tied together
For always and forever.

Anna Stienstra, Grade 6
Walter T. Bergen Middle School

I Don't Understand

I don't understand…
  why heartbreak is so tragic
  why people console themselves by putting others down
  why the world is getting meaner

But most of all…
  how people can kill
  why animals are mistreated
  why wars can't be fought with words

What I understand most is…
  why smiles are contagious
  why bears hibernate
  why sunshine cleanses the soul
  why pets are so comforting

Jessica Leech, Grade 6
Little Egg Harbor Intermediate School

Away by the Sea

One misty day, when fall was near.
A soft sound a dog did hear,
The cry of a child at sea.
So far where no one could see.

The dog, he dashed so quick did he,
To find the child by the sea.
Alas! There was no child by.
At the rock there was a shock.

The cry was of a child with glee
It was not a cry with grief.
Out at sea was his father's boat
With coming tales ready to boast.

The dog he turned away from the sea,
So far where no one could see.
Away into the misty fog
Away, away did he trod.

Daniela C. Mallack, Grade 6
Trinity Christian School

Books

Books are like stepping
Into a different world

Yet you can still
Slip between the pages
Of a book

The books are hidden
In the shelves

The words are hiding
Between the pages

To be found
By a curious mind

In a library waiting
Waiting for the day

That they get a visit
With the reader
Karinna Wildauer, Grade 6
Chatham Middle School

Dream/Nightmare

Dream
Happy, wondrous
Warming, hoping, confusing
Trance, imagination, horror, images
Scary, mysterious
Nightmare
Sophie Ghizzone, Grade 4
Our Lady of Mount Virgin School

My Mom

When I am very sad, my mom makes me glad.
She helped me ride my bike, when I was only a little tyke.
Sometimes she is mad, sad, and also very glad.
When I am sick, she makes me feel better.
When she is sick, I sometimes write her a letter.
Sometimes she will play with me and even be funny.
Her eyes are green, just like the eyes of her kitty, and she always looks pretty.
My mom dresses very well and is always swell.
When people are around her, she always makes them smile.
If I make my day a bore, she says to do a chore.
When I help my mom prepare for dinner, she calls me a real winner.
When I came to North Dover School, she helped me be cool.
My mom helped me with many things.
In fact, I would call her better than a thousand kind kings.
She knows what to say, when it's been a bad day.
My mom always helps when someone yelps.
Whenever she winks, she knows what to think
I love her so, that's what she should know.
When she goes to work, I will miss her.
So before she leaves, I will kiss her.

Joseph Randazzo, Grade 5
North Dover Elementary School

Another

Another poem; another line; another girl pretending she's fine.
Another hour; another day she wishes she could get away.
Another heartbreak; another tear; another excuse she doesn't wanna hear.
Another paper; another pen; she writes she wants to be strong again.
Another story; another line; another night that she will cry.
Another band; another song; another day passed…slowly gone.

Tamara Dietlein, Grade 6
Bartle Elementary School

Spring Fever

S o long have people tolerated cold dreary nights (ones of Poe's and my delight).
P ouring down, the rain feeds the Earth as the buds slowly become flowers.
R eacting to time and weather the birds all return to their homes for the season has come.
I nspiring young authors and artists, do the beautiful weather and skies. But, I do not appreciate summer and spring as I still hold on to winter's last thread.
N ew flowers blossoming, so colorful and cheerful, to many a one's delight. What has happened to the world so cheerful? Is no one else like Poe; am I the last to share his delights of long, cold, dreary nights?
G nats flying 'round your head, another nuisance both spring and summer share.

F or months on end it has been wonderfully cold, but now it is too warm.
E vening after evening days grow longer and nights grow shorter, after the start of spring.
V iolets blossom throughout the state catching many a one's eye.
E vening after evening days grow shorter and nights grow longer after the start of summer.
R eversing the order from nights of snow to days of beating sun.

Benjamin Glass, Grade 4
Solomon Schechter Day School

Why?

He moans, he groans
He whines, he cries
He limps, he whimpers
My dog is gonna die.

Sometimes I ask myself, why?
Why him?
What if he dies in his sleep or when I'm at school?
To me this situation is so uncool.

He tries to eat, he tries to drink
He tries to hear, he tries to see
He tries to walk, he even tries to talk
But never once has he succeeded.
My dog is gonna die.

Every time I see him, it breaks my heart in two
When he moans, I groan.
When he whines, I cry.
I ask myself, why?
Why does he have to die?

Ashley Vassiliou, Grade 5
Central School

The Shore

During the summer I go to the shore.
I walk up to the ocean,
The waves make a roar.
I love to relax and sit in the sun,
And watch the people have some fun.
The seagulls are flying by so high.
The sun is shining up in the sky.
Now I go to play in the ocean.
The waves are moving with such great motion.
I hope when I come to the shore next year,
The ocean waves are what I hear.

Lauren Oddi, Grade 5
St John's Academy

Fog

The silent, gray fog
Drifts just like a tired, lazy kitten
Looking for a place to rest
It slowly,
Like a turtle sits
Looking hard over a brown, fudge-looking harbor
In the dark quiet city
On silent haunches moves
As silent as the wind
It drifts quietly away
But will be back again
Another silent dark night

Brigid Tonry, Grade 4
Pond Road Middle School

I Want a World…

I want a world where there are no chores.
I want a world where there is more opportunities for all people.
I want a world where there are no gangs!
I pray for this world

OH!
how I pray
for
this
wonderful
world

Justin Foster, Grade 4
Evergreen Elementary School

Video Games

Oh, video games!
Oh, video games!
Video games are fun to play,
But if you play all day,
It will melt your brain away!
Your brain will go down the drain,
If you get absorbed in all that technology,
Your brain might get confused when it's time to study.
Oh, video games!
Oh, video games!
They're so fun to play…
But not all day!!!
Video games can be a lot of fun,
On a rainy day when there is no sun!
But when the sun comes back into the day,
It's time to go outside and play.

Sean Gallagher, Grade 4
St Peter Elementary School

Polar Bears

Polar bears.
Polar bears are white.
Polar bears are white and are cozy.
Polar bears are white, cozy, and eat fish.
Polar bears are white, cozy, and eat fish from the sea.
I like polar bears.

Christine Castelluber, Grade 6
Roosevelt Elementary School

Is It Heaven?

It glistens and shines in every spot,
It's really freezing but I swear it feels hot.
My hands tingle in my hot sweaty gloves,
I'm talking about the place that everyone loves.
It's truly amazing in every way,
When the snow sparkles and it's here to stay.
I love the mountains that reach the sky,
When I point my skis downhill I'm anything but shy.
This is a place where everyone should go,
It's always perfect so go with the flow!

Andrew Cohen, Grade 4
Richard Stockton Elementary School

Wind

Wind
cool, refreshing
blowing, howling, whispering
blissful, happy, chilled, soothed
breeze
Savannah Murphy, Grade 6
John Hill School

Love

A heart is fuzzy like a bunny.
Love letters are sometimes funny.
Candy hearts are sweet,
They cannot be beat.
Flowers are nice.
They give love power.
Love can fly,
Like a dove in the sky.
Love is a wonderful dream,
And I see love is not mean.
Kelly Barruffe, Grade 4
St Rose of Lima School

Bad Day

It is the worst time
of the new year,
The winds are whipping around
Like the hands of a clock.
Twigs are breaking,
The winds are howling,
and the shingles are flying like disks.
What a cold, unsatisfying day today is.
Matthew Kim, Grade 5
Cherry Hill Elementary School

Cotton Candy

Sticky, chewy, fun to eat,
Cotton candy is my favorite treat.

It comes in colors, pink and blue,
Do you like cotton candy too?

You can get it anywhere,
Just don't get it in your hair.

You can eat it on a stick,
I'm glad it's not as hard as bricks.

When you eat it you get sticky,
So when you eat it don't be picky.

Cotton candy is so neat,
That's why it's my favorite treat!
Shannon Trimm, Grade 5
St John's Academy

The Peace of the Ocean

The water of the ocean
Breaks into waves,
Washing shells and starfish
Up to the shore.
The sun's rays reflect
Off the cool water.
The creatures of the sea are playing.
Dolphins are jumping.
Turtles are diving deep, deep
Down into the sea.
Children look for sand crabs.
The ocean is peaceful.
Sara Hayet, Grade 4
Wayside Elementary School

Come with Me…

Come with me and we will peacefully
glide over the large Colorado
mountain tops.

Come with me and we will skip over
every ocean and watch the
sparkling waters

Come with me and we will dream
about a magical land where all we
do is play and relax.

Come with me and we will soar
over to Florida, Paris, Milan, or even
Ecuador and have the time of our lives.

Come with me and we will live the
life that we have dreamed of — a
life of excitement, happiness and joy!

Come with me and we will love
and care for each other because
we are a family.
Maria Alvarado, Grade 4
Lincroft Elementary School

Stars

Little dancing, twinkling eyes
Guide me through the wet night
Then come out to say their prayers
Like angels blowing in the air
Kiersten Leigh Horner, Grade 6
Little Egg Harbor Intermediate School

Sunshine

The sun is gleaming.
Shining in my face, so bright.
Summer is coming!
Kelsey Bishop, Grade 4
Stonybrook Elementary School

Football and Baseball

Football
Awesome, surprising.
Passing, tackling, running.
Goal, touchdown, homerun, trophy.
Hitting, diving, jumping.
Great, fun.
Baseball
Gordon Farley, Grade 4
Holy Family Interparochial School

A Long, Cold Winter

A long cold winter,
Of very cold weather,
When snow falls,
As light as a feather.

Long dark nights,
Short cold days,
Winter is the end,
Of fall's ways.

Baseball's over,
Football too,
There are not many sports,
That you can do.

So if you like winter,
Too bad for you,
'Cause birds are gonna fly,
Where they already flew.
Andreas M. Goergen, Grade 4
Stonybrook Elementary School

Baseball

B atting at home plate
A ction on the green colored field
S houting, "I got it," with arms extended.
E veryone happy, winning or losing.
B anging baseballs over the fence.
A ttentive eyes watching each move
L aughing in the dugout
L istening to loud cheers.
Adam Taylor, Grade 4
Solomon Schechter Day School

Spring

S prouting of beautiful flowers,
P etals show the most.
R ain makes them grow,
I n the ground they live.
N ature brings them alive.
G reat flowers are my most favorite!
Maddison Brown, Grade 4
Middle Township Elementary School #2

My Wonderland of Peace

Have you ever thought of a world full of peace?
Well, I've been doing that.
I've dreamed and thought of some people...
Blamed, abused, victimized
And of people who've collaborated...perpetrated
They are holding hands.
These people have befriended each other.
If you were in my wonderland...
A wonderland of peace...you would see...
Martin alive — his life easy,
He can love it; he's the same man...
Just and brave.
Now that it's dawned upon you,
What is your wonderland?
Mine is beautiful, full of freedom.
It's that picture in my mind...
Full of peace and distinctive hearts
That gets my mind going...
And keeps it about.
That is my wonderland...
My wonderland of peace.

Josh Musicant, Grade 5
North Dover Elementary School

Wind

Wind changed my sails when I was going one direction
Wind blew all my files in the air
Wind reasoned Katrina to hit land.

One thing in life we cannot change is wind.
The wind is always moving.
Never stopping.
We cannot overcome the power of the wind.

Kunj Bhatt, Grade 6
Thomas Jefferson Middle School

Newspaper

Newspaper
Black, white,
Pictures, news, paper,
It's read all over
Useful, thick, big
Small, smart,
Dictionary

Brittany Minetti, Grade 4
Katharine D Malone Elementary School

Spring

S unny days are coming
P urple flowers are blooming
R iver rafting time is here
I tchy with allergies
N ose running
G reat smells fill the air...too bad I can't smell them!

Aaron Tannenbaum, Grade 4
Solomon Schechter Day School

Jolly Christmas

Christmas is like playing in the snow because they're both fun
It is exciting, cheerful, and it's number one
It is acknowledged every year
By all the kids, parents, and peers

Christmas is the best to me because it's my birthday
I wish I had this amazing moment every day
I get extra presents and my family stays over
I was lucky to be born on a holiday

On this holiday nobody works, everybody stays home
Christmas is like impunity from everyone
They are safe from the glistening ice
They're footprints in the snow
Christmas is my most favorite holiday

Michael Manhart, Grade 6
Fieldstone Middle School

Happiness

Happiness is yellow.
It smells like the ocean mist.
It looks like baby bunnies hopping through a field
Of daffodils in the springtime.
It tastes like cool lemonade on a hot summer's day.
It sounds like birds singing on a spring morning.
Happiness feels like all your troubles are gone.

Maria Di Bianca, Grade 6
St Rose of Lima School

Flowers

F lowers spread out like a blanket.
L ovely colors are everywhere.
O range, pink, purple, yellow.
W atch them as they bloom.
E njoy the roses, the daisies and the tulips.
R aindrops caress their heads.
S unlight warms them all over.

Jonathan Kielmanowicz, Grade 4
Solomon Schechter Day School

Autumn Leaves

Autumn leaves are like colorful raindrops
falling from their trees.

They fall down
like feathers from pillows.

Some are red, some are green
My favorite are all of them on their trees.

Some are crunchy as you walk
some are quiet as you talk.

Anna Lee Smith, Grade 4
Lincoln Park Elementary School

Matisse

M atisse is the best dog alive!!!
A scavenger is what he is!!!
T ake him out for a walk or jog!!!
I love Matisse!!!
S ees you once, he loves you forever!!!
S o so fluffy!!!
E veryone loves him!!!

Kayla Staley, Grade 4
Main Road Elementary School

Baseball

B ats and balls
A ll-stars
S teal bases
E ager to play
B aseball rules
A great game
L ose or win
L ots of fun

Sean Cullen, Grade 4
John F Kennedy Elementary School

Spring

April is here,
I smell its fresh breeze.
Spring flowers are blooming,
I hope I don't sneeze!

Raindrops sparkle,
Birds are chirping.
Fresh wind is blowing,
Easter is lurking.

Birds are hatching,
Their chirps are subtle.
They look so cute,
When they all cuddle.

Now spring is here,
Grass is growing.
Everybody is happy,
It sure is showing!

Alyssa Piwowarski, Grade 4
Stonybrook Elementary School

That Dark Face

The night…
Yes, that mysterious stranger,
Is he friend or foe?
Only he himself knows.
For he is the night,
Yes, the night, who is
So deep, yet so,
Profound.

Peter Lim, Grade 6
Cherry Hill Elementary School

Autumn

Orange-red leaves dancing in mid air
Long, lovely tower of chocolate brown wood kiss the leaves good-bye.
Our ball of heat says "Hello" to distorted circles of white
Mother Nature preparing for a long rest.
Cold air touches everything.
Earth's animals leave our presence but fill our minds.
Different shades of green color the ground.
But just for a little while…just to take a break.

Ryan Critelli, Grade 6
Long Branch Middle School

The Great Four Seasons

The Great Four Seasons are in my mind. When spring comes up I hear the chime.
When the wind blows in and out. I feel they never doubt me out.
That's why spring is a big shout.

Summer is my favorite season. I will give you all my reasons.
The bright yellow sun is in the air. While I lay in my comfy chair.
I smell juicy hamburgers on the grill. I chill by my window sill.

Fall is warm and cold. The leaves are red and gold.
The scenery is beautiful and peaceful. I almost caught Swiper the weasel.
That's why I'm so grateful.

Winter is white and freezing. It makes me start wheezing.
I get sick and stay inside I watch my friends have snowball fights.
I get bored because I have to do chores.

These are my reasons for my Great Four Seasons!

Tyler Recinos, Grade 5
Roosevelt Elementary School

The Winning Goal

I hear the word "Pass,"
I just screamed it out loud,
not knowing what will happen next,
and out of nowhere the ball comes hurdling my way.
Without thinking I take off like a bullet,
pushing and pulling the black and white ball,
around cleats, high over heads,
and kicked through knees and legs.
I make it so far just to see a whole other challenge awaits me.
Shooting the right way, choosing the angle,
the foot, the technique, and on top of all that, the cheers.
To let them down is just so horrifying.
My heart is pounding; my feet are sweating,
"Take the shot," I think.
Then out of the blue, I kick so hard I feel light headed,
it feels like everything is standing still.
It goes in the goal
and an overflowing feeling of joy tells me that I just won the game!

Julia Godbee, Grade 5
Tamaques Elementary School

If I Were a Planet

If I were a planet,
I'd get ready to race around the sun for a new year.
I would move my arms up and down.
I would fly like a bird as I finish.
I'd clap on Pluto coming in last.
It would be a long tiring run,
If I were a planet.

Gregory Duch, Grade 4
Sicomac Elementary School

Dance

Dancing is fun I started years ago
I feel so happy when I am in a show

Smile, smile, smile always on my face
Tap, tap, tap my feet are in a chase

Jazz, lyrical, and tap I love them all
When doing ballet I must stand up tall

I take it seriously and practice all the time
My costumes are bright, glisten and shine

Long practice hours, tough competitions
I enjoy myself and dance for fun
And care the least if I have lost or won

Angela Szczecina, Grade 5
St Veronica Elementary School

What Is Yellow?

Yellow is the color of the chalk that my teacher uses,
Yellow is paper I write on.
Yellow is the sun that shines on us wherever we go,
Yellow is the cars that pass us.
Yellow is some birds in the sky.
Yellow is some shirts that we see every day,
Yellow is some chairs that we sit in,
Yellow is the stars that we see every night,
Yellow is the Shop-Rite bags that we get from shopping
Yellow is little chicks.

Troy Drexler, Grade 4
Hardyston Township Elementary School

The Flowing Wind

The flowing wind,
The blue sea water I hear,
The sand at the ground and air,
And the sunset for everyone to see
The colors: red, orange, amber
Saying "bye-bye" and sinking
On the blue pure water,
Starry night.

Franshesca Quezada, Grade 6
The Red Bank Charter School

Soaring High

On a magnificent March day,
I grabbed my colorful kite and started to play.
My cheerful kite of blue, yellow, and red,
Was enough to keep me busy from morning until bed.

My kite surprised me in a number of ways.
I watched it fly and soar for many days.
The warm sandy beach is the best place for my kite,
As I run and jump around with all my might.

My kite's tail flapped and waved high into the sky.
It waved to the birds and planes as it went by.
All of a sudden a big gust of wind blew.
It took off with my kite, and that's all I knew!

Nicole Nemeth, Grade 5
Sacred Heart School

A Flower Buds…

A flower buds in trees and in the summer breeze.
Sunflowers are golden brown, Daffodils are yellow,
Tulips are violet purple, Edelweiss is white like snow,
And Deep Red Roses planted all around.

Carley Elliott, Grade 5
St Helena School

Happiness

Happiness is yellow
It smells like daisies in a garden
It looks like a glowing rainbow
It tastes like homemade sugar cookies
It sounds like chicks chirping
Happiness feels like sitting around a warm fire on a cold day

Mariah Giri, Grade 6
St Rose of Lima School

My Family

My family is like a puzzle,
one piece gone, we break apart.
My brother,
My mom,
My dad,
And me,
Four pieces to the puzzle.
My brother is like a basketball,
always active,
always moving from one place to another.
My mom is like a pencil,
tall and slender,
erasing all our mistakes.
My dad is like a tree,
towering over me,
there to protect from harm.
My family is like a box of crayons,
one lost, makes us incomplete.

Caroline Van Kimmenaede, Grade 5
Salt Brook Elementary School

Learning from Losing
My team slaughtered the sectionals!
We made it to the states.
We won our first game.
The other team was in shame.
We made our debut to the semifinals.
We were on a trek to win.
Our team was like a mean machine!

We were lean and full of steam!
We were on a winning streak.
But our luck abated.
It wasn't meant to be.
Not this year.
Maybe next.
Michael Pansini, Grade 6
Fieldstone Middle School

Fantasy
Mighty dragons breathing flames
Holding captives, screaming dames
Unicorns, amazing sight
Phoenixes, inferno flight

Good magic and evil too
Some heal, some give the flu
Sorcerers raising hellfire
Evil kings stopped by briars

Mountains sky high, shrines for gods
Peasants' homes with rough facades
Volcanic dwellings, evil lair
Grand Palace with splendid flair

Mythic creatures, wizardry
Breathtaking lands, emerald seas
Jane Clark, Grade 6
Woodcliff Middle School

Baseball
B est sport to play
A lways keep your head in the game
S ee other teams
E xercising sport
B ad injuries
A wesome game
L oyal game, a rich game
L osing a baseball game stinks.
Richard Palmer, Grade 5
Ocean Avenue Elementary School

Snow Fall
A snowflake twirling
Floating to the icy ground
Like a white daisy.
Eleanor Wilson, Grade 4
Community Park School

The Cat That Mooed
There once was a brown cat that mooed.
He had a big attitude.
  He started to yell
  The neighbors could tell
That he wasn't really that rude.
Matthew Venable, Grade 4
West End Memorial Elementary School

Soccer
Taking breaths,
Chasing the ball,
The parents trembling with wonder,
Running hard,
You get the ball, and then…
Score!
Kerri Stine, Grade 5
West End Memorial Elementary School

Spring Is Fun!
Spring is the season of young life,
Of all the little dogs playing in the grass,
Of all the beautiful blooming flowers,
Of all the jumping baby bass,
Of all the kids playing passing hours.
  Then comes delicious days,
Of playing in the pools,
Of all the people tanning in the sun,
Of all the water balloon duels,
Of all the kids having fun.
Brittany Boykas, Grade 4
Stonybrook Elementary School

Feelings
Feelings make you feel how you should
Feelings make you feel pretty good
Without feelings your body
will feel like an empty lobby.

With feelings I'm never shy
With feelings I can fly sky high
Without feelings
I'd have a fit.

But with feelings if I wanted to sing
I could make a big hit
and with feelings my mind is lit
Without feelings
it'll be like camping
we'd be roughing it.

Because feelings make you who you are
With feelings you can go so far!
Ahmed Green, Grade 5
Roosevelt Elementary School

Summer
Summer
Sunny, hot
Swimming, boating, running
Happy, fun time, camp
Beach time
Sabrina Ben-Moha, Grade 4
Solomon Schechter Day School

Avalon
Crashing waves,
Sandy ground,
I'm with my friends,
Making sounds,
I swim with you,
You swim with me,
I love to swim,
In the beautiful sea.
Genevieve Cullen, Grade 4
Far Hills Country Day School

The Ocean
By the breezy shore
The ocean takes in seashells
Each cool summer night.
Mary Kate Repage, Grade 5
St Dominic Elementary School

A Smile
A smile can do so much,
It can cheer a frowning face,
It is the special touch,
Full of love and grace,

You see it all the time,
Don't you see?
It is worth much more than a dime,
But is always free,

A smile,
From ear to ear,
And it stays for a while,
When you see it do not fear.
Kaylie Fleck, Grade 6
Trinity Christian School

My Light
You steal my light every
Night
It's really mine 'til
A quarter to nine
People stare at you while they
Turn from me
Oh so you've heard
I'm the sun gleaming
Jillian Ostek, Grade 6
Christa McAuliffe Middle School

The Leaves
The dull leaves peacefully descend
from tall oak trees.
The blue birds loudly chirp
their beautiful melody
high in the treetops.
The cold wind blows roughly through
the dark green leaves.
The short trees are packed full of leaves,
as they tremble in the wind.
Peacefully the dreary tree trunk hardly budges.
In the dense forests
they cling to one another to keep warm.
Towering trees expand
over each other.
The remaining green leaves
hold tightly to the branches
that are swaying in the frigid wind.
Soon winter will be here.
Ashley Clark, Grade 5
Lyncrest Elementary School

Sandy Sunsets
Sunsets so beautiful,
So colorful and extraordinary.
Plants shifting,
Birds chirping.
The sun so low in the sky,
Birds fly by.
The pink, orange, and blue,
In the sky, birds flew.
Fish leaping,
Cricket wings creeping.
The ocean so calm,
We watch the palms.
The waves crashing,
Bugs and animals dashing.
The cool summer breeze,
I get a chill that makes me freeze.
Children at play,
Who could miss out on this beautiful summer day?
Nathan Orsini, Grade 5
Oxford Street Elementary School

Washington
W as the greatest president.
A s he led us to be what we are today.
S ome say he never told a lie.
H ow outstanding he was.
I n 1781 they won the war.
N o more shall the British tax us.
G eorge Washington was president for 7 years.
T he soldiers crossed the Delaware River.
O n the 3rd Monday in February we honor him.
N ow he would be proud of our country.
Patrick Murray, Grade 4
St Mary's School

St. Patrick's Day
St. Patrick's Day comes once a year.
Eating good food and having lots of cheer.
Spending time with family.
Old traditions become new.
You can have your cabbage and eat it too.
Wearing green clothes can be lots of fun.
But I can't wait until the Irish potatoes are done!
The only sad thing about all this cheer,
Is that St. Patrick's Day comes only once a year!
Catherine Fiore, Grade 5
Holy Saviour School

I Love You Extra Today
"Ooh and aah" the family went.
Over the cookies baked to fill their heart's content.

Back and forth the Valentine opened.
A love note filled with words unspoken.

Leaning forward and back the couples went,
Kissing and hugging from the moment they met.

Twirling and whirling the dancers turned,
Dancing a tango with their love to be heard.
Emily Krasnow, Grade 5
Sicomac Elementary School

Pixie Sticks
Pixie sticks are so gross
Pixie sticks I hate the most
Sugar candy that rots your teeth
You see one and grab it like a thief!

You'll do anything for one
Even SING!!!
Then you get none
Now that stings!

The pixie stick queen
As proud as can be
Has a whole bag of them
Then teases the boys and me

The dentist looks in your mouth
And what a shame
He takes out a drill
And then you know pixie sticks are to blame

I learned from this poem
That pixie sticks are bad
And when it comes to lunch
For me it will be so sad
Caroline Abin, Grade 5
Laura Donovan Elementary School

HIV/AIDS

What is HIV/AIDS? Some say it's a disease. Some say it's an infection. I say it's a monster!
Some say if you have AIDS you are dirty or cruel, but no — it just means you fell in at the wrong time and place. You do not
have to be homeless or a poor person in equatorial Africa. You could be a mother, sister, a father or a brother. AIDS is a
monster, but this monster only hurts us when we fall in love, it does not seem fair — it's not.

Ethan Kramer, Grade 5
Hillside Elementary School

Christmastime in N.Y.

Every year my mom and I go to see the New York tree.
When I see the lights it hypnotizes me.
I am in a world where there is no wrong.
The addiction to beautiful lights makes me keep staring.
It is not just the tree I love,
It is New York itself.
The smell of the pretzels that venders sell on the sidewalk,
The taste of the Cold Stone ice cream, and to touch the store windows and screaming "Mommy I want that toy!"
We also see the *Radio City Christmas Show* with the Rockettes.
I love the magic of that show they can really make you believe in Santa and reindeer and the Christmas Spirit.
It is like 500 snow days.

When we walk back to the car which is parked at the bus terminal we start to head home.
Before that though we say Merry Christmas to all the police officers whom my mother works with.
On the way home in the car we listen to the spirit-lifting Christmas music.
My mother and I talk about all the fun we have had.
I would be saying a sham if I told you that I had a horrible time.

Rebecca Fiore, Grade 6
Fieldstone Middle School

My Big Bad Brother

Having a big brother is really great, well maybe sometimes anyway.
He taught me how to make a play at the plate and how to play video games.
But wait a minute mate; it's not always great being the baby brother.
Especially when he thinks you're the favorite and everything goes your way.
You have to learn you won't get a break; he'll intimidate and infuriate.
Trying to stay with his pace may be a waste or maybe it's just fate.

But you know I really do have to say it's not so bad all the time.
My brother is good as gold when it comes to being my friend.
He's someone I can look up to and strive to be as good as in sports.
There is no one better in basketball, baseball, or football and he always picks me on his team.
No one stands a chance when we team up to play; we are money in the bank.
You have to take the good with the bad and you know I would never trade him.

Chris Marini, Grade 6
Fieldstone Middle School

Nature's Raging Frustration

The forest's light speaks to me as if it wants me in
As I enter, the sun fades to black
I hear trees crying around me as thunder roars as if the devil is calling because he's coming
Lightning strikes like the angels all bowled a strike
Massive rain rushes down like the sky is bleeding
Leaves blow like a frenzy of monkeys trying to get to a little bit of bananas
A forest fire set by young animals and myself
It becomes the only light source to shine the forest

Michael John Reardon, Grade 6
Little Egg Harbor Intermediate School

Sports

Baseball, America's favorite game
Crazy fans screaming, going insane
Mets vs Yankees what an event to see
Look! There's a baseball speeding towards me

Basketball, such an intense sport
Agile players run about the court
Shaq Daddy throwing the ball down
When it comes to dunks he takes the crown

Football, watch the games unravel
Clutch field goals make fans baffled
QB's throwing bombs to receivers
The Steelers have won now I'm a believer

Jesse Mautner, Grade 6
Woodcliff Middle School

Hockey

You skate down the ice
You try to get the puck
Also you should try to score
You should knock people out of the way
Also you should try to shoot
You should try not to go to the penalty box
You should always wear shin guards.
Also shoulder and elbow pads should be worn
You need to have a hockey stick
And you definitely need skates
Also you need to know how to shoot
And you have to be able to skate
You need to skate with a stick and the puck
You need more than one person
Also you should try to get penalty shots

Danny Leary, Grade 6
Gilmore J Fisher Middle School

The Pine Barrens

A section of the vast wilderness of nothing but Pines,
Is nothing but made of Pitch Pine,
Scrub Pine, White Pine,
That's it.
And has beautiful social bogs,
Is wet, grassy, and swampy.
The life under in the social bogs
are different than above
like sunfishes, grassy, and moccasins.
From above the land which lays poor soils,
but covered of nothing of Pines.
And they are covered with nothing but life,
like whitetails, screech owls, tree frogs.
This is a glimpse part of life in the
Pine Barrens

Robert Keil, Grade 6
Kings Academy

Stars

Stars are bright at night but invisible by day.
The moon and stars look so calm and peaceful together.
At daylight break the stars seem to have faded away
Rainy nights the stars become fogged and unseen
Soaring in the sky, so much beauty

Ardijana Kolenovic, Grade 6
Thomas Jefferson Middle School

The Amazing Play

The score was even,
And it was a pass to me,
I passed everyone you could see,
Like a buzzing bee,
Everyone cheered for me,
I ran as quick as can be,
Although I had one big fear,
To play against my peers,
I saw Joe running on the field,
I made a big shriek,
He was my own peer!

It was not over for me,
But as strange as can be,
I needed a score,
My unabated need,
Aspired me,
I took it seriously,
To confront the goal, aim, and shoot with my feet,
My special need,
has been granted for me.

Garrett Almeida, Grade 6
Fieldstone Middle School

I Am

I am the forest.
I wonder how a deer lives.
I hear little birds chirping in their nest.
I see a waterfall coming down the huge hill.
I want everyone to be safe.
I am the forest.

I pretend to be a wild animal.
I feel the rain falling on me.
I touch the smooth branches of my trees.
I worry when people are hunting.
I cry when an animal dies.
I am the forest.

I understand why they cut me down.
I say "Do not enter."
I dream that the whole world will be full of forests.
I try to make everything better.
I hope they don't destroy me.
I am the forest.

Jerry Ramos, Grade 5
Mary A Hubbard Elementary School

Dream of Life

Life is like glass,
Ready to shatter,
And they are all scattered.
Life is like one big dream
When you are ready
You wake up.

Thinking of the future and
What you will do,
Thinking of your family,
Friends and you,
Life is like one big dream
Waiting for you.

David Arabia, Grade 6
Walter T. Bergen Middle School

People

People, all different kinds
Cultures collide,
American, black, white.

We are all people
In the book of life.
African, Spanish, Arab,
We all mesh together.
In a form of people.
Some of us do not
Get along, but we have to
Stay strong.

After all,
We all hold hands,
We share the
World together forever,
For once and for all.

Jennifer Golotko, Grade 5
Laura Donovan Elementary School

Cold Days

The sky is a misty gray and black.
Thunder moves with the clouds.
And the trees want to follow.
The wind is howling like a ghost.
In the daytime sky.
As the day turns gray.
Trees are bent.
And roofs are sent away.
Slow or fast.
The trees are sweating rain.
As the day goes by.
The clouds will cry.
Until another day.

Borys Marchanka, Grade 5
Cherry Hill Elementary School

A Cool Breeze

A breeze is
A cool wind blowing in your hair.
A cool warm breeze
Blowing against your skin.
Like melted butter,
Sliding on your skin.

Harold Knight, Grade 4
Evergreen Elementary School

Who Am I?

Who am I
Who am I
People always ask me who am I
Where did I come from
I should find out then
Boy oh boy I'd like to know
Who am I who am I
Should I even know
Maybe I'm black or white
Color does not matter
God blessed me for who I am
I am glad for who I am
Big or small, dead or alive
I will always know who I am

Mario Bueno, Grade 5
The Red Bank Charter School

Acorns

Acorns fall from trees,
They are covered by the leaves,
Which blow in the windy day.

Mark Spaloss, Grade 4
Meadowbrook Elementary School

Season Change

Winter's over, spring is near,
Grass is growing, and hares are here.
Good-bye scarf, hello skirt,
Finally spring is about to lurk.
Seeing sunsets, seeing rain,
All the things I can gain.
My favorite season is about to come,
Now winter has finally run.

Victoria Liantonio, Grade 5
St Helena School

Winter/Summer

Winter
Frosty, chilly,
Playing, sledding, snowing,
Snowman, Santa, birds, swimsuits,
Writing, laughing, swimming,
Hot, fun,
Summer

Kimberly Acquaviva, Grade 5
Sicomac Elementary School

Mimi's Singing*

Mimi's singing
Makes the
Lightning dance
And the
Fish do gymnastics
Mimi's singing
Makes the
Garden grow
And the
Horses run wild
Mimi's singing
Makes the
Kangaroos jump
And the
Bluebirds chirp
Mimi's singing
Makes the
Lightning dance
And the
Fish do gymnastics

Hadley Jacobson, Grade 4
Princeton Day School
*A tribute to the poet's best friend

My Grandpa

I love my grandpa
very much.
I kiss his bald head
and say goodbye
as I head toward the
front door.
But as I turn the knob
and slowly walk out,
a pang of love strikes me
and I turn back
to hug and kiss him
until I am tired.
He pushes me gently
toward the door
that I hate to step out of.
"I love you!" I call.
He smiles and says,
"I love you too."

Kaitlyn Garcia, Grade 4
Ridge Ranch Elementary School

My Sister

Victoria loves to perform
She's the sister I adore
Definitely not shy
Such a cutie-pie
I am so glad she was born

Gabrielle Amado, Grade 6
Long Branch Middle School

Behind the Stars

What lies behind the glittering stars?
What makes them shimmer so?
Is it death or life
That sheds their light
Or is it friend or foe?
What lies beyond the mortal lives
Of which we live today?
The future is foggy,
With unclearing mist.
All that has happened
The war, the poor,
Earth is in a never-ending fight.
Yet the stars are clear,
They'll never cease.
As we pass on through all our years.
The only window,
To the life beyond,
Is through the sparkling diamonds in the sky.
Yet, what lies behind them?
What lies beyond the stars?

Molly Muoio, Grade 5
Toll Gate Grammar School

What a Wonderful Day

I love to see the trees growing new leaves.
The wind blowing in my face,
Animals running without a trace.
Birds chirping, kids slurping.
As the day goes by, family members say goodbye.
Flowers growing, streams flowing.
Kites flying, laundry drying.
People waving, children gazing.
Enjoying days in different ways.

What a wonderful day!

Alexa Limbach, Grade 4
Indian Hill Elementary School

Camp Candy

Don't you wish there was a place
Where kids can run away and play?
There are no parents and we can be free.
We could eat all the sugar we want, yippee!
There is such a place,
It's called "Camp Candy"
When playing and sugar always comes in handy.
Where kids are only in charge.
Where we can drive the coolest cars,
And we can buy tons of candy bars
Where we get toys every day,
Where you can see the candy sway.
Camp Candy is the coolest place ever.
Only if it were true,
Ohh well, whatever.

Emily Della Fave, Grade 6
Roosevelt Elementary School

5 A.M.

5 A.M. laying in my bed,
Everything is quiet, nothing is said.
Thinking about the great times that we've had,
Remembering the good, never the bad.
Getting your texts always makes me smile,
You make my day so worthwhile.
Calling you after school every day,
There's never any silence, we always know what to say.
Making me laugh all the time,
Only you could do that, one of a kind.
The poems I've written are always about us.
You're so amazing, your love is a must.
I could write on and on about my love for you,
This feeling is real, this feeling is true.
5 A.M. laying in my bed,
Thinking about you, a million thoughts in my head.

Stephanie Scrafano, Grade 6
Thomas Jefferson Middle School

True or False?

Running through the deep green meadow,
Staring at the true blue sky
You turn around and see all the lies.

Once you have noticed,
You stand there
And say it's all bogus.

As they stand there ready to lie
Not all the time passes by.

You scream, you shout
They tell you
It's not your fault.

Amber Mirza, Grade 5
Liberty Corner Elementary School

A Horrible Dream

The witches are here at night
I get scared by the scary light
I am ready to fight
But the light is too bright

I think the witches are near
And my heart is filled with fear
I think I saw a witch who looked like a bear
Oh dear!

It was a dream
It was a piece of cream
I thought back to the dream
I couldn't believe!

Rija Ahmad, Grade 5
Mansfield Township Elementary School

Loneliest Friend
Unwelcome, unwanted, sad
Forgetting, rejecting, neglecting
Loneliest person,
Left out friend,
Forgotten soul
Hiding, watching, sobbing
Lonely, small, ignored
Loneliest friend.
Elizabeth Platt, Grade 5
Durban Avenue Elementary School

Summer Sun
The hot sun shines on
The long, white, burning sidewalk
As I run along.
Ian Winters, Grade 4
Wayside Elementary School

Kittens
K ids love to cuddle them
I love them
T abby kittens are striped
T hey are too cute
E xaggerating little Angels
N ow it's time to play
S oft and cuddly little cuties
Morgan Colon, Grade 4
Main Road Elementary School

The Boardwalk
The excitement at the boardwalk
Never ends,
Memories are made
Among good friends.

Rides are rode,
And games are played,
Prizes are won
And good food is made.

Ice cream is served
From morning 'till night
Fireworks shine,
With a spectacular sight.

The sound of pinball
Is always there,
While sunburned vacationers
Stop and stare.

When it's time to leave,
The children sigh.
Little do they know,
They'll be back next time!
Michelle Garay, Grade 5
St John's Academy

Through a Student's Eyes
A is for the athletic works the Assumption teams have, during a game.
S is for the studying we do for a test.
S is for the spirit our school has as a family.
U is for the uniform that shows our pride.
M is for the merit awards that we earn through our works.
P is for our policy and our rules to help us become responsible.
T is for the thanks that we give our teachers.
I is for the inspiration we get through the year to come.
O is for the outstanding work we do all year long.
N is for the notes we take to help us learn and study.
Ryan Joyce, Grade 4
Assumption School

There's a Monster in My Desk
There it is inside my desk, waiting for me to slip.
I'm watching its every move; if it attacks I'll totally flip!
I am a frightened bug, slouching in my chair.
Why is there a monster in *my* desk, it's just not fair!
It lurks beside my book, trying to catch me by surprise.
It took me somewhat of a while to realize…there's a monster in my desk.

"THERE'S A MONSTER IN MY DESK!" I said in front of class.
The teacher yelled, "You yelled so loud you broke a glass!"
Should I confront it? I wondered in my head.
No way, I thought, I'll be dead.
My teacher walked over; she told me I was being a baby.
Being a baby? There's a monster in my desk, are you crazy?

She's going to do it, she's going to open my desk, I thought.
My teacher bent over, I backed away, just in case the monster fought.
I am so very anxious, frightened and curious.
I can't bear to watch it's just too scary!
She opened my desk, there it was; I let out a shriek.
"Mitchell," she said "this is a sham, it's not a monster.
It's your homework."…Exactly, I said.
Mitchell Vinokur, Grade 6
Fieldstone Middle School

A Sleeping Child's Savior
The bright light of the full moon swept across the darkened room,
swallowing all darkness and fears,
bringing light into a child's slumber.
Then the house is swallowed into darkness,
into nothingness, into every child's fears,
diminishing hopes, dreams, laughter, and happiness.
Wait the process has slowed, has ceased.
The light of the moon once again engulfs the house
bringing it to life once more.
The child sleeps softly under the light of the moon,
bringing back his hopes and dreams of a brighter day,
of laughter and happiness.
As daylight dawns his savior is hidden
by the warm glow of the morning sun,
not to come back again until day is gone.
Danielle Schimmenti, Grade 6
Fieldstone Middle School

I Am

I am a smart girl who loves to sing.
I wonder if ghosts really exist.
I hear the sound of my own record.
I see my favorite celebrities in front of me.
I want my own CD.
I am a smart girl who loves to sing.

I pretend to sing on stage.
I feel the love of music in my hands.
I touch my favorite celebrity's hand.
I worry about poor people in Pakistan.
I cry when people die.
I am a smart girl who loves to sing.

I understand how things suddenly happen.
I say the government should give everyone homes.
I dream to be a rock star/doctor.
I try very hard in school.
I hope my dream and my saying comes true.
I am a smart girl who loves to sing.

Asma Bahadur, Grade 6
John Hill School

Mermaid

There I was standing by the sea,
When this weird creature swam to me.
She said to me, "I'm Shelly, how are you?"
I replied to her, "I'm Jessie, how do you do?"
She said, "Let's take a swim."
She added on, "I'll show you my friend Tim"
So down we swam to the bottom of the sea,
My brain was filled with curiosity.
As the seaweed hit my face,
It scared me and I swam at a fast pace.
I swam so fast I couldn't see,
What was right in front of me.
So down I crumbled to the sea floor,
I tried to get up but couldn't anymore.
I got hurt and she was my aide,
I made friends with a little mermaid.

Jessie Vanderbilt, Grade 5
St Marys School

Living Life

Living life every day
Giving thanks in every way.
Waking up to go to school
Trying to follow every rule
So much work and so much stuff
Life can sometimes be real rough
Now I think I'm out of luck
Just remember go through things, don't give up.

Xan Dominguez, Grade 6
Thomas Jefferson Middle School

The Storm

A violent storm blows
against a small igloo standing
between two hills,
holding as tight as it can
for dear life.
The wind picks up snow and blasts it
against the domain of ice and frost.
The wind scowls at the shelter now
smashing hail from the heavens at the defenseless home,
but it stands firm.
The storm goes on for 3 hours,
until it dies,
leaving the house at peace
to nurse its wounds for its next breath.

Victor Tsyplenkov, Grade 5
Lyncrest Elementary School

Bird Calls

B aby birds are hungrily chirping.
" **I** 'm getting food," replies the mother bird.
R estlessly, they wait for her.
D ifficulty waiting, they grow impatient.

" **C** oming kids," chirps the mother bird.
A ll her babies are full of excitement.
L ovingly, the mother bird feeds her children.
L oudly, the baby birds chirp hungrily again.
S o, the mother bird goes off to find more food.

Yadid Hirschtritt Licht, Grade 4
Solomon Schechter Day School

Friendship

Friendship is a special gift
Sometimes it may give you a lift
A friend should be helping, willing to clean up a mess
That is a quality a friend should possess
A friend should be loving and caring
Very brave, but not too daring
Respectful, kind, and polite
When in dark a friend is my light
A friend should respect how I feel
When I am sad my heart is what my friend shall heal
So this is what friendship means to me
And I have a great one, can't you see?

Brianna Andersen, Grade 6
St Veronica Elementary School

Lizards

Lizards crawling on the ground
Not making a single sound
Some are munching on their food
And changing color with every mood
Few are climbing up a tree
It's truly a beautiful sight to see!

Nicole Kerrison, Grade 5
Immaculate Conception Regional School

Pat

There once was a man named Pat
Who dreamed he lost his hat
He drank a sprite
In the middle of the night
And then he petted his cat

He got caught in a pack
Everything went black
He woke up in bed
With flees on his head

He woke up with a sneeze
He got down on his knees
And said, God help me please!

David Thompson, Grade 4
Mansfield Township Elementary School

Our Solar System

Planets
Huge rocks
Turning, spinning, moving
Giving us life
Earth

Sebastian Moczulski, Grade 6
Sacred Heart Elementary School

The Sunset

Water flowing through a stream.
The faint sound of crickets,
Chirping in the distance.
The picturesque view,
Of the sun setting over the stream.
The beautiful smell of nature,
Seeping into your skin.
Trying to catch the last picture
Of the majestic sunset.

Alissa Scali, Grade 6
Christa McAuliffe Middle School

Nature Rocks

The trees are dancing
To the obsidian rock
The trees had fun times

Andrew Tsinkelis, Grade 4
Stonybrook Elementary School

My Friends

F orgiving
R eally nice
I ncredible
E verlasting
N ever gives up on you
D oes things for you
S o cool!!

Sarah Hughes, Grade 5
Our Lady of Mount Virgin School

Halloween Night

In the middle of the night
The king comes out
I walk around the pumpkin patch
And I get a fright!
Then I see the pumpkin king
He's running after me!
He's really trying to get me
But, that will never be

Nick Russo, Grade 4
Springfield Township School

Sun

The
Rays
Of
Sunshine

Like splinters of light,
Rays of sunshine fly to me.
They have become one.

Eva Cochran, Grade 5
Community School of Bergen County

Chicken

Chicken,
Chicken,
Chicken,

Tender, chewy, crunchy chicken,
Fried, barbecued, grilled chicken,
These are just a few.
Spicy chicken,
Sweet chicken,
Juicy, crispy, hot chicken,
Broiled, rotisserie, raw chicken,
Mouthwatering chicken too.
Tasty chicken,
Frozen chicken,
Don't forget stuffed chickens.
Last of all, best of all
I like
All chickens.

Henry Nguyen, Grade 5
Ridgeway Elementary School

Winter

Winter is white
It tastes like water
It sounds so quiet
It smells like chocolate
It looks like a cloud
It feels soft and cold

Jordan Bouillon, Grade 4
Main Road Elementary School

My Special Place

I'm stressed out
So I go to my special place
The tennis court
I warm up
Forgetting all my problems
I go to the baseline
Every shot releasing anger and pain…
by the end of the session
All my stress is gone
And now…I'm content
With myself and my game

Benjamin Donovan, Grade 5
Salt Brook Elementary School

Hurt

I've bruised my knee
I've scraped my elbow
I got stung
By a bee
I've pulled my hamstring in bed
I've also managed to bump my head
I've also tripped on the air
I also fell down each stair
When I have the time every day
I try to count how many medical bills
I have to pay
I've gotten sun burn in the rain
And every day it hurts
To suffer the pain

Michaela Murr, Grade 4
Toll Gate Grammar School

Only Rain

Only rain
Staring out of
The mildew covered window
The sound of rats and mice
Scampering on the floor
Door heavily locked
Wind gushing in
From an unknown place
No crackling fir
Or smells of fresh baked bread
Or warmth of overcoats
For me, only rain
Falling from the sky
The warmth for people
Who always have a way of
Seeing a better tomorrow
But for me
Only rain
Falling from the sky
Mimicking
My tears

Lucia Schnetzer, Grade 6
Bartle Elementary School

My Weakness: Annoyances
There are things that annoy me so much, I could scream,
Like the screech of nails on a chalkboard,
Or when your friends don't tell you "secrets,"
Or when you can't get any privacy in your room,
Or when you can't find the remote,
Or when your mom is on the phone and you need it,
Or your obnoxious brothers.

These things infuriate me like a flea on a dog,
A bee stinging in the same spot,
Continuous replays on TV,
A ticking clock when you are trying to sleep,
These are my weaknesses,
When they happen, I am a bomb, EXPLODING,
They may be easy to ignore,
But not for me!
Rebecca Noonan, Grade 6
Fieldstone Middle School

What Is Orange?
When I see orange
I see a juicy tangerine!
When I think of orange
I think of an orange submarine!

Orange is…
The scarf my grandma knitted me!
Orange is…
The color of a shimmering key!

Orange is…the color
Of a raft in the bay!
Orange is…a sunset
On a warm day!

When I think of orange…
I think of May!
I think of my favorite color
In a great way!
Lauren Murphy, Grade 5
Sandman Consolidated Elementary School

Halloween
On Halloween I could sight
A black cat that was about to bite
There were witches lined up all ready to fight
But, they took off on their very long flight
Brant Cooper, Grade 4
Springfield Township School

Sleepy Sleepers
Sleepy sleepers sleep through the sleepy night
And the next day they don't have to sleep
Until the sleepy night comes again.
Christian Kuehl, Grade 5
Springfield Township School

The Little Red Hen
Once there was a little red hen,
In fact, she wasn't even red, she was white,
Why she was called the little RED hen I don't know,
But let's get back to the story.

Being hungry she wanted to make some bread
"Will you help?" she asked her friends.
"NO WAY!" the lazy friends said,
So hen went to the field to get the wheat,
Went to the mill to make it into flower,
And went home to bake it.
But hen was tired, she asked her friends for help,
But they all said "NO WAY!"
What a bunch of lazy couch potatoes.
So the little red hen baked the bread,
Her so called friends wanted some,
Hen said, "NO WAY!"
She gobbled up the bread.

And she became really fat,
Let the truth be told,
This story should be named,
The Fat White Hen.
Sierra Bagish, Grade 5
Salt Brook Elementary School

I Am
I am a dog,
jumping and quick, going with the wind,
not wanting to stay in one spot.
I am New York City,
crazy and curious, always wanting to do something.
I am a valley,
back and forth, always changing my mind about everything.
I am soccer,
never stopping, always trying to reach my goal.
I am a pencil,
sharp and useful, always wanting to keep on writing.
Victoria Starr, Grade 5
Salt Brook Elementary School

Where It's Beautiful
I wish I could be where it's beautiful.
Where the sun shines down on you.
The ocean seems to speak.
The ocean tells me that she won't hurt me.
She's powerful, but graceful and beautiful.
I love it when it's sunset,
And the sun kisses the sea,
As it slowly goes down.
I wish I could be where it's beautiful.
The most beautiful place in the world.
Kayla Maggio, Grade 6
Thomas Jefferson Middle School

Summer

It's very hot today,
The children went outside to play,
Because it's summer!

It's eighty degrees outside,
Let's go get ice cream,
Because it's summer!

It's almost September,
It's almost time for school,
Because it's summer's end!

Collin Pierlott, Grade 4
St Peter Elementary School

I Love Cats

I love cats.
My cats love to sleep on me.
My cats are spazzes at home.
My cats are fluffy, soft, nice, and playful.
I pet my cats almost every day.
I love my cats a lot.

Jodie Brill, Grade 4
Franklin Township Elementary School

Nature's Leaves

Falling leaves gliding
In the air over benches
People crunching them
Under their feet as they walk
Watching the leaves decompose

Ashley Ortiz, Grade 5
Springfield Township School

The Rain Family

When I go outside, raindrops fall.
My sister Katie rushes to the mall.
My Aunt Debra dries her hair.
Baby Sadie runs in her underwear.
Mom and Dad cuddle together.
When rain comes, it is the best weather.

Ebony Davis, Grade 5
Lanning Square Elementary School

Halloween

Halloween is the best.
It's better than all the rest.
I love to get gum and candy.
It's really fine and dandy.
You see a lot of scary things.
Oh, the fun Halloween brings!
Walking outside I advise.
There you'll see a wonderful surprise.
Ghosts, ghosts everywhere,
And goblins and witches to spare.

Alessandra Ricci, Grade 4
St Rose of Lima School

Derek

Derek
Nice, smart, generous, respectful
Brother of Courtney
Love of dogs, the Falcons, and football
Who feels happy when the Giants win a football game
Mad when the Red Sox win a game,
And sad when I lose a Pee Wee football game
Who needs water, food, and P.S.P.
Who gives money to charity, my best attitude, and 100% to my team
Who fears clowns, robbers, and kidnappers
Who would like to go to Hawaii, visit Disney World,
And be a professional football player
I am a resident of Wyckoff on Birchwood Drive
Ajamian

Derek Ajamian, Grade 4
Sicomac Elementary School

Snowy Day

Snow is descending from the wan sky like a dreamlike continuum.
It fell to Earth's soft snowy blanket swiftly and silently.
The tiny snowflakes started out fierce and rough
and ended like a light feather.
The Earth's surface is like a mother
waiting to catch her baby in her arms.

Rajwoana Ahmed, Grade 5
Lyncrest Elementary School

On a Spring Morning…

…I hear birds chirping.
…Mom's cooking smells so sweet.
…there's dew on the grass.
…I see bunnies hopping and jumping across the backyard.
…I see colorful flowers that take my breath away.
…sometimes I lie on the grass and look up at the clouds forming beautiful designs.
…I sadly think about how the day will have to end.
…I look forward to going to sleep and waking up on another spring morning.

Kathleen Bratyanski, Grade 4
Long Memorial Elementary School

Stratton Mountain, VT

Snowy, steep, bumpy, metal poles, dropped mittens,
and hundreds of heads on the liftline.

Talking, shouting, speeding snowboarders, kids clanking their poles,
skis and snowboarders on rails, and people getting scraped up on ice.

Calm, energetic, challenged, and interested.

Snow like a white blanket. Moguls as big as tortoise shells.
Slopes as steep as backs of chairs.
Stratton is wide, tall, and long.

Josh Beckerman, Grade 5
Salt Brook Elementary School

My Mom

My mom is always there for me.
She says she will always care for me.
When I'm sick and in bed
She comes in and rubs my head.
My mom can be fun
When we are out in the sun.
She likes to play basketball
Even if she hits the ball against the wall.
She makes me laugh
And we always have a blast.
Sometimes she can be mad.
But inside I can see she can be happy just like me.
And when I'm sad she will make me glad
By playing video games with me.
My mom is not just a mom.
She's my friend until the end.
So when she's gone I'll be sad.
But will always remember what we had.
Then I'll think of her and be glad.

Salvatore Smith, Grade 5
North Dover Elementary School

Family Reunion

As a beautiful melody fills the room
My companions and I waltz to the tune
Accompanied by my sister's sweet voice
My brother plays a song of their choice

Mom sways in with a tray full of snacks
My cousins reach for potato chip packs
Gram and Aunt argue 'bout what is the best
Lemon pie with or without the zest

Because I am terrible at Monopoly
Grandpa laughs and slaps his knee
Playing Rummy, Kim puts down an ace
Mike gives her our family's victory chase

Worn out with tons of happiness
Because we played five games of chess
Relaxing with my family, I lay
Boy, do I love Family Reunion Day!

Gabrielle Laut, Grade 5
Old York Elementary School

The Mixed Rainbow

Blue is the color of the bright sky in April.
Red is the color of a caring heart.
Yellow is the color of the sun in the summer.
Purple is the color of a beautiful scented rose.
Orange is the color of the sand on the beach.
Green in the color of grass swaying in the wind.

Julie Mintz, Grade 5
Sicomac Elementary School

Springtime

Springtime is finally here.
Springtime is my favorite time of year.
It's the time of fun and joy.
You can also play in sand with your favorite toy.
I would love to lay down.
When school comes I arrive with a frown.
Springtime has come to an end.
Summer is just around the bend.

Steve Adrianzen, Grade 5
Immaculate Conception Regional School

The Lucky Charm

I am a little four-leaf clover.
I live in a town called Dover.
I bring lots of good will;
I am sometimes found over a hill.

I am usually the color green;
I am always seen.
You can see me day or night;
I truly am a magnificent sight.

You think about me on St. Patty's Day
In the warm bright sun is where I lay.
Usually my days are bright and sunny,
But I have to watch out for that hungry bunny.

Natalie Fairman, Grade 5
Sacred Heart School

Vacation/Work

Vacation
joyful, adventurous,
loving, playing, relaxing.
New Jersey shore, Atlantic City, Caribbean, Las Vegas.
tiring, hating, waiting,
frustrated, annoyed.
Work.

Javier Gonzalez, Grade 4
Christ the Teacher School

The Strange Kid

There once was a kid who was interactive
Yet he was very attractive.
But all of that changed
And he became deranged
Because he became *radioactive*.

Aengus Walker, Grade 5
Sicomac Elementary School

My Shiny Sneakers

Nikes oh Nikes I miss you so much,
it wasn't me who threw you in the dump.
Nikes oh Nikes you were so shiny and clean,
Nikes oh Nikes I wish you would come back to me.

Matthew Garramone, Grade 6
Franklin Elementary School

Good Night, Sleep Tight
Good night, good night, sleep tight
little one
As you crash into a pondering dream
We sit and wait and watch you 'til morn'
Then talk about your wonderful dream
Now that the day is slowly ending
Your energy is all worn out
As I tuck you into bed I say once more,
"Good night, good night sleep tight
little one."
Cassidy Ann Greenberg, Grade 6
Little Egg Harbor Intermediate School

Giant Pandas
Pandas furry and soft,
black, white and large
from China and Japan
eating bamboo and grass
chubby white bodies
big, round heads
dark black eyes
living in bamboo forests,
fat and friendly
black ears and a white head.
Jonathan Foligno, Grade 4
Lincoln Park Elementary School

Sports and Games
I play a lot of sports and games.
They all have complicated names.
Some are an hour or two,
Some are just for you.
Sports are mostly played outside,
Some games you have to hide.
Sports are fun and great to play,
But I wouldn't do it all day.
Playing sports and games is really fun.
So try to play with everyone.
Daniel Ambrosino, Grade 4
St Rose of Lima School

Football
I am brown and white.
I'm thrown in the air
By someone who cares.
I am played on a large, green field.
I am kicked.
I'm punted by a punter.
I'm carried by a runningback.
I'm thrown by a quarterback.
Now I'm done.
What am I?
David Sandnes, Grade 4
Christ the Teacher School

The Wind
The wind outside is roaring.
It throws the branches around.
There are no birds flying.
The sky is darkening.
The fog is slowly coming.
It's getting cold and crummy.
So go inside, and turn up the heat.
Get cozy!
Grant Hessman, Grade 5
Cherry Hill Elementary School

Wrestling
To wrestle is a fight,
With all your vigor and all your might,
Months of work, months of training,
Through all the struggling and straining,
To feel the glory of the winning,
And the joy of the pinning.
Paul Sullivan, Grade 6
Trinity Christian School

Storm
A fierce storm hits town
Everyone went to shelter
The storm passed quickly
Kevin Martina, Grade 4
Loring Flemming Elementary School

Spring's Sensations
Snow never refuses its sensation
Because it's an abomination
In white it covers our nation
Snow never refuses its sensation

Rain never fights its sensation
It lets down blue upon our nation
Some people say it's an abomination
Oddly, I don't think it's an abomination
Rain never opposes its sensation
Amethyst V.R. Carey, Grade 6
Gilmore J Fisher Middle School

Winter
I love winter
when it is cold outside
I have to get my old clothes
jump out in the snow
but I know I will be cold
"Winter is here!"
I shout with cheer
I make snowmen
It is fun
I don't miss the sun
because winter is here!
Amanda Peek, Grade 5
Christ the Teacher School

Spring
In spring,
When you hear that ping,
You know baseball has started.
But when Jeter parted,
You should at least bunt.
What a stunt!
Why would a baseball player quit?
I am having such a fit!
Ted Walker, Grade 5
Lafayette Elementary School

My Mom
I love my mother
Because she is so caring
She also loves me
Chris Torres, Grade 6
John Hill School

Snowboard Designs
Snowboard designs,
So colorful with darts and hearts,
Arrows and sparrows,
Webs and heads.

Snowboard designs
Green and red,
Blue and white,
Pink and black,
Lines and vines words and birds,
Dots and locks.

I snowboard too!
Snowboard designs,
I love them with bright colors.
Tyler Ricci, Grade 4
Sundance School

Spring Flowers
S pectacular flowers are blooming
P ink flowers on the trees
R ed vibrant flowers spreading all over.
I vory flowers, white as ghosts.
N ectars perfuming the air.
G rabbing the attention of bees.

F ragile flowers, petals flying
L ilies trumpeting the season.
O h, how the spring flowers boast.
W ild roses taking charge.
E ager buds waiting to grow
R ising up from head to toe.
S pectacular flowers are blooming.
Cheli Kalina, Grade 4
Solomon Schechter Day School

The Tragedy of 9/11

People saw planes flying low.
"What will happen?"
"I don't know?"
Then they saw the planes crash.
Everyone started to dash.
Many loved ones were lost that day,
They are still looking for them today.
There were many heroes
Including police officers, doctors, and firemen
When will things be back to normal, when?

Caroline McCann, Grade 6
Chatham Middle School

Cleaning My Room

I do not like to clean my room.
I do not like to use a broom.
I like to have my room a mess
even though my mom's a pest!
I do not want to clean today.
I want to go outside and play.
It's too hot and nice outside,
I want to play on the slip 'n slide.
The cleansers smell so horrible,
It's enough that I have to clean the cat's litter bowl.
The vacuum sounds so loud to me,
Why can't I let my room just be?
Cleaning my desk, putting things away,
I just don't like that, what more can I say?
I have friends to play with and things to do,
cleaning my room is the last thing that I want to do!
Why does everything have to be just so?
I don't understand I just don't know.

Kaitlyn Ennis, Grade 4
Mansfield Township Elementary School

If I Were a Mud Pie

If I were a mud pie,
I'd shimmer and splatter, oozing with mud.
I'd feel like a plop of slime.
I'd stay as still as an old tree and form a clop of gooey dirt.
I'd jump and jiggle my fat gooey belly.
I'd try to move my legless body like a crab with no claws.

Rachel McNally, Grade 4
Sicomac Elementary School

A World Where Everybody Matters

I wish for a world where we all loved one another,
Where you would treat everyone like a sister or a brother,
A world where there would never be room to discriminate,
Because when you discriminate it only generates hate,
I wish for a world there was no more pain or war,
Where people wouldn't make fun of one another anymore,
Where no matter what, everyone would be created equal,
Our Lord god loves us all, for we are all His people

Angel Strouse, Grade 6
St Margaret Regional School

Pets All Around

Look at all these pets I found,
    They jump up, down, and all around.
There are rabbits, dogs, lizards, and cats,
    I wouldn't even mind if you got me some rats.
Some are trained
    And some are often blamed.
Some pets could be mischievous,
    But very few are devious

Lauren Peoples, Grade 5
Most Holy Redeemer School

Spring

S pring is finally here!
P laying baseball outside.
R abbits hopping around.
I ce cream on a sunny day.
N ice day to go out and play.
G oing to the park.
T he flowers smell so nice.
I love the spring!
M y brother is starting his basketball season.
E aster will be coming soon.

Erin Batz, Grade 4
St Mary's School

St. Peter School

I go to a very cool school,
The school is St. Peter School!
It has the best principal, Sr. Alice!
She lets us have skating parties at the Cherry Hill Skating Rink!
She makes sure the children are well-educated
We learn all subjects from math to English, religion, too!
Everyone here is honest and kind,
She makes sure of that!
She makes sure we are happy, too!
She's the best, yes, she is!
These are the reasons I love St. Peter School!

Devon Caputa, Grade 4
St Peter Elementary School

Ode to Oreos

Oh Oreo, I remember the first time
I enjoyed your sweet vanilla cream filling
And your chocolate cookie outside
Oh Oreo, there is so many ways to eat you
But I love taking off one of your cookies
And licking some of your filling
And then eating you in one bite
Oh Oreo, in 50 years from now
You will still be America's favorite cookie
And you will still be my favorite cookie

Julia Loria, Grade 5
Salt Brook Elementary School

Spring

In spring, the sun comes out.
I go outside and shout!!!
The flowers bloom.
The leaves are growing.
And the heavy rain is falling.
You go out and play,
On a great, sunny day.
The animals come out.
The spring break is on.
And school is done!

Ania Januszko, Grade 4
John F Kennedy Elementary School

Spirit of Christmas

Bells are ringing,
The fire is crackling,
Carolers are singing,
Snow is falling,
The tree stands high and proud,
For the lights are a shining,
Ornaments are a twinkling,
And
The spirit of Christmas is in
The air

Darsey Schulaka, Grade 6
Great Meadows Regional Middle School

Spring Break

School is out
And about!

Easter is coming
As we hear all the birds humming.

No math or grammar
I'm free from all that matter.

We go on vacation here and there
Hopefully I won't see a bear!

The ice cream man comes around
Playing that musical sound.

T-shirts and shorts
Playing on basketball courts.

We're having fun
In the new sun!

Playing with friends
Not writing with pens.

School is out
And about!

Christina Monteleone, Grade 5
St Rose of Lima School

Mother Nature

Her hair is as free as the autumn breeze.
Her hands are as gentle as the slow-moving ocean waves stroking the shore.
She is as strong as the screaming thunder on a cloudy day.
She is as loud as the glass shattering as if it is destroying everything in sight.
Her children are the grass, the snow, and the rain.
Her perfume smells like the fresh winter air.
Her lips are as red as the bright red rose in the spring.
Her name is Mother Nature.

Maya Bensalem, Grade 5
Hillside Elementary School

Monster Madness

I have a friend with a case of "Monster Madness"
When I see her, I get a case of "Monster Sadness"
She screams in the night
And give me a fright
She always says she sees a monster
I think this case really haunts her
Most of the time a monster isn't the case,
It's her 6 year old brother with his friends John, Paul, and Chase.

Alexis McGinn, Grade 5
Most Holy Redeemer School

Love

Love is pink.
It smells like roses.
It looks like a big, happy, smiley face smiling at you.
It tastes like a chocolate cake with your name on it.
It sounds like the mmm sound you make after you have eaten your favorite candy.
Love feels like the joy you get when someone gives you flowers.

Brianna Kane, Grade 6
St Rose of Lima School

The Night Sky

The bright stars twinkle in the night sky,
as they shine it becomes dark.

When dusk approaches I stare at the moon in the sky,
it looks very high.

I wonder what the gleaming lights are coming from,
my brother says it's only the headlights on the cars.

The moon is yellow when it glows,
you could tell it really shows.

The moon and the stars are yellow and gold,
if I'm outside too long I'll shiver and get cold.

You can't see the clouds in the middle of the night,
that's when stars come in handy because they create a lot of light.

Watching stars is fun to do,
it could make your dreams come true.

Melanie Cieciuch, Grade 4
Lincoln Park Elementary School

Opa
You've met up with the Lord,
for He will guide you to freedom,
but remember that I love you, and I'm happy you're at peace.

Take me in your arms, to hug me as hard as you can,
and love me as a third daughter, for I love you as a father.

Keep me as yours, and never forget me, your granddaughter,
as I will never forget you, my grandfather.

I asked you to help me in the darkest of times,
which you did, but it's not the same.
You're not here anymore.
Help me when I need help,
whisper in my ear of what your thoughts are,
and help guide me to success.
Love me as your granddaughter, forever.

You're in a dark, but peaceful sleep, resting in comfort,
now you've entered the gateway to Heaven.

Take me with you as your granddaughter
to love and care, forever.
I love you so much, so remember Dein Schatz, Briana.
Briana Setnitzky, Grade 6
Fieldstone Middle School

Happiness
H olding on to those precious moments.
A ble to feel free when you smell those wonderful scents.
P eople all around you have fun for a while.
P raying for the joy of your soul and smile.
I n the valley of hopes and dreams.
N othing is good as what it seems.
E xpressing your face is nothing but fun.
S howing your spirit feels like you won.
S hining yourself into the sun.
Sidney Rada, Grade 6
Thomas Jefferson Middle School

The Flowers
Flowers are pretty, flowers are nice
Flowers just make everything right

With all the colors of the rainbow you see
It looks like a beautiful, beautiful tree

Although they attract many bees
Just be as free as you can be

And enjoy the many species
The flowers can and may be.
Sadie Ramos, Grade 5
St Veronica Elementary School

The Lenten Season
The season of Lent
Is a time to repent.
Purple is the color of the Holy King,
It's time to praise God and sing.

This is when you are praying and fasting,
Forty days it will be lasting.
This is the time when you are forgiving,
You look at the life you have been living.

The resurrection of Jesus Christ is on Easter Sunday,
For all the children it is a fun day.
Lent is not a time to be funny,
But the children love to see the Easter Bunny.
Justine Fairman, Grade 6
Sacred Heart School

The Vacuum Cleaner and the Sweeper
Said the vacuum cleaner to the sweeper,
"you are really a fine cleaner,
you're a handsome piece of plastic.
Are you not, not, not?"

"Your bristles are so amazing,
and your plug is so electrifying,
and your cord is so terrifying
when you are on."

"Though I would not call you noisy,
you are strong and tall and skinny
and I am sure you're never whiny
would you be my wife?"

So without the least delay
They were married in Green Bay,
and they are still happy today,
They have no strife.
Shira Damari, Grade 4
Solomon Schechter Day School

Drums
The love for the drums
Is deep in my heart
But in the band
I'm a small part
I'll practice day and night
To make sure I'm ready for the limelight
When we play for the crowd
Some think we're good but some think we're loud
When I hear people
Clap their hands
I know we have
The best band
Josh Knighten, Grade 6
Springfield Township School

Slap Shot
I took a slap shot,
That was so fast,
It cracked the glass,
That hit the hat,
Off the hockey fan,
That was so fat,
And that puck did a,
Back tuck and landed on,
The mat!!
Mark VanVlaanderen, Grade 4
Stonybrook Elementary School

Christmas
Presents for Christmas
Having delicious cookies
Presents are coming
Julia Alspach, Grade 4
Main Road Elementary School

Spring Is Here
Spring is here.
It's the best time of the year,
So give a spring cheer.
To let all know spring is here.

It's the best time of the year.
And now Easter will be here.
So without any fear…
Let's all give a spring cheer.
Dominiquea Trotter, Grade 4
St Mary's School

What Happens in My House
My mom works all day.
She never has time to play.
My dad works at the store.
Until they close the door.
My brother jumps around.
While my sister sits down.
My family is busy.
While at home I take it easy.
Isaac A. Garcia, Grade 4
Trinity Christian Academy

Signs of Fall
Beautiful red and yellow leaves
A very cool relaxing breeze
People hanging up wreaths
People jumping into piles of leaves
Mouth-watering pumpkin pie,
Birds flying south in the sky
Ghosts and goblins saying "Boo"
I am scared! How about you?
Those are the signs of fall
Isaiah Torney, Grade 5
Ridgeway Elementary School

The Night
The night is a black blanket
covering the sky
Like the day it will die
But comes back every day
Day and night take turns that's what I say
At night animals sleep
Even ones in the deep
Not much of a glimpse of a thing
But after the night birds sing
Anderson Vilefort, Grade 6
Kawameeh Middle School

After the Thunderstorm
Where is the thunder?
It must have gone to bed.
The angels have stopped bowling.
Now peace is here instead.

The bright sun is shining,
Through the glistening trees.
Now peace is settled on Earth.
Don't come back thunder, please!
Emily Wolsch, Grade 6
Chatham Middle School

Humpty Dumpty
Humpty Dumpty is an
egg
so of course, when he falls
he'll break his
head
Now he is
broken
and not as
tall
but my question is
why would you sit
on a
wall?
Someone put that egg back together.
I don't know that guy's name
but he helped Humpty Dumpty
regain his fame.
Alexandra Schlobohm, Grade 5
Salt Brook Elementary School

A Great Feeling
A great feeling,
Like catching a fly ball,
Like having a good day at school,
Like learning a new skateboard trick,
A great feeling!
Christopher Seager, Grade 4
Wayside Elementary School

The Garden
As I look upon the full beautiful garden.
Colorful flowers and roses brighten.
When it rains the soil always hardens.
Then when the big shiny sun shows.
The vegetables and fruits always glow.
As I taste the best sweet fresh peach
Full moonlight tender love talk.
Blowing through the garden walk.
Delightful dancing stars.
Surrounding my mom's embracing arms.
Pierre S. Parra, Grade 6
Thomas Jefferson Middle School

Get Well Soon!
Get well soon,
You're turning maroon!
If you're sick in the head,
You should go to bed.
If you're sick in the stomach,
You should read a love comic.

If you have the flu,
I feel sorry for you.
If you have a fever,
You should seek a fat beaver.
If you go to work,
You'll go berserk.
If you stay home,
You'll be left alone.

If at any rate,
You feel very great,
Then you go to work,
And your boss'll go berserk.
Now say good-bye
It's time I pass by…
Pavel Temkin, Grade 4
Princeton Charter School

Spring
I hear the crickets chirping
In the night spring sky
As I look at the stars
That are up so high
Nadine Filemban, Grade 5
Belhaven Avenue Middle School

Summer
S ummer is great!
U nicorns run freely.
M ice hid from hawks.
M acaws come get food.
E agles soar high.
R ainbows shine over the lakes!
Samantha Cases, Grade 4
Main Road Elementary School

A Little Chair

I went in a room,
I saw a little chair,
It was next to a broom.
It sat there and stared.

I saw a little chair,
It was brown and old.
It sat there and stared,
My Dad took it and yelled, "Sold!"

I said, "Who you sold it to?
That chair was good!"
"That guy with the little shoe.
He bought it 'cause it was made of wood."

"That chair was good!"
It was next to a broom.
"He bought it 'cause it was made of wood."
I went in a room.

Joshua Williams, Grade 6
Lanning Square Elementary School

What Is Green?

Green is the color of grass,
green is the leaves on a tree.
Green is an apple that is good.
Green is when you dump gas in a fire,
green is hope to lift your spirit.
Green is paper from a tree,
green is my favorite color!

Cody Travolta, Grade 4
Hardyston Township Elementary School

Sunshine on a Rainy Day

I am wishing for sunshine on a rainy day
It is quite useless — some would say
I need to acknowledge the thought —
That the sun will always go
Waiting for sun is like waiting for grass to grow
But I wait anyway

The bright lightning flashes oh so near
It lights up the dark blue sky
Goose bumps appear on my bare skin
The horror is in sight
Now more than ever
I am wishing for sunshine on a rainy day

Then suddenly there was a streak of pale yellow light
The intensifying winds had finally faded
The violent winds had come to an end
And this short brief moment proves
That even on the darkest of days
You should wish for sunshine on a rainy day

Deanna Magda, Grade 6
Fieldstone Middle School

Who Am I?

I am sweet, caring, and athletic.
I wonder what I will be when I get older.
I hear the laughter of my brother and sister.
I see my family after my long hard day.
I want to be a first grade teacher.
I am sweet, caring, and athletic.

I pretend that I am a teacher.
I feel great when I am with my sister.
I touch my warm cozy bed at night.
I cry when my sister is mean to me.
I am sweet, caring, and athletic.

I understand you can have more than one friend.
I say "If you are nice to others they'll be nice to you."
I dream of being a first grade teacher.
I try to do my best in school.
I hope I will be a nice teacher.
I am sweet, caring, and athletic.

I am Carmen Imbimbo.

Carmen Imbimbo, Grade 5
Sicomac Elementary School

Ned, What Is He?

Hey, there's Ned!
Did you know that he's red?
I met him while he was flying around my bed.
Then he bumped his head.

He was messing up my best bedspread
and acting like an airhead.
He went after my piece of bread.
"I'm hungry," he said.

After he was fed, he fluttered his wings and read.
Can you guess what is my little friend Ned?
Why he's a ladybug, you silly, silly Fred!

Elizabeth Wasdyke, Grade 5
Sacred Heart School

A Crazy Day

The sky is dreary
The clouds are gray
It's warm outside
What a crazy day!
The trees are dancing with each other
Moving along you hear them mutter.
The wind blows strong in different ways
as it turns into a sunny day.
A rainbow appears so beautiful and bright
I can tell it will be a beautiful night.

Amanda Longobardi, Grade 5
Cherry Hill Elementary School

Spring

I am spring.
You know me for bringing life back
after a cold winter.
My enemy is cold weather,
because it freezes me.
My best friend is the sun,
because it helps me grow.

Maxine Abustan, Grade 4
Christ the Teacher School

Fear

In the darkness, in our minds,
Lay a power, we cannot find.
All alone, in the cold, cold night,
It catches up to us, and gives us a fright.
It crawls within us, in and out.
It eats our spirits, and makes us shout.
In the corners of our minds,
Locked up, not hard to find.
It's that shiver down your spine,
When you know you're out of line.
Lost forever in our nightmares,
Face them now, if you dare.
That teddy you hold, oh so dear,
Covers that shadow of what we call fear.

Chandni Rathod, Grade 6
Thomas Jefferson Middle School

Roof Dancers

With a tap-ity-tap and a
Click-ety-click on the roof
the rain it dances,
I lie in bed I hear the noise.

Boom! Boom! The thunder aroars.
As the music flows —
I dance in my sleep!

Lauryn Fields, Grade 4
Middle Township Elementary School #2

Winter's Beauties

The sound of hot cocoa going into a cup
Just waiting for me to drink up

Winter, wonder, white,
Shining glory makes me want to drift
Into the snow slowly

I feel so peaceful and calm
Making me want to never set my alarm

Yummy white marshmallows
Chewy and all makes me
Never want to go back to fall

Gregory Burdea, Grade 5
Bartle Elementary School

The Jolly Party

Tall, gray trees stand guard over a small, white house
A small, white house all wrapped up in crisp soft snow
A sleek horse gallops by the house pulling a sleigh full of people
Inside this house there is a party going on
A very jolly party indeed
People are running in and out like little ants
And joyful children are having snowball fights in the yard
The windows are aglow with light
And music dances out into the yard
When it is all over people say their good-byes
And think of what a jolly party this has been!

Meg Beane-Fox, Grade 5
Sandman Consolidated Elementary School

Life

Life is hard
You can't do lots of things with your life that you want to
Like going out of town or down south
to see your grandmother.

Life is hard
Sometimes people make you do things you don't want to do
Like forcing you to try drugs or tell you to rob
a jewelry or corner store.

Life is hard
Because when you're a kid you have to go to school
And do lots of class work or homework
Filled with hard math problems.

Life is hard
Because when you want something from your mom or dad
They say, "No, you can't always get everything you want."
Which is tough to hear.

Life is hard
But you have to live with it
And try your best to keep up with everything so that you can be
a success.

Dajah Jordan, Grade 5
Roosevelt Elementary School

Discrimination

The same old blood! The same red-running blood!
And yet, no one cares about the fact that
We are all human, we are all the same,
And not one of us should have to toil more than the other.
Why do we care whether or not we're the same or different?
Because we're all not the same, we're different.
On the outside they look tough and mean,
But on the inside, I bet they're all weeping with fear,
They're hiding their feelings behind a brick wall,
Where not even the best of bombs could destroy it.
If we keep this up, the world will turn into a blank road;
Where we're all destined to go down without fixing the problem.

Megan Campbell, Grade 6
Chatham Middle School

The City

Bustling people moving about
Shoving as if they see no one there.
City slickers and tourists separating
Like water and oil
With tourists surrounded in a vast sea of cars.

Walking around gazing at scenery
Wondering where to visit next.
Tall buildings galore surrounding the gawkers
With slickers walking by
As if nothing was there.

Trying to get by the people staring at the statues
That have always been there from the beginning.
It's kind of irritating when so many are there.
You get used to it though after so many times
Of watching people flagging down taxis that are already full.

Whoever you are, slicker or starer,
The city is always a busying place.
With jobs to go to or statues to stare at,
Many apartments allow
All the time in the world.

Justin Patel, Grade 6
Allen W Roberts Elementary School

Gone*

I had a friend who went away.
She's not coming back for another day.
We had some fights, agreements too.
We even shared the same shoes.
I miss her much, she misses me too.
I know because I call her every month or two.
Hopefully, I'll see her soon.
Yeah probably in a year or two.
I had a friend who went away.
Maybe to return another day.

Ariana Barnhardt, Grade 5
Hillside Elementary School
*Dedicated to Jordan Sterner

Tree

I am a tree.
You know me for growing fruit.
I was born when God created the Earth.
I live anywhere.
My best friend is rain,
because he allows me to grow.
I fear people chopping me down.
I love the animals,
because they keep me company.
And I dream of being the tallest tree on Earth.

Jessica Fowler, Grade 4
Christ the Teacher School

My Wonderful Mother

My mom is the best.
She's definitely better than all the rest.

She likes fat free French Vanilla.
Cappuccino and cookies in two.

Haircutting she used to do.
I get my haircuts for free.
She is the greatest haircutter there could be.

Cleaning the house
She likes to do.
But cleaning up
After the flood made her blue.

That's my wonderful mother.

Chase Mancini, Grade 4
Franklin Township Elementary School

People

People
People swimming in a pool
People waiting to go to school
People yelling over here
People at parties giving cheer
People waiting to be recognized
Hey look over there, some famous guys.

Kaitlyn George, Grade 4
Katharine D Malone Elementary School

My Family

I have a mom, dad, 2 sisters, a nana, and a cousin.
My mom is nice
She make good rice
She is scared of mice.
My dad works at QVC
As seen on TV
He loves to call me Minnie Me.
I have 2 sisters that bug me
But I know they really love me.
I have nana that's crazy
And she started taking care of me
When I was a baby.
My cousin is a very young lady
And she is very crazy.
So you know about my wonderful and crazy family.

Tajah Harrison, Grade 5
The Red Bank Charter School

Clouds in the Sky

Too high to jump
Too hard to fly
But I'm still waiting for that day
When I can just fly away

Corinne Mulvanerton, Grade 6
Immaculate Conception Regional School

Beyond

I sit in my room staring out the window,
Thinking of what is beyond it.
Beyond the window
The sky and those twinkling little stars.
What is beyond these walls,
That fence that keeps me in so tight.
Except when I'm out there,
Traveling that world I have to call home.
I shiver in fright
Lonely in a crowd of a million.
I look around
Not so lonely anymore.
So think of me,
And where I'll be.
I'll be beyond it all.
Beyond the past.
Beyond the present.
Beyond the future.
I'll be there my friend.
Emily Boltner, Grade 6
St Veronica Elementary School

Homework

I do not like homework
The dog ate it.
It is past my bedtime.
The cat tore it up.
Please do not make me do it.
Dad put it in the shredder.
Are you kidding?
I am not doing that.
I will pay you $50.
Oh fine I will do it.
I will not do it tomorrow.
Logan Nadel, Grade 4
Mansfield Township Elementary School

Oceans

Oceans
High tides
Swimming, surfing, fishing
Crashing waves of blue
Beautiful
Erin Lockwood, Grade 6
Sacred Heart Elementary School

Raptor

A speedy lizard
Swift, fierce dinosaur
Clawing, carnivore
A reptilian creature
Crushing, injuring, damage.
Aamir Razak, Grade 4
Mansfield Township Elementary School

Parents

My home
My dad will play with me
My parents are funny and kind
Parents
Omar Chaudhry, Grade 6
John Hill School

The Performance

It's the time,
It's the moment,
You've waited oh so long.
Now's your chance,
Now you can shine,

You go out,
A brand new person,
To pretend,
Be in someone else's shoes.

The spotlight in your eyes,
But you don't even try to block it,
You don't even care,
You're doing what you want,
Tonight, it's all about you.

How everyone wants to be you,
Out there with flowers all around,
People came to see you,
The performance has begun.
Kate-Lynn Brown, Grade 5
Brayton Elementary School

A World Without

A world without separate lives,
All should be equal.
A world without
violence and despair.
We could have hope,
and love to share.
No fighting, stopping wars
we don't need them anymore.
What we need is peace,
love, and happiness
to get us through
this life we are living in.
Without a world like that
to be living in,
it is meaningless to walk
through life without a friend.
No more discrimination
in this great nation.
We need peace,
We need love,
We need life for everyone.
Olivia Suarez Onorato, Grade 6
St Margaret Regional School

Comet

I am hurling through space.
With a tail of fire.
With a speed unimaginable.
And in a blink of an eye, I'm gone.

I come and go so quickly.
And I go faster and faster.
Until I hit the Earth.
And create a huge fiery crater.
Daniel Perez, Grade 4
Christ the Teacher School

Spring

Spring is here!
Come one and come all,
Come outside,
Forget about the mall.

The sounds are pretty.
All different colors,
Flowers are nice,
I've been outside for hours.

My dog is jumping.
He is having some fun,
He's running around,
And he is blocked by the sun.
Nicole Williams, Grade 4
Stonybrook Elementary School

Angelina Is Cute When She…

Angelina is cute when she
Blows bubbles from her mouth.
Angelina is also very cute
When she laughs loudly.
Angelina is cute when she
Puts her hands behind her head.
Angelina is cute when she
Makes her bottom lip quiver.
Angelina is also cute when
She rolls over on the ground.
What cute things will she do next?
I may soon find out.
Lauren Grippaldi, Grade 5
Robert B Jaggard Elementary School

New York Giants

The New York Giants,
They are a great football team,
They have lots of fans,
They are very powerful,
The colors are red and blue.
Taylor Kapp, Grade 4
Mansfield Township Elementary School

Time

Time is an illusion
made up, something we only see
something made up, a hypocrisy
like the hypocrisy of a democracy we use
lies, lies, never the truth,
"it's over, it's over"
that's what they say
but they know that there'll always be another day,
till the clocks stops dead,
the clock will never stop,
'cause time's just somethin' we made up in our head

Evan Larsen, Grade 6
Friends School

Play

Play, play that's what kids are all about
Kids love playing and that's without a doubt.
We can run, jump, hop, and swing (have fun)
And when we're playing we can do anything…
We can run, dip, glide, and even slip and slide
So when we're through we creep and creep and fall asleep.

Kayla Michele Jackson, Grade 5
St Helena School

My Best Friend

My best friend is very loving you see
She is trustworthy and caring you will agree
She is there for me when I need her
She will always be around
She always cheers me up
BEST FRIENDS FOR LIFE!!!
We are like sisters
She is my teddy bear that I bring everywhere
We have a friendship know one else has
We have been friends for as long as I can remember
We do everything together
No one can come between us
Our friendship will never end
We are two peas in a pod
Who will always be Best Friends

Brielle Zakashefski, Grade 6
Our Lady of Mount Virgin School

My Neighborhood on a Summer's Day

Lily pad green trees,
Swaying gently in the warm breeze.
Kids having tons of fun,
Playing in the hot steamy sun.
Adults lazily walking by,
With children who are sometimes shy.
Slow moving cars that slink by like snakes,
Being careful not to slam on the brakes.
Bikes, balls, bats thrown everywhere,
If we never eat dinner, I certainly don't care!

Robyn Czapkowski, Grade 6
Christa McAuliffe Middle School

Easter Sunday

Easter Sunday is happy and great,
A special time to celebrate.
This wonderful day is full of joy,
For everybody, girl and boy.
The churches are decorated here and there,
With many who sing with happiness and care.
Parents watch us find Easter eggs,
As we search hard and strain our legs.
This day isn't just about candy and searches,
It's a time for Christians to go to their churches.
Where they remember a certain someone named Jesus,
That special person who loves us and frees us.

Amanda Del Grosso, Grade 6
Sacred Heart School

Appreciation

I'm Babe Ruth's bat.
He's the one
who got all the fame.
Why not me?
I was the one
who hit all the balls.
I was the one
who suffered.
I sat in the dugout
with all the gum
and sweaty socks.
That was then,
but now…
I'm in the Hall of Fame.
To be nice,
I shared it with him.

Kaitlin Keen, Grade 6
Lower Alloways Creek Elementary School

Spring

S pring breaks sunny weather
P laying children smile
R ainbows glistening in the sunlight
I ll children's fevers disappear
N o one is sad in the super sunny sunshine
G arden flowers bloom and shine

Hally Maule, Grade 4
West End Memorial Elementary School

Snow

I sleep by a little window in my house with all my lights on.
When I wake up it will be dawn in this little town of mine.
The snow will cover the pine trees like my warm coat.
While I am sleeping by the little window of mine I will know,
Tomorrow there will be lots of snow.
That will be nice.

Johnny Petronis, Grade 5
Sandman Consolidated Elementary School

Let's Take a Walk

Let's take a walk for all the people that are holding tears inside their eyes and fears inside.
Let's take a walk for all the people that won't let go of hiding under the sheets
Because they're afraid that they can't compete with their life ahead.
So come on and take a walk with me so you can see what your future's going to be
Let's take a walk, walk, walk
Let's take a walk down to the projects to see drugs' horrors and effects
Let's take a walk down the street to the school for kids living in fear 'cause their moms are on drugs
And their pops are gone so they get no love and feel as if they don't belong
Let's take a walk for all the people that tried to hold me back and inspired me to write this rap and express the way I feel
Let's take a walk for all the mothers living with a broken heart
Because they're living on welfare and could no longer bear the pain in the game of life
Let's take a walk for the women that suffered for being a caring wife
Let's take a walk for all the people living with HIV and STD's
Let's take a walk for all the families lending a helping hand and still stand strong even though no one understands
Let's take a walk for all the caring men and the young girls and women that were raped under and above the age of 10
Let's take a walk for all the haters that are sipp'n on hater-aid because they know they can't make it where I am

Let's take a walk

Aisha Rivera, Grade 6
Cleveland Elementary School

A Day with the Farmer

Early in the morning the rooster starts crowing.
The farmer needs to wake up for he has mowing.
The obnoxious dog starts to bark.
It is already 6:00 a.m. however it is still dark.

After he finishes mowing he needs to gather his crops.
After he needs to pull out the weeds.
The farmer was tired, hungry, and sore after his long hard day.
His trek back to the barn seemed to be far, far away.

He wanted to see ham on his dinner plate.
So he picked up his pace to a quicker rate.
By the time he got home his stomach was a growling bear but some food would hit the spot.

He found out that it was hot prime ribs in the pot.
After his delicious dinner he looked at his wife and said "I am going to bed."
Before he fell asleep he read his book how to be a better farmer.

Kyle Van Den Heuvel, Grade 6
Fieldstone Middle School

Waking Up

Yup, it's that time of day, that we hate, I should say
Waking up is never fun because when you crack open your eyes and you still think it's 1
When that annoying alarm starts to beep you really wish you could go back to sleep
Slowly walking out of bed you usually trip, or fall, or hit your head
You smack the alarm wishing you had a hammer then when you look in the mirror you get even madder
Your hair looks like you got struck by lightning it appears very very frightening
You get out your clothes for school since you aren't in bed you feel like a fool
You go to brush your hair and flip it back you tie your shoes and pack your backpack
Stuffing breakfast down your throat you throw on your coat
You kiss your mom goodbye wiping her lipstick off of your eye
You run outside and close the door then you really wish you wouldn't have to wake up anymore.

Carly Brady, Grade 5
St Rose of Lima School

Winter

Rolling around in the white sparkling snow.
So cold you can see your breath when you blow.
You make a snowman all short and fat.
And add a shiny, silky hat.
School is out because snow is covering the street.
A big white blanket of smoothed out sleet.
You start a wild snowball fight.
You send snowballs soaring through the air with all your might.
Outside in the freezing weather you are shaking.
You can smell the warm cookies your mom is baking.
You rush inside to get warmed up.
You drink hot chocolate in a very hot cup.
You watch the shimmering snowflakes come on down.
But when it melts your smile becomes a frown.
So go out in the snow today.
Or the snow will be gone and you can't play.
Don't take this precious time to rest.
Because…winter is the best.

Rachel Weaver, Grade 4
Richard Stockton Elementary School

The Birth of Stars

I see one star sparkling with light.
It looks so lonely all by itself.
Snap!
In a flash the stars come out.
Hundreds, millions!
As quick as they were gone, they were there.
And that I think is the birth of stars.

Jessica S. Bush, Grade 4
Community Park School

I'm So…

I am so lazy…
Could you pick that up for me?
I am so classy, you'll be asking…
"Where you get that from?"
I am so wicked, I'll put a spell on you.
I am so determined, when I want something, I get it.
I am so tired…
Could you carry me to my bed?
I am so forgetful…
That reminds me, I forgot my homework,
I am so magical.
Don't you see I have a wand?
I am so hideous.
I mean, look at my hair!
I am so cranky.
Get me my breakfast, NOW!
I am so silly, I will have you laughing your pants off.
I'm so appreciated,
people love me all over the world.

Juanice Williams, Grade 6
The Jersey City Community School

My Dog Bear

My dog is very quick,
And his hair is very thick.
His coat is white and brown,
And you never see him frown.

He likes to play with a ball,
And in the leaves of the fall.
He like to play with a stick,
And my face he likes to lick.

This is all about old Bear,
From his actions to his hair.
I really love that dog of mine,
Although his breath isn't fine.

Kevin Good, Grade 5
Immaculate Conception Regional School

I Am

I am a nice and peaceful girl
I wonder why things always change
I hear silence when I think
I see nature changing beneath me
I am a nice and peaceful girl

I pretend my dog is with me
I feel my mom and dad's hands holding mine
I worry about my family and I dying
I cry when I think about bad things happening
I am a nice and peaceful girl

I understand some things aren't true
I always wonder why
I dream that God is next to me
I try to be kind to all
I hope wars will end
I am a nice and peaceful girl

Jessica Mertz, Grade 4
Meadowbrook Elementary School

If Life Were Easy

If life were easy there would be no challenges.
Everything would be perfect.
Every person would be the same as everyone else.
But life isn't that way and there is no such thing as perfect.
Everyone is unique.
If there weren't challenges life would be easy.

Hamsa Fayed, Grade 6
Roosevelt Elementary School

School in the Summer

School in the summer is no fun
When you bring your bag home and it weighs a ton
Work is a drag, no matter what
Some kids like it. I think they're nuts.

Nicholas Hammell, Grade 5
Springfield Township School

For I Wish I Were "Freedom"

I wish…
I were freedom,
For I would let people live longer.
I wish I were freedom,
I would make people free.
I wish I were freedom,
For peoples' rights would rise.
If I were freedom,
I would make all wars end.

Joseph Caraccio, Grade 4
St Joseph School

Tree House

A tree house
A hideout to you and me.
A comfort, a happy place
A calm house to you and me.
My real home, my imagination
A warm place to you and me.
A palace, a dungeon
An imagination to you and me.
A fun place, a secret place
A home to you and me.

Christine Cremonni, Grade 6
Chatham Middle School

Spring

Spring has flowers sprouting,
Colors like yellow and blue.
Spring makes children come shouting,
To sparkling grass with dew.

Spring has birds all singing,
Songs from morning 'til night.
Spring has animals bringing
Their babies to see the light.

Gardeners are all planting,
From crops to colored flowers.
Children now come panting,
After many endless hours.

This is what makes spring beautiful,
From morning when you look out,
To night with a lull so peaceful,
For that is what spring's about.

Karen Baltazar, Grade 5
St Veronica Elementary School

Air

The air is misty
It is cool in the hot sun
Air is wonderful

Yash Varma, Grade 5
St Helena School

Winter Forest

Trees covered in white sparkly snow
White sparkly grass
In a white sparkly land
Beautiful in its own way.
All animals curled up
Silver streaks in their hair
Like creamy milk
In a bowl
In a never-ending way.

Kaitlin Kline, Grade 4
Pond Road Middle School

Spring Is Here

Spring, spring, spring is here
Flowers bloom and all kids cheer
Birds fly back all snow clears
But, for every F comes a tear
Strong winds come blowing us down
Up we go but down we fall
Drip, drip, drip the angels cry
Winter's gone bye, bye, bye
Saint Patrick's Day green all around
Leprechauns making little sounds
Rabbits jumping side by side
Easter's here come outside
Scary thunderstorm stop the madness
Come out rainbow join the gladness
Skies of blue clouds of white
Grass of green, black for night
Spring is good, windy, bad
But, spring, spring, spring is here

Gabriella Snead, Grade 6
Gilmore J Fisher Middle School

Quiet/Loud

Quiet
Peaceful, calm
Sleeping, dreaming, thinking
Nice, easygoing — aggravating, horrible
Screaming, yelling, crying
Noisy, annoying
LOUD

Nora Ellmann, Grade 5
Hillside Elementary School

Mother Nature

Mothers here, Mothers there,
Mothers are anywhere,
Some are tall, some are short.
You can't see her, but she's there,
Mother Nature.
She is there.

William Fox, Grade 4
Friends School

A Very Windy Day

Trees are crying,
Howling like ghosts.
Branches are swinging like dancers.
You can hear the roar of the wind,
Yelling at the trees.
Shingles are flying,
Wind is crying.
Today is a dreadful day.

Brittany Lapadula, Grade 5
Cherry Hill Elementary School

Smelly Man

There once was a smelly old man,
who lived in garbage cans.
The garbage truck came,
and he went insane,
That was the end of the smelly old man.

Noëlle Nebbia, Grade 4
Meadowbrook Elementary School

Love Can Last

Love is great
love is good
keep love in our neighborhood
if love is lost
it will not be found
it will not flow around
and our hearts will not grow profound.

Caitlin Donohue, Grade 6
St Joseph's School

Summer Forever

The ocean breezes fly by,
the seagulls dance in the sky,
the smell of the salt from the sea.
Like a bird, I am free!
The feel of the sand, the sun on my face.
Bring sunblock just in case!

Gabriella Guerrera, Grade 6
St Veronica Elementary School

I Want a World…

I want a world
that's sweet as candy.
I want a world
with no drugs, and no gangs.
I want a world
with no violence and no wars.
I want a world
with jobs for everyone.
I want a world
with no theft.
This is the world I want!

Amy Lopez, Grade 4
Evergreen Elementary School

I Made a Mistake

I went to the classroom to see the teacher,
I made a mistake…and found a creature.

I went to the kitchen to make a shake,
I made a mistake…and made an earthquake.

I went to Florida to see Miami,
I made a mistake…and misplaced my Grammy.

I went to the dictionary to look up a word,
I made a mistake…and found Big Bird.

I went to the computer to play a game,
I made a mistake…and found Notre Dame.

I went to the store to get food,
I made a mistake…and found a dude.

I went to the bathroom to take a shower,
I made a mistake…and fell in baby powder.

I went to the guidance counselor to find a friend,
I made a mistake…and found the end.

Matthew Grassi, Grade 4
Sicomac Elementary School

The Most Influential Woman in My Life

Mary
Beautiful, kind
Reading, sharing, biking
She is always there to help me
Mom

Stephanie Solly, Grade 5
Ridgeway Elementary School

Being a Mountain

If I were a mountain
I'd sit crossing my legs
waiting for the wind to wear me down.

My muddy-colored shirt and green mossy pants
would become a rugged cone
that touched the sky.

My head would rest on the cream-colored clouds,
and the stars would be my lamplight in the dark.

The trees would be my blanket
with the roots clinging to me
as if they were holding on for dear life.

I would have the animals to talk to
when I am lonely
so I'd feel as if I were at home.

Grace Tellado, Grade 4
Sicomac Elementary School

Perfection

I watched in awe as she took long strides down the halls
Her hair tousled with perfection,
She waves to everyone; sickening to watch yet sweet,
And who I long to be is she.

She sits down in class and pays attention,
But really she is passing notes,
She is a liar,
And yet she is who I want to be.

She is caught bullying someone,
But then she blames the person for her behavior,
The teacher believes her,
And now I realize that who I long to be is me.

Toni Kitsopoulos, Grade 6
Chatham Middle School

What Is Pink

Pink is the color
Of flowers in a vase.
Pretty frilly bows.
And a baby's face.

Make-up is pink.
So is perfume.
It's the little sister
Of maroon.

Tough men are pink.
Girly girls too.
It's bubble gum and it's
A ballet shoe.

When I think of pink,
I think of a ribbon.
I think of the wonderful
Breast Cancer Coalition.

Pink's a lot of things
Like, joy and happiness,
But it's definitely not
Sorrow and sadness!

Brandi Brooks, Grade 5
Sandman Consolidated Elementary School

Baseball

Baseball is a lot of fun,
In the field, you have to run.
When the pitcher pitches the ball,
You hope you can hit it over the wall.
Baseball is a tough sport, so don't get mad
If you do bad.

Christopher Lyons, Grade 5
Our Lady of Mount Virgin School

Mr. Fishbone

I am Mr. Fishbone.
I go into your trash.
I look for sunken treasures,
Like green beans and hash.

I take your gum,
from underneath your chair.
Then chew it for a while,
until it tastes rare.

I have revealed secrets.
That no one has ever heard,
like Susie is a trembling failure,
and Michael has an anonymous bird!

If you have lost something valuable
only call me.
The only doubt you'll have
is I may keep it…you see!
Nicole Liebeknecht, Grade 5
St Rose of Lima School

The Dancing Dog

There once was a dog from France
Who wanted to learn how to dance
He didn't know how
So he took a bow
And then began to prance.
Danielle Holland, Grade 5
Springfield Township School

Yesterday

Yesterday, the sky turned green.
Yesterday, apes drove cars.
Yesterday, trees spoke.
Yesterday, pollution stopped.
Yesterday, evil was wiped out.
Yesterday, wars ended.
Yesterday, in my imagination.
Madeline Moore, Grade 5
Liberty Corner Elementary School

With These Hands

With these hands I will compose
a novel that people will read,
and discover new places in their hearts

With these hands I will end war,
and bring world peace
to us and other countries

With these hands I do my best
to help others
to have a better time next time
Harry Clewell, Grade 5
Salt Brook Elementary School

The Beauty of the Beach

The waves crash against the shore, taking in sand.
And giving us dozens of tiny, colorful shells to play with.
I pick up a few shells and shake them around in the palm of my hand.
They make a sweet, jingling sound like a thousand Christmas bells
Ringing all at once.
I roll around in the crystal, white sand.
I pick up a handful of sand and let it slide through my fingers.
I pick up another handful and throw it up in the air.
It comes down on me like dry rain.
A hermit crab scuttles past me, dragging its mobile home behind it.
It burrows under the sand and becomes invisible, hidden underground.
Seagulls hop about around me, begging for food.
When they see that I have refused, they skim the ocean
Looking for their own lunch of fish.
A large shell washes up on the beach.
I put it against my ear and hear the ocean's echo.
As the dandelion sun meets the horizon, the sky fills with a mixture
Of scarlet, gold and fuchsia.
I fall asleep there, on the sand.
With the waves still splashing against the shore,
The sunset in the sky, and dream about the beauty of the beach.
Claire Gates, Grade 4
Indian Hill Elementary School

He's Ripped, He's Stained, He's Teddy

Mom, don't throw Teddy away!
Although he has rips and stains he is still my best friend!
You have to throw Teddy away!
Teddy is definitely a devastated bear.
Mom don't throw Teddy away!

He has rips, one eye and stains.
You have thrown Teddy away!
Since you got Teddy when you were born you drooled on him,
Played in the mud with him and played with Teddy on the playground.
You even took a bath with him.
Since the first stain I had an aspiration to throw that ratty thing away!
Mom please don't throw Teddy away!
Alexa Kastan, Grade 6
Fieldstone Middle School

My Mom

My mom shows her love in so many ways.
When she is happy, she makes me cookies.
She also gives me lots of kisses.
She even lets me go to my friend's house.
She helps me in math.
She also likes cleaning up my mistakes.
She is funnier than my friends Mark and Krissy.
When I am not around she always misses me.
To me my mom is like the sun.
I love it when she calls me her "honey bun."
If my mom entered the best mom contest; she would win 1st prize.
I love my mom but she loves me more.
Reginald Brown, Grade 6
Trinity Christian Academy

Death or Life — Unborn Children

Every day we think and say,
Why do YOU choose this way?
We pray, and pray, and pray all day,
But one more life is taken away.

You are a person that is blinded from that start
Don't you realize that there in your body
Beats another little heart?

When I see you I pray and pray,
I hope that you won't choose that way

God will forgive you
Yes He will,
He will forgive you,
And I will too.

Someday we hope you understand,
That abortion is not that way in this land.
We hope the day will finally come,
When all abortion, is gone, and done.

Candace Turner, Grade 6
Sacred Heart Elementary School

My Best Friends

My friend Madi is so cool,
She really rules the school.

My friend Keri is so funny,
Her personality is very sunny.

My friend Geena likes to shop,
Till she really drops.

My friend Amanda is really nice,
But I know she is scared of mice.

Don't feel bad if you lose a friend,
Because you have plenty more to stay to the end.

Hayley Pascoal, Grade 4
St Rose of Lima School

Sameerah (Mom)

Beautiful, honest, nice, harmless
Related to Lee and Tysheach
Cares deeply about her children, brothers, her job and J.R.
Who feels love and peace.
Who needs her children, food, home and love
Who gives a helping hand and care
Who fears losing her children, and strong words
Who would like to see her children grow-up.
Resident of Somerset, New Jersey.

Dajhier McCutchen, Grade 4
Franklin Park Elementary School

The Mystical Woods

I heard of a place that my grandpa told me about.
It was called THE MYSTICAL WOODS.
I thought it wasn't real but the name sounded good.
Then one day I saw a book.
I was interested so I took a look at the book.
When I finished reading the first twenty pages
I entered a world filled with magical sages.
They looked at me and when I looked at them
For some reason they handed me a mystical gem.
When they gave the gem to me it surrounded me with light.
Then I entered a dark town filled with night.
I walked into the castle and I saw the king.
He was a short king.
Then he saw me and he was frightened so he sent me away.
At first I was mad but then I was glad
Because I could tell my grandpa about all the fun I had had.

John Haiduk, Grade 5
St John's Academy

The Magical Sea

I can feel the wind in my hair,
My toes are sinking in the sand.
The oceans waves are crashing on the beach.
With the suns shining reflection,
Feeling the warm sea water on my toes.
It is very peaceful by the sea.

Carly Bornmann, Grade 4
Stonybrook Elementary School

Pop-Pop

The little girl got into her dress.
Today was her day for show and tell.
She went to school with a picture,
because her Pop-Pop couldn't show, but she could surely tell.

She bet he'd love to be there,
with her clinging to his arm.
Like before the leaving of her Pop-Pop
and his lovely charm.

In front of the class she stood.
Facing the class and showing them her pride.
Starting to talk about the man in the picture,
the man who had recently died.

"He took me on the ferris wheel.
He walked with me in the park.
He let me sit on his lap.
And he held me in the dark."

"He loved to see me smile.
I loved his soft touch.
I just wanted you to know,
I loved my Pop-Pop very much!"

Jae Li, Grade 6
Fieldstone Middle School

Spring
S ounds of the bird's tunes;
P eople enjoy the peaceful noons.
R abbits are hopping in the sun's rays.
I nside or outside kids will play.
N ow it's spring, not winter, not fall.
G oodbye winter, snow and all.
Jackie Prezant, Grade 4
Solomon Schechter Day School

Love Is Coming
V alentine's Day is coming.
A rrows from Cupid are flying.
L ove is coming soon.
E veryone deserves love.
N ight ends but love never does.
T here is love in the air.
I love the sweet chocolate candy.
N o one should be hated.
E very day the air should be full of love.
S oon Cupid's arrows will hit you.

D elicious candies to receive.
A lot of candy for me to eat.
Y ou will be in my heart every day.
Chunli Bent, Grade 4
St Mary's School

Books
Books bring me joy
Unlocking everything.
All kinds of feelings
They can bring to you.
Books may make you happy
When you are sad.
Books take you to places
You wish you had been.
Turning pages never knowing
What may come next
It can be ongoing.
Until the end of the book
When the last words are read,
You never know what can fill your head.
Joseph Peluso, Grade 4
Edward H Bryan Elementary School

Spring Is the Best
Spring is coming.
Children are running.
Birds are humming.
Sun is shining.
Bunnies are hiding.
Bells are ringing.
Spring is the best!
Brittney Papa, Grade 4
John F Kennedy Elementary School

Life Is a Contradiction
Life is a contradiction.
It's messy, but it's neat.
I know, but I'm not sure
why I'm standing on a street.

I'm cleaning my room,
but it's already clean.
I'm fixing the ends
of the spaces in between.

I'm able to think,
but I can't.
I know that it's dead,
but I'm watering my plant.

Life is a contradiction,
as weird as it may sound.
There are people doing weird things.
You just have to look around.
Gabriela Riccardi, Grade 4
Charles Olbon Elementary School

Mars
There once was an old lady from Mars,
That loved to eat different candy bars,
She loved to eat nuts,
She was a big klutz,
No wonder that lady was from Mars!
Ashley Zufolo, Grade 4
Meadowbrook Elementary School

Esther's Sweaters
There once was a girl named Esther,
who wore sweaters of polyester.
But then came the time,
when the moths did their crime.
She could no longer wear polyester.
Fernanda Paixao, Grade 6
Fieldstone Middle School

Higher Than the Clouds
Shooting in the air
No one would even dare
To run down the aisle
Or jump out on a crocodile
Rapidly bumping through the sky
You look out and you're very high
It's fun to fly in the air
I can't wait to be there,
Shooting down, the wheels pop up,
Now all we need is to back up.
It's very late.
Now let's get to our gate!
Max Kauderer, Grade 4
Solomon Schechter Day School

Me
I am silly
I hear music
I see my family
I wish I could be rich

I feel happy when I read
I feel frustrated when I don't read
I get angry when I lose something
I am puzzled by my teacher
I dream about money
I wonder what I will be
I plan to teach
I hope some day I will get married

I know I am smart
I understand my life
I learn many things
I value my life

I love everybody
I am afraid of snakes
I am embarrassed when I snort
I am proud of how I look
I am me.
Casey Mac Vicar, Grade 4
Nellie K Parker Elementary School

Frosty Fun
Pine trees covered in white
The crunching of snow below my feet
The crisp air
The freezing cold of winter creeping in
Hot chocolate waiting for me inside
Winter is here
Casey Sullivan, Grade 6
Long Branch Middle School

My Dog
I love my dog
Almost more than my sister
I like to play fetch with him
I feed him and pet him
I remember the day we bought him
He cried the whole way home
Although it was annoying
He still was my dog
I love him like a brother
The German Shepherd was small then
Now he is huge
He licked my face
With that slobbery tongue
At first I hated it but now I love it
He is my dog
Brian Bulger, Grade 5
Tamaques Elementary School

Sunny Days

Sunny days
Sunny days
The sky which speaks with glee
The sun gleams as it obliterates fear…
The trees swishing in a faint noise
The birds sing in the vacant, vast air.
Sunny days you shall sparkle until twilight
Sunny days
Sunny days

Hassan White, Grade 6
Great Meadows Regional Middle School

Little Blue Bird

F lying through the sky, there was a bird.
L owering its left wing.
Y oung and beautiful was the bird.
I nching higher and higher into the sky.
N avy blue was the color of the bird.
G oing to the nest to go to sleep,
 The very next day, the bird didn't wake up
 But his spirit is still with us.

Raquel Lesser, Grade 4
Solomon Schechter Day School

The Teacup

I stare at the sparkling teal blue cup,
 As I touch the shimmering handle.
 All the green tea is steaming hot,
As it makes the polka dots go swimming.
 Bathing in the beautiful gold tulips
 Laying on the dancing pink stripes.
Moving to the beat that the tea kettle makes,
 Singing it a song.
 The teacup makes so many things
 Seem like they're not impossible.
The busy teacup makes me feel like I'm lucky.
 I see the sparkling teal blue as,
 I touch the shining handle.

Maria Hershey, Grade 5
Tamaques Elementary School

Basketball

Basketball, I love the sport,
I love running down the court,
I dribble, dribble, shoot, shoot,
Love to throw to the hoop.
The crowd cheers and goes wild,
Each parent looking for their child.
Coach says we do great,
She also says don't be late.
Remember H.E.A.R.T. and B.E.E.F. too
Watch out the ball's headed straight for you.
This sport is my favorite, I try not to fall,
I love all my teammates but the game most of all!!!

Gabrielle Gillen, Grade 5
St Joseph Grade School

I Play Football

I play football out not in,
my favorite team is the Miami Dolphins!
Not the Giants and not the Saints,

I love football so much,
I play football with my Dad…
my mother just doesn't understand.

I watch football every week
and I even have a football for an antique!

Every time they score a touchdown
I say WOW!

My favorite position is the quarterback,
not the fullback.

At the beginning of the game,
the payers stampede,
the flags are waving,
the crowd is full of screams!

I love cheering for my team!!!

Mark Kudla and Danny Edman, Grade 4 and Grade 2
Sundance School

Hi, Bye

Here you are again saying bye,
Every time we see each other it's always hi.
Why do we keep saying hi and bye.
Why can't it just be hi and not bye.
Just tell me why hi and bye keep coming around.
I hope when you say bye this time you will come back.
Do not say bye ever again.

Kiara Black, Grade 6
Trinity Christian Academy

My Bird Buckbeak

My bird is no average bird.
Sometimes I think he is magic.
He sings, he dances
He, he has a true passion for music.
Do you know why?
He sings Beethoven!
Sometimes when I'm feeling sad
I feel like flying away with him.
He is just great.
Oh, and by the way, did I say he could talk?
He can, a little, but the best thing he can do is…
He can call my dad's name.

I love my bird!

Michael Tomasetto, Grade 4
St Peter Elementary School

My Accident
Mom said, "Never bother the dog."
I didn't listen.
I went to play with my dog,
but she didn't want to play.
I bothered her some more.
I went up behind her, and pulled her tail.
She bit me on the cheek!
I had to sit and wait
till the ambulance came!
I got eight stitches in my left cheek!
I learned it was an accident
not to listen to my mother.
Katie Gowey, Grade 5
Durban Avenue Elementary School

When I'm Older
When I am older my bones will ache
And my teeth will break
And when I am older I will be clumsy
And when I am older, I will shake till I break
Billy Perry, Grade 4
Stonybrook Elementary School

A Day by the Bay
I'd love a day by the bay
Where I can dream the day away.
Along the sands, my day is planned.
Boarding, boating and getting a tan,
To building a castle in the coarse sand.
Collecting seashells big and small,
Sea glass, sand dollars, I love them all.
The horizon, blue with boats splashing by,
As planes pulling banners zoom through the sky.
The boardwalk, the snack bar, the ocean spray in the air,
As the cool breeze rushes through your hair.
What I would do when the sky is blue to spend a day at the bay.
Evan Caltavuturo, Grade 5
St John's Academy

The "Good" in Good Friday
On Good Friday we remember Jesus dying on the cross,
Everyone is feeling sad for this terrible loss.
On this day Jesus taught us how we should forgive,
Even if others do not agree with how we choose to live.

This is indeed a memorable dark, dreary day,
For some people it may even cause melancholy and dismay.
We remember that by dying he opened Heaven's gates,
To eternal life for us, where he will patiently await.

Good Friday is an appropriate name for this holy day,
Jesus gave us eternal life in Heaven where we could stay.
Our savior, Jesus Christ paid the ultimate price,
By redeeming our sins with his loving sacrifice.
C.J. Puzo, Grade 6
Sacred Heart School

Shadow
I love my Shadow
because he's like my shadow,
he follows me,
wherever I go he will always be.
He's black and he's white
and he's cute as can be,
when I go to the kitchen he comes with me,
he runs, he plays, he scratches and bites,
but no matter what
he is still my puppy.
Jessica Ann Poletti, Grade 6
Little Egg Harbor Intermediate School

Ode to Spring
Oh spring, oh spring
You make me feel alive
The start of a new, beautiful year right by my side
With birds humming and singing, flowers blooming with joy
The world is a beautiful garden with nature and life.
Oh spring, oh spring
What amazing things you bring
Leaves and flowers, new life and new memories
Oh spring, oh spring
The joy you bring
You tell me the secret that summer is near
Jessica McGregor, Grade 5
Salt Brook Elementary School

A Very Special Egg
Once a hen laid an egg
But then a snake came so she started to beg
The hen pleaded don't eat my chick
Or I will be forced to throw a brick
And break your leg!
Shannon Fox, Grade 5
Springfield Township School

Prejudice
What is this I see before me?
Violation, injustice, back-stabbing,
Criticism and pain…like a spear through the heart?

Giving me…the thought of…something monstrous?
No! This shall not be!

We will stand through!

Let the spear hurt but,
Prejudice cannot hurt,
It may hurt the enslaved person,

But not the free soul.
Paige Hackett, Grade 5
Winslow Township School No 6

Spunky Girl

I love her a lot.
She likes to play.
Spunky loves the outdoors, cold or hot.
She snuggles with me on a rainy day.

I've noticed that she likes both girls and boys.
Spunky likes walks around town.
She loves her toys.
She'll cheer me up when I'm down.

I call her my puppy,
My mom calls her Marshal.
Her love for us
Is never partial.

On her towel she loves to lay.
With her toys she loves to play.
She's my best friend.
Her love for my family will never end.

Heather Van Voorhis, Grade 6
Kings Academy

Figure Skating

Figure skating is as fun as rides at a carnival.
When you spin, it is like you're on the spinning teacup.
When you jump into the air, it's
like you're being scared in the haunted house.

When you speed up, you feel the fresh air
like when you're riding a roller coaster.
When you put one leg up, you go unsteady
like when you're on a ferris wheel.
Figure skating is such a graceful and exciting sport!

Min Jung Kim, Grade 4
Christ the Teacher School

Skiing in Lake Tahoe

I was off the chair lift
and ready to glide down the mountain.
I was feeling very alive and awake.
Whoosh
My skis were starting to slide down the steep mountain.
I could feel the freezing snow
and ice flying on the lens of my ski goggles.
I could hear the skis screeching as I turned.
I was leaning so far forward
I thought I would fall down the mountain.
I am going faster and faster.
I keep turning and turning.
I come to a quick stop.
I clear off my ski goggles
and get back on the ski lift.

Drew Palumbo, Grade 5
Tamaques Elementary School

Night Time

The moon shines brightly in the sky at night
Time so peaceful and so quiet
The chirp of crickets can be heard
Even the sound of nearby birds,
The trees and shrubs cast eerie shadows
Up upon the grassy meadow
Stars dot the sky, trillions by the square
The soft blowing breeze so gentle and fair
Night can seem quite magical
Do you not agree?

Francesca Falzon, Grade 5
St Helena School

Pillows in the Sky

Pillows in the sky.
They will move from left to right.
In the heat they will rumble.
In the cold they will tumble.
They are white.
They will snow.
They will rain.
They can travel from here to Spain!
They are pillows in the sky.
They are soft like silk.
They are white like milk.
They can be rough, but not so tough.
They are like white little feathers.
They are black in bad weathers.
They look like pure white leather.
They are oversized cotton.
They are shaped like buttons.
But there is nothing to fear, they are in the atmosphere.
They are pillows in the sky.

Ryan Appleby, Grade 5
Oxford Street Elementary School

Always Benevolent to Me

My au pair is always benevolent to me.
Everything I do is ok to her.
She never yells when I do something wrong.
She's like a guy giving away a billion dollars to a poor family.
Her kindness is very noticeable
She is like a purple person in a yellow world
I try not to be bad.
But sometimes I yell and scream anyway.

When you have two obnoxious sisters
That are always yelling and screaming
It is hard not to yell.
She has the authority
To yell at me whenever she wants
But she never does.
She is like a poor person giving money to charity
My au pair is always benevolent to me.

Fred Guss, Grade 6
Fieldstone Middle School

All Alone

I'm all alone nobody's here I'm all alone.
My mother's out my father's sick. The TV is broken, I cannot fix.
I watch the clock tick two and through, I have a needle, I start to sow.
I sow my thoughts, I sow my dreams, and I thread my loneliness reap the seams.
I've made a blanket of many designs. Of many lands, of many kinds,
I fall asleep, my many thoughts, they start to creep.
I dream of friends, I dream of the sea. I drift away with the manatees.
They carry me to a vast land of meadows and swamps. I meet a fairy, her name is Dot.
She creeps close to me and whispers in my ear "Why on earth are you here?
You should be enjoying life every day; don't let your loneliness rot you away.
Whenever you're lonely just close your eyes, and think of a delightful surprise."
I open my eyes, it's morning again. I feel the warmth of my home wrap around me.
I look out the window, I see a bumble bee.
I'll never forget what that dream taught me.
Don't let life make you feel alone and empty.
For every day is brand new. I always enjoy it and so should you.

Shanell Sorrells, Grade 6
Sampson G Smith Intermediate School

Nature's Colors

If I were red I'd be a cardinal perched on a fir tree.
If I were orange I'd be the rising sun on a prairie filled with flowers.
If I were yellow I'd be a rapid cheetah running on a savanna.
If I were green I'd be a tropical rain forest in Central America.
If I were blue I'd be an ocean wave in the deep blue sea.
If I were purple I'd be a rose in a flower garden.
If I were all these colors I'd be a rainbow glistening in the sky overlooking the world.

Ahsan Ali, Grade 5
Sicomac Elementary School

If I Were a Rainbow

If I were red I'd be a soft rose petal in a lovely garden.
If I were orange I'd be a bright bold sun giving light to the world.
If I were yellow I'd be a cool glass of lemonade sitting by the pool.
If I were green I'd be the stem of a tulip in the park.
If I were blue I'd be a pool waiting for kids to take a swim or I'd be the bright bold sky for the world to see.
If I were pink I'd be a polka dot on a little girl's favorite skirt.
If I were purple I'd be a violet in a soft meadow.
If I were all of these colors I'd be a bright vibrant rainbow stretching across the sky after a rainstorm.

Lindsay Costigan, Grade 5
Sicomac Elementary School

White

White is the color of a beautiful orchard swaying in the wind,
White is the color of a puffy cloud floating in the sky,
White is the color of a magician's hand doing a trick right before your eyes,
White is the color of a blank piece of paper with millions of ideas just waiting to be drawn on,
White is the color of a graceful swan gliding on the water,
White is the color of freshly, fallen snow ready to build a snowman,
White is the color of the stripes on the American flag,
White is the color of purity and innocence.

Jaclyn Spielsinger, Grade 5
Sicomac Elementary School

Friends

F riends are always there for you.
R eady and eager to help.
I have fun with my friends.
E specially when we go places.
N othing is better to do than play with a friend.
D on't be mean and friends will come to you.
S miling is what you'll do if you have a friend.

Natalie Mazouz, Grade 4
Solomon Schechter Day School

In the Still of the Night…

…the gleaming moon shines through my open window.
…a slow breeze blows my curtains.
…leaves rustle quietly.
…the night creatures bustle around my yard.
…I open my eyes slowly to see what is going on.
…the next thing I know, it's morning.
…I enjoy the peacefulness

Dane Ferolin, Grade 4
Long Memorial Elementary School

Being a Rainbow

If I were a rainbow
I would reach across the ocean,
stretch my colors over Earth,
and wait for someone to find my gold.

My colorful clothing as wet as the ocean,
my head sticking above the clouds,
and swaying with the wind.

Looking down around me,
I stand on leaves as silent as the wind,
and I creep away, not seen or heard.

I jump across the ocean from country to country,
I go to find more gold,
and I dissolve with the wind.

Brendan Woo, Grade 4
Sicomac Elementary School

Poetry Is…

Poetry is expressing yourself,
Poetry belongs on a bookshelf.
Poetry is an idea, ripe and blooming,
Poetry can be gentle or booming.
It gives you a great feeling inside,
It makes you feel so alive.
It never dies or loses its touch,
There's no such thing as writing too much.
So next time you have to write a poem,
Let your imagination roam!

John Macejka, Grade 5
Sicomac Elementary School

Friends

Friends are special, there's no doubt,
When you fight you'll work it out.
Many different unique themes,
Many different hopes and dreams.

Some friends are happy, some always sad,
But I am always very glad,
To be with them until the end.
I love all my great, great friends!

Some short, some tall,
Doesn't matter at all!
Some solemn, some funny,
Some have bunnies!

My life would be incomplete,
My future swept from under my feet,
Without my friends.

Filomena Martini, Grade 6
Walter T. Bergen Middle School

My Life

My life began as a wee little thing
I always thought I was a king
As I got older soccer became my sport
I loved playing basketball on the court
It was so cool that we had a boat
All my friends would sit and gloat
When I was 5, I sat and cried
Only because my Poppy died
When I moved I was 7
I met my new friend, Kevin
My new school was so big and bright
I wish I could go all day and night
My teachers are nice, my friends are better
On the playground we love the weather
At age 8 my life was great
My friends and I love to skate
At age 9 a team I'm with
We are so good it is no myth
At age 10 I think I know
I love to snowboard in the snow
I'm turning 11 so watch me grow!

Joseph Finley, Grade 5
North Dover Elementary School

Index

Author Autograph Page

Author Autograph Page

Author Autograph Page

Author Autograph Page

Author Autograph Page

Author Autograph Page

Author Autograph Page

Author Autograph Page

Author Autograph Page

Author Autograph Page

Author Autograph Page

Author Autograph Page